# The Divine Vision of Radha Krishn

"The Divine Vision of Radha Krishn" tells about the philosophy, history, and the practical form of the eternal tradition of *raganuga* style of devotion to God in Supreme Divine form, Radha Krishn, as described in the Upnishads, the Bhagwatam and in the writings of other historical Masters of Vrindaban, India. It also tells about the Vision of His Divinity Swami Prakashanand Saraswati whose transmuted Grace materialized in the form of Barsana Dham and Shree Raseshwari Radha Rani Temple in the U.S.A.

The supreme form of God, the kinds and classes of Saints, the absolute state of the Blissful superiority of various forms and abodes of God in a progressive manner, the Divine secret of Krishn's descension on the earth planet, the ultimate secret of the creation, the philosophies of all the *Jagadgurus* along with the Shat Sandarbh of Jeev Goswami, the Divine sovereignty of Shree Raseshwari Radha Rani, the description of Barsana Dham and the devotional guidelines for a devotee of Radha Krishn are the main topics of this book, which, if correctly understood and positively followed, will bring you closer to Radha Krishn. This is what "The Divine Vision of Radha Krishn" is.

✳✳

*Bhakti-yog-rasavatar*
Jagadguru Kripalu Mahaprabhu,
the supreme Divine descension
of this age, whose transmuted
Grace has appeared in the form of
*"The Divine Vision of Radha Krishn"*

His Divinity Swami
Prakashanand Saraswati
*the foremost disciple of—*

# The Divine Vision
# of Radha Krishn

H.D. Swami Prakashanand Saraswati

*Published by:*
International Society of Divine Love
Barsana Dham, Austin,TX, USA

BL1225
.R27
P7
1997x

Library of Congress Catalog Card Number: 97-071727
ISBN 1-881921-05-0
❦

**International Society of Divine Love**
Barsana Dham, 400 Barsana Road, Austin, Texas 78737
Ph: (512) 288-7180 • Fax: (512) 288-0447

# Endorsements

This is probably **the first book in the English language that reveals the true Divine form of Radha Krishn, Divine Vrindaban and *raganuga bhakti*.** It fulfills the devotional quest of everyone longing to receive Divine love and vision.

**The work resolves amicably the religious conflict of *advait vad* and the *Vaishnav* philosophies and removes all the existing fallacies that prevailed for centuries and confused simple hearted devotees.** It gives immense pleasure to the inquisitive scholars who wish to know the supreme form of God in general and to the devotees of Shree Radha Krishn in particular.

The work of Shree Swamiji, I am sure, will be highly appreciated and acclaimed all over the world, it provides the authentic information about all the aspects of soul, *maya*, *brahm*, creation, *karm*, *gyan*, *yog*, *bhakti*, etc.

> **Prof. Dr. Jayamanta Mishra**, *Ph.D., Vyakaran-Sahityacharya,*
> *Ex-Vice Chancellor (K.S.D.S. University, Darbhanga),*
> *Ex-Sr. University Professor and Head, Dept. of Sanskrit,*
> *Bihar University, Muzaffarpur, Darbhanga, India*

❁

**The true meaning of '*avatar*' as interpreted in the book, "The Divine Vision of Radha Krishn," by Swami Prakashanandji Maharaj is the real, correct and true definition and description of '*avatar*'. Till now scholars and writers have been misinterpreting this word as per their own misconceptions and ideas.**

Whatever is written in this book on "Radha Krishn" and "*bhakti*" is remarkable and reveals the true Divine form of Lord Krishn and Raseshwari Radha Rani.

Your efforts are laudable and praise worthy and provide most authentic information on all the aspects of a soul. The book is a treasure of Divine knowledge and worth preserving.

**World Religious Parliament and Universal Sanatan Dharma Foundation conveys profound thanks to H.D. Swami Prakashanandji Maharaj for**

publishing this Divine book for the benefit of common man, Spiritual leaders, Saints and all of his *bhaktas* in Divine service.

> **Acharya Prabhakar Mishra,** *President, World Religious Parliament and Universal Sanatan Dharma Foundation, New Delhi, India.*

❦

For the unparalleled and remarkable revelation of H.D. Swami Prakashanand Saraswati, "The Divine Vision of Radha Krishn," and the manifestation of Radha Rani's Divine supremacy and Her true form of devotion through his teachings, the World Religious Parliament has honored him with the title of "विश्वगौरव" which means "the Divine Glory of the entire world."

WORLD RELIGIOUS PARLIAMENT
(विश्व धर्म संसद्)
K-40-B, LAJPAT NAGAR II, NEW DELHI-110 024 (INDIA)

विश्वगौरव सम्मानपत्र

वेदवेदाङ्गादिनिखिलशास्त्रपरम्परासुखाब्धाली, अखिल संस्कृतवाङ् मयसंरक्षण–प्रचार–प्रसारप्रखार समग्र–आर्षसनातनमर्यादाजीवनपद्धतिसदाचारपरायण, 'सर्वभूतहिते रतः–वसुधैव कुटुम्बकम्' की सदभावना से ओतप्रोत,

अनन्त श्रीविभूषित श्री **H.D. SWAMI PRAKASHANAND SARASWATI**
निवासी **INTERNATIONAL SOCIETY OF DIVINE LOVE, BARSANA DHAM, AUSTIN, U.S.A.**

को अन्तर्राष्ट्रीय अधिवेशन में विश्वगौरव सम्मानपत्र से विभूषित किया जाता है ।

एतद्देशानुसूलस्य        सकाशाद्व्रजजगन्मन ।
स्वं स्वं चरित्रं शिक्षेरन् पृथिव्यो सर्वमानवाः ।

World Religious Parliament is pleased to confer

The Title of Vishwagaurav

In recognition of his meritorious contribution for World Development

through        **SERVICES OF SUPREME GODDESS RADHA RANI**

श्रीमद्जगद्गुरू
Chairman
Presentation Committee        Acharya Prabhakar Mishra
१।१०।३६        International General Secretary
World Religious Parliament.

❦

Rev. Swami Prakashanand Saraswati, the founder of the International Society of Divine Love, is a well known personality in the sphere of the spiritual world.

Shree Swamiji has written a number of authentic books which are greatly enhanced by the fact that they are assets to the devotees. These books are one of the relatively few books in English about the true Divine wisdom of India.

**Really "The Divine Vision of Radha Krishn" is a *shastra* for devotees of Priya Priyatam.** This book brings Radha Krishn closer to those who read it attentively. **We should be grateful to Rev. Swamiji for one of the most authoritative expositions of the spiritual wealth of India ever to be published.** Shree Swamiji's contribution in the realm of *raganuga bhakti* is really great and highly commendable.

> **Dr. Krishnaji,** *M.A. (Hindi, English, Sanskrit), Ph.D., D.Litt., Principal Institute of Oriental Philosophy, Vrindaban, India.*

"**The Divine Vision of Radha Krishn**" is the "**book of the century**". It appears as if Swami Prakashanandji has been a witness of Radha Krishn *leelas* in the moments of his Divine ecstasy.

It is commendable that Swamiji has wonderfully adapted the doctrine of synthesis 'सर्व सिद्धान्त समन्वय' which removes all the differences.

It can be announced joyfully to the national and international lovers and adorers of *Braj ras* that "The Divine Vision of Radha Krishn" - the book of the century will certainly reveal to its readers the way to realize the vision of Radha Krishn.

> **Premlata Paliwal**, *Director Vrindaban Shodh Sansthan*
> *(Research Institute), Vrindaban, India.*

❀

Science and technology have taken great strides during the second half of the 20th century but it appears that spirituality has been on the wane during this period. And if spirituality declines, there can be no doubt that mankind will suffer a catastrophe, and perhaps the signs of such a catastrophe are becoming distinctly visible. Today the scenario the world over is ethnic violence, religious and social oppression, and corruption of unimaginable dimensions. But let us not be without hope. The situation can be redeemed but only through spirituality and the gospel of love. In this context, the message and teachings of His Divinity Swami Prakashanand Saraswati as contained in his book "**The Divine Vision of Radha Krishn**" **presents a practical and progressive approach to the dilemma of the modern man.**

**It is astonishing to find Shree Swamiji's penetrating perception of the complexities of human nature and the marvellous manner in which he co-relates the teachings of all of our ancient scriptures (the Vedas, the Puranas, the Upnishads, the Brahm Sutra and the Gita).** His masterly exposition that the actions of God are beyond human reasoning and what may often appear to be faulty or mistaken are only God's way of showering Grace upon mankind, is unique and enchanting.

Shree Swamiji's total absorbment of his self to Radha Krishn inspired him to establish Shree Raseshwari Radha Rani Temple at Barsana Dham.

His message, though rooted in deep philosophy, is marked by clarity and simplicity and is pragmatic. **We need the teachings of Shree Swamiji.**

> **Justice Ram Nandan Prasad**, *M.Sc., B.L. Visharad,*
> *New Delhi, India.*

❀

"The Divine Vision of Radha Krishn" by Swami Prakashanand Saraswati is a spiritual discourse that answers all the concerns of humankind.

> **K.V.S. Rama Sarma**, *Editor-in-Chief, National Herald,*
> *New Delhi, India.*

"The Divine Vision of Radha Krishn" brings a feeling of completeness. For scientists, this book represents a once in a life time opportunity. It brings to their attention the missing link that they are seeking. In order to successfully accomplish any research task, the first and most important step is to establish the correct hypothesis (correct understanding of the starting point). The author provides them with the description of creation and working of the universe. This is done in such a fashion that may enlighten modern scientists and physicists sufficiently to resolve their long term quest of finding the first substance of creation and determine the exact model of the universe.

**Dr. Mark Pasula**, *Ph.D., President, Signet Diagnostic Corp., West Palm Beach, Florida, U.S.A.*

❀

As a researcher, I find it fascinating to study ancient scriptural writings in view of the current state of scientific knowledge. It is quite remarkable how accurately many of these writings describe the way we now understand the universe.

Shree Swamiji has taken the oldest and most complete scriptures of all, and described their meaning in simple terms (in "The Divine Vision of Radha Krishn") that everyone can understand. Furthermore, some of the concepts he relates may very well be incorporated into quantitative theories in the relatively near future.

For example: consider the description of 'time' as an omnipresent energy. In the standard way, such an energy leads to a corresponding 'time force', and this could then explain why time always moves in one direction. Another example: Shree Swamiji explains that when a black hole dies its mass goes back into energy and a new galaxy appears.

It is possible to take the view of our surroundings as presented in the Upnishads and explained by Shree Swamiji, and interpret it in the light of todays understanding of the laws of physics and our presently incomplete cosmological models. It is highly likely that a future generation will soon see that these eternal writings are indeed a valid description of the universe around us.

**Dr. Joel Broida**, *Ph.D., quantum physicist, San Diego, California, U.S.A.*

❀

Congratulations on your noble efforts to publish the book "The Divine Vision of Radha Krishn" and disseminate this wisdom to transport us to the highest planes of bliss.

**Prof. Dr. Lokesh Chandra**, *Member of Parliament (Rajya Sabha), New Delhi, India.*

❀

In "The Divine Vision of Radha Krishn" Shree Swami Prakashanand Saraswati has summarized the knowledge from more than four hundred Vedic scriptures in a simple and easy to understand language and has explained the entire philosophy of God realization.

My deepest gratitude to Shree Swamiji whose Divine Grace has manifested itself in the form of this book for the benefit of all sincere seekers of God's love.

> **Dr. Ivan Plavec**, *Ph.D., Director of Research, Systemix, Inc., Palo Alto, California, U.S.A.*

❀

**"The Divine Vision of Radha Krishn"** by H.D. Swami Prakashanand Saraswati **is the first book in the English language to discuss the true Divinity of Radha**. Radha and Krishn are one and the same, but They appear in two forms. This concept is very elegantly clarified in chapter four.

**Another unique feature of this book is a listing of "fifteen most important fallacies that misled simple hearted devotees for centuries". One that caught my immediate attention points out that the correct spelling and pronunciation is 'Krishn' and not 'Krishna'.** Any one with some knowledge of Sanskrit (or even of Indian languages like Hindi, Marathi or Gujarati) will agree! Similar comments hold for *yog*, *karm* and several other Sanskrit words used in the English language.

On the whole **the book provides a very fresh and interesting reading and must be read by anyone interested in spiritual writings.**

> **Prof. Kuldip C. Gupta**, *Ph.D., Hindu University of America, Colorado, U.S.A.*

❀

"The Divine Vision of Radha Krishn" offers a significant insight into the philosophy and religious ideals of one of the most prominent branches of devotional Hinduism. Herein a notable teacher of Hindu theism expounds in detail the major spiritual concepts that underpin the religion of devotion to Radha Krishn.

Anyone who wishes to understand the devotion to Radha and Krishn will find this book an invaluable source of information from within the tradition itself.

> **Dr. Nick Sutton**, *Ph.D., lecturer in Eastern Religions, Edge Hill University, Lancashire, England*

❀

"The Divine Vision of Radha Krishn" authored by H.D. Swami Prakashanand Saraswati is a treasury of knowledge about *bhakti* and *gyan* in general and the philosophy of '*avatar*' in particular. Swamiji has rightly given a new interpretation of *avatar* using the word 'descension'. **The first book of its own kind which** describes *avatar* in three forms, *poornavatar, anshavatar, gunavatar* and correlates the same with Lord Krishn and Ram who were *poornavatars* in real sense. The book will interest not only scholars studying Hinduism in depth, but others too.

> **Dr. Shyam Singh Shashi**, *Ph.D., D.Litt., author, Padmashri, New Delhi, India*

The book is the first of its kind that has been ever published so far. There is absolutely no doubt that the publication of this book is a great treasure for the Hindu community world over and for others who have interest in Hinduism.

I am extremely glad that our **Pujya Swamiji Maharaj has put an end to the 2,000 year old controversy of** *advait vad* and *Vaishnav* philosophy.

> **H.H. Swami Buaji**, *founder, Indo-American Yoga-Vedanta Society, New York, U.S.A.*

H.D. Swami Prakashanand Saraswati has given a rare treasure of inspiration for those who have a sincere longing and deep desire in their hearts to experience God's Divine love.

**All the Upnishads, Puranas, Uppuranas, Gita, Ramayan and many devotional books, as well as the philosophies of all the *Jagadgurus* are incorporated in such a way as if the ocean of knowledge in these books is churned and solidified into one book, that would be "The Divine Vision of Radha Krishn."**

I have been trying to experience and understand the deeper meaning and the differences between different practices of worship of God, and methods of meditation, which have become popular these days. After reading Swamiji's book I feel more comfortable to follow the path of *bhakti* the way Swamiji describes in His book and guides innumerable souls on this path. Many of my questions have been answered and clarified.

I personally feel very grateful to Shree Swamiji for imparting his Divine knowledge into this book and am ever thankful for his Grace that I have had the opportunity to read it.

> **Prof. Adarsh M. Kumar**, *Ph.D., University of Miami, Miami, FL, U.S.A.*

# Contents

## PART ONE

### भगवत् तत्त्वज्ञान एवं रागानुगा भक्ति

### Understanding the Supreme
### Divine Truth and *Raganuga* Devotion
❀

## (2) The charm of Radha Krishn love, sequence of Divine abodes, Their Blissful superiority, and *Gyanis* falling in love with Krishn.

## (3) The Vedas, the Bhagwatam, and the *rasik vanis* gradually reveal the absolute supreme form of God and His Divine love.

## (4) The descension of Radha Krishn is an opportunity for all the Divine powers to serve Them.

# 3. Soul, *Maya*, God, and the Creation as Described in Our Scriptures.

## (1) General description of soul, *maya* and God, and the Divine identity of the soul.

## (2) *Maya.*

## (3) The creation.

## (4) *Brahm* (God).

## 4. The Total Substantiated Philosophy of Soul, *Maya*, and God, and Absolute Supreme *Brahm*.

## 6. Detailed Explanation of *Bhakti*.

### (1) *Bhakti* (Divine and devotional).

### (2) Kinds of *karmas, karm yog,* kinds of *sanyas,* and four kinds of desires.

### (3) The progressive description of *bhakti* in our scriptures. Your relationship with Krishn and *gopi bhao.* Form of God realization in *raganuga* tradition, *bhao bhakti,* and *sattvic bhao.*

### (4) All the Divine powers are dedicated to Radha Krishn. Fallacies that create confusion, and the ignorance and pride that block the Grace of Krishn. Explaining ' ये यथा मां प्रपद्यन्ते '.

## 7. The Practical Side of *Raganuga* Devotion.

## 8. Kinds, Classes, and Nature of Saints.

## 9.  Summarizing the Philosophy of Soul, *Maya*, God, the Blissful Superiority of the Divine Abodes, and the Fallacies that Block the Path to Krishn.

जयश्रीराधे

## PART TWO
### राधानुग्रह एवं बरसाना धाम
## The Grace of Shree Radha and Barsana Dham

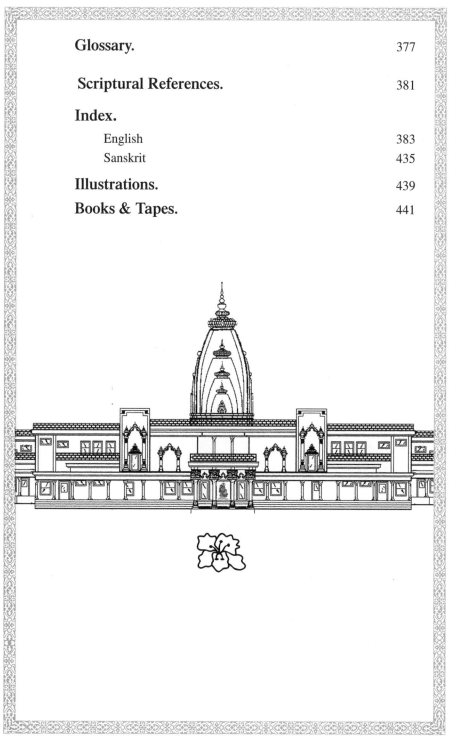

नमामि वृन्दावनमेवमूर्ध्नी वदामि वृन्दावनमेववाचा ।
स्मरामि वृन्दावनमेवबुद्ध्या वृन्दावनादन्यदहं न जाने ॥

(वृ.म. 17/95)

*"God realization is not the consequence of any practice. It is a Divine gift which is received through His Grace when a devotee's heart and mind conceive an unbreakable oneness with his Divine beloved, Radha Krishn, where even the desire of love dissolves in the loving feeling of His absolute nearness."*

*Shree Swamiji*

**To a devotee of Radha Krishn who is longing for His Divine vision and love:**

*"Life is short, and the opportunity is exceptional. Don't waste it in idle talks and illusive entertainments of the world. The mistake could be irreparable, and you may not even get a chance to repent...*

*Remember Radha Krishn every moment. Love Him, serve Him, live for Him, and you will recognize that Radha Krishn are really very close to you."*

*Shree Swamiji*

# Foreword

My deepest regards to my beloved Divine father His Divinity Swami Prakashanand Saraswati (Shree Swamiji) whose Grace has enlightened thousands of souls around the world and they have found the true path to God. His simple, direct, and authentic teachings and explanations of Indian Vedic literature relate to the ancient Masters of Vrindaban who revealed the supremacy of Radha Krishn Bliss.

India has had the privilege of having hundreds of Saints who taught the path of *raganuga bhakti* (*divine-love-consciousness*), but, in thousands of years, this is the first time this path of devotion to God has been brought to the West in its real, true and original form without any coloring of dogmatic religious beliefs.

On October 15 and 16, 1994, a great historical event transpired when we inaugurated our Barsana Dham *Ashram* in Austin, Texas. This *Ashram* provides the same Divine atmosphere as it was during the time of our ancient Masters and Sages. A sincere, good-hearted person, who visits Barsana Dham feels inspired with deep feelings of love for God. This loving affinity for God is a precious gift which is beyond compare.

Devotees, who know about the Divine pastimes and plays *(leelas)* of Krishn in Braj (India), when they visit Barsana Dham, begin to feel that they are really in Braj. While seeing the devotional *(leela)* places of Barsana Dham they imagine that the *leelas* of Radha Krishn are still happening here as they had happened 5,000 years ago.

At the end of the Inauguration event of 1994 we decided to have the Deity Establishment Ceremony of Shree Raseshwari Radha Rani on the Sharad Poornima of 1995. On that particular occasion and at the request of the devotees, Shree Swamiji decided to grace them with such a book which has all the devotional and philosophical information in a simple and easy to understand format. Thus "The Divine Vision of Radha Krishn" was created.

To make it more valuable for everyone, Sushree Meera Devi and Priya Dasi added detailed information about Barsana Dham and Shree Raseshwari Radha Rani Temple in the U.S.A., the International Society of Divine Love, and our contributions to the world, along with a brief biography of Shree Swamiji which is very inspiring to a devotee of Radha Krishn.

I strongly suggest that you read these writings with a devotional heart and mind. If you take these words directly into your heart you will receive answers to your devotional prayers and questions, whatever you have, and you will feel close to Radha Krishn.

September, 1995                                          Peter Spiegel

# Introduction

"The Divine Vision of Radha Krishn" is a practical guide for all who sincerely desire to experience the loving Bliss of any form of God, especially Radha Krishn, and perceive His supreme Divine beauty, because the procedure of devotional *bhakti* for receiving the Divine vision of any form of God is the same. **One should know that God is not the subject of intellect, only His devotional form and philosophy is the subject of pure and faithful intellect.**

In this book we have incorporated the theme and philosophies of all the scriptures. There are more than two hundred Upnishads, thirty-five Puranas and Uppuranas, many other devotional books like the Narad Bhakti Sutra, the Panchratra, etc., the Gita, the Bhagwatam and their explanations by other Saints ( टीका, भाष्य ), the *darshan shastras* and *smriti granthas*, history books (Ramayanam, Mahabharat), hundreds of books by Roop, Sanatan and Jeev Goswami and other Saints of Braj on devotion, dedication, *leela*, philosophy and biography, etc., several books of *advait marg,* and all the *bhashyas* on Brahm Sutra including Jeev Goswami's Shat Sandarbh with their explanations ( टीका ) etc.

The paths of *karm, gyan* and *yog* with their outcomes along with all the classes of *bhakti* are described to evaluate the simplicity and the greatness of *raganuga bhakti* which is the main path of Divine love realization. The philosophies of all the *Jagadgurus* have been described and their differences reconciled. The practical aspects of *raganuga* devotion, the pitfalls of the path, and their remedies are also explained. Traditional, conceptual, and intellectual misbeliefs, mistakes, and fallacies have also been removed and explained.

There is most controversial situation between *advait vad* and the *Vaishnav* philosophy which has never been reconciled in the last thousands of years. But we have given a new dimension to it in this book that ends the conflict. In doing so we had to consider all the aspects of Shankaracharya's writings and also his personal feelings.

The puzzling factors for the scientists that relate to the creation and working of this universe, the weakness of the uncertainty principle of the quantum theory and the first particle of the universe are also described.

There are very few words in the English language whereas there are hundreds of technical words in the Sanskrit language which are used in our scriptures to explain the Divine theory. They could be described but not translated. So we have used a number of original terms of Sanskrit in these writings (with their explanations) to elucidate the Divine truth in an exacting manner, and also to provide a guideline for a Sanskrit scholar to easily relate to our explanations. Thus, this book is the concentrated essence of more than 400 scriptures and it describes the most intricate philosophies of the Divine world.

In this way, from a prideless, open minded, highly educated scholar to a simple-hearted devotee, this book may enlighten the devotional path of every sincere and faithful ( श्रद्धावान् ) soul who desires to receive the Grace of Radha Raseshwari Krishn of Divine Vrindaban. A day may come when you may really receive Their Divine vision. I will feel most happy if I have helped you in any way. All the time while I was writing, I only felt Her Grace that took the shape of this book. I know nothing but Her love and kindness. I can only sing Her glory.

जयति रासेश्वरी, जयति श्रीराधिके ।
जयति कृष्णात्मिके, कृष्णप्राणाधिके ॥
नवरसविस्तारिणी, रतिरसप्रदायिनी ।
जयति मम स्वामिनी, जयति मम जीवने ॥

Radha Ashtmi, 1995.                    Swami Prakashanand Saraswati

# PART ONE

## भगवत् तत्त्वज्ञान एवं रागानुगा भक्ति
## Understanding
## the Supreme Divine Truth
## and *Raganuga* Devotion

जयति रासेश्वरी, जयति श्रीराधिके । जयति कृष्णात्मिके, कृष्णप्राणाधिके ।
नवरसविस्तारिणी, रतिरसप्रदायिनी । जयति मम स्वामिनी, जयति मम जीवने ॥

# भगवत् तत्त्वज्ञान एवं रागानुगा भक्ति

❋ श्रीराधे ❋

नमामि नवनागरीगौराङ्गीकृपालयाम् ॥

❋

श्यामानन्दरसैकसिन्धुबुडितां वृन्दावनाधीश्वरीं
तत्स्वानन्दरसाम्बुधौ निरवधौ मग्नं च तं श्यामलम् ।
ताट्टक् प्राणपरार्धवल्लभयुगक्रीडावलोकोन्मदा-
नन्दैकाब्धिरसभ्रमत्तनुधियो: ध्यायामि तास्तत्पराः ॥

❋

# 1.
# The Eternal Truth of Our Scriptures and *Raganuga Bhakti.*

## Radha Krishn and Their Divine abode.

The Divine supremacy of Shree Raseshwari Radha Rani is detailed in the Radhikopnishad, the Radha Tapniyopnishad, the Devi Bhagwatam (ninth canto), and all the writings of the *rasik* Saints of Vrindaban. Shree Shukdeo Paramhans, about 5,000 years ago, described the personality of Shree Radha at three places in the Bhagwatam and only in a few words, because the form of Radha is for adoration and for evolved devotional experiences through the *raganuga* tradition of devotion, not for intellectual analysis.

Radha Herself is Krishn, so Radha and Krishn are one and the same, but They appear in two forms ( येयं राधा यश्च कृष्ण: ).

Their names are Divine powers which were introduced by the descended Saints through their teachings and writings.

Our main scriptures, like the Upnishads, the Gita and the Bhagwatam, are eternal and Divine. From time to time they are reproduced by a descension of God on the earth planet for the good of the souls. The Upnishads, which are part of the Vedas, were introduced by the creator Brahma even before the beginning of human civilization. The Gita was said by Krishn Himself in 3138 B.C. and the Bhagwatam was written by Bhagwan Ved Vyas around the same time.

The Bhagwatam tells in the eleventh canto that sometimes at the end of the 28th *dwapar* (a Vedic system for the calculation of time) Radha Krishn descend on the earth planet. We have a very systematic style of calculating the cycle of time. Accordingly, since the recent re-formation of this earth planet, Radha Krishn have appeared a number of times. Their recent descension (appearance) was 5,000 years ago. The Bhagwatam also tells (in the first canto) that Krishn is the absolute beauty and the supreme form of God, Whose virtues fascinated the foremost *Yogi* Shukdeo to the extent that, forgetting his Divine transcendence, he fell in love with Krishn, memorized the whole of the Bhagwatam, and always remained absorbed in Radha Krishn love.

Their eternal abode, Divine Vrindaban, (the Divine world) is limitless, beyond the existence of material time and space, omnipresent, and stands in its own glory. It is the expansion of Radha Krishn's personal Bliss, and is beyond the comprehension of a material mind. It is perceivable by a soul only through the Divine eyes received by Their Grace on the complete purification of the heart through the practice of *raganuga bhakti*.

## Devotion to Radha Krishn is eternal.

Devotion to Radha Krishn is called *rasopasna* or *raganuga bhakti* or *divine-love-consciousness*. Our eternal scriptures, the Upnishads, say,

"रसो वै सः ।"
"ईशावास्यमिदं सर्वम् ।"
"कृष्ण एव परो देवस्तं ध्यायेत्तं भजेत् ।"

It means, "The supreme Divine power is Bliss Himself. He is omnipresent in this world. He is (Radha) Krishn. Remember Him, worship Him, adore Him, and enjoy the sweetness of His love." **Thus we know that devotion to Radha Krishn (the path of *divine-love-consciousness*) is eternal.**

The Devi Bhagwatam also tells about the other forms of God that are innate in the form of Radha Krishn. They are: Shiv, Vishnu, Lakchmi, Parvati and Durga, etc. Their form is also eternal. In general, the Upnishads say that those who attain the vision of any of those forms of God are liberated from the bondage of *maya*, become Divine like God, and enjoy the Divine happiness. But, at one place, it says that those who attain the Grace of Radha Krishn enjoy a still deeper aspect of Divine Bliss called Divine love (तं रसेत् तं भजेत्).

This is the Divine secret of Radha's personality which is extensively revealed in the writings of the Saints of Vrindaban, where they describe the indescribable superiority of Radha's beauty, charm, and love in all the *leelas* of Divine Vrindaban (*leela* means the playful Divine acts of Radha and Krishn).

Most of the *Jagadgurus* emphasized the greatness of Radha Krishn. Shankaracharya worshipped Krishn. Nimbarkacharya, Vallabhacharya and Jeev Goswami (of Madhvacharya religion) described the greatness of Radha Krishn in their writings.

The Upnishad says,

"तस्य शक्त्यस्त्वनेकधा ह्लादिनी सन्धिनी ज्ञानेच्छा क्रियाद्या
बहुबिधा शक्तयः तास्वाह्लादिनी वरीयसी ।"

It means that God has many powers, *ahladini, sandhini,* etc. *Sandhini* is the 'almighty' power of God, whereas *ahladini*, the 'Divine love' power of God, is the main and supreme power which already includes the 'Divine Bliss' of other forms of God. **To reveal this secret the Devi Bhagwatam said that God Vishnu etc. appeared from the Divine body of Radha Krishn.**

During the descension period of Radha Krishn, 5,000 years ago, the *gyani* and *yogi* Saints who came to Braj and happened to see Krishn found true Divine happiness in Him and became His devotees forever. The *bhakt* Saints of other forms of God, who came to Braj at that time and happened to see Krishn, experienced an enhanced blissfulness in the vision of Krishn.

These instances explain that Radha Krishn are the prime source of all kinds and forms of Divine happiness. **It means that a sincere and true devotee of God, following any religion, may find peace and happiness in a place where pure devotion to Radha Krishn is done.**

## The kinds of Divine Blissfulness of God.

Our scriptures categorize the experiences of the Divine Blissfulness of God as: (a) *brahmanand*, (b) *bhagwadanand*, and (c) *premanand*. They are received according to your sincere submission and loving attachment to God, and your conception about the particular form of God you wish to attain. The Divine blissfulness of God, of any of these three kinds, is experienced with the Grace of God only after complete purification of the heart.

Krishn says in the Gita,

" ये यथा मां प्रपद्यन्ते तांस्तथैव भजाम्यहम् । "

"I Divinize that form of God which a devotee has conceived in his heart before God realization (because all the forms of God are within Me)."

All the religions and Saints say, "You have to love God and leave worldly attachments." This is called devotion or *bhakti*, and this has to be done by everyone desiring God realization, irrespective of his faith, religion or belief. The differences are only in the concept of the form of God in various religions of the world because they deal with only one form of God. Indian scriptures explain all the forms of God along with Their relative inter-submissive supremacy.

God is only one for all the souls of this universe. He has many forms and names and, with all of His forms and names, He is omnipresent. Those who lovingly surrender to the impersonal *(nirakar)* form of God, after God realization, experience a kind of 'unidentified unlimited joyous peacefulness' in their heart. Such unidentified Bliss is called *brahmanand.* Those who lovingly adore a personal form of God with a desire to be blissful and see His glory, after God realization, perceive and enjoy the 'Blissful Divine happiness' in the Divine abode of their adored form of God. Such a Divine Bliss is called *bhagwadanand* or the Blissfulness of *sandhini* power (the almighty form of God). Those who lovingly adore the personal form of God as Radha Krishn, desiring only to receive Their love and serve Them, after God realization, perceive and enjoy the 'loving sweetness of Krishn love or Radha Krishn love.' They also enjoy Their loving association in Golok or Divine Vrindaban. This is supreme Divine Bliss and is called *premanand.* It is related to *ahladini* power (the Divine love form of God).

We can also understand it like this: All the forms of God and Their abodes, mentioned in our scriptures, exist eternally in the Divine dimension.

सर्वे पूर्णाः शाश्वताश्च देहास्तस्य परात्मनः ।

When only the physical structure of this universe was created and there were no souls, God still existed in the universe as an omnipresent Divine power. He was then called *nirakar brahm.*

When the celestial worlds were created and the souls came into being, the eternal almighty forms of God, like Vishnu, Lakchmi, Durga, Shiv, Parvati, etc., descended along with Their abode in the celestial space of this *brahmand* and became involved in disciplining and maintaining it according to the uncountable *karmas* of the uncountable souls. These personal forms of God are called *bhagwan,* the almighty. Sita Ram and Radha Krishn also appeared on this earth planet for a short period of time. Their main work was to give Divine love to Their dedicated devotees, so They are called *premavatar* (the loving descension of God). Krishn gave the maximum limit of Divine love *(premanand)* that a soul could receive, so He is called *poornavatar* (the supreme descension of God) and *poorntam-purushottam-brahm* (the supreme Divine love form of God).

**The formless *brahm*, the almighty *bhagwan*, and the loving form of God, *premavatar*, are all one, yet there are blissful qualitative differences in Them.** The simultaneous existence of the mono-dualistic state of God is absolutely beyond the comprehension of human intellect, because it is the miraculous work of *yogmaya*, the personal supreme power of God. Jeev Goswami wrote six volumes called the Shat Sandarbh which explains the theory of self-submissive state of various powers and forms of God. Finally, it explains the excellency of Divine love and Radha Krishn.

His work is called *'achintya bhedabhed vad'* which means, 'the philosophy of simultaneous mono-dualistic state of the Divine forms of God which is intellectually inconceivable.' It means it has to be taken with faith according to the writings and teachings of our great Masters. So, we believe in the writings of our *acharyas* and follow their advice. *Acharya* means those great Masters in whose name the existing religions, stating devotion to a personal form of God, were formed. They have clearly explained that *brahmanand* is included in *bhagwadanand*, and *bhagwad-anand* is included in *premanand*. This is the reason that if a sincere devotee or even a Saint, worshipping any form of God, visits Braj in India, he feels at home because Radha Krishn descended, lived, and played for many years in Braj. We have established the same kind of spiritual environment in Barsana Dham, U.S.A.

## What is *rasopasna* or *raganuga bhakti*?

The greatness of *premanand* is very difficult to understand intellectually, but, to Grace the souls, Krishn Himself explained it playfully. **The stories of Indra, Brahma, Shiv and Lakchmi in Krishn *leelas* have special messages.**

The surrender of the celestial king, god **Indra**, explains that Krishn's descension was Divine. The apology and submission of the foremost *gyani, yogi* and the creator of this world, **Brahma**, reveals the truth that the form and the Bliss of Krishn is beyond and above *brahmanand* and is also beyond the Divine intelligence of a Saint. He is the supreme form of God *(poorntam purushottam brahm)*.

God **Shiv**, who Himself is a form and embodiment of *bhagwadanand*, expressed His gratitude when allowed to see baby Krishn, and **Maha Lakchmi** could not receive the Bliss of *maharaas*, She only enjoyed the apparent beauty of the playful actions of Radha, Krishn, and the *Gopis*. These instances explain that *premanand,* or the excelling sweetness of Divine love of Radha Krishn, is above and beyond *bhagwadanand* (the Divine happiness of other forms of God).

The Bliss of Radha Krishn is called *'ras'* or *'rag'* in Sanskrit. The total expansion of the Divine abode of Radha Krishn along with all the eternal Saints of that abode are the form of this Bliss. When Krishn descended 5,000 years ago in Braj (now called Mathura district), He brought thousands of Saints of His Divine abode who appeared in Braj. They were called the *Brajwasis*. Radha Krishn lived among them and played with them. Those *Brajwasis* loved Radha Krishn more than their own soul, and they established an example of loving devotion to Radha Krishn. The path of devotion that follows the loving pattern of those *Brajwasis*, and reveals the *ras* (bliss) of Radha Krishn, is called *rasopasna* or *raganuga bhakti.*

## The desire of your inner self.

When your mind begins to understand that you are eternally related to your Divine beloved Radha Krishn, your heart begins to feel an affinity for Them, and when you truly understand this truth, your heart ceases to desire for worldly things and in its place remains a deep longing to meet your soul-beloved, the eternal couple, Radha Krishn. You understand that you belong to Radha Krishn and that your life is to receive Their Divine love. This is true knowledge of the 'self' and the knowledge of all the Divine knowledges.

## The form of *raganuga bhakti.*

Correct understanding of the Divine truth, the decision to gradually renounce worldly attachments, and faith in a Divine Master and Radha Krishn's gracious kindness, induces a subtle longing in a dedicated heart that desires to meet Radha Krishn in Their Divine form in this lifetime. The loving feelings of a humbly submitted heart at the lotus feet of Radha Krishn appear in the form of tears of love. These tears of love further clean and purify the heart and the devotee begins to feel a kind of relational closeness and affinity with Radha Krishn, Their names, Their *leelas,* and Their Divine abode.

Such feelings of love and longing (without any request for any kind of material gain or comfort from Radha Krishn), followed by continuous remembrance of Their name and the *leelas,* develop and create a stable 'devotional base' in the depths of the devotee's heart. This is called *bhao,* and devotion with such a *bhao* is called *bhao bhakti* or *raganuga bhakti* or *divine-love-consciousness.* Such a *bhao bhakti* is initially introduced in the heart of a dedicated devotee with the Grace of some *rasik* Saint.

The Divine truth revealed in this chapter is explained in great depths in the following chapters. **The second chapter** gives detailed information about Radha Krishn ( राधा कृष्ण तत्त्व ) along with other Divine powers. **The third and the fourth chapter** explains the total philosophy of all the *Jagadgurus* including *achintya bhedabhed vad* that relates to soul, *maya,* creation, and *brahm.* It also explains the absolute supreme form of *brahm.* **The fifth and the sixth chapter** tells all about the practical side of heart purification practices and *bhakti.* **The seventh chapter** relates to the practical side of *raganuga bhakti* and the Grace of a Saint that reveals the Divine love of Radha Krishn. **The eighth chapter** explains the kinds, classes and the general nature of Saints. **The ninth chapter** is the summarized information of most of the philosophies which are explained in this book.

# 2.

# *Sat-Chit-Anand* Krishn.

## (1) Our main scriptures and the system of describing God in our scriptures.

### What are our main scriptures?

Our scriptures are Divine powers and Divine writings revealed by God or a power of God Himself. (a) They show the path to God Who has uncountable Divine powers and many personal forms of absolute Divine nature. (b) They also explain the absolutely intricate manifestation, working, establishment, function and the process of the creation of the universe with unlimited number of souls of unlimited past *karmas*. The intertwined complex cause and effect situation of the *karmas* create the destiny of a particular living being and causes many kinds of variation in the nature and likings and dislikings of a soul. Accommodating all of these factors and situations, our scriptures advise a soul what is the best thing for him to do. There are five categories of Divine scriptures:

(1) **The Upnishads, the Gita and the Bhagwatam.** These are the three prime scriptures. More than two hundred Upnishads are available nowadays. They are part of the Vedas and are produced in the world through the creator of this planetary system, Brahma, before the beginning of human civilization. The Gita is said by Krishn Himself when He descended on the earth planet for the first

time. Radha Krishn have descended many times according to the Divine schedule. The Gita is the simplified essence of all the Upnishads. It is in simple Sanskrit in 700 verses and it was again reproduced in the latest descension of Krishn 5,000 years ago.

**The Bhagwatam** was produced by a descended power of God, Ved Vyas. It incorporates the philosophies of the Gita and all the Upnishads, and furthermore it describes the creation of this universe in great detail along with the Divine history of 155.521973 trillion years, when our planetary system was originally created. The descriptions in the Bhagwatam that make it the scripture of top-most importance are the *leelas* of Krishn, the philosophy of Divine love, and the description of *Gopi's* love for Krishn.

(2) There are thirty-five **Puranas and Uppuranas, and two history books, the Ramayanam and the Mahabharat.** The Puranas go into great detail telling the stories related to the celestial and Divine happenings among celestial gods and goddesses and the Divine forms of God or Goddess. Every Puran tells, in detail, the stories about a particular form of God. Thus, many of the stories are repeated with some variations in them. They also tell about *maya* and the creation, and that is also repeated in them. The Ramayanam tells the philosophy of Divine love and the life history of Bhagwan Ram when He descended on the earth planet. The Mahabharat is also a history book that tells the Divine history of India prior to 3102 B.C.

The above mentioned scriptures and many more were reproduced by Ved Vyas between 3202 and 3072 B.C. The Bhagwatam says that these scriptures explain the theme of the four Vedas, so they are called the fifth Ved.

" ऋक्यजुःसामाथर्वाख्या वेदाश्चत्वार उद्धृताः ।
इतिहासपुराणं च पञ्चमो वेद उच्यते ॥ " (भा. 1/4/20)

(3) The six *darshan shastras,* called the six schools of philosophy, are: Nyay by Gautam, Vaisheshik by Kanad, Poorv

Mimansa by Jemini, Sankhya by Kapil, Yog Darshan by Patanjali and Uttar Mimansa, called the Brahm Sutra, by Ved Vyas. They are all individually expounded philosophies on a particular aspect which is already in the Vedas and also in the Gita. The first two establish the details of reasoning and logic of how to prove the existence of a substance, material or Divine. The third one explains about the Vedic rituals that reveal the luxuries of the celestial abodes. The fourth and the fifth one explains how to introvert the mind by the deep thinking (धारणा) of the impersonal form of God and by the practice of *yog*. The sixth one, which is most important among all the six, deals with the philosophy of soul, *maya* and God.

(4) The fourth category of our scriptures are **the writings of our *Jagadgurus*** on the Gita, the Brahm Sutra (also called the Vedant Darshan) and the Upnishads, and **the Shat Sandarbh of Jeev Goswami.** The prime *Jagadgurus* are: Shankaracharya, Nimbarkacharya, Ramanujacharya and Madhvacharya. Their detailed writings explain the philosophy of soul, *maya*, God, creation, Divine omnipresence, the goal of human life, forms of God and the form of liberation, etc. Jeev Goswami's writings are: Sat Sandarbh, Bhagwat Sandarbh, Parmatm Sandarbh, Krishn Sandarbh, Bhakti Sandarbh and Preeti Sandarbh. They are collectively called the Shat Sandarbh. They are the most explanatory philosophies related to the various forms of God, Their self-submissiveness, and Their Blissful superiority. The description of soul and God is clearer in his writings as compared to others. There are detailed commentaries on the third and fourth categories of scriptures by other Saints and there are hundreds of books on the philosophies of the personal and impersonal devotions to God.

Shankaracharya explained only the *chid* (the formless or *nirakar*) part of God. The other four *Jagadgurus* said that the *nirakar brahm* is established in *purushottam brahm*, the omnipresent all-virtuous personal form of God, Who is kind and gracious. Jeev Goswami further elaborated the self-submissive Blissful superiority of the personal forms of God. He revealed this Divine secret that the supreme, all-Blissful, and all-loving form of God is Krishn. Vallabhacharya and Nimbarkacharya also said the same thing in their writings.

(5) In this category comes **the writings of all the *rasik* Saints of Braj** who were engrossed in the Divine love of Radha Krishn (*'ras'* means the Bliss of Divine love and *'rasik'* means the one who has attained that Divine love of Radha Krishn). There are detailed explanations of the love, Grace and kindness of Krishn in these writings. Hundreds of such books were written by our *rasik* Saints. The most important ones are: Bhakti Rasamrit Sindhu (explaining the devotional philosophy), Ujjwalneelmani (telling more about Divine Vrindaban, Radha, Krishn, *Gopis* and Their Divine ecstasies, etc.) and Radha Sudhanidhi (telling more about Radha's Divine loving form and Her limitless kindness). Then there are hundreds of books in Sanskrit and in Hindi language that tell about the *leelas* (the Divine plays) of Radha Krishn. They reveal the intimate Divine secrets of the Divine realm. They also tell about the absolute excellence of the Divine love (the *premanand*) that could be experienced by the souls of the world.

All the five categories of scriptures finally refer to the same absolute Divine truth, Krishn, Who is paraphrased as "सत्यं परं धीमहि" in the beginning and almost at the end of the Bhagwatam.

Briefly counting, there are more than 400 scriptures mentioned above. Reconciling the controversies that appear to a material mind, and considering all the aspects of all the scriptures, we are going to explain the absolute Divine truth of all the scriptures as explained in the Bhagwatam ( सर्ववेदान्तसारं हि ) and which is attained through *raganuga bhakti.*

## Definition of God.

God is eternally existing omniscient and omnipresent personality of Bliss ( सच्चिदानन्द ) and Grace with unlimited number of powers that could be categorized in three forms: Divine intellect, almightiness, and Divine love ( चित् तत्त्व, संधिनी, आह्लादिनी ).

All the powers of God are absolute, naturally self-submissive, and of unlimited potency, having Their specific personal form and name. All the personal forms of God have Their own Divine abode which is the expansion of Their own form. Their name, form and abode are omnipresent and eternal, existing in Their own Divine dimension.

## Can God be intellectually understood?

Now the question is: Are these powers, abodes and forms of God one or many, and whether They are all independent, interdependent or dependent? Again, are they different or non-different in nature? The answer is both, 'no' and 'yes' in every situation, which means it is impossible to intellectually understand, because our every thought is based on material perception which represents full duality caused by the time and space manifestations of *maya*.

The whole universe is evolved of two main factors, time and space ( अक्षरात् संजायते काल: ) in a constantly changing and aging manner that causes birth and death of every existing thing. Thus our thinking is based on these factors. So, technically we cannot imagine the differential and non-differential existences of simultaneous mono-dualistic nature of the various forms of God.

This situation is called ' विरुध्य धर्माश्रय ' in our scriptures which means the two opposites simultaneously existing at the same place and at the same time. It is described in a style as, " अणोरणीयान्... " etc. "He is minute, He is absolutely big. No. He is neither minute nor big. He is female. No. He is male, etc. He is simultaneously everything." There are many such self-contradictory statements for God. Finally it is said, " यो बुद्धे: परतस्तु स: " "God is beyond the understanding of human mind."

In fact, God can never be intellectually understood, but it is also a fact that His devotional philosophy can certainly be understood by a faithful devoted mind so that the person can easily establish his faith in Him, recognize his relationship with Him, and thus, start his devotion and proceed towards God realization. That's the reason that our scriptures and Saints tell a lot about His name, form, Grace, virtues and kindness.

But still there is one problem. These scriptures that include the Upnishads, the Puranas, writings of *Jagadgurus* and other Saints are the Divine outcome that need a Divine mind to exactly understand their theme, which again brings an aspirant to the same improbable situation, because he has only a faithful heart but an ignorant mind.

On his own, no matter how great a scholar a person is, when he reads the stories of the Puranas and the various philosophies of our *Jagadgurus,* he finds it confusing. What happens then is that he formulates his own philosophical ideas and sticks to it. I have seen many people who are truly devoted to God but their devotional understanding about the ultimate form and Bliss of God is not correct. They have pride of their own learning and understanding so it's hard to convince them because the teachings only enter into such a heart and mind which is willing to accept its mistakes (श्रद्धावाँल्लभते ज्ञानम्). **Thus, for the benefit of the humble seekers of God's love, we are now going to explain all the aspects of God and God realization, the Divine oneness, and the Blissful superiority of various forms of God as simply as possible.**

## The style of describing God in our scriptures.

One thing we must keep in our mind is that our scriptures have a system of describing the spiritual facts. Just like a person who keeps his most valuable thing in the safest place, similarly, **our scriptures describe the intimate Divine secrets very exceptionally,** and the topic of general worship is described everywhere in abundance.

Ninety-three percent of our Vedas describe about the attainment of celestial luxuries and general worship to various forms of God for receiving material happiness and liberation. The term used to this effect is *'bhukti mukti prad.'* Only seven percent of the verses of the Vedas include the Upnishads. The Puranas describe general worship and devotion (*sakam bhakti*) for *dharm, arth, kam* and *mokch* which means the same as *bhukti* and *mukti* (attainment of material prosperity and liberation). But one thing is there, they all emphasize on *bhakti,* which means devotion to a personal form of God like Shiv, Durga, Ganesh, etc.

There is a secret behind such statements. The descriptions of devotion for material gain is an allurement to enter into devotion. Just like a mother promises to give chocolate to her five year old boy if he goes to school, but her desired intention is to discipline the boy and to encourage him into proper study. So, the desired intention of all the scriptures is to introduce devotion for only God realization, not for material indulgence. That's why where Poorv Mimansa and the Vedas describe the fascinating enjoyment and the attainment of celestial sensualities, the Upnishads, the prime part of the Vedas, totally condemn it by saying:

"इष्टापूर्तं मन्यमाना वरिष्ठं नान्यच्छ्रेयो वेदयन्ते प्रमूढाः ।
नाकस्य पृष्ठे ते सुकृतेऽनुभूत्वेमं लोकं हीनतरं वा विशन्ति ॥"

(मुं. 1/2/10)

It means that those who praise and desire for celestial luxuries are totally and perfectly ignorant because they are running after an illusory hope of fulfillment that would never happen. They could however do pure *bhakti* and attain Divine Bliss forever.

## The philosophy behind the stories of Puranas and other scriptures.

The descriptions of the Puranas and other scriptures relate to three main things: (1) The importance of human life, and the importance of *bhakti* and God realization through *bhakti*. (2) The absoluteness and oneness of all the forms of God, and (3) the graciousness of the Divine actions.

(1) We will tell you a few stories as an example. Once Ved Vyasji saw a worm running away from the road with the fear of

THE DIVINE VISION OF RADHA KRISHN

being crushed under a cart which was coming in the same direction. He came to him and said, "Why do you have so much attachment to your body? That's no good. Finally when you receive a human body, do *bhakti* and find God." The worm listened carefully and accepted the teaching. In the meantime the cart came and killed the worm. Later on, after many incarnations, he became sage Maitreya. Another story is of Naradji. In his previous life he was the son of a maidservant whose father was unknown. He received the teachings of sages, devoted himself to God, and in three lifetimes he became God realized (Skand Puran, Maheshwar Kumarika Khand).

We should not take such stories literally. Another place it is mentioned that Brahma produced Naradji along with nine other sages from his mind. They were unborn sages. They just appeared. These descriptions seem to be absolutely confusing, but they are not. The fact is that all the *rishis* and sages mentioned in the Puranas and the Upnishads are eternal Saints. They were never ordinary souls. They appear along with the creation at certain times. Thus the above two stories are simulations. Naradji and sage Maitreya acted like ordinary souls to practically teach the human beings: **(a) the importance of human life, (b) the importance of *bhakti* (devotion to God), and (c) the importance of God realization over any other commitments, duties and responsibilities of life.**

(2) Once God Shiv came to Ayodhya to see Bhagwan Ram and desired to stay longer. Shiv then assumed Himself as a priest, came to Bhagwan Ram and asked Him if he could relate the Shiv Puran. Bhagwan Ram consented and the priest (Shiv) began to tell the stories. In the end it happened that Ram became Shiv and Shiv became Ram. It was an amazing scene... After some time Ram again became Ram and Shiv became Shiv.

There are many such stories about the other forms of God. **It tells the oneness of all the forms of God like Shiv, Durga, Vishnu, Ram and Krishn.** They all worship each other at certain occasions just as Bhagwan Ram worshipped Shiv in Rameshwaram before

going to invade Lanka and Shiv always adored Ram as described in the Ramayanam. All the Puranas define their related God as *brahm*. It means that **all the forms of God are absolute and one. The worshippers of one form of God should not disrespectfully criticize or condemn other forms of God. Such an act becomes a spiritual transgression.**

(3) There are certain stories in our Puranas, etc. that appear to be like the worldly acts of anger, jealousy, greed and lust, etc. Take one example.

Once in the Vaikunth abode of Supreme God Vishnu, His three sweethearts, Goddesses Saraswati, Ganga and Lakchmi, entered into a conflict which was started by Saraswati because She was really envious of Ganga. All the four were there in the same room. Saraswati said to Vishnu, "You are sitting like a dumb and wicked husband. You love Your sweetheart Ganga more than Myself and it's not fair. You should be loving all of us equally." Saying so, She rushed in anger to grab Ganga by Her hair. Lakchmi tried to meddle politely. Vishnu, seeing the situation warm up, sneaked out of the room. Quarrelling went high, Saraswati angrily gave *shap* to Ganga to go to the material world and become a river. Ganga did the same to Saraswati. Seeing this, Saraswati became furious on Lakchmi, saying, "You are sitting like a log and not favoring Me, so You also go to the material world and become a Tulsi plant." Thus, Tulsi plant, river Ganga and river Saraswati appeared in India. (Saraswati river existed a long time ago when Rajasthan province was not a desert. Now this river does not exist.)

In a worldly sense '*shap*' could be translated as 'curse.' But the Divine actions are always gracious, so '*shap*' is 'श्रेयप्रद,' **an unusual act to Grace the souls.** So we see that because of that Divine quarrel millions of souls are being devotionally benefited. That's Grace. Similarly all the worldly-like actions of ignorance and emotions, or any unusual or illogical looking actions of God and Divine Personalities mentioned in the Ramayanam, the Puranas or anywhere else should be taken as a Divine and gracious act.

They are meant, (a) to Grace an individual, or (b) to Grace the souls of the world in general, or (c) to establish a religious or devotional discipline, or for any other reason, because a Saint is one with God and God Himself is the form of Grace. Actions of God, Goddess or Divine Personalities are beyond human intellect and beyond material logic.

**Thus, one should not even imagine any worldliness in the Divine acts. They could be of any style, kind and nature, but they are only gracious. Implying materiality in Divine actions and behaviour or comparing Their actions with our worldly actions are grave transgressions.**

## The soul of the Puranas, the essence of the Upnishads and the Bhagwatam.

As mentioned earlier (in this chapter), **the intimate Divine secrets are very exceptionally revealed.** There are certain stories to ascertain these facts. For instance: Shiv joins *maharaas* as a common *Gopi* along with His consort Parvati. Vishnu was never recognized by the *Gopis* in *maharaas*. Lakchmi only enters Divine Vrindaban but She cannot taste the Bliss of *raas* or *maharaas*. Sita's maidens and Ram's devotee Saints of Dandak forest seek for the entrance in Braj with Their Grace to experience *maharaas ras* which Sita and Ram could not give. These stories reject the theory of total oneness of all the forms of God as explained earlier. **Now we will explain the topic of difference in non-differential absoluteness.**

To reveal the Divine secret of Blissful superiority and to compliment the above stories, the Radhikopnishad says that the creator of the whole universe supreme God Maha Vishnu ( नारायणोऽखिलब्रह्माण्डाधिपतिरेकोंऽश: | ) is only a fraction of Krishn's absolute supremacy. Radha and Krishn are one ( तस्य ह वै द्वेतनु: | प्रकृते: प्राचीनो नित्य: | ). They Both adore each other (राधा भजति श्रीकृष्णं स च तां च परस्परम्‌| ), still Radha is the life and soul of Krishn (प्राणाधिष्ठात्री सा देवी | ) so He adores, worships, submits and surrenders to Radha. He cannot deny Radha's will.

"सर्वेशः सर्वशास्ताऽहं राधां बाधितुमक्षमः । " (दे.भा. 9/4/17)

"कृष्णप्राणाधिदेवी सा तदधीनो विभुर्वतः । " (दे.भा. 9/50/17)

Radha is the queen of Vrindaban and it is Raseshwari Radha who reveals the Bliss of *maharaas.* Thus Shukdeo, who kept Radha hidden in his heart all the time like the most valued treasure, reveals this secret in the beginning of Raas Panchadhyayi of the Bhagwatam and tells ( वीक्ष्य रन्तुं मनश्चक्रे योगमायामुपाश्रितः। ) that Krishn took the permission of Radha Rani before doing *maharaas,* because Krishn's excelling beauty, charm and love is Radha. Radha Herself is Krishn, or Radha is Radha and Radha is Krishn. So, with this phrase, Shukdeoji tells the prime supremacy of Radha in the *leelas* of Divine Vrindaban. Thus the Radhikopnishad further says ( सैव यस्य प्रसीदति तस्य करतलावकलितं परमधामेति । ) that only with the Grace of Radha one can understand and experience the sweetness of the Divine love of Vrindaban.

Among hundreds of thousands of verses of the Upnishads, the Puranas, and the Bhagwatam, just a few verses reveal the real truth of Radha Krishn's supremacy.

Among the 200 Upnishads that are available nowadays, almost all of the Upnishads tell about liberation or becoming like God ( अमृतत्वं च गच्छति ॥ न च पुनरावर्तते ॥ स मुक्तो भवति ॥ स नारायणो भवति ॥ मत् सायुज्यमेति ॥ कृतकृत्यो भवति ॥ ) in the abode of God. This is the Bliss of Divine almightiness called *bhagwadanand.* Only at one place it is said, " कृष्ण एव परो देवस्तं ध्यायेत्तं रसेत्तं भजेत् । Krishn of Vrindaban is the Supreme Blissful form of God. Love Him, serve Him and remember Him. Then you will experience the Bliss of Vrindaban which is called *ras* or *premanand.*"

**Now you can imagine how precious and rare this *prem ras* or *premanand* (the Divine love of Radha Krishn) is.** That's why Vyasdasji says, "श्रीशुक ताहि प्रगट नहिं कीन्हो जानि सार को सार । Shukdeoji did not openly describe the personality of Radha in the Bhagwatam because She is the most precious one. Her love is the essence of the essence of the Divine *ahladini* power."

**The Upnishads only at one place tell this Divine secret which is the soul of the Puranas and the final essence of the Upnishads. It says,**

"तास्वाह्लादिनी वरीयसी । परमान्तरङ्गभूता राधा । कृष्णेन आराध्यत
इति राधा । कृष्णं समाराधयति सदेति राधिका । गान्धर्वेति व्यपदिश्यत
इति ॥ " (रा. उ.)

"God has many Divine powers. Out of which two are main: (1) *ahladini* and (2) *sandhini*. *Ahladini* is the supreme power. The most intimate state of *ahladini* power is Radha. Krishn adores Radha, that's why She is called Radha (the one who is adored). Radha also adores Krishn." The same supreme *ahladini* power is Radha and Krishn, so Both are one.

*Sandhini* power is called *aishwarya shakti* which means the almighty power. Almighty power is subordinate to *ahladini* power (the Divine love power) which is Radha Krishn, Who are the supreme Divine love forms of God.

## Explaining the oneness of all the forms of God along with Their Blissful superiority.

To explain this superiority for a common man, the Devi Bhagwatam explains in its own style,

"एतस्मिन्नन्तरे विप्र सहसा कृष्ण देहतः ।
आविर्वभूव दुर्गा सा विष्णुमाया सनातनी ॥
...वामार्धाङ्गाच्च कमला । ...वामार्धश्च चतुर्भुजः ।" (दे.भा. 9/2/54, 55, 64)

It means that all the forms of God and all the Goddesses (Lakchmi, Durga, Vishnu and Shiv, etc.) came out from the personality of Radha Krishn. These are almighty forms, that's how all of Them have some weapon in Their hands. This story tells three things: (1) All the forms of God and Goddesses are the various forms of the same one God. (2) All of the forms of God and Goddesses are substantially one and are all absolute, and (3) the form of Radha Krishn is the supreme form of God. That's how They all emerged from Them because They reside in Radha Krishn.

# (2) The charm of Radha Krishn love, sequence of Divine abodes, their Blissful superiority, and *Gyanis* falling in love with Krishn.

🕉

### What is the excellency of Radha Krishn love? Radha, the *Mahabhao*.

Chaitanya Mahaprabhuji who was the descension of Radha Herself revealed the Divine secrets for the devotees desiring Divine love.

After this *brahmand* (world) was created, Radha Krishn, in Divine Vrindaban, decided to again appear as Chaitanya Mahaprabhu. Ved Vyas mentioned this descension in the Puranas as, "शचीसुतः ।" (भ. पु.) "चैतन्यनामः हरिः" (नृ. पु.)

Mahaprabhuji accepted the Bhagwatam as the explanation of the Brahm Sutras (अर्थोऽयं ब्रह्मसूत्राणाम् ।). From time to time he revealed certain devotional and Divine secrets in his speeches. They are all stated in the Chaitanya Charitamrit. His eight verses of devotional teaching, called Shikchashtak, are very famous. The Bhakti Rasamrit Sindhu, the Brihad Bhagwatamrit, the Shat Sandarbh and many more books written by his disciples, Roop, Sanatan and Jeev Goswami, are the expositions of Chaitanya's direct Grace that showed the secrets of devotion and revealed the explicit philosophy of the forms of God, His Blissful superiority and its attainment. The disciples of Chaitanya Mahaprabhu whose names appear in the Chaitanya Charitamrit were all descended Saints.

Mahaprabhuji freely distributed the Divine love of Radha Krishn through his chantings of the Divine name to everyone who came to him with a faithful heart. He said in the Shikchashtak that loving and humble association of the heart and mind with the Divine name of Radha Krishn (through chanting and remembrance) gradually reveals the bliss of devotion *(bhakti)*. This is the essence of all the spiritual practices. **But, unless the devotional procedure and the devotional goal is clearly established in the mind, the devotion does not even start. Devotional goal means precisely which form of God a devotee desires to realize, and devotional procedure means exactly what he has to do during his devotions to achieve that particular Blissful form of God.** Just doing something for God or following any kind of religious or devotional discipline will not give you God realization. It will be considered only a 'good action,' not devotion. (The devotional aspects will be explained in the fifth, sixth and seventh chapters.)

What are the various forms of God and what is Their Blissful superiority, Mahaprabhuji has Himself explained. It dispels the confusion arising out of contradictory looking statements and stories of the Puranas and the other scriptures. He says,

"सत् चित् आनन्दमय कृष्णेर स्वरूप, अतएव स्वरूपशक्ति होय तिन रूप । आनन्दांशे ह्लादिनी सदंशे संधिनी, चिदंशे संवित् जारेज्ञान करिमानि । ह्लादिनी सार अंश तार प्रेम नाम, आनन्द चिन्मय रस प्रेमेर आख्यान । प्रेमेर परम सार महाभाव जानी, सेइ महाभाव रूप राधा ठकुरानी ॥"

"God Krishn is *sat-chit-anand*. This is His personality as absolute *brahm*. It is His *swaroop shakti* which appears in three forms. *Sat* appears as *sandhini* (the almighty power of God), *chit* appears as *samvit* (the omniscient-absolute-unlimited-knowledge aspect of God), and *anand* appears as *ahladini* (the personal Bliss of God). The essence of *ahladini* is called *prem tattva* (the Divine love power), and the absolute essence of *prem tattva* is *Mahabhao* (महाभाव). This is Raseshwari Radha Rani."

*Mahabhao* is Radha *tattva*. *Mahabhao* is the personal characteristic of Radha. *Mahabhao* is the absolute culmination of

Divine love power where the absolute almightiness of God mergingly disappears. Only Krishn, the supreme God ( पूर्णतम पुरुषोत्तम ब्रह्म ), understands about *Mahabhao* Radha, but when He tries to fathom the depth of it, His Divine consciousness merges into the loving sweetness of Radha, the *Mahabhao*. Thus, Radha Herself is the absolute knower of Herself. Still Radha and Krishn are one or Radha Herself is Krishn. You can also say that Krishn is the beauty of *Mahabhao* (सौन्दर्य) and Radha is the charming and exciting sweetness of *Mahabhao* (माधुर्य). So, when Radha sees Krishn, She also drowns in the charm of Krishn's beauty.

This 'love' of Radha Krishn is like the life force and the sole essence of the whole of the Divine phenomena. Thus, (a) all the forms of God and Goddesses known as almighty powers are naturally self-submitted to Radha Krishn, just like your physical body naturally follows the will of your mind. (b) Almighty forms of God have Their Blissful form of Divine regality which a Saint experiences in Vaikunth. It is somewhat like a king to his subject's relationship and preferences. (c) The loving form of Radha Krishn is the highest form of Divine Bliss. It reveals such a 'love' that is beyond words and beyond imagination. It is so marvellous that even Goddess Maha Lakchmi cannot describe it. That makes it exceptionally special and great. Just think, if the sandalwood tree bears a flower, how deep and how exciting would be its fragrance? This is the excellence of Radha Krishn love as compared to the Blissfulness of Vaikunth.

## The sequence of Divine abodes of all the forms of God.

" गोलोकनाम्नि निजधाम्नि तले च तस्य
     देवीमहेशहरिधामसु तेषु तेषु ।
ते ते प्रभावनिचया विहिताश्च येन
     गोविन्दमादिपुरुषं तमहं भजामि ॥ " (ब्र.सं. 43, बृ.भा. 2/27/93)

" शिववैकुण्ठमिति तदुपरि कृष्णस्थानं गोलोकाख्यं इति । "

(पुरुषार्थबोधिन्योपनिषत् 6 प्रपाठक)

" श्रीवृन्दावनस्यैव प्रकाशविशेषे गोलोकत्वम् । " (कृष्ण संदर्भ 116)

The Upnishads and other scriptures say that Golok is the extension of Vrindaban Dham. Both are the abodes of Radha Krishn which is above the abode of Maha Vishnu, Shiv and Goddess Durga.

Although all the Divine abodes are omnipresent and are all absolute, yet, for general devotional understanding, their sequence is described according to their Blissful superiority. There are three sections: (1) almightiness (भगवदानन्द, *bhagwadanand*), (2) Divine love mixed with almightiness ( ऐश्वर्यमिश्रित प्रेमानन्द ) and (3) pure Divine love ( प्रेमानन्द, *premanand*). The first one is called Vaikunth which is the abode of all the almighty forms of God and Goddess like Vishnu and Lakchmi, Shiv and Parvati, Ganesh, Durga, Kali, Kartikeya, and also all other affiliated forms of God and Goddesses. In the second category there are two abodes, Saket of Bhagwan Ram and Sita, and Dwarika of Krishn and Rukmini. The last one, *premanand*, which is pure Divine love, is called Golok and Vrindaban, the abodes of Radha Krishn.

Sanatan Goswami says,

" श्रीवैकुण्ठेऽतुलसुखभरप्रान्तसीमास्पदेऽस्यायोध्यापुर्यां
तदधिकतरे द्वारकाख्ये पुरेऽस्मिन् ॥ "          (बृ.भा. 2/5/249)

" गोलोक इति गूढोऽपि विख्यातः स हि सर्वतः ॥ " (बृ.भा. 2/5/80)

" रासो हि तस्य भगवत्त्वविशेषगोप्यः सर्वस्वसारपरिपाकमयो व्यनक्ति ।
उत्कृष्टतामधुरिमापरसीमनिष्ठां लक्ष्म्यामनोरथशतैरपि यो दुरापः ॥ "
                                              (बृ.भा. 2/5/150)

"The Divine Bliss of Vaikunth is extensively great. (It is uncountable times greater than the Divine euphoria of *brahmanand* which is the most talked about topic of impersonal *vedant*.) But the Divine Bliss of Saket (Ayodhya) abode is greater. The Divine Bliss of Dwarika is still greater. The Divine Bliss of the famous abode Golok is very deep, profound and above all. But the unimaginable Divine Bliss of Vrindaban abode, the *raas ras*, is something that exceeds the limits of the Divine Blissfulness of all the Divine abodes."

He further says, "God has a supreme Divine secret, and that supreme secret is His supreme Divine love which is not experienced by His own almighty Divine form Maha Vishnu and Maha Lakchmi. That's why it is a supreme secret. That supreme Divine love is Radha Krishn and Their eternal Divine abode Vrindaban. Their love and the Bliss of Vrindaban is called *raas ras* which is the absolute exposition of Divine sweetness, Divine love, Divine charm, Divine beauty, Divine relationship and Divine intimacy."

All of the Divine almighty forms of God along with Their abodes descend into the celestial space of each and every *brahmand* of this universe to maintain the discipline of the material management. They exist as an embassy or branch office of Their eternal Divine abode Vaikunth and remain until the total dissolution of that *brahmand*. To Grace the souls with Divine love, Bhagwan Ram and Krishn also descend on every earth planet of this universe, representing Their abodes, Saket (Ayodhya), Dwarika, Golok (Braj) and Vrindaban, for a short period of time, but on a regular basis according to the Divine schedule. Sita Ram come for about eleven thousand years and Radha Krishn come for more than one hundred years on the earth planet.

Bhagwan Ram, Dwarikadhish and Krishn are all the forms of Divine love, the *ahladini* power. It means that Krishn Himself is Dwarikadhish and Ram, but the last two forms have a touch of almightiness or Godly glory. So the loving sweetness of Their abode, as compared to Golok, is impaired to the extent of the existence of almightiness.

A little boy is happily playing with his mother. She goes to an evening party. The boy follows her, but now his playfulness and the resultant happiness is restricted. Next day the mother goes to the school where she is the Principal. The boy also goes to the school, but in that situation his playfulness with his mother is fully restricted. Just like the social and official dignity restricts the flow of lovingness and the intimate behavior for both, the mother and the boy. Similarly, we can understand that in the presence of Godly dignity the playfulness and the delightful sweetness of the Divine love remains dormant to that extent.

Although same Krishn is Dwarikadhish, same Krishn is Ram, and same Krishn is Vishnu (Shiv and Durga). In this way, Krishn Himself represents different kinds of Divine powers in Their respective Divine abodes. So, His form is also changed accordingly. In Vaikunth with four arms as Vishnu He represents full Godly dignity, the Divine almighty power called the *sandhini shakti*. Durga with eight arms and Shiv with ash-smeared body are also in Vaikunth. In Saket as Ram, He represents *ahladini* (the Divine love) power with a part of Godly glory. In Dwarika as Dwarikadhish He represents *ahladini* power with a minimal association of *sandhini* power. In Golok as Krishn, with flute and peacock feather diadem, He represents pure *ahladini* power in its full Divine love glory. In Vrindaban the same Krishn represents the servitude of His soul Radha when His flute sings only Radhey name.

One may ask why am I saying that Krishn represents Himself as Vishnu, why not Vishnu as Krishn. The reason is that it is not so. You should know that too many 'why's, and how's' are intellectual indulgence and God is beyond intellect.

The Upnishads say that *ahladini* power is the supreme personal power of God ( तास्वाह्लादिनी वरीयसी ) that holds all the powers including *sandhini* power within itself. Krishn is the form of *ahladini* power so He is called *poorntam purushottam brahm* (the supreme personality of God). Thus all the forms of God reside within Krishn, whereas all the forms are absolute and are Divinely one.  Also, all the forms are the various forms of Krishn Himself representing Their respective Divine powers with varying Blissful elegance.  **Thus, there is an absolute oneness with definite Blissful differences in all the forms of God.  This, simultaneous non-differential difference (*bhedabhed*), is the natural feature of God Krishn which is established by the *yogmaya*, Radha, Who is the essence and life force of *ahladini* power.**

Now the gist is that, in a natural self-submissive manner, all the forms of God reside within the form of Krishn and all the forms of Goddess reside within the form of Radha.  Yet They have Their own abode, representing a particular form of Divine Bliss.

Their Blissful superiority is beautifully described in the Brihad Bhagwatamrit in great detail when Gop Kumar once saw Krishn in a dream and desired to meet Him and experience His love.  Searching for Krishn love he visits the celestial abodes up to Brahm *lok,* and then from Vaikunth to Golok (Braj).

First he goes to the celestial abodes and finds that people there enjoy the abundance of luxury, earned out of lots of austerity, good deeds and Vedic rituals done in their previous lives.  But they are jealous of others because some of them have better enjoyments.  He crosses the celestial abodes and reaches Brahm *lok* where he finds Divine peace.  In Brahm *lok* he meets all the Vedas, Upnishads, Puranas, Bhagwatam and other scriptures in their original Divine physical form.  He also meets Goddess *Bhakti* there.  He crosses Brahm *lok* and sees the most pacifying *brahm jyoti,* the formless Divine light, which is the power of absolute liberation, the *kaivalya mokch.*  It did not interest him so he goes further and sees God Shiv Who escorts him to Vaikunth where he meets God Vishnu.

God Vishnu greeted him with great love and affection and asked him to live forever in His abode.  Gop Kumar finds that Vaikunth is the true form of Divine Bliss.  Each and everything there is unlimited times more blissful and exciting than the limitless pacifying euphoria of *brahm jyoti* called *brahmanand.*  Still he is not very happy. He finds that all the unlimited affection, love and caring of Bhagwan Vishnu for him always holds a king-like Godly dignity that suspends the feeling of personal intimacy between them. Gop Kumar is longing for his personal intimate friend Gopal Krishn, not God friend Vishnu. So he proceeds further to Saket *lok*.

He finds consolence with the affection of Bhagwan Ram. He recognizes that things here are much more attractive and beautiful than Vaikunth and the Blissfulness of Saket is loving and lovingly exciting. He lives there for a long time but his heart is still longing to enjoy the sweet loving playfulness of Gopal Krishn which was not available in Saket. Bhagwan Ram, seeing his wish, advises him to go to Dwarika.

He comes to Dwarika, sees Krishn, and in loving excitement he faints. Krishn runs to him and lifts him to His lap. Gop Kumar comes to consciousness and, finding himself very close to Krishn, he feels very happy. Later on he associates with sage Narad and Uddhao. They tell a lot about Braj *leela* and express the greatness of Golok and Braj (both are the same). He lives there happily. Whenever he sees the beautiful face of Krishn he feels very contented, but still he lacks to see the loving playful intimacy of Krishn where he can freely hug Him, kiss Him, play with Him, eat with Him and live with Him.

Naradji tells Gop Kumar, "Whatever you are longing for, is not available in Dwarika. **Braj *leela* is the intimate part of Krishn's Divine loving plays, rarely described in our scriptures. Very few *bhaktas*, who know this secret, desire to receive that kind of Divine love of Krishn.**" He further says,

"Away from all kinds of Godly dignity, formality, protocol and etiquette, Krishn intimately reveals His intimate self and He attends to every desire of the *Brajwasis*. He feels happy in serving them with His boundless love. ( अनुव्रजाम्यहं नित्यं पूयेयेत्यङ्घ्रिरेणुभिः l ) This kind of love is only seen in Golok. Along with Himself,

Krishn also brought Golok in India which is called the Braj. So, O Gop Kumar! You must go back to Braj where, with the Grace of your Divine Master, you will find true Krishn love whose excellence exceeds all kinds of Divine Blissfulness found in Vaikunth, Saket and Dwarika abodes." Thus, Gop Kumar comes back to Braj and, with the Grace of his Master, he experiences the Bliss and intimacy of the Divine loving plays of Krishn.

There is still one more Divine abode of Radha Krishn, the Divine Vrindaban, which is the crown jewel of all the abodes, where the Bliss of *raas* and *maharaas* surpasses even the Blissfulness of Golok.

## The forms of God and Their Blissfulness as described in the Bhagwatam.

The Bhagwatam beautifully describes the total oneness of all the forms of God and says,

" वदन्ति तत्तत्त्वविदस्तत्त्वं यज्ज्ञानमद्वयम् ।
ब्रह्मेति परमात्मेति भगवानिति शब्द्यते ॥ " (भा. 1/2/11)

But further it says,

" यद्वाञ्छया श्रीर्ललनाऽऽचरत् तपो विहाय कामान् सुचिरं धृतव्रता । "
(भा. 10/16/36)

" नायं श्रियोऽङ्ग उ नितान्ततेः प्रसादः
स्वर्योषितां नलिनगन्धरूचां कुतोऽन्याः । " (भा. 10/47/60)

It means, "The God realized Saints ( तत्त्वविदः) tell that that absolute truth is indisputably one (अद्वयम्) but it is indicated by the words, *brahm, parmatma,* and *bhagwan*." Further it says, "The supreme bliss of Radha Krishn love received by the *Gopis* was deeply desired by Maha Lakchmi, and, to obtain that, She did devotional austerity for a very long time but She could not receive it." These references reveal two important facts which are very easy to understand. They are: (1) All the Divine forms of God described as *brahm, parmatma* and *bhagwan* are substantially one, but still (2) They have definite qualitative differences of Blissful superiority, that's why even Maha Lakchmi desired for that.

Jeev Goswami, in the Parmatm Sandarbh, goes in great detail explaining the three forms of one absolute *brahm*, Krishn. In fact, the whole of Parmatm Sandarbh is the explanation of this very verse.

We can understand it like this: A happy guy is frolicking with his son and feels 'very happy'. He is then called 'the father.' He goes to his office and dictates letters to his secretary. He is still 'happy'. He is then called 'the boss'. He gets tired of work and goes to sleep. Now he is neither a very happy father nor a happy boss. He is just useless, 'sleeping peacefully'. He can't even recognize his own self, so he cannot recognize his peacefulness. He will know it when he is awake, but at that time he won't be sleeping.

Like these three situations of the same person, there are three eternally existing forms of God, referred to as *bhagwan* (the loving form), *parmatma* (the almighty form) and *nirakar brahm* (the formless, inactive and virtueless state of God). *Nirakar brahm* is called *avyakt shaktik nirgun nirakar brahm* ( अव्यक्तशक्तिक निर्गुण निराकार ब्रह्म ) which means an absolutely formless state of God (*brahm*) where all of His powers and virtues are absolutely dormant, so they are of no use. **The *nirakar brahm* does not even recognize its own absolute identity, then how could it recognize its dormant Divine Blissfulness.** Such a form of *(nirakar) brahm* is established in *sandhini* form of *(purushottam) brahm*, the almighty God, and *sandhini* form along with *nirakar brahm* is established in the *ahladini* form of *(poorntam purushottam) brahm*, Krishn. **Thus it is only the personal form of God that recognizes the absolute identity of *nirakar brahm* within Himself.**

## The Divine love of Bhagwan Krishn.

With this sequence of description (*brahm, parmatma* and *bhagwan*) Ved Vyas indicates the sequence of Blissful superiority of these forms of God called *brahmanand, bhagwadanand* and *premanand.*

Although all the forms of God are Blissful but the *nirakar brahm* is a state of no-experience. So Sanatan Goswami says,

"सुखगन्धोऽपि नास्ति यत् ।" (बृ.भा. 2/2/171)
"यथारोग्ये सुषुप्तौ च सुखं मोक्षेऽपि कल्प्यते ।
परन्त्वज्ञानसंज्ञोऽयमनभिज्ञप्ररोचकः ॥ " (बृ.भा. 2/2/172)

It means, "It is assumed that there is Divine happiness in *brahm* but, in fact, the described happiness is like a relief from sickness, or the state of deep sleep." A person has stomach pain. He takes some medication and the pain is gone. He feels happy. Then he rests and now he is sound asleep *(sushupti).* He is free from all kinds of pains of the world. He is in an *advait* state where he cannot feel or experience anything. *Brahmanand* of the liberated souls is like this.

Now remains the two main forms of Bliss, the almighty God *(parmatma,* the *sandhini shakti)* and the loving form of God *(bhagwan,* the *ahladini shakti).* As explained earlier, the Bhagwatam tells the same thing that ( कृष्णस्तु भगवान् स्वयम् ) Krishn Himself is *bhagwan* and the Bliss of His love that He revealed in Braj, during His descension period, is desired even by the supreme Goddess Maha Lakchmi (the almighty form of God).

## The qualitative excellence of Divine love.

The Bliss of God in any form and style is always absolute, unlimited, eternal, and of total contentment. There cannot be any quantitative difference in any two kinds of Divine Blissfulness. That's why a soul receiving the Bliss of any form of God is always Divinely contented forever.

For instance: A *Gwalbal* (playmate) is dancing and admiring the sound of the flute played by Krishn. A *Gopi* comes by, hears the flute, sees Krishn and drowns in Krishn love. Both are contented in Krishn love in their own style. The *Gwalbal* never even thinks that the *Gopi's* enjoyment of Krishn love is greater than his, and the *Gopi* never thinks that She is enjoying more of Krishn love than the *Gwalbal,* because both are experiencing the limitless love of Krishn. It is the same with a Vishnu *bhakt*, Shiv *bhakt*, or Krishn *bhakt*. They are all contented with their own Divine experience.

Now the question is, why does the *sandhini* power, Maha Lakchmi, praise the greatness of *Gopi's* love for Krishn, long to embrace the footdust of those *Gopis,* and desire if they could Grace Her with Krishn love? It shows that there is something very special that makes Krishn love the highest; and that is the difference of relational sweetness which ranks according to the sequence of the Divine abodes, explained earlier.

**This superiority of excellence of Divine love that reveals relational intimacy with Radha Krishn in a more and more exalted manner, which Jeev Goswami has said as 'relational closeness with Krishn,' is a kind of multiplying absolute richness into absolute Blissful existence at every step of relational proximity. Even Brahma and Shiv cannot describe the greatness of such a Divine love because it is beyond the Divine language of the Vedas. But it is the limitless kindness of Shree Raseshwari Radha Rani that She awards this Divine love to every soul faithfully coming to Her.**

## References of *Gyanis* falling in love with Krishn.

The Divine love of Krishn has such an amazing character that it may evoke the totally absorbed (*brahm-leen*) mind of a foremost *yogi* and incline it to fall in deep love with Him. It so happened with **Paramhans Shukdeo** that only two simple verses of Krishn *leelas* evoked his absolute transcendence.

" हरेर्गुणाक्षिप्तमतिर्भगवान् बादरायणि: ।
अध्यगान्महदाख्यानं नित्यं विष्णुजनप्रिय: ॥ " (भा. 1/7/11)

The virtues of Krishn excited him to such an extent that he studied the whole of the Bhagwatam, and after that he remembered only Radha, the *yogmaya*, the life-essence of Krishn's all-greatness. The Bhagwatam further says,

" आत्मारामाश्च मुनयो निर्ग्रन्था अप्युरुक्रमे ।
कुर्वन्त्यहैतुकीं भक्तिमित्थम्भूतगुणो हरि: ॥ " (भा. 1/7/10)

"The fascination of Krishn's love and beauty is such that those whose minds are absorbed in the Divine *turiya* state of *brahmanand* (like Shukdeo), those whose minds are free from *mayic* bondage and are Divinely contented in themselves (like Sankadik), those *Gyanis* and *Yogis* who happened to come to Braj and were amazed to find their own imperceptible *brahm* in the most loving form, and those whose minds are engrossed in the Bliss of Vaikunth (like sage Narad), also selflessly love and adore Krishn." When Naradji thought of giving an example of how a Krishn devotee should be, the words *"yatha braj-gopikanam"* came out of his heart. It means one should love Krishn like the *Gopis* of Braj whose every breath was to please Krishn.

The amazing topmost *Yogi*, **Brahma**, who created this whole world out of empty space, and the first prime receiver of the Vedic knowledge, when he comes to Braj and sees the supreme *brahm* Krishn playing with *Brajwasis*, bursts into tears of loving emotion and, rebuking his pride of Divine knowledge, he says to Krishn,

" अहो भाग्यमहो भाग्यं नन्दगोपव्रजौकसाम् ।
यन्मित्रं परमानन्दं पूर्णं ब्रह्म सनातनम् ॥ "  (भा. 10/14/32)
" तदस्तु मे नाथ स भूरिभागो भवेऽत्र वान्यत्र तु वा तिरश्चाम् ।
येनाहमेकोऽपि भवज्जनानां भूत्वा निषेवे तव पादपल्लवम् ॥ "

(भा. 10/14/30)

"Who would not envy the luck of the *Brajwasis* whose personal friend is supreme *brahm* Krishn Who cares to fulfill all of their wishes." Further he says, "I would feel the luckiest one in the world if I am given a chance, in this lifetime or in another lifetime, to be born in Braj even as a peacock or even a flowering tree or a bush, so I can be in Your service of some kind and thus become one of Your loving beings."

**Jagadguru Shankaracharya**, who introduced the non-dualistic *(advait)* philosophy of absolute oneness of soul and *brahm,* now, for himself, longs and desires for the Grace of Krishn and says,

" उदासीनः स्तब्धः सततमगुणः सङ्गरहितो
भवांस्तातः कातः परमिह भवेज्जीवनगतिः ॥ " (प्र.सु. 245)

"Oh my beloved Krishn! Your *nirakar* form *(brahm),* which is neutrally static, aloof, dissolute and devoid of Divine virtues, never interests me. What will happen to me if You are like that? No. I cannot bear Your separation. You have to Grace me, and reside in my heart with Your loving face (that entices the heart of all the *Gopis*)."

A very famous *Gyani* and *Yogi* of the early 16th century, **Madhusudan Saraswati**, the writer of Advait Siddhi, after seeing the beauty of Krishn, says, " कृष्णात्परं किमपि तत्त्वमहं न जाने । "

"Krishn is the supreme *brahm*. There is nothing beyond Krishn that I know of." He describes in the Bhakti Rasayan that all the forms and powers of God reside within Krishn, and the Bliss of Golok is of the highest quality that exceeds the Blissfulness of all other Divine abodes of other forms of God.

# (3) The Vedas, the Bhagwatam, and the *rasik vanis* gradually reveal the absolute supreme form of God and His Divine love.

## Why the Vedas describe so little about the Bliss of Divine Vrindaban?

There are two reasons: The first one is that the *leelas* of Golok and Vrindaban are the intimate Divine revelations and are Divinely most precious, so they are briefly indicated in the Upnishads. The second and the main reason is that the Vedas (Upnishads) are affiliated with the *sandhini* (almighty) power. Their approach is only up to Vaikunth *lok,* so they don't really know the internal matters of Golok and Vrindaban. **They know the philosophy and the facts of Krishn's abodes but they don't know much about the leela-Bliss of these abodes.** At the end of every Upnishad when they tell about the outcome of the Divine knowledge, Grace of God, or *bhakti,* they say just one thing, *mokch* or *brahm sayujya,* which means liberation. Few Upnishads say, " तद्विष्णोः परमं पदं सदा पश्यन्ति सूरयः, " which means, "entering the abode of God." Even while describing the greatness of Krishn Bliss in the Krishnopnishad, it says, " देहबन्धाद्विमुच्यते इत्युपनिषत् ।," which means a Krishn devotee receives liberation from the bondage of *maya.* It clearly indicates that their reach is only up to *sat-chit-brahm,* the liberation and the almighty forms of God, not the loving Bliss of *ahladini* power.

## The Puranas are also affiliated with the *sandhini* power of God.

They tell a little more about Golok and Radha Krishn. " इतिहासपुराणं पञ्चमं वेदानां वेदम् । " The Puranas like the Devi Bhagwatam, the Skand, the Padm, the Brahmand, also Narad Panchratra and Brahm Sanhita, etc. tell more about Radha Krishn and Golok and they explain briefly about Vrindaban. But, the description of Krishn *leelas* and other happenings, related to Krishn and Radha with other forms of God and Goddess, etc., are described in a very dry manner in these Puranas with no real feelings of love. It is like a press reporter, who has no understanding about music, reporting about the happenings of a classical concert, or an eight year old boy telling details about a romantic story played in a classical dance.

It is clearly seen when, in the very end after a detailed description of *raas leela* and *nikunj leela* of Radha Krishn, the Brahm Vaivart Puran says, " श्रीकृष्णचरितं रम्यं चतुर्वर्गफलप्रदम् । " It means that, with the Grace of Radha Krishn, devotees receive the material benefits and liberation, called *dharm, arth, kam* and *mokch,* where the truth is that, according to the Bhagwatam, a devotee of Krishn rejects all kinds of *mayic* luxuries and all the forms of liberations for the service of his beloved Krishn.

When Ved Vyas wrote the Vedas, the Puranas and even the Brahm Sutra, he taught it to his ordinary disciples. But when he wrote the Bhagwatam, his very last work, he could not find anyone in the world at that time who could understand and hold the Divine truth of the Bhagwatam in his heart. He then meditated and saw that Shukdeo was the only one who had such a capability, but he was absorbed in such a Divine state of transcendence *(brahmleen samadhi)* where nothing in the world could wake him up.

Ved Vyas knew this secret that the Bliss and power of Krishn love is above all the Divine powers and experiences. So he told one of his disciples to go where Shukdeoji was laying in *samadhi* and to sing two verses of Krishn *leelas* from the Bhagwatam. The disciple did so.

The Divine virtues of Krishn entered the heart of Shukdeo and evoked his *brahmleen* state. Shukdeo opened his eyes, saw the man singing the verses, followed him, came to Ved Vyas and learned the Bhagwatam. After teaching the Bhagwatam to Shukdeo, Ved Vyas felt very happy, and Shukdeo, conceiving the Bliss of the Bhagwatam, entered into a kind of conscious *samadhi* of Divine love of Radha forever.

The Vedas were revealed by Brahma before the beginning of human civilization. They tell about the futility of *mayic* creation, the bondage of the souls and the absoluteness of God, and also about *karm, gyan,* renunciation, and *bhakti.*

" भक्तिरेवैनं नयति । भक्तिरेवैनं दर्शयति । भक्तिवश: पुरुष: ।भक्तिरेव भूयसी ।" (वेद; प्रीति संदर्भ 65) " यस्य देवे परा भक्ति: ।" (श्वे. 6/23) " जुष्टं यदा पश्यति ।" (मुं. 3/1/2) " उपासते पुरुषं ये ह्यकामा: ते शुक्रमेतदतिवर्तन्ति धीरा: ।" (मुं. 3/2/1)

These verses tell the potential greatness of *bhakti*, but they do not describe the absolute Divine goal of a soul. They describe only, **(a) liberation from *mayic* bondage (*mukti*) and (b) receiving union with God in His abode.** They are unaware of the *leela* Bliss of Radha Krishn. So are most of the Puranas.

**Thus we know that the goal and approach of the Vedas and the Puranas are up to worldly and celestial (*dharm, arth, kam*) happiness, the liberation (*mokch*), and the Divine Bliss of the almighty God only. They do not take us to the *premanand* of Radha Krishn, the Bliss of Divine Vrindaban.** That's why, whenever they describe any Divine abode they go into an extreme detail about the riches of that abode, like the roads of that abode are paved with precious stones, mirror frames are made of sapphires, candles have enlightened rubies, and colorful gems enlighten the house, etc. etc.

## Which scriptures truly explain about Vrindaban Bliss?

(1) The Bhagwatam takes you beyond the field of *sandhini,* the almighty power, and reveals the Bliss of the Divine love, the *ahladini* power. It tells much more about the *leelas* of Krishn and also about *maharaas,* the intimate Divine Bliss of Radha Krishn. It is in fact the Bhagwatam which has really revealed the supremacy of Krishn love above all other forms of God.

(2) Then there are *'rasik vani,'* the writings of *rasik* Saints, that tell in full detail about the *leelas* of Radha, Krishn and the *Brajwasis.* Roop Goswami, Sanatan Goswami, Jeev Goswami, Swami Haridas, Hit Harivansh, Nimbarkacharya, Vallabhacharya, Nanddas, Surdas, Dhruvdas, Vilvamangal, Krishndas, Vyasji, Gadadhar-bhatt, Nagridas, Bhagwat rasik, Jaideo, Radhavatar Chaitanya Mahaprabhu and many more *rasik* Saints revealed the *leelas* of Radha Krishn along with the true devotional philosophy for all the souls of the world.

The writings of *rasik* Saints are further explanations of the Divine secrets that are indicated in the Vedas. That's why it is said, "वेद रसिकन की बानी." It means that the writings of *rasik* Saints are the true Divine knowledge of the Divine realm and are the detailed explanations of the Divine theme briefly described in the Upnishads (like Radhikopnishad and Gopaltapniyopnishad), and also the true explanation of the famous Vedic phrase, "रसो वै स:".

## The Bhagwatam and the *rasik vani* are the essence of the Vedas and beyond the Vedas.

Ved Vyas wrote the Bhagwatam especially to reveal the supreme loving *leelas* of Krishn's descension and taught it to a God realized Saint, Paramhans Shukdeo.

One verse tells what is in the Bhagwatam,

" धर्मः प्रोज्झितकैतवोऽत्र परमो निर्मत्सराणां सतां
वेद्यं वास्तवमत्र वस्तु शिवदं तापत्रयोन्मूलनम् ।
श्रीमद्भागवते महामुनिकृते किं वा परैरीश्वरः
सद्यो हृद्यवरुध्यतेऽत्र कृतिभिः शुश्रूषुभिस्तत्क्षणात् ॥ " (भा. 1/1/2)

**(What is *dharm*?)**

*Dharm* means adopting a system of living with certain spiritual practices to elevate the *sattvic* state of a person from normal to good and from good to God. **There are two kinds of *dharm*, *par* (primary) and *apar* (secondary). *Apar dharm* is of three kinds: (a) social, (b) Vedic, and (c) religious. It is also called 'good deed' or 'dharm'.**

(a) Doing any kind of good deed, giving selfless charity, helping the poor, sincerely doing some kind of social service, being truthful, honesty in business, doing his family duties properly, etc. (b) Following the four orders of life according to Hindu religion called **varnashram dharm,** and observing all kinds of Vedic rituals. (c) Worshipping celestial gods, religious fasting, observing social and family religious formalities and rituals, and worshipping any form of God and Goddess (occasionally or regularly) with a desire to improve or maintain family prosperity. It also includes pious austerity of any kind, and *yogic* practices according to Yog Darshan. In general you can say that such practices that relate to *sattva gun* and evolve *sattvic* qualities of a person are called *'apar dharm'*. These practices can only take a person up to *satya lok* which is the last and topmost celestial abode of the *mayic* world.

" योगस्य तपसश्चैव न्यासस्य गतयोऽमलाः ।
महर्जनस्तपः सत्यं भक्तियोगस्य मद्गतिः ॥ " (भा. 11/24/14)

*Par dharm* relates to God realization only. It is also called **bhakti, para bhakti, devotion, devotional action** or **devotional karm.** It is of three kinds: (a) Desiring for liberation (*mokch*) or desiring for any kind of *mayic* sovereignty from God but wholeheartedly worshipping God like *Bhakt* Dhruv. (b) Wholeheartedly and selflessly worshipping any form of God, other than Krishn, and (c) selflessly adoring Radha Krishn to receive Their pure Divine love.

The Bhagwatam relates with the third kind of *par dharm* or *para bhakti* to the supreme Divine love form of God, Krishn, that reveals *premanand.* That's what is meant by, 'धर्मः प्रोज्झितकैतवोऽत्र परमः.' It is for those pious hearted people whose mind is settled (as it has understood the deceptiveness of the *mayic* attraction and the futility of worldly happiness) and heart is desiring for Divine love ( निर्मत्सराणाम्).

The Bhagwatam is also for the Divinely enlightened *Gyanis* and *Yogis* ( सताम्) as a last chance to receive Krishn love before they leave their physical body ( तथा परमहंसानां मुनीनाममलात्मनां भक्तियोग-विधानार्थम् । भा. 1/8/20 ). There is an example of Madhusudan Saraswati who received Krishn love after experiencing *brahmanand* (the Bliss of the impersonal aspect of God).

The great sage Ved Vyas has revealed ( वास्तवं वस्तु) the supreme Divine form of God, the supreme *ahladini tattva,* the supreme *yogmaya,* Radha ( योगमायामुपाश्रितः ), and the *leelas* of Krishn in the

Bhagwatam. It eliminates the total bondage of *maya* ( तापत्रयोन्मूलनम् ) and provides the absolute Bliss of the soul, the Divine love ( शिवदम् ). When we have such a scripture that gives all the philosophical understanding and also tells all about Krishn devotion, then there is nothing to do with other scriptures and their methods of devotion ( किं वा ).

( कृतिभिः means सुकृतिः, a pure hearted selfless devotee having good devotional *sanskars,* and शुश्रूषुभिः (हृदयंगमं करोति) means to conceive the theme and the Bliss of the Bhagwatam in the heart.)

Whenever such a devotee begins to conceive the Divine loving *leelas* of Krishn in his heart and mind, Krishn immediately enters his heart and stays in his heart ( सद्यो हृद्यवरुध्यतेऽत्र कृतिभिः शुश्रूषुभिस्तत्क्षणात् । ).

*Sadyah* word is used to explain the fact that through *raganuga* method of devotion the *bhao* of Krishn is revealed in the heart very soon as compared to other forms of devotional practices prescribed in other scriptures. According to the Bhakti Rasayan, when a devotee's heart softens and melts with the deep feelings of love and longing, his mentally conceived form of Radha Krishn begins to reside in his heart all the time ( द्रुते चित्ते प्रविष्टाया गोविन्दाकारता स्थिरा । ). At that time the devotee's heart assumes a kind of oneness with Radha Krishn and he begins to feel Their constant presence near him. This state of *divine-love-consciousness* is described by the word हृद्यवरुध्यते in the above verse.

**The Bhagwatam is the manifested Bliss (*ras*) of the Divine love of Krishn which has been indicated by a very important phrase of the Upnishad, "*raso vai sah.*" *Sah* is Krishn, because its qualitative word *rasah* relates to *ahladini* power, not *sandhini* power.** So it is said,

" पिबत भागवतं रसमालयम् । "

"The Bhagwatam is the nectar of the pure Divine Bliss. Just drink it forever without fussing around." Vallabhacharya, Chaitanya Mahaprabhu, all the *Jagadgurus* and all the *rasik* Saints of Braj respected it and accepted it as the prime scripture, because it is the essence of all the Upnishads and the scriptures, and it reveals the supreme Bliss of God.

The Bhagwatam tells only about the selfless devotion to Krishn which has no worldly ambition or even desire for liberation. **Thus, the goal of human life, according to the Bhagwatam, is not just to receive liberation from *maya*, it is to receive the selfless Divine love of Radha Krishn as *Brajwasis* have received.**

Krishn Himself says,

"न पारमेष्ठ्यं न महेन्द्रधिष्ण्यं न सार्वभौमं न रसाधिपत्यम् ।
न योगसिद्धीरपुनर्भवं वा मय्यर्पितात्मेच्छति मद्विनान्यत् ॥ " (भा. 11/14/14)

"My devotee does not desire the kingship of this world, the amazing powers of *yog,* the effulgent throne of god Indra, the throne of Brahma, or even liberation. He only desires Me and My selfless Divine love."

**Keeping the Krishn *leelas* of the Bhagwatam as a basic guideline, the *rasik* Saints of Braj elucidated the description of all the *leelas* in great detail and adorned the philosophy of Krishn love of the Bhagwatam by uncovering this fact that it was the Grace of Radha that manifested *maharaas*.** Thus the true Divine love form of Radha Krishn and Their *leelas* were revealed by these Saints, the sweetness of which is unknown to the Vedas.

## The descended *rasik* Saints revealed the qualitative superiority of the Divine Bliss to the world (the five *bhao*).

These writings are in Hindi, Bangla and Sanskrit languages. The *leelas* of Radha Krishn in Hindi language are written in the form of songs. Saints saw the Divine *leelas* happening and described it. These songs are called *'pad.'* The devotional philosophy, the Blissful superiority of the *leelas* and also the detailed descriptions of Vrindaban and Golok, are all written in these books. Some are in Hindi and some are in Sanskrit. Some of the disciples of Chaitanya Mahaprabhu wrote books in Bangla language.

There are many personal eternal associates of Radha Krishn in Divine Vrindaban, like Lalita, Rangdevi, etc. They descended on the earth planet with the will of Radha and They themselves revealed these facts. Roop, Sanatan, Jeev, Haridas, Nanddas, etc. were all descended Saints.

They also described in detail the adornments and the ornaments of Radha and Krishn and all about Them. **Now, from their writings, we know the classifications of the relational Bliss of God. They are:** *shant bhao* **(the relation of a subject to his gracious king),** *dasya bhao* **(the relation of a loving servant to his kind master),** *sakhya bhao* **(fraternal relationship),** *vatsalya bhao* **(maternal relationship), and** *gopi bhao* **or** *madhurya bhao* **(total submission to Divine beloved Krishn). There is also a** *'samanjasa bhao'* **that falls between** *vatsalya bhao* **and** *gopi bhao* **and is experienced in Dwarika abode.**

All of these Divine relational sweetnesses can be experienced in absolute form. Progressively they are sweeter and sweeter and amazingly more and more charming and exciting than the previous ones in the same sequence. This is the sequence of the Divine Blissful superiority. The last one is *gopi bhao,* the love of Radha Krishn as experienced in Divine Vrindaban.

The first one is experienced in Vaikunth, the abode of the almighty power. Basically, the second and third ones are experienced in Saket, and the second, third and fourth ones are experienced in Dwarika, the abodes of *ahladini* mixed with almighty power. The third, fourth and fifth ones are experienced in Golok, the abode of the full bloom *ahladini* power, and the fifth one in its full glory is experienced in Divine Vrindaban, the abode of Radha Rani, the *Mahabhao.* Saket abode also has *vatsalya bhao* and Dwarika abode has a partially selfless kind of *bhao* called *samanjasa bhao.*

## (4) The descension of Radha Krishn is an opportunity for all the Divine powers to serve Them.

🦚

### The eternity of Divine abodes, descension of Radha Krishn, and an opportunity to serve Them.

All the Divine abodes of all the forms of God are eternal and omnipresent. The devotee Saints who reach those abodes reside there forever. The almighty forms of God (Vishnu, Shiv, Durga etc.) also have Their transitory abodes in every *brahmand*. During the *maha pralaya* (the total dissolution of the whole universe) these abodes are terminated and are absorbed and transferred to their original and eternal abode. When the universe again comes into being, after limitless time lapse, the branches of these Divine abodes of almighty forms of God again appear in every *brahmand*. Thus, the original eternal Divine abodes are never effected with the dissolution or creation of the universe.

The Divine loving *leelas* of Vrindaban are eternally happening in uncountable styles. Radha Krishn, in Their eternal Divine abode Vrindaban, always desire to give more and more love to everyone in that abode. Vrindaban is the expansion of Radha's own personality. Everything of that abode including space, air, perfume of flowers, soil, dust, etc. is all Radha's manifested love in various forms.

### The descension of Radha Krishn is a Divine blessing to everyone.

Radha Krishn descend on the earth planet to Grace everyone ( मुख्यं तस्य हि कारुण्यम् ). (a) They Grace the souls by revealing Their love and *leelas* for them which are even beyond the understanding and reach of the creator Brahma and Maha Lakchmi, and (b) They give an opportunity to all the Divine powers so they can receive Their association.

As explained earlier, the *ahladini* power is the life and soul of *sandhini* (almighty) power, and Radha Rani is the life of *ahladini* power. Divine Vrindaban is the personal expansion of Radha Rani. So, almighty powers cannot enter the *leela* places of Divine Vrindaban. It's a natural loving instinct that everyone desires to serve his soul. These Divine powers get the chance to serve their soul beloved Radha Krishn when They descend in the material world, because, at that time, all of them can descend on the earth planet, live there in any form, and then serve Radha Krishn and *Brajwasis*.

In our scriptures there are examples of this kind that Shiv, Brahma (येनाहमेकोऽपि भवज्जनानां भूत्वा निषेवे तवपाद पल्लवम् ।), Narad, Maha Lakchmi and the Vedas in Their Divine form came and lived in Braj. In fact, all the almighty Divine powers came and lived in Braj, felt extremely blessed and served Radha Krishn during the descension period.

" तत्तन्महाप्रेमविहारकामः कस्मिन्नपि द्वापरकालशेषे ।
गोलोकनाथो भगवान् स कृष्णः
कृत्स्नांशपूर्णोऽवतरत्यमुष्मिन् ॥ " (बृ.भा. 2/5/92)

"नानात्वमात्रैरिव वर्तमानैः सर्वैः स्वरूपैः सममद्वयः सन् ॥ " (बृ.भा. 2/5/93)

" एकः स कृष्णो निखिलावतारसमष्टिरूपो
विविधैर्महत्त्वैः ॥ " (बृ.भा. 2/4/186)

The Brihad Bhagwatamrit says the same thing in its own style that Bhagwan Krishn, incorporating all other forms of God within Himself, descends on the earth planet.

श्रीकृष्णोऽवतरति तत्तदंशावताराणामपि प्रवेश इति यदुद्दिष्टं तद्यथा तत्र ।
" एते चांशकलाः पुंसः कृष्णस्तु भगवान् स्वयम् । " (भा. 1/3/28)

यतः स्वयं भगवत्यवतरति सर्वेऽपि ते प्रविष्टा इति ॥ (कृष्ण सन्दर्भ. 90)

" त्वं ब्रह्म परमं व्योम पुरुषः प्रकृतेः परः ।
अवतीर्णोऽसि भगवन् स्वेच्छोपात्तपृथग्वपुः ॥ " (भा. 11/11/28)

" स्वेच्छामयस्य " इत्यनुसारेण स्वेषा सर्वेषामेव भक्तानां या इच्छा
तां पूरयितुमुपात्तानि ततस्ततः स्वत आकृष्टानि पृथग्वपूंषि
निजतत्त्वाविर्भावा येन तथाभूतः सन्निति ॥   (कृष्ण सन्दर्भ. 90)

" स भवान् सर्वलोकस्य भवाय विभवाय च ।
अवतीर्णोंऽशभागेन साम्प्रतं पतिराशिषाम् ॥ " (भा. 10/10/35)

The general meaning of all the above verses is that when
Krishn descends all the Divine powers and Divine forms of God
and Goddess descend along with Krishn or separate from Krishn.
They live in some form in Braj, enjoy the loving Grace of Krishn,
feel grateful and in some way find an opportunity to serve Krishn.

The Bhagwatam gives a crystal clear view of the whole
situation. It says that Maha Lakchmi desired to receive the Bliss of
*Gopi* love. She did extreme renunciation and devotion to obtain it
but She could not. " यद्वाञ्छया..." (भा. 10/16/36) and " नायं श्रीयोऽङ्ग..."
(भा. 10/47/60).

During *maharaas* when Krishn played on his flute to call the
*Gopis* for *maharaas*, its sound passed through the Vaikunth *lok*
and reached the ears of Bhagwan Vishnu and Lakchmi. (To
distinguish Vishnu and Lakchmi of Vaikunth abode from the Vishnu
and Lakchmi of every *brahmand*, the word '*Maha*' is added, like
Maha Vishnu and Vishnu. Otherwise, in general use, Vishnu or
Maha Vishnu and Lakchmi and Maha Lakchmi are the same.)
Bhagwan Vishnu, with a deep sigh said, "Lakchmi! There is going
to be *maharaas* in Braj (Vrindaban)." Lakchmi asked, "Then why
are We sitting here? We should go and join the *maharaas*." Vishnu
said, "No, it is beyond our rights." Lakchmi insisted to go and
Vishnu resisted. Finally, Lakchmi decided to go on Her own, and
She came to Braj. But, to Her dismay, She was not allowed to join
the *leela* of *maharaas*. She remained standing outside the *leela*
place and simply watched it happening like the other celestial gods
and goddesses who were also allowed to watch.

Watching a Krishn *leela* or even joining in any playful act of Krishn is one thing and experiencing the Blissfulness of that *leela* is another. It is like the two boys who are watching a home video. The first one gets a thrill when he sees his mother on the screen and says, "See, she is my mother." The other boy says, "Yeh, she is pretty." He could only appreciate her beauty not the love as the first boy felt. So, the gods and goddesses, along with Brahma and Lakchmi, only enjoyed the beauty of the playful acts of Radha Krishn and *Gopis*, not the Bliss of *maharaas* which was way beyond their reach. These instances reveal (a) the unrivaled supremacy of the Bliss of Radha Krishn *leelas*, and (b) the true humble desire of the Almighty powers to serve Krishn by revealing and establishing His glory of Divine love.

Lakchmi is the supreme Goddess of Vaikunth, the great *sandhini* power. How could She have made such an ignorant mistake of ignoring Vishnu? In fact, She did not. When She discovered that Radha Krishn are going to do *maharaas*, She found a great chance to serve the Queen of Her heart, Shree Radha, and the Lord of Her mind, Krishn. Thus, She went ahead and, with such an act, She established the absolute supremacy of the power of Divine love, and the absolute greatness of the Bliss of *maharaas* and the *leelas* of Radha Krishn in Vrindaban. In this way, without going into intricate brain wrecking theological details, She revealed this truth so perfectly that even a simple faithful person can easily understand it, which thousands of verses of the philosophical descriptions of the scriptures could hardly do. She felt so happy and excited after successfully doing Her service that She forgot to sit down. She entered into a dreamy conscious *samadhi,* kept standing with folded hands and watched *maharaas*.

In the tenth canto, Gopi Geet of the Bhagwatam, the *Gopis* say, "जयति तेऽधिकं जन्मना व्रजः श्रयत इन्दिरा शश्वदत्र हि । With the descension of Krishn, the glory of Braj is enhanced and Lakchmi is now permanently residing in Braj." It means that Lakchmi was there in Braj all the time during the descension period. She came before the arrival of Radha Krishn and glorified the Braj with abundance of natural beauty, and so, bypassing the natural law, all kinds of perfumed flowers bloomed throughout the year. When the Goddess of Vaikunth, Lakchmi, was the exterior decorator, who could imagine the beautifications of Braj. In this way, all the powers of God experienced the boon of Their being and tried to serve Radha Krishn and *Brajwasis* whenever and wherever They found any opening.

## The appearance of Krishn.

There are certain religious fallacies which have been popularized so much in the society that they have totally clouded the Divine truth. One of them is that Vishnu came as Krishn and Ram, which relates to certain references of the celestial events. We are now going to see how much they have been misinterpreted.

Once, when demon Kans and his associates tormented the society, celestial gods approached Vishnu for help when Brahma, within himself, heard a Divine voice ( गिरं समाधौ ) which he related to the gods. It said, "Don't worry, the supreme God knows your problems. He Himself ( वसुदेवगृहे साक्षाद् भगवान् पुरुष: पर: I ) is coming to eliminate the demons and establish peace. You all go and take birth in Braj." (Bhag. 10/1/21, 22, 23) Devki had already desired to have almighty God, Vishnu, as her son and she was already granted her wish in her past lifetime.

" एतद् वां दर्शितं रूपं प्राग्जन्मस्मरणाय मे । इत्युक्त्वाऽऽसीद्धरिस्तूष्णीं भगवानात्ममायया । पित्रो: सम्पश्यतो: सद्यो बभूव प्राकृत: शिशु: ॥ "

(भा. 10/3/44, 46)

Krishn said, "O Devki, I appeared as Vishnu in front of you just to remind you of your past wish." Saying so, Shukdeoji says that Krishn became a small baby. Vasudev then took baby Krishn to Gokul, a nearby village about six miles from Mathura where, from the very next day, He started His Divine loving *leelas* at the house of Nand Baba and Yashoda which we all know.

" यास्यामि पृथिवीं देवा यात यूयं स्वमालयम् । यूयं चैवांशरूपेण शीघ्रं गच्छत भूतलम् ॥ " (ब्र.वै.कृ. 6/61)

The Brahmavaivart Puran in Krishn-janm-khand, Chapter 6, tells that once gods and goddesses went to Golok with a request to save them from the terror of demons. Krishn assured them and said that He, along with Radha and other *Gops* and *Gopis,* is coming soon and that they should also descend in Braj.

The Garg Sanhita says that,

" परिपूर्णतमं साक्षाच्छ्रीकृष्णं श्यामसुन्दरम् ।
ज्ञात्वा नत्वाऽथ तं प्राह देवकी सर्वदेवता ॥ श्रीदेवक्युवाच,
हे कृष्ण हे विगणिताण्डपते परेश गोलोकधामधिषणध्वज आदिदेव ।
पूर्णेश पूर्ण परिपूर्णतम प्रभो मां त्वं पाहि परमेश्वर कंसपापात् ॥ "

(ग.सं.गो. 11/34, 35)

Seeing Krishn, the supreme personality of God, Devki (the mother of Krishn) prostrated and said, "O Krishn, the prime creator of the universe, God of almighty God, Lord of Golok, the absolute *brahm,* the supreme Divinity, the absolute supreme personality of God, my beloved Lord, please save us from the evil demon Kans."

There is nothing confusing in these statements, just the bare fact that killing of the demons is the work of might, the almighty God. It is not an act of Divine love, so Krishn, acting as Vishnu, killed the demons, and Krishn, as Beloved of *Brajwasis,* did all the loving *leelas* which are beyond the reach of Godly almightiness. That's why the Bhagwatam says that the Vedas are still trying to find the footdust of the *Gopis* of Braj so they can also receive a drop of the nectar of the Divine love of Radha Krishn, but they have not yet found it ( त्वद्यापि यत्पदरजः श्रुतिमृग्यमेव । भा. 10/14/34).

In the descension days, all the forms of God came with Krishn and all the forms of Goddesses came with Radha and, assuming a celestial or a human form in Braj, They stayed in Braj and received the privilege of doing some service and being near Radha Krishn and *Brajwasis.* Brahma says (*naumidya*), "O Krishn, You are adored and worshipped by everyone, either in this world or in the Divine world."

By reviewing all the Divine facts and the statements of all the five categories of scriptures, it is thus comprehended that God Himself is absolute and unlimited Bliss Who has many omnipresent forms of mono-dualistic nature which are distinguished according to Their Blissful superiority. The sweetest and the supreme form of God is Krishn Whose life-essence is Radha. So, **in one verse, Radhavatar Shree Chaitanya Mahaprabhuji gives the total devotional understanding for a devotee.** He says,

" आराध्यो भगवान् व्रजेशतनयस्तद्धाम वृन्दावनं
रम्या काचिदुपासना व्रजवधूवर्गेण या कल्पिता ।
श्रीमद्भागवतं प्रमाणममलं प्रेमा पुमर्थो महान्
श्रीचैतन्यमहाप्रभोर्मतमिदं तत्राग्रहो नापरः ॥ "

"This is the essence of the total Divine knowledge that Krishn is the Divine Beloved of your soul. So, to receive the selfless Divine love of Krishn, Whose eternal Divine abode is Vrindaban, is the only goal of your life. (He Himself was Radha so, by using the word Vrindaban He is indicating to that form of Krishn Who is absorbed in the love of Radha, the *Mahabhao*. In this way he is referring to Both Radha and Krishn.) You should adore Him, worship Him, love Him and live for Him. The examples of such a devotion are the *Gopis* of Braj whose every thought was Krishn love and whose every breath desired the happiness of Krishn. The impartial and fair representation of the total Divine truth is the Bhagwatam, which is the final and ultimate scriptural authority. It enunciates the absolute greatness of Krishn love (which He revealed in *maharaas*). This is the advice and proclaimed philosophy of Mahaprabhu Shree Chaitanya which should be accepted with faith and followed by everyone who desires to taste the sweetest nectar of Divine love. He should not mingle with the philosophies of other scriptures or the writings of such people who do not humbly adore Radha Krishn of Divine Vrindaban, (as it may end up in confusion, disappointment and loss of devotional feelings. The human life is precious and short. It should not be wasted in intellectual gambling. It must be used for the experience of Krishn love)."  ❀ ❀ ❀

# 3.
# Soul, *Maya*, God and the Creation as Described in Our Scriptures.

## (1) General description of soul, *maya* and God, and the Divine identity of a soul.

### Soul, *maya*, and *brahm* (God).

Ved Vyas wrote the Brahm Sutra and then he wrote the Bhagwatam, where he revealed that the supreme *brahm* of the Brahm Sutra is Krishn. The Brahm Sutra and the Bhagwatam, both, he started with the same phrase *'Janmadyasya yetah.'* But when Shankaracharya wrote his *advait bhashya* on the Brahm Sutra, he ignored the personal form of God. Then, the *Vaishnav acharyas* and Masters, who came after that, contradicted the philosophy of Shankaracharya and emphasized the personal form of God. As a reflex action, the followers of *advait* philosophy stressed on the *advait vad,* which became like a non-ending debatable situation for the intellectuals. Although the philosophy of the personal form of God was always on the plus side, still this situation was somewhat confusing to simple faithful people as to which side to follow.

The writings of our *Jagadgurus* and great Masters, called *bhashya* and *teeka* ( भाष्य, टीका ), are in Sanskrit language. They use certain logical terms of the Nyay Darshan to describe a fact. These descriptions sometimes go into extensive details just like writing a forty page judicial judgement for a simple yes or no, which is, of course, necessary for the sake of justification, but it is much less intelligible for a common man. We can guess it by the fact that Shankaracharya explained the first *sutra* (अथातो ब्रह्म जिज्ञासा) in about five pages of the book which 'Shree Bhashya' contradicted and interpreted in more than one hundred pages. It gave detailed reasonings to explain that Shankaracharya carefully picked only such phrases and verses of the Upnishads that showed or appeared to be showing the impersonal side of *brahm.*

To learn *vedant* (the Brahm Sutra and all of its *bhashyas*) one has to study Sanskrit, then he has to study Nyay Darshan (to some extent). Only then he can start studying *bhashyas* of the *Jagadgurus* which is like a lifelong project to study all of them in proper order. I remember, once when I was in Kashi, a principal of a Sanskrit college (in his late fifties) who had three Masters degrees in Sanskrit ( साहित्य, न्याय, वेदान्त ) came to see me. He was holding a big book in his hand. During the conversation I asked him what was that book about. He said, "It is Shree Bhashya which I am studying nowadays." Imagine, he was the principal of a college with lots of academic degrees and still he was studying the *vedant.* So, we can see how extensive are these studies.

For these reasons, in general, the study of all the *vedantas* along with the supporting books of all the *Jagadgurus* is not possible, and a 'little knowledge' is always dangerous.

Thus, to facilitate this situation, to make this total knowledge available to the seekers of God's love, and to clarify the argumentative aspects of *advait vad,* we are going to put together all the important verses of (1) the Upnishads, (2) the Gita, (3) the Bhagwatam and (4) the Brahm Sutra that have been commonly used in the *bhashya*s of *Jagadgurus* to establish their philosophy of (a) soul, (b) *maya* and (c) God *(brahm).*

This chapter gives you all the above mentioned verses with their actual meanings, and summarized meanings, category-wise (soul, *maya*, and God), so that, without studying all of our *darshan shastras* and the *vedantas*, you yourself can understand their general theme. It also includes the topic of the creation with such scientific explanations which are still unknown to scientists and physicists.

The next chapter explains the total expansion of the Divine world. The intricate philosophies of all the *Jagadgurus* and *achintya bhedabhed vad* are substantiated and explained with further details that were not explicitly revealed earlier. Also, the *advait* philosophy of God Shiv's descension, Shankaracharya, is justifiedly reconciled and explained with a new vision to settle the intellectual disputes that have prevailed for the last two thousand years.

## General concept of soul, *maya* and God.

Now we will learn about the Divine identity of the soul, the existence of *maya* and its qualities, the omnipresence of God, and the supreme life force of the Divine existence.

" भोक्ता भोग्यं प्रेरितारं च मत्वा । सर्वं प्रोक्तं त्रिविधं ब्रह्ममेतत् ॥ "

(श्वे. 1/12)

" अजामेकां... । अजो ह्येको जुषमाणोऽनुशेते... । " (श्वे. 4/5)

" विष्णुशक्ति: परा प्रोक्ता क्षेत्रज्ञाख्या तथापरा ।
अविद्या कर्मसंज्ञान्या तृतीया शक्तिरिष्यते ॥ " (वि.पु. 6/7/61)

" कृष्णेर आनन्त शक्ति ताते तिन् प्रधान ।
चिच्छक्ति, मायाशक्ति, जीवशक्ति नाम ॥
अन्तरङ्गा बहिरङ्गा तटस्था कहि जारे ।
अन्तरङ्गा स्वरूपशक्ति सबार ऊपरे ॥
सत् चित् आनन्दमय कृष्णेर स्वरूप ।
अतएव स्वरूपशक्ति होय तिन रूप ॥ " (चै.च.)

The Shvetashvatar Upnishad said, "All that exists is *brahm*, but there are three things in it. All the three things are eternal. (a) The *maya*, which has three qualities, *sattva*, *raj*, and *tam*, and according to these qualities it creates this amazing and alluring world. (b) The uncountable souls, who become emotionally attached with the *mayic* entertainments, and (c) the supreme God Who is the controller of both, but He is absolutely unaffiliated with the qualities of *maya*."

The Vishnu Puran explains, "God's own personality is called *para shakti,* which is also known as *'swaroop shakti'* which means 'the personal Blissful power.' This power has two naturally affiliated powers, (a) *chetragya shakti* or *jeev shakti* (all the souls), and (b) *avidya* or *maya shakti* ( *shakti* word means power)."

The Chaitanya Charitamrit further specifies, "Out of uncountable powers of God Krishn, *swaroop shakti, maya shakti* and *jeev shakti* are the main. *Sat-chit-anand* is called the *swaroop shakti* of Krishn." *Swaroop shakti* of Krishn means His personal Blissful form and personality. It includes all the Divine abodes and all the forms of God and Goddess (explained in Chapter 2). It also includes *chid-brahm*, the *nirakar* aspect of God. *'Swaroop'* word means 'personal.'

"*Maya shakti* and *jeev shakti* are the two very close affiliates of *chid-brahm* or *chid shakti* of Krishn. But these two have their own characteristics. *Jeev shakti* is Divine and *maya* is non-Divine. *Maya* is lifeless, blissless and creates illusive blissfulness of a short-lived nature that fascinates and distracts the living beings (souls), so it is called the external power ( बहिरंगा शक्ति, *bahiranga shakti*) of God. So, *sat-chid-anand* is Krishn's personal Blissful form *(swaroop shakti),* and *jeev* and *maya* are the eternal affiliates of His personal form."

*Jeev shakti* (*jeev* means soul): This term collectively refers to all the uncountable souls. This is called *tatastha shakti* ( तटस्था शक्ति ), the neutral power of God Krishn. It means that *jeev shakti* is a power of God Krishn, but it is not a part of His personal power *swaroop shakti,* and also it is not a part of *maya shakti.* Souls are unaware of the Divine Bliss and are ignorantly attached to the attraction of *maya.* All the souls are live. *Maya shakti* is lifeless

(यथा सतः पुरुषात्केशलोमानि). It is called *bahiranga shakti* (the external power of God Krishn) which means that its qualities tend to create extroverted understanding (ignorance) in the mind of the souls (पराञ्चिखानि व्यतृणत् स्वयंभूः) that takes them away from God. *Swaroop shakti* is called *antaranga shakti* (अन्तरंगा शक्ति) which means that it is the intimate personal power of God. It is the personality of God.

The Chaitanya Charitamrit tells more about it and says that the form of *swaroop shakti* is *sat-chid-anand.* This is Krishn. The *'sat'* of Krishn is called *sandhini shakti* (the almighty power), the *'chit'* of Krishn is called *samvit shakti* (the Divine intellect), and the *'anand'* of Krishn is called *ahladini shakti* (the Divine love power). Sometimes *swaroop shakti* is also referred to as *chit shakti*, but normally *chit shakti* means the Divine intellect part of God.

The Divine form and abodes of *sandhini shakti* and *ahladini shakti* have already been explained in the previous chapter. **The details of *chit shakti* including soul, *maya* and creation, and the supreme personality of God *(brahm),* are the main topics of this chapter.**

The philosophy of soul, *maya* and their relation to God has been extensively described by our great Masters and *Jagadgurus,* called *bhashya* on the Brahm Sutra. At some places it appears disputable, although in fact, it is not, because they had to describe the inconceivable Divine truth into material language. We are now going to relate these philosophies in a straightforward and simplified manner so that you can easily understand them. **All of the important verses with their literal meanings that have been related in the *bhashyas* of the *Jagadgurus* regarding soul are as thus:**

## The Divine identity of a soul (the original text).

**The Upnishads:**

(a) " बालाग्रशतभागस्य शतधा कल्पितस्य च ।
भागो जीवः स विज्ञेयः स चानन्त्याय कल्पते ॥ " (श्वे. 5/9)

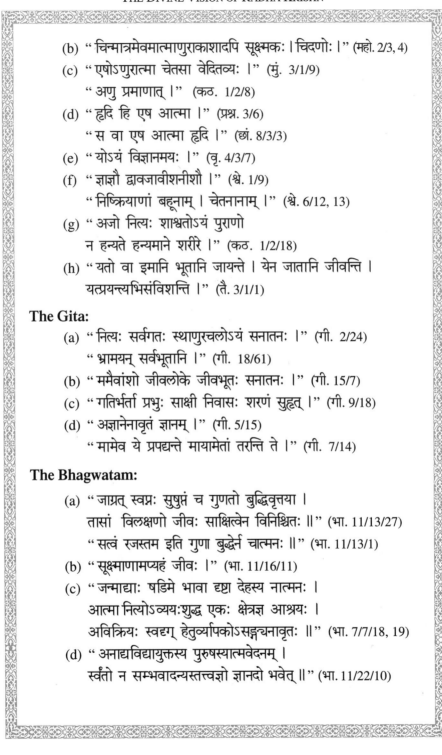

(b) "चिन्मात्रमेवमात्माणुराकाशादपि सूक्ष्मकः । चिदणोः ।" (महो. 2/3, 4)

(c) "एषोऽणुरात्मा चेतसा वेदितव्यः ।" (मुं. 3/1/9)

"अणु प्रमाणात् ।" (कठ. 1/2/8)

(d) "हृदि हि एष आत्मा ।" (प्रश्न. 3/6)

"स वा एष आत्मा हृदि ।" (छां. 8/3/3)

(e) "योऽयं विज्ञानमयः ।" (बृ. 4/3/7)

(f) "ज्ञाज्ञौ द्वावजावीशनीशौ ।" (श्वे. 1/9)

"निष्क्रियाणां बहूनाम् । चेतनानाम् ।" (श्वे. 6/12, 13)

(g) "अजो नित्यः शाश्वतोऽयं पुराणो

न हन्यते हन्यमाने शरीरे ।" (कठ. 1/2/18)

(h) "यतो वा इमानि भूतानि जायन्ते । येन जातानि जीवन्ति ।

यत्प्रयन्त्यभिसंविशन्ति ।" (तै. 3/1/1)

## The Gita:

(a) "नित्यः सर्वगतः स्थाणुरचलोऽयं सनातनः ।" (गी. 2/24)

"भ्रामयन् सर्वभूतानि ।" (गी. 18/61)

(b) "ममैवांशो जीवलोके जीवभूतः सनातनः ।" (गी. 15/7)

(c) "गतिर्भर्ता प्रभुः साक्षी निवासः शरणं सुहृत् ।" (गी. 9/18)

(d) "अज्ञानेनावृतं ज्ञानम् ।" (गी. 5/15)

"मामेव ये प्रपद्यन्ते मायामेतां तरन्ति ते ।" (गी. 7/14)

## The Bhagwatam:

(a) "जाग्रत् स्वप्नः सुषुप्तं च गुणतो बुद्धिवृत्तया ।

तासां विलक्षणो जीवः साक्षित्वेन विनिश्चितः ॥" (भा. 11/13/27)

"सत्त्वं रजस्तम इति गुणा बुद्धेर्न चात्मनः ॥" (भा. 11/13/1)

(b) "सूक्ष्माणामप्यहं जीवः ।" (भा. 11/16/11)

(c) "जन्माद्याः षडिमे भावा दृष्टा देहस्य नात्मनः ।

आत्मा नित्योऽव्ययःशुद्ध एकः क्षेत्रज्ञ आश्रयः ।

अविक्रियः स्वदृग् हेतुर्व्यापिकोऽसङ्ग्यनावृतः ॥" (भा. 7/7/18, 19)

(d) "अनाद्यविद्यायुक्तस्य पुरुषस्यात्मवेदनम् ।

स्वतो न सम्भवादन्यस्तत्त्वज्ञो ज्ञानदो भवेत् ॥" (भा. 11/22/10)

(e) "भगवानेक आसेदमग्र आत्माऽऽत्मनां विभुः ।" (भा. 3/5/23)

(f) "अखिलदेहिनामन्तरात्मद्दक् ।" (भा. 10/31/4)

## The Brahm Sutra:

(a) "नेतरोऽनुपपत्तेः ॥" (ब्र.सू. 1/1/16)

(b) "भेदव्यपदेशाच्च ॥" (ब्र.सू. 1/1/17)

(c) "अस्मिन्नस्य च तद्योगं शास्ति ॥" (ब्र.सू. 1/1/10)

(d) "ज्ञोऽत एव ॥" (ब्र.सू. 2/3/18)

(e) "उत्क्रान्तिगत्यागतीनाम् ॥" (ब्र.सू. 2/3/19)

(f) "नाणुरतच्छुतेरिति चेन्नेतराधिकारात् ॥" (ब्र.सू. 2/3/21)

(g) "स्वशब्दानुमानाभ्यां च ॥" (ब्र.सू. 2/3/22)

(h) "अंशो नानाव्यपदेशात् ॥" (ब्र.सू. 2/3/43)

  "अपि च स्मर्यते ॥" (ब्र.सू. 2/3/44)

(i) "गुणाद्वा लोकवत् ॥" (ब्र.सू. 2/3/25)

(j) "तद्गुणसारत्वातु तद्व्यपदेशः प्राज्ञवत् ॥" (ब्र.सू. 2/3/29)

(k) "सैव हि सत्यादयः ॥" (ब्र.सू. 3/3/38)

(l) "विशेषानुग्रहश्च ॥" (ब्र.सू. 3/4/38)

(m) "सम्पद्याविर्भावः स्वेन शब्दात् ॥" (ब्र.सू. 4/4/1)

  "मुक्तः प्रतिज्ञानात् ॥" (ब्र.सू. 4/4/2)

(n) "भोगमात्रसाम्यलिंगाच्च ॥" (ब्र.सू. 4/4/21)

## The Upnishads.

The Upnishads say that, (a) the soul is very subtle and small. If you could divide the very tip of your hair by one hundred times and again divide it by hundreds of times, whatever is left, the soul is still smaller than that. (It is just an example.) It means that the soul is smaller than anyone's imagination. अनन्त्याय means, the soul takes uncountable forms of life in uncountable species. Also, अन्त means death and आनन्त्य means death of the death, which indicates that the ultimate liberation of the soul is also possible ( कल्पते ).

(b) This soul is only *chit* (pure Divine intellect), *anu* (infinitesimal), and subtler than the space. (c) The soul is definitely infinitesimal. (God is absolute-*chit* and soul is described as the infinitesimal-*chit*, which means that soul is a part of the absolute *chit,* God.) (d) It resides in the heart of a person (not in the brain area).

(e) विज्ञानमय: means the soul which is substantially the *chit*, the partial Divine intellect, is naturally self-enlightened or you can say that it is a self-enlightened *chit*.

(f) The soul (along with body and mind) is the enjoyer of the *mayic* world. It is eternally ignorant. There are uncountable number of dormantly live ( निष्क्रय, चेतन ) souls.

(g) The soul is अज , निय , शाश्वत , and पुराण: . It means it was never created. Its infinitesimal form is stable and eternal. (It maintains its *chit* identity and remains the same even after liberation.) It never changes. It remains the same in all the forms and bodies it takes, and even during the total dissolution period *(maha pralaya).* Death of the physical body does not affect it in any way.

(h) All the unlimited number of souls reside in the supreme God (*brahm*) during the creation and also during the total dissolution period.

## The Gita.

Krishn says in the Gita that, (a) the soul remains eternally the same forever. It takes uncountable forms of life and travels everywhere in the *mayic* field but these changes do not affect it. It was never born. Its form as a soul is stable and eternal. There are uncountable souls.

(b) Souls are part of My Divine personality. All the souls are eternal. ( जीवभूत: word means all the souls. It refers to the total collective form of all the souls which indicates that it is a separate power of God Krishn apart from Krishn's personal internal power. All the powers of God are included in the personality of Krishn.)

(c) The souls are not only part of My personality, they also have personal relationship with Me. I am their ultimate goal (until they come to My abode they cannot relax and they cannot be settled). I am their protector and I am the one Who Graces them with Divine love and knowledge. I am their loving supreme God. I am the observer of the *karmas* of all the souls. (I feel very happy if any soul begins to think of Me, so I am always watching him and I wish that he should remember Me wholeheartedly so that I can Grace him with My Divine love.) All the souls reside within Me, I am the home of all the souls. I am the refuge of the souls. (When they humbly surrender to Me, I organize Divine guidance for them so that they can experience My Divine Grace, do devotion and come to Me.) Finally, the souls have very sweet and intimate relationship with Me (like the *Brajwasis*).

(d) But, the Divine knowledge that reveals their relationship with Me is eternally blemished by the *bahiranga maya shakti*, and, in its place, remains the ignorance which is opposite to the Divine knowledge. (Human beings have forgotten their true Divine relationship, that's why Saints and scriptures have to remind the souls about their Divine relationship with Krishn.) When they understand this truth and singlemindedly surrender to Me, their veil of ignorance is broken with My Grace.

## The Bhagwatam.

The Bhagwatam describes that, (a) the awakened state, sleep, and the state of deep sleep etc., are the states of the *mayic* mind. The actual soul is different. It is the prime enlivener of the mind and, at the same time, it is also a neutral kind of uninvolved onlooker of the mind. Mind contains the three *gunas* of *maya*. (b) It is the subtlest and the minutest thing in the universe.

(c) Birth, physical existence, growth, deterioration, old age and death, are the six consequences of the body, not of the soul. Basically, the soul is eternal, indestructible, pure on its own or unadulterated, individual, form of Divine intellect (Divine *chit*), animator of mind and senses ( आश्रय ), non-changing or non-degrading, self-enlightened on its own like the sun ( स्वदृक्, स्वयं प्रकाश ), silent onlooker and the enlivener of your mind which does all the actions (so it is called हेतु: ), life giver to the entire body by its own virtue ( व्यापक , as said in the Brahm Sutra, 2/3/23: अविरोधश्चन्दनवत् ), unallied by the other souls, and evident.

(d) But, the soul is eternally blemished by the *maya*. The mind of a person, on its own, can never know, receive, obtain or experience the Divineness or the Blissfulness of the soul. It has to be awarded to him by another Divine personality. (e) Bhagwan Krishn, Who is the Soul of all the souls, omnipresently exists (in all the souls) even during the state of absolute dissolution of this universe. (f) Krishn is the Soul of all the unlimited number of souls and He is looking at the souls all the time with kindness ( ईक् ), which indicates that the souls have loving relationship with Krishn.

The fact is, that the *chit shakti* of Krishn cannot be eternally influenced by the *maya* which, by itself, is a lifeless and dependent existence. It means that there is another section of *chit* power which is of that kind, and which accumulates all the souls. This section of *chit*, which is the accumulated form of all the souls, is also a special kind of Divine existence so it is also a power ( शक्ति ) of Krishn, called the *jeev* (soul) *shakti*. Because the individual souls are like a tiny fraction of the *jeev shakti*, the souls are also called a fraction or a part of God Krishn. So, the Brahm Vaivart Puran says that in all the uncountable *brahmandas*, souls are a fraction of a part of Krishn ( समस्तब्रह्माण्डे श्रीकृष्णांशांशजीविनः ॥ 15/106).

## The Brahm Sutra.

Ved Vyas in the Brahm Sutra says that, (a) soul is not Bliss (only God is Bliss). (b) Soul is separate from Blissful God ( द्वा सुपर्णा । ज्ञाज्ञौ द्वावजा ) as it is clearly stated in the Upnishads. (c) The Upnishads and other scriptures command the necessity of soul's devoted union with Blissful God (so that the soul could receive its true enlightened form as pure Divine *chit* and also become Blissful with His Grace). The same thing is further said in the Upnishads:

(मुं. 3/1/2)  " जुष्टं यदा पश्यति । "
(तै. 2/7)  " रसꣳ ह्येवायं लब्ध्वाऽऽनन्दी भवति । "
(मुं. 3/2/1)  " उपासते पुरषं ये ह्यकामाः । "
(श्वे. 6/23)  " यस्य देवे परा भक्तिः । "
(श्वे. 1/10)  " तस्याभिध्यानाद् योजनात् तत्त्वभावात् । "

(d) Soul is pure Divine *chit* ( ञ ). (e) Soul is described to be travelling from one space to another (from mundane earth planet to celestial abodes and back), and from one body to another (on the same planet in different species of life), so it is definitely a spot-existent thing. (f) (Soul has an infinitesimal form.) If someone asks that, why *'atma'* word is used in the Upnishads to represent the omnipresent Divinity when the soul is infinitesimal?  Like,

(वृ. 4/4/22)  " एष महानज आत्मा योऽयं विज्ञानमयः
सर्वस्यवशी सर्वस्येशानः सर्वस्याधिपतिः । "
(ऐ. 1/1/1)  " आत्मा वा इदमेक एवाग्र आसीत् । "

The answer is, that *atma* word is used for both, soul and God. Wherever the almightiness or Divine omnipresence is related, it only means God, not the soul ( इतराधिकारात् ).  (g) Because soul is related as अणु (infinitesimal) in the Upnishads ( एषोऽणुरात्मा । ) and also its individuality, ignorance and limitedness is seen and experienced by every human being.

(h) Souls are uncountable, individual and are part of God as described in the Upnishads and the Gita, " पादोऽस्य विश्वा भूतानि त्रिपादस्यामृतं दिवि । " (पु.सू. 3) " एको वशी निष्क्रियाणां बहूनाम् । " (श्वे. 6/12) " ममैवांशो जीवलोके जीवभूतः सनातनः । " (गी. 15/7) The words *nana, bhutani* and *jeevbhootah* ( नाना, भूतानि, जीवभूतः ) are plural, which means the unlimited number of souls; and the words *anshah* and *padah*, ( अंशः, पादः ) are singular, which means the one single collective form of all the souls called the *"jeev shakti."* *Tripad* ( त्रिपाद ) means *sat-chit-anand brahm* with all of His eternal Divine abodes.

(i) If someone thinks how a tiny soul, residing in the heart, could give life to the whole body, it is simple to understand. Just like a candle sitting at one spot enlightens the whole room, similarly the radiance of the soul enlivens the mind and the whole body. (Mind resides in the brain area as well as heart area and soul resides in the heart area, that's why you feel your real 'self' only in these two places but still the entire body is felt as the field of your real own self.)

(j) Wherever the greatness of the soul is mentioned in the Upnishads it is related only to the Divine substantial similarity of the pure infinitesimal *chit* of the soul ( अणुचित् ) with the Divine *chit* ( विभुचित् ) of God, because both are Divine. तद्गुण means the Divine quality of God, not His Divine powers or Divine virtues, because: (k) the Divine virtues like omnipresence, almightiness and omniscience etc., are the virtues of God, not of the soul. (l) The selfless devotion *(bhakti)* easily reveals the Grace of God (which terminates the *mayic* bondage of the soul). (m) It is told in the Upnishads ( शब्दात् ) that the soul then receives its true Divine identity as pure *chit* and with its (infinitesimal) pure form it enters the Divine realm. The Upnishads repeatedly tell that such a soul is fully liberated from the bondage of *maya* forever.

(छां. 8/3/4) " अस्माच्छरीरात्समुत्थाय परंज्योतिरूपं सम्पद्य
स्वेनरूपेणाभिनिष्पद्यते । "

(मुं. 3/2/6) " न स पुनरावर्तते । परामृताः परिमुच्यन्ति सर्वे । "

(n) Those souls who receive only liberation *(kaivalya mokch)* lose their personal identity and spontaneously enter and remain with their infinitesimal pure *chit* form ( अणुचित् ) in the Divine *chit* part of God (called *jeev shakti*). But those who have desired to experience the Divine Bliss of their adored form of God and to be with Him, after the termination of *mayic* bondage, receive a Divine body and enter the Divine abode of their beloved God. There they enjoy and experience the absolute Bliss of that abode in the same amount as their beloved God experiences. This similarity with God is only in experiencing the Divine Bliss.

# The definition of soul.

Considering the Divine facts and the statements of all the scriptures, the form and situation of the soul could be defined as thus:

"Souls are eternal, live, infinitesimal *chit*, unlimited in number, constant, unchanged in any situation (even liberation), individual and forming a fractional part of the *jeev shakti* of God Krishn which is the collective form of all the unlimited souls and is affiliated to *chid brahm* ( चिद् ब्रह्म ) which is the personal power of Krishn. That's why souls are called part of God Krishn's personality ( हरेरंशम् ) and have all kinds of normal to sweetest relationships with Krishn. The substantial quality of infinitesimal *chit* and the omnipresent absolute *chit* of God is exactly same, like an endless ocean of pure water and a drop of pure water, or an unlimited fire and a spark of it. So there is a qualitative similarity between a soul and God. Souls, the infinitesimal Divine intellect (the *chit*), are eternally blemished and influenced by *maya* which has made them ignorant beings who are self-convincingly fallen for the charming deceptions of the *mayic* world. This situation could be changed when a human being takes the refuge of the supreme power, God, and understandingly submits and devotes himself fully to His Grace which breaks the eternal *mayic* bondage, brings the soul to its pure *chit* form and awards Blissful synonymity of the soul with that form or abode of God he had previously conceived in his mind."

**Jeev Goswami precisely and clearly describes the form of the souls. He says,**

" जीवशक्तिविशिष्टस्यैव तव जीवोंऽशो न तु शुद्धस्येति ।"

(परमात्म संदर्भ, 39)

"Material souls are not part of the pure *chit*, the *swaroop shakti* of Krishn (otherwise they would have been naturally Blissful). They are part of the *jeev shakti* of Krishn."

He further describes, "(1) This *jeev shakti* is separate from the *chit shakti* of Krishn although it is of the same characteristic.

(2) It is neutral (*tatastha*), and (3) all the individual souls of the *jeev shakti* maintain their individuality even after liberation. Merging of the *Gyanis* with *brahm* only means receiving a Divine similarity with *brahm*."

(1) " विष्णुशक्तिः परा प्रोक्ता । " (वि.पु. 6/7/61) इत्यादि विष्णुपुराणवचने तु तिसृणामेव पृथक्शक्तित्वनिर्देशात्, " अपरेयमितस्त्वन्याम् । " (गी. 7/5) इत्युक्तम् ।

(2) उक्तञ्च तटस्थत्वं श्रीनारदपञ्चरात्रे, " यत्तटस्थन्तु चिद्रूपं स्वसंवेद्याद्विनिर्गतम् । रञ्जितं गुणरागेण स जीव इति कथ्यते ॥ " " तयोरन्यः पिप्पलं स्वाद्वत्ति " (मुं. 3/1/1) इत्यादौ ॥

(3) मोक्षदशायामपि तदंशत्वाव्यभिचारः स्वाभाविकशक्तित्वादेव । अतएवाविद्याविमोक्षपूर्वक-स्वरूपावस्थितिलक्षणायां मुक्तौ तल्लीनस्य तत्साधर्म्यापत्तिर्भवति । " निरञ्जनः परमं साम्यमुपैति " (मुं. 3/1/3) इत्यादि श्रुतिभ्यः ; " इदं ज्ञानमुपाश्रित्य मम साधर्म्यमागताः । " (गी. 14/2); अतएव " ब्रह्म वेद ब्रह्मैव भवति " (मुं. 3/2/9) इत्यादिषु च ब्रह्मतादात्म्यमेव बोधयति ॥ (परमात्म संदर्भ, 37)

He says, "*Jeev shakti* has unlimited number of souls. They are of two kinds: eternally pure souls and eternally blemished souls which are under the bondage of *maya*. The eternally pure souls of *jeev shakti* are eternally Blissful. They are called the *parikar*, the 'eternal associates' of God."

तदेवमनन्ता एव जीवाख्यास्तटस्थाः शक्तयः । तत्र तासां वर्गद्वयम् । एको वर्गोऽनादित एव भगवदुन्मुखः, अन्यस्त्वनादित एव भगवत्पराङ्मुखः । तत्र प्रथमोऽन्तरङ्गाशक्तिविलासानुगृहीतो नित्य भगवत्परिकररूपः ॥ (परमात्म संदर्भ, 47)

Now we know that a person has to terminate his *mayic* bondage with the Grace of God and then his soul can resume its innate Divine Blissful form, because all the souls are exactly like the *chit shakti* of Krishn.

There is one very great thing in the favor of souls that they can attain and experience any kind of Divine Blissfulness from Vaikunth to Divine Vrindaban through proper devotion, which is not possible for the almighty Divine powers of Krishn.

## Jeev shakti.

Soul (*jeev*) is अणु चित् (the infinitesimal *chit*), *jeev shakti* is असीम चित् (the unlimited *chit*) and *chid brahm* is विभु चित् (the omnipresent *chit*). All these three are substantially the same, but physically and constitutionally different.

There is nothing in the material world which is omnipresent. All the matter in the world is made of either atoms, or particles or wave particles like light rays. There is always a gap between the two particles that separates them and makes them individual, so nothing in the world, not even the magnetic field, could be technically called omnipresent. It could only be unlimitedly existing in the endless space. Similarly, the only difference between *chid brahm* and *jeev shakti* is that **jeev shakti is unlimited and absolute but not omnipresent,** and *chid brahm* is unlimited, absolute and omnipresent, and souls are non-stationary, spot-existent, infinitesimal individual beings.

*Jeev shakti* cannot be omnipresent ( विभु ) because omnipresence means only *one* absolute power and souls are uncountable in *jeev shakti*. Omnipresence relates to a particular Divine dimension. For instance, all the forms and abodes of God, described in Chapter 2, are omnipresent in their own dimension. *Chid brahm*, the personal *chit* power of Krishn, is also omnipresent. The name, form, *leelas*, virtues, abode, Saints (their body, mind and senses) and the affiliated Divine powers of that particular Divine abode are one (dimension) because they are all included in the personality of that form of God, or you can say that they are the expansion of the personality of that form of God. This is all the amazing work of the personal power of God called *yogmaya*. *Jeev shakti* is not a Divine dimension of that kind because the souls within it are unlimited in number and are totally individual. **So it is not one and single absolute power. It is a multiple absolute power.** No two souls can be absolutely one. So, *jeev shakti* is unlimited and absolute and is affiliated to the omnipresent *chid* power of Krishn.

# (2) *Maya.*

## The existence and form of *maya* (the original text).

### The Upnishads:

(a) "अजामेकां लोहितशुक्लकृष्णां वह्वीः प्रजाः सृजमानां... ।" (श्वे. 4/5)

(b) "ज्ञाज्ञौ द्वावजावीशनीशावजा होका भोक्तृभोग्यार्थयुक्ता ।" (श्वे. 1/9)

(c) "मायां तु प्रकृतिं विद्यान्मायिनं तु महेश्वरम् ।" (श्वे. 4/10)

(d) "क्षरं प्रधानममृताक्षरं हरः क्षरात्मानावीशते देव एकः ।" (श्वे. 1/10)

(e) "विद्याविद्ये निहिते...। एकं बीजं बहुधा यः करोति ।" (श्वे. 5/1, 6/12)
    "स ईक्षत । स इमाँल्लोकानसृजत ।" (ऐ. 1/2)

### The Gita:

(a) "प्रकृतिं पुरुषं चैव विद्ध्यनादी उभावपि ।" (गी. 13/19)

(b) "भूमिरापोऽनलो वायुः खं मनो बुद्धिरेव च ।
     अहंकार इतीयं मे भिन्नाप्रकृतिरष्टधा ॥" (गी. 7/4)

(c) "दैवी ह्येषा गुणमयी मम माया दुरत्यया ।
     मामेव ये प्रपद्यन्ते मायामेतां तरन्ति ते ॥" (गी. 7/14)

(d) "मयाध्यक्षेण प्रकृतिः सूयते सचराचरम् ।
     हेतुनानेन कौन्तेय जगद्विपरिवर्तते ॥" (गी. 9/10)

### The Bhagwatam:

(a) "ममाङ्ग माया गुणमय्यनेकधा ।" (भा. 11/22/30)
    "सत्त्वं रजस्तम इति प्रकृतेर्गुणाः ।" (भा. 6/12/15)

(b) "शक्तिः सदसदात्मिका माया ययेदं निर्ममे विभुः ॥" (भा. 3/5/25)

(c) "पुरुषः प्रकृतिर्व्यक्तमात्मा भूतेन्द्रियाशयाः ।
     शक्नुवन्त्यस्य सर्गादौ न विना यदनुग्रहात् ॥" (भा. 6/12/11)

### The Brahm Sutra:

(a) "तदधीनत्वादर्थवत् ॥" (ब्र.सू. 1/4/3)

(b) "भावे चोपलब्धे ॥" (ब्र.सू. 2/1/15)

(c) "सत्वाच्चावरस्य ॥" (ब्र.सू. 2/1/16)

(d) "असद्व्यपदेशान्नेति चेन्न धर्मान्तरेण वाक्यशेषात् ॥" (ब्र.सू. 2/1/17)

(e) "जन्माद्यस्य यतः ॥" (ब्र.सू. 1/1/2)

## The Upnishads.

The Upnishads describe *maya* as a lifeless potential power of God that has kept unlimited number of souls under its bondage since eternity. They say that,

(a) *Maya* is eternal. It has three qualities, *tam, raj* and *sattva,* representing its evil, selfish and pious characteristics. The Upnishad illustrates it as black, red and white. It creates this amazing universe that qualifies with these three qualities of *maya* everywhere.

(b) This eternal *maya* is the field of material enjoyment for the souls, that's how it keeps them under its total influence. (c) It is a power of God and is controlled by God. (d) The world it creates is not stable. It slowly perishes to death and then to rebirth. Its working is enforced by the power of God (because it is lifeless on its own).

(e) The *chit*-soul and anti-*chit maya* dependently reside in God. With one single *mayic* energy God creates this amazing multiform universe. God just thought, and the universe was created.

## The Gita.

The Gita tells that, (a) soul and *maya* are both eternal. (b) Earth, water, fire, air, space, mind, intellect and ego are the eight prime energies (aspects) of *maya*. (c) Krishn says in the Gita that *maya* is My power. It has its own characteristics and qualities (*sattva, raj* and *tam*). It is limitless and has a strong grip on all the souls, so it is extremely difficult to cross. But when a soul wholeheartedly surrenders to Me, he crosses the ocean of *maya* with My Grace. There is no other way to cross it. (d) *Maya* cannot create the universe on its own (because it is lifeless and mindless), so it needs My inspiration to evolve, and to keep on running in the form of the existing world.

## The Bhagwatam.

The Bhagwatam explains that, (a) *maya* is a power of Krishn. It has three *gunas, sattva, raj* and *tam, which* appear in every form of its endless manifestation. (b) *Maya*, which is like a cross between 'truth' and 'fake,' is a power of God with which He creates this universe. (c) *Maya,* along with souls and its prime energies, is unable to create this universe on its own. It depends on God to inspire it.

## The Brahm Sutra.

The Brahm Sutra describes, in logical detail, about *maya (prakriti)* in Chapter 4 of Part 1, and about creation in Chapter 1 of Part 2. It also describes the details of the evolution of space, fire, water and earth etc. in Chapter 3 of Part 2. Here is the general meaning of the important *sutras.*

(a) *Maya* resides in God and is controlled by God. Its utility as an exhibitor of the universe is subjected to God's help.

(b) The presence of the universe (effect, कार्य) proves its eternal subtle existence (cause, कारण ), because cause reveals the effect and effect always contains its cause within it, like a tiny seed becomes a tree and then the tree itself contains its own seed. (c) *Mayic* world in its subtle energy form already existed in God as an absolute energy or power ( सदेव सोम्येदमग्र आसीत् । छां. 6/2/1) before the evolution of this universe. **Its subtle existence was a truth and its manifested existence is also a truth.**

(d) This *sutra* clarifies the meaning of " असद्व्र इदमग्र आसीत् । ततो वै सदजायत । तदात्मानं स्वयमकुरुत ॥ " तै. 2/7. It says that there are two stages of the universe ( धर्मान्तरेण ), the evolved perceived stage and the unevolved non-perceivable stage. The word असत् refers to its non-perceivable stage, and the word आसीत् tells its non-perceivable existence ( वाक्यशेषात् means the last word which is आसीत्). The word आसीत् means 'to exist.' So the literal translation of this verse is, "This universe existed like nothing in the very beginning." It means the universe eternally exists, either in its subtle form or in its evolved form.

(e) This *sutra* refers to " यतो वा इमानि भूतानि जायन्ते... " तै. 3/1. It tells that this universe evolves from God, exists in God, and dissolves back in God.

Shankaracharya defines *maya* as thus:
" सदसद्विलक्षणाऽसौ परमात्मसदाश्रयाऽनादिः ।
सा च गुणत्रयरूपा सूते सचराचरं विश्वम् ॥ 99 ॥ "
" माया ब्रह्मोपगताऽविद्या जीवाश्रया प्रोक्ता ।
चिदचिद्ग्रन्थिश्चेतस्तदक्षयं ज्ञेयमामोक्षात् ॥ 105 ॥ " (प्र.सु.)

He says, "*Maya* creates this amazing illusory universe that consists of unlimited static and non-static beings. It has three *gunas*, *sattva, raj* and *tam*. It is an undelineable ( अनिर्वचनीय ), non-Divine, lifeless existence that eternally resides in God, and is controlled by God. It is of two kinds. The main one is called '*maya*' which is directly under the control of God. The other one is called '*avidya*.' It is created by the souls and it resides in the souls. *Maya* forms an unbreakable knot ( चिज्जड़ग्रन्थि ) that stays until the soul is liberated."

## The definition of *maya*.

Taking into account all the statements of the scriptures, *maya* could be defined as:

"A non-Divine, lifeless energy which is a totally dependent power of God. It eternally exists as an affiliate to the *chit shakti* of God Krishn where it has eternally enslaved unlimited number of souls of *jeev shakti* with its anti-Divine character ( अविद्या ). That's why it is called *bahiranga* (extroverted) *shakti*." *Bahiranga* means introducing such perceptions that take a soul's mind away from God.

"The character or the qualities of *maya* are *sattva, raj* and *tam,* that pervade and exist in every phase of *mayic* existence. They appear as pious, selfish and evil qualities of the mind. They introduce positive, creative, and negative forces of the cosmos. *Maya* also has three forms of ego called *man* (emotional mind), *buddhi* (intellectual mind) and *ahankar* (the ego), and five kinds of perceptions (hearing, touching, seeing, tasting and smelling) that are related to its five main aspects of energies (space, air, fire, water and earth) that evolve into the form of this universe."

## (3) The creation.

🌺

### Powers involved in creation.

God Himself, and God-enlivened three lifeless powers, *mool prakriti, kal,* and *karm* ( मूल प्रकृति, काल, कर्म ), are involved in creation. They remain all the time in this universe along with all the souls. *Mool prakriti* is the original cosmic power, *maya*. Apart from its three qualities, it also has the power of 'attraction' ( आकर्षण ) that appears as gravity and other attracting forces of the universe. Ved Vyas says,

"ज्ञानिनामपि चेतांसि देवी भगवती हि सा ।
बलादाकृष्य मोहाय महामाया प्रयच्छति ॥"

"The material and sensual attraction of *maya* for human beings is so great that highly evolved *sattvic gyanis* may also fall for this *mayic* attraction and drown into worldly mire."

*Kal* is the 'time' energy ( अक्षरात् संजायते काल: ) that resides in God, and is enlivened and produced by God. The Bhagwatam says,

"स काल: परमाणुर्वै यो भुङ्क्ते परमाणुताम् ।
सतोऽविशेषभुग्यस्तु स काल: परमो महान् ॥" (भा. 3/11/4)

"The time energy *(kal)* initiates the functioning of the universe since the awakening of *maya* and until the total dissolution of the universe. It is very powerful. It predominantly stays in every phase of *mayic* creation and its existence." ( ततोऽभवन्महत्तत्त्वमव्यक्तात्काल-चोदितात् । भा. 3/5/27)

During the creation when all the *mayic* energies (space, fire, ego, etc.) resume their individual shape, they come to a dead stop because of their inability to create this universe on their own. At that time God evokes the power of the *karmas* of all the souls that mechanically guides *maya* what to do. At the same time, God Himself omnipresently helps the entire creation to evolve and He becomes everything. The Bhagwatam and the Upnishad say the same thing.

" सोऽनुप्रविष्टो भगवांश्चेष्टारूपेण तं गणम् ।
भिन्नं संयोजयामास सुप्तं कर्म प्रबोधयन् ॥ " (भा. 3/6/3)
" इदं सर्वमसृजत । तत्सृष्ट्वा तदेवानुप्राविशत् । तदनुप्रविश्य
सच्च त्यच्चाभवत् । निरुक्तं चानिरुक्तं च । निलयनं चानिलयनं च ।
विज्ञानं चाविज्ञानं च । सत्यमभवत् । यदिदं किं च ।" (तै. 2/6)

In this way *maya*, along with *kal* and *karm*, creates this universe with the help of God.

## Creation and dissolution.

The universe has two states, creation and dissolution ( सृष्टि व प्रलय ), that eternally keep on rotating one after another, and will go on forever ( यथेदानीं तथाग्रे च पश्चादप्येतदीदृशम् । भा. 3/11/13). It never started. Thus, the cycle of creation and dissolution, *kal, karm, maya* and souls are all eternal. During the dissolution period, (which is unimaginable) all of these (*kal, karm, maya* and souls) remain in God in an absolutely subtle *nirakar* and dormant state. During the creation, all the souls are reborn according to their existing living status at the time of previous dissolution, like a frog becomes a frog and a human becomes a human. ( यथा पूर्वमकल्पयत् । न कर्मविभागादिति चेन्नानादित्वात् ॥ ब्र.सू. 2/1/35 )

## *Nirakar* and *sakar* form of *mayic* creation.

*Maya* perpetually goes on assuming its form from *nirakar* to *sakar* and from *sakar* to *nirakar* (*nirakar* means having no perceptible form and *sakar* means perceptible form).  During *maha pralaya* ( महाप्रलय ), the total dissolution period, *maya*, along with all of its powers and celestial gods and goddesses remains in a totally *nirakar* state.  During creation, with the help of God, *maya* evolves and assumes its *sakar* state, and its *nirakar* celestial gods and goddesses along with their celestial abodes become *sakar*.  During *maha pralaya,* all of these gods and goddesses along with their abodes *(bhuva, swah, maha, jan, tap* and *satya)* again go back to their lifeless, *nirakar*, dormant state, and the *mayic* world also dissolves back into its original lifeless, *nirakar* dormant form, and stays in God.

**So it is the celestial (*mayic*) gods and goddesses who become *sakar* from *nirakar* and then go back to their original *nirakar* state,** not the Divine forms of God like Shiv, Durga, Bhagwan Ram, etc.  Constantly changing state, is the nature and the characteristic of *maya*, and eternally constant state, is the nature of the Divine.  **Divine abodes and forms of God are eternal and unchanging and exist in Their own Divine dimension.**

I don't know how such a wrong and materialistic ideology, that *nirakar brahm* becomes *sakar,* got so much popularity.  It is pure *mayavad*, the product of *mayic rajogun*.  It could be the effect of *kaliyug* and the selfish and egoistic bent of human mind that yields to surrender to anyone for his personal comfort, but he hesitates to surrender to his eternal friend Krishn (or any other form of God) Who could make him Blissful forever.

## The physical nature of *mayic* creation (motion, aging, and variation).

Motion, aging and variation ( गति, विकृति, भिन्नता ) are the three main natures of *mayic* creation.

**Motion:** We can see that nothing in the universe is static.  Planets, galaxies, clusters, all of them are moving.  There is movement everywhere in every phase of the creation.  This movement is given by the time energy *(kal)*.  Time has a nature to always move forward, (never backward) and to move in a circular motion ( काल चक्र ). So, from a tiny atom to the visible universe, everything is in motion. **The force of time energy, along with other factors, promotes movement in the space, that's how all the physical bodies appear to be moving away in the cosmos.**

**Aging:** Everything in this creation is always aging. *Maya* is termed as *char* ( क्षरं प्रधानम् ). It means the one which is never stable, and is always declining. It has four aspects: formation, declination, death and rebirth. It thus forms the cycle of birth and death for every existing thing in the universe from a tiny plant to a human being and from a particle to a galaxy. Since the day anything is born it starts aging, and immediately after its death it enters into the process of being reborn. It could be the death of a living being (soul), or a controversial natural body like a 'black hole.' It is a *mayic* axiom that birth follows death and death follows birth, and, during its lifetime it keeps on aging, fading, waning, declining or deteriorating.

**Variation:** Everywhere in the world we see variations. It is of two kinds, general and incidental. General variation is the amazing common nature of *maya* where the appearance of each and everything in the world, less or more, differs from one another. We know that the face of every person and his fingerprints are different. Not even that, every leaf of a tree or even every DNA is different from one another. Scientists have not yet discovered much about the DNA but if they could reach to that level of technological development, which is not possible, they may see that the body of every DNA is slightly different from the other.

The second kind of variation which is incidental is the outcome of the individual and collective (active and inactive) *karmas* of all the uncountable souls living in that particular area. We see some good and bad incidents happening all the time in our life and around us.

From a minor road accident to a major catastrophe that occurs in the world, we call it 'accident,' which literally means a happening that has randomly happened.  Physicists have a term 'uncertainty principle' which they use to justify the sudden uncertain behavior of particles in the theory of quantum mechanics.  It is like a 'suspense account' in a financial balance sheet.  The universe is full of such incidental irregularities, although it is running in a precisely organized pattern.

Astronomers observe very little of such incidental happenings in the universe but a lot is happening inside.  A planetary system dies and another is born.  A galaxy dies and somewhere in the space a new galaxy is being formed.  Many unpredictable disasters may also happen.  For instance: We don't know for sure when and where a big meteorite is going to hit the earth planet, or a comet may collide, or a volcano may erupt, or polar snow might melt, or the earth may topple from its axis, thus changing the location of its north pole.  Many such unknown happenings lie in the heart of the future.

A person is driving, the car swerves and falls into a fifteen-foot ditch.  He comes out of the smashed car with only a few bruises.  The same person, after some time, goes to buy vegetables, slips on the curb of the road, breaks his leg and he is admitted in the hospital.  A cyclone hits and blows the beach houses, killing many people, but a little baby is safely thrown aside.  Four people are travelling in a car.  A truck hits, three die on the spot and one survives.  A grandmother suffering from long term sickness prays God to lift her up from the world but she does not die and her young grandson dies from a sudden heart attack.

Even an ordinary man of India would say it is all the effect of one's own *karmas* (past and present), but  scientists only call it bad luck.  **God's powers don't make mistakes.  They have reasons for every single happening.**  Would you like to open an account in such a bank where the computer has a .001% uncertainty.  It means that one in a thousand entries may go wrong.  A one million dollar deposit may be recorded as only one dollar, and no one could guarantee that it won't be you.  You wouldn't like to deal with such a  bank.

There is nothing 'uncertain' in the universe. From the formation of a galaxy to its final death, all the happenings are controlled by the force of *karm* of the souls. It is a power that conducts and controls every single happening of the physical universe. **So we have fully controlled incidental happenings, not uncontrolled.**

## Purpose of creation and the science of *karm*
( भोक्ता, भोग्यम् ).

**Creation is only for the souls. It provides facility for the souls to understand the kindness and Bliss of God and do devotional actions so that they can cross the bondage of *maya* and reach God.**

The world is created in such a way that every being likes certain things and dislikes certain things of this visual world. This is common to every soul. Human beings have one more aspect. They develop an attachment for certain things and certain people in the world. This attachment multiplies their experience of liking and disliking which is called enjoyment or suffering.

There are certain rules of this world. If you intentionally hurt someone in any way or break some kind of law, you deserve to be punished for your bad deed, and if you intentionally help someone in any way or follow certain religious rules, you deserve to get a reward for your good deed. They are called *'karmas.'* But the punishment or reward that a human being receives, is determined according to the intensity of his intention and the kind and class of the person he has hurt or helped. It means, whether that person is an ordinary selfish being, or an evil one, or a good person, or a God-fearing person, or a pious person, or a devotee. Again, if he is a devotee, what kind and class of devotee is he. It is all taken into consideration. Eating or killing birds and animals for personal interest is also a bad deed because you inflict pain into them. The rule of doing good or bad *karm* applies to human beings only, not the lower species, because they don't have intellectual intention, they live with their instincts.

The punishment of bad *karmas* is material suffering and the reward of general good *karmas* is material enjoyment. You don't instantly receive the good or bad outcome of your *karmas* because the period of undergoing the consequences of a *karm* is longer than the actual length of the time spent in doing that *karm*. So, as a general rule, a portion of all the *karmas* of one lifetime is given to be fructified as a destiny of the next lifetime and the rest of it is stored in the totally unconscious part of the human mind. In this way there are unlimited *karmas* stored in the mind. They are called *sanchit karm* ( संचित कर्म ), and the portion of past lives' *karmas* that become the destiny of the present lifetime are called *prarabdh karm* ( प्रारब्ध कर्म ). While undergoing the outcome of your *prarabdh karm,* you also keep doing a great number of new *karmas* every day. This new *karm* is called *kriyaman karm* ( क्रियमाण कर्म ).

*Kriyaman karm* has an impact on the effects of the *prarabdh karm* in a person's life. All the thoughts and the actions of a person which have a desire or motivation is classified as *karm*. So, the philosophy of *karm* is quite extensive and complex, but we are only concerned with the *prarabdh karm* or the destiny of a soul in this chapter. Like human beings, other souls of lower species also have their destiny (to enjoy and to suffer) which refers to their previous life as a human being when they were free to do any kind of good and bad action in the world.

Gravity is considered to be a weak physical force of the atoms but collectively it becomes so evident and strong that it regulates the running of the entire system of all the galaxies and their clusters. *Karm* is a much more powerful non-physical energy. It is the collective manifestation of all the unlimited *karmas* of all the unlimited number of souls in the universe. Everything that takes birth has a destiny and that destiny is governed by the force of *karm*. Accordingly, our earth planet's destiny, which includes all of its major events, is governed by the collective force of the various classes, categories and intensities of *karmas* of all the souls residing on this planet, and a galaxy's physical destiny is governed by the collective force of the *karmas* of the souls residing in that galaxy, and so on. An individual soul's destiny is governed by his own *karmas,* but the visual world has to provide the instant physical set up to provide the experience of the outcome of the destined event. That's how if a person is not destined to get hurt in a car accident, he won't, but the others will if they are so destined.

## *Maya* provides facility for a soul to do *kriyaman karmas.*

*Maya* is called *bhogya* ( भोग्यम् ) and soul is called the *bhokta* ( भोक्ता ) in the Upnishads. *Bhogya* means the field of experience, and *bhokta* means the experiencer. The main purpose of the creation is to provide the field for doing new *karmas*, the *kriyaman*, so that every soul should have a chance to understand the truth, do the devotion to God, break his *mayic* bondage with the Grace of God, and receive the Divine Bliss forever which the Ved describes as *raso vai sah* ( रसो वै सः ). But, in doing so, this *maya* has to provide the field for the experience of all kinds of (good, bad and devotional) *karmic* consequences of a soul. **Thus, this world is the field of doing new *kriyaman karm* and, at the same time, undergoing the consequences of *prarabdh karm*.**

## The definition of creation.

Animated by God, the lifeless ( जड़ ) *maya,* with the help of its two lifeless forces *kal* (the time energy) and *karm,* evolves itself into the form of this universe along with unlimited number of souls within it where gracious God is also omnipresent with all of His Divine forms.

*Maya* also evolves the mind and body of the souls with its five senses. The senses perceive their relative objects in the world which are created by *maya* to be naturally attractive to the mind. Thus, *maya* keeps the mind of the person firmly attached in the world by developing a deep liking for it. The person, with a hope of receiving real happiness (which is nothing but a fascinating mirage of ignorance of his own mind) develops a deep desire for worldly things, and thus he creates his own bondage of deep worldly attachments (called *avidya*).

The time energy moves the whole universe forward in a circular-like motion, with all of its multiple manifestations of the three *gunas,* where the force of *karm*-energy creates and controls the variations of the physical situations as well as the events of this visual world according to the individual soul's destiny and collective souls' destiny. The destiny of the earth planets of the galaxies and the galaxies themselves are formed at the time of their origination and it is on the basis of the various classes of the collective *karmas* of all the souls residing within that area.

Instability of the existing situation and the limitation of the (constantly aging) life-span of everything that is born, is the inherent character of *maya.* Thus, from an ordinary planet to the entire universe, everything meets its death and it is created again; and this cycle of birth and death continuously goes on in a perpetual order which will never end because it never had a beginning. It is eternal.

## The creation of the universe is still a mystery to the physicists.

Modern physicists, many of whom still hang on to a very naively described Big Bang theory which has six major faults, are trying to locate the first particle of the cosmos that created the galactic system, and thus are trying to solve the mystery of the origin of the universe. This fact, in the terminology of modern quantum theory, was already described a long time ago in one of our scriptures, the Nyay Darshan, where it says," न प्रलयोऽणुसद्भावात् ॥ परं वा त्रुटे: ॥ " (4/2/16-17). It means, "the non-divisible, nonphysical, motionless and constant kind of 'absolute particles' are the cause ( कारण ) and the very first phase of this creation."

It is just an indication of the situation. It does not go into detail because it is not a necessary knowledge in regard to the development of the *sattvic* values of mankind.

The creator Brahma, who created our planetary system (only from the mere space energy) similar to other uncountable planetary systems of this cosmos, himself describes the chronology of this creation. It is as thus:

" तस्माद्वा एतस्मादात्मन आकाशः सम्भूतः । आकाशाद्वायुः । वायोरग्निः । अग्नेरापः । अद्भ्यः पृथिवी । पृथिव्या ओषधयः ।ओषधीभ्योऽन्नम् । अन्नात्पुरुषः । स वा एष पुरुषोऽन्नरसमयः ॥ " (तै. 2/1)

He says, "From God, and promoted by God, the 'space' energy manifested itself in the form of livable space ( आकाश ) as we observe today. This was the first phase of subtle and omnipresent manifestation. From the space and in the space, another energy, that creates movement in the space, and also moves the space with the help of time energy, appeared. It was called *vayuh* ( वायु : ). This was the second phase. Then that energy further evolved itself into the form of omnipresent heat ( अग्निः ) energy. This was the third phase of subtle omnipresent manifestation. All these three energies remain together." As a rule, a subtler energy remains omnipresent in the subtle energy, and so on.

After that, the first phase of physical manifestation started, and the omnipresent heat energy materialized itself into: (1) absolute particles, to (2) very subtle particles, to (3) subtle particles, to (4) tiny particles, to (5) sub-particles and then to (6) the particles that could be compared to photons.

"The particles took the shape of atoms and molecules ( आपः ) and then the physical planetary systems ( पृथिवी ) came into being. Then the atmosphere was created, and air, fire and water were grossly materialized to provide the living facility for the souls. Then life began, and firstly vegetation appeared ( ओषधयः ). Then plants, trees, fruits, grains ( अन्नम्), insects, animals and birds, etc. appeared; and then human beings ( पुरुषः ) appeared." **This is the sequence of creation described by the Creator himself.** The function and affiliation of the other two powers, *kal* and *karm*, that help *maya* is described earlier.

The 'absolute particles' are not particles in a technical sense. They only represent the positive and negative aspect of *mayic* energy in an unlimited number of subtle and abstract-like omnipresent non-divisible existence. It is only the miracle of *maya* that represents such a phenomena of creation which is beyond comprehension. So, this energy remains continuous and omnipresent in the space and yet it represents unlimited abstract numericals of positive and negative entities. This is the **first** stage.

At the **second** stage, the omnipresence of this energy starts to break, and at the **third** stage the omnipresence is broken and negative (-) and positive (+) particles begin to emerge from an ocean-like omnipresent heat energy. At the **fourth** stage, the negative and positive particles come to their actual individual shape which are **the first physical (tiny) particles of this creation**. These tiny particles are of two kinds: (1) active (+) and (-) particles, and (2) dormant (+) and (-) particles. Attraction, motion and change; these inherent characteristics of *maya* become evident and the (+) and (-) tiny active particles, attracted to each other, gain their velocity and immediately start joining to each other. Dormant (+) and (-) particles also join the active (+) and (-) particles. Thus, changing their shape by joining more and more in number and gaining more space of movement, **they form three kinds of sub-particles (0, +, -) in the fifth stage.** Even number of collection of (+) and (-) tiny particles become **neutral sub-particle** (0), and uneven number of collection of (+) and (-) tiny particles become **positive charge** (+) or **negative charge** (-) **sub-particle.** Their shape and intensity of (+) or (-) charge depend upon the kind and the total number of tiny particles that are attached together. These sub-particles still keep on joining together and, in the **sixth** stage, many kinds and classes of the three categories of (+), (-), (0) particles are born. Some of these particles are even smaller than a photon and some are approximately the same as a photon.

These particles are the foundation blocks of all the prime particles of an atom. Thus, every prime particle has hundreds of tiny particles. Some of them which are on the surface act as the radiance of that prime particle. So, every prime particle has its own kind of radiance or force pattern of varying strength. Now we see how simple and how complex is the formation of an atom. Like the digital 0's and 1's together could create any kind of picture, the tiny negatives (-) and positives (+) create all kinds of atoms. The nearest and simplest example about breaking the omnipresence of absolute particles could be like when you make cottage cheese from boiling fresh milk, the evenly present substance of cottage cheese in the milk slowly starts breaking, and finally the whole substance, in a condensed form, turns into cottage cheese and starts floating.

Our technology is not good enough even to faintly observe photon-like particles. It is a very very long way to observe the 'tiny particles,' and even if we could do so, what would be the usability of it? After discovering nuclear fuel we entered into a grave problem of its waste disposal. Our nuclear defense schemes ended up into global insecurity. Unless we follow the advice of the creator God and try to be humble, forgiving, helping others and developing our own inherent good qualities by worshipping the supreme God (Who is our Divine beloved and eternal friend), all the materialistic efforts may end up into disappointments by being less productive and more destructive. However, we have described the first particle of the creation along with the functioning of the universe and the purpose and system of creation in an easy to understand style.

## (4) *Brahm* (God).

❀

### *Brahm*, the supreme Divinity (the original text).

**The Upnishads:**

(a) " रसो वै सः । " (तै. 2/7)

" आनन्दो ब्रह्मेति व्यजानात् । " (तै. 3/6)

(b) " एको देवः सर्वभूतेषु गूढः सर्वव्यापी सर्वभूतान्तरात्मा ।

कर्माध्यक्षः सर्वभूताधिवासः

साक्षी चेता केवलो निर्गुणश्च ॥ " (श्वे. 6/11)

(c) "सत्यं ज्ञानमनन्तं ब्रह्म ।" (तै. 2/1)

(d) "सत्यं विज्ञानमानन्दं ब्रह्म ॥" (बृ. 3/9/28)

(e) "अणोरणीयान्महतो महीयान् ॥" (कठ. 1/2/20)

(f) "स्वरूपं द्विविधं चैव सगुणं निर्गुणं तथा ।" (गो.उ.ता.)
"भगवन्नखण्डाद्वैतपरमानन्दलक्षणपरब्रह्मणः
साकारनिराकारौ विरुद्धधर्मौ । विविधविचित्रानन्तशक्तेः ॥
सर्वपरिपूर्णस्य परब्रह्मणः परमार्थतः साकारं बिना
केवलनिराकारत्वं यद्यभिमतं तर्हि केवलनिराकारस्य गगनस्येव
परब्रह्मणोऽपि जडत्वमापद्येत ॥ तस्मात्परब्रह्मणः परमार्थतः
साकारनिराकारौ स्वभावसिद्धौ ॥" (त्रि.महा. 2)

(g) "न तत्समश्चाभ्यधिकश्च दृश्यते । परास्य शक्तिर्विविधैव
श्रूयते स्वाभाविकी ज्ञानबलक्रिया च ॥" (श्वे. 6/8)

(h) "दिव्यो ह्यमूर्तः पुरुषः स बाह्याभ्यन्तरो ह्यजः ।
अप्राणो ह्यमनाः शुभ्रो ह्यक्षरात् परतः परः ॥" (मुं. 2/1/2)

(i) "सर्वेन्द्रियगुणाभासं सर्वेन्द्रियविवर्जितम् ।
सर्वस्य प्रभुमीशानं सर्वस्य शरणं सुहृत् ॥" (श्वे. 3/17)

(j) "तमेकं गोविन्दं सच्चिदानन्दविग्रहम् ।" (गो.पू.ता.)

(k) "कृष्ण एव परो देवः । तं भजेत् ।" (गो.पू.ता.)
"तस्याभिध्यानाद् योजनात् तत्त्वभावात् ॥" "उपासते पुरुषं
ये ह्यकामाः ॥" "यस्य देवे परा भक्तिः ॥" "जुष्टं यदा
पश्यति ॥" (श्वे. 1/10; मुं. 3/2/1; श्वे. 6/23; मुं. 3/1/2)

(l) "न तत्र सूर्यो भाति न चन्द्रतारकं नेमा विद्युतो भान्ति कुतोऽयमग्निः ।
तमेव भान्तमनुभाति सर्वं तस्य भासा सर्वमिदं विभाति ॥" (मुं. 2/2/10)
"तद्विष्णोः परमं पदं सदा पश्यन्ति सूरयः ।" (गो.पू.ता.)
"तच्चानिर्वच्यमनिर्देश्यमखण्डानन्दैकरसात्मकं नित्यवैकुण्ठं विभाति ।
निरतिशयानन्दाखण्डब्रह्मानन्दनिजमूर्त्याकारेण ज्वलति ॥" (त्रि.महा. 1)
"सलोकतां समीपतां सरूपतां सायुज्यतामेति ।" (कलि.)

## The Gita:

(a) "परं ब्रह्म परं धाम पवित्रं परमं भवान् ।
पुरुषं शाश्वतं दिव्यमादिदेवमजं विभुम् ॥" (गी. 10/12)

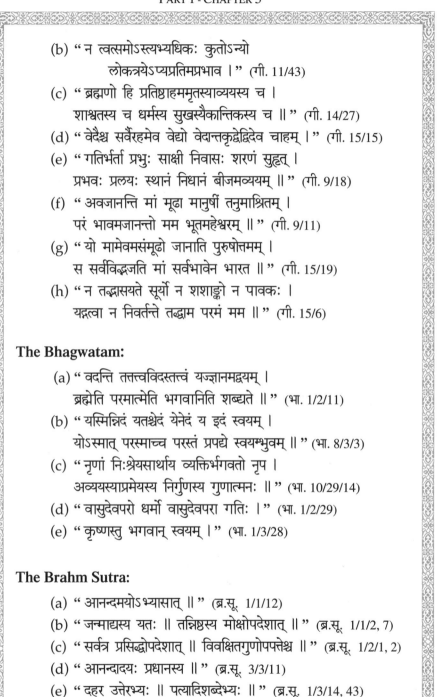

(b) "न त्वत्समोऽस्त्यभ्यधिकः कुतोऽन्यो
    लोकत्रयेऽप्यप्रतिमप्रभाव ।" (गी. 11/43)

(c) "ब्रह्मणो हि प्रतिष्ठाहममृतस्याव्ययस्य च ।
    शाश्वतस्य च धर्मस्य सुखस्यैकान्तिकस्य च ॥" (गी. 14/27)

(d) "वेदैश्च सर्वैरहमेव वेद्यो वेदान्तकृद्वेदविदेव चाहम् ।" (गी. 15/15)

(e) "गतिर्भर्ता प्रभुः साक्षी निवासः शरणं सुहृत् ।
    प्रभवः प्रलयः स्थानं निधानं बीजमव्ययम् ॥" (गी. 9/18)

(f) "अवजानन्ति मां मूढा मानुषीं तनुमाश्रितम् ।
    परं भावमजानन्तो मम भूतमहेश्वरम् ॥" (गी. 9/11)

(g) "यो मामेवमसंमूढो जानाति पुरुषोत्तमम् ।
    स सर्वविद्भजति मां सर्वभावेन भारत ॥" (गी. 15/19)

(h) "न तद्भासयते सूर्यो न शशाङ्को न पावकः ।
    यद्गत्वा न निवर्तन्ते तद्धाम परमं मम ॥" (गी. 15/6)

**The Bhagwatam:**

(a) "वदन्ति तत्तत्त्वविदस्तत्त्वं यज्ज्ञानमद्वयम् ।
    ब्रह्मेति परमात्मेति भगवानिति शब्द्यते ॥" (भा. 1/2/11)

(b) "यस्मिन्निदं यतश्चेदं येनेदं य इदं स्वयम् ।
    योऽस्मात् परस्माच्च परस्तं प्रपद्ये स्वयम्भुवम् ॥" (भा. 8/3/3)

(c) "नृणां निःश्रेयसार्थाय व्यक्तिर्भगवतो नृप ।
    अव्ययस्याप्रमेयस्य निर्गुणस्य गुणात्मनः ॥" (भा. 10/29/14)

(d) "वासुदेवपरो धर्मो वासुदेवपरा गतिः ।" (भा. 1/2/29)

(e) "कृष्णस्तु भगवान् स्वयम् ।" (भा. 1/3/28)

**The Brahm Sutra:**

(a) "आनन्दमयोऽभ्यासात् ॥" (ब्र.सू. 1/1/12)

(b) "जन्माद्यस्य यतः ॥ तन्निष्ठस्य मोक्षोपदेशात् ॥" (ब्र.सू. 1/1/2, 7)

(c) "सर्वत्र प्रसिद्धोपदेशात् ॥ विवक्षितगुणोपपत्तेश्च ॥" (ब्र.सू. 1/2/1, 2)

(d) "आनन्दादयः प्रधानस्य ॥" (ब्र.सू. 3/3/11)

(e) "दहर उत्तरेभ्यः ॥ पत्यादिशब्देभ्यः ॥" (ब्र.सू. 1/3/14, 43)

(f) "सर्वोपिता च तद्दर्शनात् ॥ सर्वधर्मोपपत्तेश्च ॥ न प्रयोजनवत्त्वात् ॥
लोकवत्तु लीलाकैवल्यम् ॥ " (ब्र.सू. 2/1/30, 37, 32, 33)

(g) " तदव्यक्तमाह हि ॥
अपि च संराधने प्रत्यक्षानुमानाभ्याम् ॥ " (ब्र.सू. 3/2/23, 24)

(h) "ध्यानाच्च ॥ स्मरन्ति च ॥ " (ब्र.सू. 4/1/8, 10)

(i) " अपि च स्मर्यते ॥ विशेषानुग्रहश्च ॥ अतस्त्वितरज्ज्यायोलिङ्गाच्च ॥
अनाविष्कुर्वन्नन्वयात् ॥ " (ब्र.सू. 3/4/37, 38, 39, 50)

(j) " भोगमात्रसाम्यलिङ्गाच्च ॥ " (ब्र.सू. 4/4/21)

## The Upnishads.

The Upnishad says, "भोक्ता भोग्यं प्रेरितारं च मत्वा सर्वं प्रोक्तं त्रिविधं ब्रह्म-मेतत् । (श्वे. 1/12) तथा - बृहत्वाद् बृंहणत्वाच्च यद् ब्रह्म परमं विदु: । (वि.पु. 1/12/ 57)."

*Brahm* is defined as the one Who is the Great and Who makes (other souls) great. Everything that exists is *brahm*. It has its two unusual powers. One is *maya*, the lifeless existence, and the other is *jeev shakti* which is live Divine *chit* but under the grip of *maya*. (Both are explained earlier.)

These two are the eternal affiliates of the main and supreme Divine power, God, the supreme *brahm*. The personal Blissful Divinity of *brahm* is called the *swaroop shakti*.

The Upnishad says about God *(brahm)* that,

(a) He ( स: ) is the supreme Bliss.

(b) He ( देव: ) Himself is within everything that exists. He is omnipresent, He is the Soul of every soul, He is the giver of the outcome of every soul's *karmas,* the whole universe is within Him, He is the onlooker of every soul's *karmas*, He is the supreme life force ( चेत: ) that gives life to every one (all the souls and *maya*), and yet He is only Divine ( केवलो निर्गुणश्च ). *Sattva, raj* and *tam* are called the *gunas* ( गुण ) which are the qualities of *maya*. God does not have *mayic* qualities, He is only Divine, so He is called *nirgun* ( निर्गुण ) which means He is bereft of *mayic gunas*.

(c, d) *Brahm* is supreme unlimited eternal intellect and Bliss.

(e) He is so minute that He is omnipresent in every particle of the world, and He is so great that He engulfs the unlimited expansion of the whole universe.

(f) God has two forms: Personal form with all of His Divine virtues ( सगुण ), and impersonal form with no virtues ( निर्गुण). God Maha Narain (the first supreme spiritual Master of Shankaracharya's religion) says that the main form of God is His personal form. He also has an impersonal Divine aspect. Thus, He has two eternal forms, personal and impersonal (*sakar* and *nirakar*). He has amazing unlimited Divine powers, so He can have such self-contradictory Divine situations. The impersonal (*nirakar*) aspect cannot independently stay on its own. It has to stay in the 'Personal' form. It would be lifeless like the 'space' without the personal form, because the personal form of God is the 'life factor' of the whole of the *nirakar* realm (which also includes *jeev shakti*).

(g) God is supreme, no one is equal to Him then who could be bigger than Him. He has unlimited Divine powers.

(h) He is Divine. He does not have *mayic* form ( अमूर्तः ), but He has eternal Divine form ( पुरुषः ), and that Divine form, from every aspect and from every angle, is eternal and unborn. He is beyond the realm of material life factor ( अप्राणः ), material mind ( अमनाः ), and the souls ( अक्षरः ).

(i) He has no material-like senses, yet He is the enjoyer of all the five kinds of Blissfulness. He is the supreme Lord and the controller of everything, yet He is the refuge and eternal friend of all the souls.

The above two verses specially specify that, although, the Divine body of God has a resemblance to human form but His Divine body is omnipresent, eternal and beyond all the limitations that appear in a material body.

(j, k)  His Divine body is ( विग्रहम् ) the eternal embodiment of pure Divine Bliss and knowledge and He is Govind, Krishn.  So, wholeheartedly, selflessly and lovingly dedicate yourself to Him because He is ( परो देवः ) the supreme form of God among other forms of God.

(l) His Divine abode is beyond the *mayic* light of any kind, like: sun, moon, stars, fire and lightning.  It is established in its own Divinity and it is the expansion of the Personal form of God Who is the enlivener of this cosmic existence.  The selfless earnest devotees always desire for that Divine abode (where they could live with their beloved God).  The Upnishad also tells about the eternal Vaikunth abode of Maha Vishnu which is the personified excellence of absolute Divine Bliss.  (There is an extensive description of Radha Krishn's Divine abode, Vrindaban, in the words of Maha Vishnu in the Samrahasyopnishad.)  The devotees who reach these Divine abodes receive closeness with their beloved God according to their devotional conception in their devotional period.  It is termed as *salokya, saroopya, samipya* and *sayujya.*

## The Gita.

The Gita says that, (a)  Krishn is supreme *brahm*.  He is the absolute refuge (of all of His powers).  He is absolutely pious.  He has personal form ( पुरुषः ).  He is primordially present in the universe ( आदि देवः ) as the supreme controller.   He is unborn and He is eternally omnipresent.

(b) Krishn is supreme *brahm*.  No one is equal to Him, then who could be greater than Him.  The glory of His greatness shines in all the abodes.

(c) Krishn Himself says in the Gita, "Absolute *nirakar brahm* which is the abode of liberation ( अमृतस्य ), eternal (*apar* and *par*) *dharm*, and unlimited Divine Bliss (that is seen and experienced in Vaikunth, Saket and Dwarika abodes), are all established in Me." (The scripturally prescribed religious, moral, social and devotional discipline, designed to promote and elevate the *sattvic* qualities of a soul with its final goal to find God, is called *dharm.* *Apar* (secondary) *dharm* is general religious discipline, and *par* (primary) *dharm* is pure devotion *(bhakti)* to God to receive His Grace. The first one is also called the *varnashram dharm* ( वर्णाश्रम धर्म ) and its prescribed discipline and practice changes from time to time according to the social and devotional status of the person. The second one ( पर धर्म ) is non-changing and eternal.)

Further Krishn says,

(d) "I am the supreme God *(brahm)* Who is indicated by all the Vedas ( सर्वे वेद यत्पदमामनन्ति । कठ. 1/2/11 ) and thus, I am the Divine knowledge, I am the knower (of My Ownself), and I am the knowable ( ज्ञान, ज्ञाता, ज्ञेय ), because I am the producer of the Divine *vedantic* knowledge of ( वेदान्त कृत् ) God and God realization."

(e) "I am the ultimate goal, protector, master, observer of *karmas*, residing place, refuge and the Divine beloved of all the souls. I am the original source ( बीजम् ) of all the souls. They reside within Me in all the four phases of the creation (evolution, dissolution, creation and non-creation)."

(f) "The ignorant people slightfully believe ( अवजानन्ति ) that I appeared in a *mayic* body on this earth planet. They do not understand the absoluteness and Divineness of My descension ( परं भावम् ). I am the Supreme Master and the originator of *maya* and its manifestations. (So I don't have to oblige *maya* to enter its realm. I thus appear in My own supreme Divine love form and all the celestial gods and goddesses serve Me during My descension period.)"

(g) "Those intelligent souls who know Me as the supreme personality of God ( पुरुषोत्तम ) are the true knowledgeable ones. Knowing so, they adore Me wholeheartedly by all means."

(h) "My Divine abode is eternal and beyond *mayic* existence. Those who reach My abode remain there forever."

## The Bhagwatam.

The Bhagwatam says that, (a) there are three titles of the same God, *brahm, paramatma* and *bhagwan* (according to the representation of His Divine virtues).

(b) This whole universe emerges from Him, stays in Him, and functions with His help. Although He has modeled Himself in the form of this universe, yet He is unaffected and unattached with the entire creation. With all of His virtues, He Himself exists in His own glory ( स्वयंभूः । स्वे महिम्नि । छां. ).

(c) The same supreme God, Krishn, Who has uncountable Divine virtues ( गुणात्मनः ), Who is beyond the three *gunas* ( निर्गुणः ), Who is beyond the reach of *mayic* intellect and Who is always absolute in every situation ( अव्यय ), appears in this world and reveals His *leelas* to provide facility for the souls to do devotion and reach Him.

(d, e) Krishn Himself is the supreme God. His devotion is the ultimate commitment of a soul, and His abode is the ultimate goal of a soul.

## The Brahm Sutra.

The Brahm Sutra says that, (a) God is Bliss Himself, and this fact has been repeatedly said in the Upnishads. (b) From Whom and in Whom, the creation, the existence and the dissolution of this universe happens, He is God. The one whose mind is devotionally established in God ( तन्निष्ठः ) receives liberation from *maya*. (c) This fact has been related in all the scriptures, that the absolute Divine virtues and powers, as explained in the Upnishads, relate to God only.

" सत्यसंकल्पः सर्वकर्मा सर्वकामः सर्वगन्धः सर्वरसः ॥ "
(छां. 3/4/2) " एतत्सत्यं ब्रह्मपुरं । एष आत्मा अपहतपाप्मा
विजरो विमृत्युर्विशोको विजिघत्सोऽपिपासः सत्यकामः
सत्यसंकल्पः सोऽन्वेष्टव्यः स विजिज्ञासितव्यः ॥ " (छां. 8/1/5)

सर्वगन्धः *sarv gandhah* word indicates that He has many kinds of sweet relationships with all the souls.

(d) Out of all of His Divine virtues, the Divine Blissfulness is the main. (e) In *dahar vidya*, the eighth chapter of Chandogya Upnishad (stated above), *atma* word refers to God. The Shvetashvatar (6-7) says, "पतिं पतीनां..." which means that He is the supreme Master, Lord and God the almighty for all the souls, and the supreme controller of the universe.

(f) The Upnishads say that He has all the Divine powers. All the *dharmas* are established in Him. He is self-complacent. But, only out of natural kindness and graciousness ( लीला कैवल्यम् ), He, like the bountiful Grace of selfless Saints, has created this universe (so that the souls could come to Him by following the path of *bhakti*).

(g) He is beyond *mayic* intellect and senses ( यो बुद्धेः परतः ). *Pratyakch - anumanabhyam* word refers to both forms of God, *sakar* and *nirakar*, and it says that, through selfless devotion and dedication His Divine form could be visualized, or His impersonal form could also be attained if so desired, but both, *sakar* and *nirakar* forms, are attainable through devotion *(bhakti)* as said by the Up-nishads, the Gita, and the Bhagwatam.

" उपासते पुरुषं ये ह्यकामाः । " (मुं. 3/2/1)

" जुष्टं यदा पश्यति । " (मुं. 3/1/2)

" तस्याभिध्यानाद् योजनात् तत्त्वभावात् । " (श्रे. 1/10)

" भक्त्या त्वनन्यया शक्य अहमेवं विधोऽर्जुन ।
ज्ञातुं द्रष्टुं च तत्त्वेन प्रवेष्टुं च परंतप ॥ " (गी. 11/54)

" भक्त्याहमेकया ग्राह्यः । " (भा. 11/14/21)

" मामेव ये प्रपद्यन्ते । " (गी. 7/14)

(h) Engross your mind in Him (lovingly and faithfully). Remember Him (with a feeling of relational closeness). (i) The two *sutras* (36 and 37) explain the exceeding potency of *bhakti* against other *sattvic* practices as said in the Gita, "नाहं वेदैर्न तपसा..." (11/53). It means that the study of *vedant*, austerity, charity or following any kind of general *dharm* does not reveal God. Only selfless *bhakti* reveals God.

Further, the *sutras* 38 and 39 say that, through *bhakti,* the Grace of God (as mentioned in the Upnishads, धातुः प्रसादात् । श्वे. 3/20 । यमेवैष वृणुते । कठ. 1/2/23) is easily and quickly received (तस्याहं सुलभः । गी. 8/14 । क्षिप्रं भवति धर्मात्मा । गी. 9/13). Thus, *bhakti* is the sure and the superb means of God realization (अहो बत श्वपचोऽतो गरीयान् । भा. 3/33/7), as it entices the heart of supreme God Krishn (अहं भक्तपराधीनः । भा. 9/4/63 । अनुब्रजाम्यहं नित्यम् । भा. 11/14/16). *Sutra* 50 further says that a person living a family life should do selfless *karmas* and *bhakti* with sincere feelings and humbleness. (It is called *karm yog.*)

(j) This is one of the most important statements of the Brahm Sutra. After liberation, soul receives a synonymity with his desired form of God. (In liberation through *gyan marg*, the soul stays with *nirakar brahm* without a body.) In liberation through *bhakti marg*, the soul receives a Divine body. With that Divine body he enters the Divine abode of his beloved God where he receives a synonymity with Him. But this synonymity is only in experiencing the Divine Blissfulness of that abode. It has no concern with the administration or the creation of the universe in any way. Soul becomes totally pure and unblemished and after God realization it never comes back under the bondage of *maya.*

## The definition of *brahm.*

Taking into consideration the writings of all the scriptures stated above, God (*brahm*) could be defined as thus:

"God *(brahm)* is absolute, eternal, omnipresent Divine personality Who has uncountable amazing powers that unfold such Divine states which are incomprehensible to the material mind."

"He is only one; no one is equal to Him. He has two forms, *sakar* and *nirakar*, whereas the *nirakar* form, which is like a dormant existence of mere Divine intellect called *chit* ( चित् ) and has no apparent Divine virtues or powers, is inseparably established in the personal form of God."

"His *sakar* (personal) form is beyond *mayic* names, forms, *gunas*, senses and nature, so He is called *avyakt, nirgun, nirakar, niranjan,* etc. But He has Divine body, Divine names, Divine virtues and His Divine abode, so He is called *sagun sakar brahm* (*bhagwan*). His Divine mind, body, senses and powers are all omnipresent so He is mentioned to be functioning without the need or help of the senses."

"Bliss-Grace-Knowledge is His personality. With this form He is omnipresent in the universe and also resides in every soul. He is master of *maya*, friend of every soul ( सखायाः ), controller of the whole universe through *karmic* power, and protector of His devotees with whom He has all kinds of sweet relationships. Out of kindness He descends in the world in His original Divine form to reveal the easiest path of His attainment, the *bhakti*, which is also an eternal Divine power related to His power of Grace."

"The supreme form of God is Radha Krishn. His Divine abode is eternal and beyond *mayic* existence where His devotee Saints go and live with Him, forever."

" ईश्वरः परमः कृष्णः सच्चिदानन्दविग्रहः ।
अनादिरादिगोविन्दः सर्वकारणकारणम् ॥

वेणुं क्वणन्तमरविन्ददलायताक्षं, बर्हावतंसमसिताम्बुदसुन्दराङ्गम् ।
कन्दर्पकोटिकमनीयविशेषशोभं, गोविन्दमादिपुरुषं तमहं भजामि ॥

यस्यैकनिःश्वसितकालमथावलम्ब्य,
जीवन्ति लोमविलजा जगदण्डनाथाः ।
विष्णुर्महान् स इह यस्य कलाविशेषो,
गोविन्दमादिपुरुषं तमहं भजामि ॥ " (ब्र.सं. 1, 30, 48)

The first knower of the Vedas and the Upnishads, the creator Brahma, says in the Brahm Sanhita,

"Govind Krishn is supreme God and the prime cause of the cause of this universe. He is the supreme eternal form of absolute *sat-chit-anand brahm* as described in the Vedas."

"I worship and adore Krishn, the supreme Lord, Whose beautiful complexion appears to be like a newly rain laden cloud. Who plays on His flute and wears a peacock-feather-diadem. Who has lotus eyes and Whose charming beauty defeats the grace of uncountable cupids."

"The materially unimaginable long lives of celestial lords like us is only one single breath of the supreme Creator Maha Vishnu, and that Maha Vishnu is only a fraction of Krishn's powers. I worship and adore the supreme God Krishn."

(The form of Radha Krishn, other forms of God and Their abodes along with Their Blissful superiority is already explained in Chapter 2.)

The Chaitanya Charitamrit says,

" आनन्दांशे ह्लादिनी सदंशे संधिनी
चिदंशे संवित् जारे ज्ञान करिमानि ।

कृष्णके आह्लादे ताते नाम ह्लादिनी
सेइ शक्ति द्वारे सुख अस्वादे आपनी ।
सुख रूप कृष्ण करे सुख आस्वादन
भक्त गणे सुख दिते ह्लादिनी कारन ।

ह्लादिनी सार अंश तार प्रेम नाम
आनन्द चिन्मय रस प्रेमेर आख्यान ।

प्रेमेर परम सार महाभाव जानी
सेइ महाभाव रूप राधा ठकुरानी । "

" महाभाव चिंतामणि राधारस्वरूप
ललितादि सखी तार काय व्यूह रूप । "

"Krishn's personal form is *sat-chit-anand*. *Anand*, the Divine Bliss, is recognized as *ahladini* power; *sat*, the eternal almighty existence, is recognized as *sandhini* power; and *chit*, the Divine intellect, is recognized as *samvit* power." The Vishnu Puran (1/12/69) also tells the same thing, " ह्वादिनी संधिनी संवित् त्वय्येका सर्वसंश्रये । "

"*Ahladini* is the main power that contains the other two. *'Ahlad'* word means the deep intimate absolute Bliss, love and happiness, so it is called *ahladini*. This is Krishn's own personal power that rejoices Krishn. Krishn Himself is the form of Love, and He rejoices Himself with His own power of love, the *ahladini*. This is the power that makes the soul Blissful."

"The concentrated essence of *ahladini* power is called the 'Divine love power' ( प्रेम, प्रेम तत्त्व, रस ), like the concentrated perfume of rose flowers in an essence form. This is the power that manifests the loving *leelas* of Krishn."

Further, "The absolute essence of the Divine love ( प्रेम तत्त्व ), and the absolutely culminated state of all the exciting, loving and thrilling aspects of the Divine love power is *Mahabhao*. That *Mahabhao* is Shree Raseshwari Radha Rani, the supreme Queen of Divine Vrindaban. She is like *chintamani* (a mythical jewel) that awards everything one wishes. Radha can give anything to Her devotee including God Krishn and Herself. Her eight personal aides, Lalita etc., are the expansion of Her own personality."

So, Radha Krishn are the absolute supreme *brahm* in two forms.

यस्या: क्रीडं चन्द्रमा देवपत्न्यो दृष्ट्वा मग्रा आत्मनो न स्मरन्ति ।
वृन्दारण्ये स्थावरा जंगमाश्च भावाविष्टां राधिकां तां नमामि ॥

# 4.

# The Total Substantiated Philosophy of Soul, *Maya*, and God, and Absolute Supreme *Brahm*

( जीव माया ब्रह्म तथा पूर्णतमब्रह्म के सिद्धान्त का प्रतिपादन ).

## (1) Soul and *maya*.

### (i) *Tattvamasi* (तत्त्वमसि).

All the Divine philosophies relate to soul and the realization of the absolute Bliss. Its practice starts only after the correct understanding of soul and God relationship. First we take one of the most important statements of the Vedas, *tattvamasi*.

The Ved did not say *tadevattvam*. It said *tat-tvam-asi*. So it incorporates all the three kinds of relationships with God, (1) *tat sadrisham* ( तत् सदृशम् ), (2) *tadansham* ( तदंशम् ), and (3) *tasya tvam* ( तस्य त्वम् ), *asi* ( असि ).

(1) Substantially soul and God are both Divine. That's all. This aspect of relationship is 'neutral relationship,' and it is related to *nirgun nirakar brahm* ( चिद् ब्रह्म ) of *yogis* and *gyanis*. (2) Being substantially same as God, soul also has a constitutional relationship where it is a fractional part of God's *sachchidanand* personality ( हरेरंशम् । अमृतस्य वै पुत्राः ). It is called '*shant bhao*.' It is like the relationship of a subject or a loyal servant to his king. This is related to the *sandhini shakti* ( संधिनी ) of God. (3) Being

substantially same and constitutionally a fractional part of God's personality, soul also has intimate and loving relationships with his beloved God because he belongs to Him ( तस्य ). This is related to the *ahladini shakti* ( आह्लादिनी ) of God. तत्सदृशम् *(tat sadrisham)* aspect is included in तदंशम्*(tadansham)*, and both are included and established in तस्य त्वम् *(tasya tvam)*. Thus तस्य त्वम् is the main and complete relationship of a soul to God. *Tasya tvam* **means you belong to Him and He is your Divine beloved.**

## (ii) Form of soul.

*Chit shakti* ( चित् शक्ति ) of God has two eternal forms: one is the original, absolute, unlimited and omnipresent *chit shakti* and the other is called *jeev shakti* which is also absolute and unlimited ( असीम ) but not omnipresent ( विभु ); because it consists of unlimited number of individual and infinitesimal ( अणु ) souls which are substantially the same as the original *chit shakti*. The individual souls are like hydrogen atoms of the ocean or like grains of rice in a mountain of rice.

*Jeev shakti* **is further of two kinds and both are unlimited.** One is the **pure** *chit* that consists of unlimited number of pure souls that reside in each and every Divine abode of God and are called the eternally liberated souls, or the eternal associates of God, or *nitya siddha mahapurush* ( मुक्त जीव, परिकर अथवा नित्य सिद्ध महापुरुष ). The other is **blemished** *chit* **or** *maya* **affected** *chit* that also contains unlimited number of souls which are possessed by *maya*, the anti-*chit* ( अचित् ) power. This *mayic* bondage is eternal and firm, but it could be terminated with the Grace of God. They are called *mayic* souls ( माया बद्ध जीव ). Thus all the souls are part of *jeev shakti* which is a power of God ( समस्तब्रह्माण्डे श्रीकृष्णांशांशजीविनः । ब्र.वै.15/106), so they are called part of God.

Soul is part of *chit*, so it is only *chit*, it is not a knower ( ज्ञ, चित् खण्ड, ज्ञोऽत एव ). Its *chit* quality remains absolutely dormant until it receives a personal identity. Only then the soul becomes a knower. It is seen in the world that ( सुखमहमस्वाप् सन् ) a happily sleeping guy

knows about his happy sleeping only when he wakes up, not while sleeping. So, the knower has the knowledge. 'Knowledge' and 'knowingness' are two separate things. Knowledge (ज्ञ) itself has no knowledge of its being knowledgeable, because knowingness is an active quality which cannot be activated in an absolutely impersonal state just like the dormant knowledge ( ज्ञ ) of a person in deep sleep.

Initially, soul is *nirakar chit* (impersonal). When it receives a personal identity with the Grace of God and receives Divine mind, body, and senses, its dormant *chit* quality becomes active and appears in its fullness and then the Divinely enlightened soul becomes the form of Divine knowledge. Only then he experiences the absolute Divine Bliss ( आनन्दी भवति ).

During creation, the soul receives a material identity and has material mind, body, and senses which are formed of *maya,* the anti-*chit* power. Although, the *chit* quality of the soul is activated, but the 'knowledge' of the person is modulated according to the character of *maya* which is anti-Divine, and so, it is naturally attracted towards the *mayic* field. It is like seeing a refracted vision through multicolored translucent glasses. So, such an understanding which is derived of sensual perception, is called ignorance because it does not relate to the pure knowledge of the *chit*. It is totally conditioned to *mayic* existence, because the means of receiving the knowledge (the mind and senses) and the source of receiving the knowledge (the *mayic* world) both are material. But, **this ignorant understanding could be broken by accepting correct knowledge of the path to God, because every soul is always searching for the absolute Bliss which is not the character of this world.** The *mayic* bondage of the soul cannot be terminated and it cannot receive its pure Divine form unless it receives the Grace of God.

Those *mayic* souls who follow the principles of *nirakar brahm* and accordingly receive liberation with the Grace of God, receive their original *nirakar chit* form with dormant *chit* qualities, and stay in the same state in the *jeev shakti,* forever.

## (iii) Form of *maya*, and the form of *mayic* bondage.

*Maya* is an anti-*chit* power which is dependently established in *chid brahm,* having its full effect on the unlimited number of souls of *jeev shakti* since eternity. It is lifeless and mindless. Its flow is against God (पराञ्चिखानि व्यतृणत् स्वयंभू:); it has three *gunas*; it is unstable; it runs in a cycle of life and death; it creates a perfect duality; its happiness is fickle and its appearance is deceptive. That's how it is called anti-*chit*.

For a God realized Saint the characteristics, *gunas*, and the defilements of *maya* do not exist, still the outer appearance of this world exists. That's how, remaining in his own Divine state and observing the omnipresent Divinity, he lives and behaves in the world. But, for an ordinary soul, its total existence is perfectly real because *maya* is an eternal power of God.

There are two kinds of *maya*, (1) the original *maya* which is a power of God, and (2) the soul's own creation which appears as worldly desires, hopes and attachments that cause grief, pain and pleasure. It is called *avidya* or *moh* (अविद्या, मोह). It is totally fake because it is only an imagination of the mind that appears as desires, attachments, pains and pleasures, but it appears very real to a human mind. That is why it is called illusion or mirage.

The soul has to terminate his own creation first, then God will naturally cancel the bondage of His *maya*. This is the procedure. So, for God realization, the second *maya (avidya)* is more important than the first one, because this is the main obstacle in the path to God. That's why Shankaracharya, ignoring the first one, describes the second one (in his *bhashya*) in an exaggeratingly mystical manner and says that the total creation is fake and imaginary. Had he literally meant what he said, he would have been contempting his own statements because, in that case, he himself along with his body, words, teachings, writings and the earth he walked upon would have been proved fake and nonexisting, but it is not so. It is thus very obvious that his indication of fakeness of *maya* refers to *avidya* (ignorance), the attachment of souls in the world, which he himself corrected in the verses 99 and 105 of his last work where he proclaimed that *maya* is a power of God, so that the true aspirants of God should not be confused with the style of the writing he used in his *bhashya*. (*Bhashya* means the detailed description on the Brahm Sutra.)

Along with *maya* two powers, *kal* and *karm,* are also involved in the creation of this universe, but they are all lifeless, so God has to initiate them to work. **Kal, karm, maya and souls always remain together.** During *maha pralaya,* in *nirakar* form, they dormantly reside in God. During the creation period also they reside within God and God remains omnipresent in the universe.

**Celestial gods and goddesses are** *mayic* **powers and are** *nirakar* **and lifeless like** *maya.* **They only come to life and assume a** *sakar* **form when God initiates His power and the universe is created along with uncountable** *brahmandas.*

## (2) The supreme *brahm.*

### (i) Significance of the word *brahm* and the absolute greatness (अद्वितीयत्व) of *brahm.*

*Brahm* (or God) is a general word for the Divinity or the Divine existence. It is like the word 'color' which has no tangible meaning on its own unless it is specified as blue color or red color, etc. You may say 'blue' or you may say 'blue color,' both are the same, but when you say only 'color,' it only classifies the substance, meaning you know that it is color, not food or drink, but you cannot buy, or obtain, or even imagine 'color' unless you specify it as blue, green or white, etc. One more thing, the word 'color' entered the dictionary only to facilitate the description of the colorful world which already existed.

Similarly, the word *brahm* signifies only the quality, greatness, and Graciousness of the Divine existence. You should know that not just *brahm* (God), but a 'form' of *brahm* (God) is recognized, experienced, worshipped or perceived; and a form of *brahm* is a specific Divine power or a specific Divine existence which already has an eternal abode and name like Vishnu, *chid (nirakar) brahm,* Durga, Ram, etc.

When you say that you want to get your living room painted in a fancy color, you really mean a color. So whenever a scripture says the word *brahm,* it definitely refers to a particular Divine form or power of *brahm* (God). That's why *brahm* is generally referred as 'He' ( स:, देव: ) which is to signify His Divine personal form (the word He also includes She).

" तस्य शक्त्यस्त्वनेकधा । " (रा. उ.)

" न तत्समः । परास्य शक्तिर्विविधैव श्रूयते स्वाभाविकी -

ज्ञानबलक्रिया च । " (श्वे. 6/8) " सखायाः । " (मुं. 3/1/1)

**The word *brahm*, formed from the root word *brihe*** (बृहि वृद्धौ; वृंहति बृंहयति इति ब्रह्म । बृहत्वात् बृंहणत्वाच्च तद् ब्रह्म । ), **means the absolute extensiveness of its own powers and its greatness to make others (souls) great.** The word सखायाः ( सौख्यम्, सौख्यार्थम् ) represents the personal relation and the gracious kindness of God upon all the souls. He is called by many names like *par-brahm, para shakti,* etc. He has many kinds and classes of Divine powers and Divine virtues which are relatively subjected to Him. **He is one and absolute and there is no one equal to Him** yet He is a Divine friend to all of the souls.

## (ii) He reveals His knowledge through His own words, the scriptures, which are eternal and Divine, so He is knowable through scriptures ( शास्त्रगम्य ).

यो बुद्धेः परतः । "He is beyond the limits of human intellect." There are three ways of receiving and conceiving any kind of information in the mind and thus forming an understanding: (1) by direct perceptions ( प्रत्यक्ष ), (2) by intelligent guess about a preconceived situation ( अनुमान ), and (3) by accepting any kind of documentary evidence or verbal statement of a right person ( शब्द ).

The first two are out of the question because God is beyond *maya* and *mayic* perceptions. Only the third one, which are our prime scriptures revealed by God Himself including the writings of our great Masters, called *aapt vakya* आप्त वाक्य, are the means of understanding and developing faith in God and His path of realization. The human mind is, (a) material, (b) finite by all means, (c) subjected to the qualities of *maya,* (d) conditioned to the dimensions and manifestations of time and space, and restricted to its own inadequacies of vanity, attachments and willfulness, etc., whereas God is, (a) Divine, (b) absolute, unlimited and eternal, (c) beyond the field and qualities of *maya*, and has amazing, inconceivable and unlimited Divine powers, (d) beyond the concept of *mayic* time and space, and has unlimited Divine virtues. So the facts about God should be taken with faith. One thing you must know that God is God, so He is beyond your material logic. He may have any kind or form of Blissful Divine existence that may appear impossible to a human mind.

## (iii) His omnipresent Divine personality ( सर्वव्यापक साकार ब्रह्म ).

" सर्वव्यापी स भगवांस्तस्मात्सर्वगतः । सर्वेन्द्रियगुणाभासं...
सर्वस्य प्रभुमीशानं सर्वस्य शरणं सुहृत् । अपाणिपादः...
तमाहुरग्र्यं पुरुषं महान्तम् । एवं स देवो भगवान्वरेण्यः ।
एको देवः... साक्षी चेता केवलो निर्गुणश्च । धातुप्रसादात् ।
देव प्रसादात् । सैव यस्य प्रसीदति । " (श्वे.)

The Upnishad says, "The supreme gracious God, *bhagwan,* is omnipresent with His Divine personal form." His personal appearance, like His arms, legs, body, face, decorations, etc. are fully described in the scriptures, but still, His functioning is not restricted to the use of His bodily organs (like *mayic* bodies). It means that He does not have to run to reach somewhere because He is already there, or He does not have to use his eyesight to know or see something because He always knows everything. That's how the Upnishad paraphrases this Divine phenomena by the words *sarvendriya...*, *apani...*, *sahasra...*, etc. "सहस्रशीर्षा पुरुष: सहस्राक्ष: सहस्रपात् । विश्वतश्चक्षुरुत्... । " (श्वे.)

These verses specially indicate the omnipotence of God's absolute and omnipresent perception and functioning, and, at the same time, they also indicate the omnipresence of His Divine body, otherwise they would not have used the words like (पाणिपाद:, अक्ष:) hands, feet, eyes, etc. They would have used simple words like ( सर्वज्ञ:, सर्वद्रष्टा ) all-knowing, all-perceiving, etc.

It is an obvious fact that no one can personally relate to an omnipresent formless existence, and there cannot be any real tangible experience of the Divine Bliss of God unless He is perceived. So, God has a Divine body which is perceivable. He is the form of Bliss and Grace.

For the creation and the maintenance of the universe He does not have to do much from His Divine body. He simply thinks, looks and smiles ( वीक्षितं, स्मितम् ), and it is all done. So, His body is mainly for the happiness of His devotee Saints. **It is an amazing miracle of the Divine world that unlimited, absolute, endless and omnipresent existence of the Divine Bliss of God infinitely concentrates into His Divine body and the devotee Saint experiences the unlimited absoluteness of God's Bliss in His vision. This is the miracle of His unlimited power of Grace that makes it happen. With such a Blissful form, God is omnipresent.**

God has uncountable Divine virtues. He is described as *sagun sakar brahm* ( सगुण साकार सविशेष ). He is called सर्वकर्मा, सर्वरस:, सत्य संकल्प: , etc. which means that He does and He could do everything simply by thinking, and He has all kinds of Blissful qualities and powers. स ईक्षत । स इमांल्लोकानसृजत । (तै.) He thought to create, and the whole cosmos was created.

God in His personal form is absolutely beyond the *mayic* qualities, nature, forms, names, manifestations and intellect. So He is also called *nirgun nirakar*, etc. ( निर्गुण, निराकार, आग्राह्य, अचिन्त्य इत्यादि । ' निर्गुन ब्रह्म निरंजन... कौशिल्या के गोद । ')

Sometimes in one verse both facts are related. For instance: "दिव्यो ह्यमूर्तः पुरुषः ।" ( मु. 2/1/2 ). "His personality ( पुरुषः ) is Divine. He has no (*mayic*) form ( अमूर्तः )." If someone translates this verse as 'His Divine personality ( पुरुषः ) has no form', it would be like yelling at someone and saying, 'Hey, do you know I have no tongue in my mouth.' 'He' word means a 'personal form.' The words सः (He), देवः (He, Lord), पुरुषः (He, the personality of God), ईशः (the supreme controller) have been liberally used for God in the Upnishads. One Shvetashvataropnishad used these words forty-four times in its six chapters.

**So, now we know that God (*brahm*) is always *sakar* and omnipresent.** He is called *nirgun, nirakar, achintya,* etc., because He is beyond *mayic* name, form and *gunas,* and He is called *sagun sakar,* etc. because His Divine personality has uncountable Divine virtues and powers.

## (iv) His Divine virtues.

All the virtues of God are related to His Divine personal form ( ज्ञानबलक्रिया च ). His knowledge, almightiness, will and action are all, in some way, related to Gracing the souls and Saints with His Blissfulness. His Bliss and Grace appear in uncountable forms. His limitless Divine beauty, charm, joy, love, etc. are forms of His Blissfulness, and His unlimited kindness, forgiveness, graciousness and affection, etc. ( दीन दयालु, करुणा सागर, भक्त वत्सल ) are the forms of His power of Grace.

## (v) His main forms of eternal existence ( ब्रह्म की नित्य अभिव्यक्ति ).

The absolute *brahm* has four main forms of eternal existence: (a) *Mahabhao* ( महाभाव ), (b) *leela purushottam* (लीला पुरुषोत्तम ), (c) *purushottam* ( पुरुषोत्तम ), and (d) *nirakar brahm* ( अव्यक्तशक्तिक निराकार ब्रह्म ).

**(a) *Mahabhao.*** This is the state of *brahm* where the unlimited Divine knowledge mergingly loses its identity. This is such a Divinely unimaginable state of the Divine which is absolutely absolute by all means, so this is called *Mahabhao.* This is Radha, Raseshwari. She has two eternal forms, Radha and Krishn, so Both are one. Her abode is Divine Vrindaban.

**(b)** *Leela purushottam.* The magnificence of Divine love, that reveals the intimacy of your personal Divine relationship with your beloved God, is *ras* ( रस: ); and the actions and doings of the Divine beloved, that increasingly enriches and glorifies that *ras*, is *leela.* So, the One Who manifests such *leela ras* is *leela purushottam.*

There are three forms of *leela purushottam*: Krishn, Dwarikadhish and Bhagwan Ram. Their Divine abodes are Golok, Dwarika and Saket. Radha Krishn are in Golok, Rukmini Krishn (Dwarikadhish) in Dwarika and Sita Ram in Saket. Krishn is called Dwarikadhish in Dwarika. Krishn is also called *poorntam purushottam brahm* and Ram is called *maryada purushottam* because His *leela ras* is somewhat restricted to certain disciplines ( मर्यादा ).

**(c)** *Purushottam.* Maha Vishnu (or Narain) is called *purushottam.* He resides with Maha Lakchmi in Vaikunth abode which reveals the unlimited Blissful almightiness of *brahm* (and holds all the almighty forms of God and Goddess).

**(d)** *Nirakar brahm. Nirakar brahm* is eternally *avyakt shaktik,* which means that it omnipresently exists as formless, virtueless, nameless and mindless *chit* ( चित् ) that has no definite identification because it is bereft of *mayic* qualities and has absolutely dormant Divine qualities. So it is called, '*nirgun nirakar nirvishesh brahm,*' ' निर्गुण निराकार निर्विशेष ब्रह्म I .'

" अदृष्टमव्यवहार्यमग्राह्यमलक्षणमचिन्त्यमव्यपदेश्यमेकात्म-
प्रत्ययसारं प्रपञ्चोपशमं शान्तं शिवमद्वैतम् ॥ " (मां. 7)

The Mandukyopnishad expresses the existence of *nirakar brahm* in a denial form. It says that it is such a dormant Divine absolute existence ( शान्तं शिवमद्वैतम् ) that cannot be observed, cannot be imagined, cannot be told, and cannot be described, because it has no active properties that could be described ( अलक्षणम् ). It is simply an inconceivable Divine existence.

It is also called *chid-brahm* or *chit-shakti*. *Chit* literally means inactive Divine intellect or knowledge.

Ignorance is compared with darkness and knowledge is compared with light, so *chit* is also considered an enlightened knowledge or intellect. But, factually, it is not Divine light, it is only Divine intellect ( चित् ) without mind. So *nirakar brahm* is live but inactive (dormant). It is mere Divine intellect ( ज्ञान स्वरूप ).

*Sagun sakar (brahm) bhagwan* has the Divine mind, not the *nirgun nirakar brahm*. So *sagun sakar bhagwan* is the knower ( ज्ञाता ) of *nirgun nirakar (chid) brahm*. *Nirgun nirakar brahm* does not even recognize its own identity as *chit* ( ब्रह्म केवल ज्ञानस्वरूप है, ज्ञाता नहीं है । ) because it is mindless; that's why it is inactive and called *akarta* ( अकर्ता ). One person is dead forever and another one is unconscious forever. Carefully think over the situation. You will find that, for his own self, the second person is also like dead forever because he will never acknowledge his identity. It is the third person, who observes both, can recognize the live identity of the second person, but it is of no use for the unconscious person. This situation of *brahm*, where it is of no use, is called *avyaoharya* ( अव्यवहार्य ).

A soul, in its pure state, is an exact replica of such *nirgun nirakar brahm* in a tiny form, so it is also called *brahm*. A *mayic* soul, when he receives liberation ( कैवल्य मोक्ष ) according to *gyan marg,* receives the same Divine state of unacknowledged-self. This is what Jagadguru Shankaracharya described in his *advait bhashya* of Brahm Sutra where he asserted that *brahm* is निर्गुण, निराकार, निर्विशेष, ज्ञानस्वरूप and अकर्ता (virtueless, formless, having no attributes, just the mere Divine intellect, and inactive). This description of his is also in relation to the pure soul which, qualitatively, bears the same description.

Associates of *nirakar brahm*: *Jeev shakti* and *maya shakti* (described earlier) are the two associates of *chid brahm* and are the powers of *sagun sakar bhagwan*. *Maya* **is established in** *chid* ***brahm*, and** *jeev shakti* **resides parallel to** *chid brahm*, **and all the three are established in** *sagun sakar bhagwan*. *Chid brahm* and *jeev shakti* are both called *chit* ( चित् ) and *maya* is called anti-*chit* ( अचित् ) because, (a) it is lifeless, and (b) it has anti-Divine character.

## (vi) The three natural qualities of *brahm* (God), His personal forms, functions and Divine dimensions ( भगवत्स्वरूप व भगवद्धाम ).

The absolute supreme God is also mentioned as, ***para shakti, swaroop shakti, atmmaya, yogmaya*** etc.

(a) **Natural qualities of God.** He has three natural qualities or nature ( स्वभाविक गुण ): *sat, chit* and *anand*. All the three qualities remain in all the three where one remains prime and prominent and the other two qualify it. Thus, all the forms and powers of God have all the three qualities with one main quality.

(b) **Practical aspect of these qualities or their specific powers.** The practical aspect of *sat* or the power of *sat* ( स्वाभाविक गुण की शक्ति ) is called *sandhini* (the almighty power) or ***sandhini shakti***. The practical aspect of *chit* is called *samvit* or ***chit shakti*** or *gyan shakti* (the Divine intellect) or *chid brahm;* and the practical aspect of *anand* is called *ahladini* or *hladini* or ***ahladini shakti***. Now, according to the above description, *sandhini shakti* is also qualified with *chit* and *anand; chit shakti* is also qualified with *sat* and *anand;* and *ahladini shakti* is also qualified with *sat* and *chit*. But *chit shakti*, in its initial form, is always *nirakar (nirakar brahm* or *chid brahm)* and dormant, like the dormant intelligence of an unconscious mind. For that reason, its qualifying *anand* quality also remains dormant. Only its *sat* quality which is 'existence' remains perfect. (Initially, *sat* word means 'eternal existence'.) Thus, the function of *chit shakti* is only seen in *sakar brahm (sakar* forms of God).

*Ahladini shakti*, along with its qualifying *sat* and *chit*, has three forms: (1) *ahladini shakti*, (2) *prema shakti* or *prem tattva* (the Divine love power) and (3) *Mahabhao*, where *prema shakti* (or *prem tattva*) is the essence of the Bliss of *ahladini's* intimate excellence, and *Mahabhao* is the absoluteness of the absolute *prem tattva*. (*Tattva* means the essential substance of a particular Divine power.)

"ह्लादिनी सार हि प्रेम बखानी । प्रेम सार राधा ठकुरानी ॥ " (चै.च.)

(c) **The Divine dimension ( दिव्य धाम ).** All of these powers have their own personal Divine dimension called abode ( धाम, लोक ) which is unlimited and omnipresent. The dimension of *sandhini* is called Vaikunth; the dimension of *ahladini* is called Saket and Dwarika; the dimension of *prema shakti* is called Golok and the dimension of *Mahabhao* is Vrindaban. The absolute *brahm* glorifies every abode in two forms, male and female.

(d) **Innate self-submittedness of the Divine powers to Their supreme enlivener.**

" तास्वाह्लादिनी वरीयसी, परमान्तरङ्गभूता राधा । "

In your own personality, your body does everything happily whatever your mind says, because body is naturally submitted to the mind, and body and mind both live for happiness so they are the natural servant of happiness. This is just an example and you should know that an example has only partial resemblance. So, not exactly but something like that, in the Divine world, all the almighty powers including *jeev shakti* are self-submittedly established in the Divine love power ( प्रेम तत्त्व ) which is established in *Mahabhao* Radha. **It is a miracle of the Divine world that all the powers, freely glorifying their own Divine dimension (abode धाम), are established into Their next superior power, and in this way They form the supreme absoluteness of one single God (*brahm*).**

**'Bliss' is the 'life aspect' of the Divine realm.** So, from this angle of view, we say that Radha *tattva* gives 'life and Bliss' to Divine love power, the *prem tattva* ( आत्मा तु राधिका तस्य ), and *prem tattva* gives 'life and Bliss' to *sandhini tattva*. That's how they are naturally established and self-submitted to their source of Bliss which is their life giver. That's how, in a progressive style, the Blissful superiority exists in all the Divine abodes, of which the culminating point is Radha *tattva* ( परमांतरगंभूता ).

For the same reason it is said that Radha is the soul of Krishn and Krishn is the soul of *sandhini tattva* (Maha Vishnu and Lakchmi, etc.) and all the souls ( तस्येदं शरीरम् ).

Thus, Vaikunth, Saket, Dwarika, Golok and Vrindaban are the abodes whose Blissful superiority progressively increases up to Vrindaban abode. Vaikunth is the abode of Divine almightiness, Saket and Dwarika are the abodes of Divine love ( प्रेम तत्त्व ) mixed with almightiness, Golok is the abode of pure Divine love, and Vrindaban abode is like the eternally full bloom flower of Divine love.

One should not think that the description of Blissful superiority makes the other one inferior. This is another miracle of the Divine world that there is no experience of lowness by the Saints of any of these abodes. They are all Divinely contented in the absoluteness of their Blissful experience. Still there are certain enriching superiorities of the Divine love which makes it special. They are like multiplying absolute magnificence into absolute Bliss.

(e) **Functions of *sat*, *chit* and *anand* powers** ( सच्चिदादि गुणों का कार्य ). *Sat shakti* relates to action ( क्रिया ), *chit* to the Divine knowledge ( ज्ञान ), and *anand* to the Grace ( इच्छा ) and the experience of Bliss. Thus, ***sat shakti*** appears as the name, form, action *(leela)*, virtue, the Divine abode and its magnificence, etc. of all the forms of God. It also includes the creation of the universe ( नाम, रूप, ऐश्वर्य, क्रिया, लीला, गुण, धाम तथा सृष्टि आदि कार्य ).

***Chit shakti*** appears as the Divine mind of all the forms of God. It includes omniscience, omnipotence, Godliness and sentience of Its Own Divine dignity, powers and virtues, etc. In Golok and Vrindaban it also appears as the knowledge of the loving sweetness of the *leelas*, and the love and beauty of Radha and

Krishn ( दिव्य ज्ञान, दिव्य बुद्धि, सर्वज्ञता, अन्तर्यामित्व, सर्वशक्तिमत्ता, भगवत्ता तथा स्वैश्वर्य गुण शक्ति आदि का ज्ञान, इत्यादि । राधा कृष्ण को परस्पर एक दूसरे के अनुराग, लीला रस, प्रेमातिशयिता व सौन्दर्य माधुर्यादि का ज्ञान । ).

*Anand shakti* appears as the Grace, kindness, affection to all the souls and Saints, experience of Own Bliss, and self-complacency, etc. in all the forms of God. Same power imparts liberation, *Bhakti* or Divine love to a devotee. In Golok and Vrindaban it is the essence of *ahladini* power and gives the experience of unimaginable love of Radha and Krishn to each other, and to Their associates ( कृपा, करुणा, दीनदयालुता, ज्ञान-भक्ति-प्रेम दान । महाविष्णु आदि का स्वानन्दानुभव, आत्मारामत्व इत्यादि । राधा कृष्ण को परस्पर एक दूसरे के प्रेमरस का अनुभव, तथा परिकरों को ब्रज रस, युगल रस का अनुभव । ).

As an axiom, an 'existence' is the existence of a power that qualifies every aspect of its own being by its natural qualities, character and virtues. Thus, God is recognized and experienced according to the virtues of His powers like *sandhini, ahladini,* etc., in their respective abodes which are all intimately related to their supreme source of Divine Bliss, Radha Krishn of Divine Vrindaban, the abode of Radha Rani.

Although, the same *chit* word has been used for the Divine mind of all the forms of God, but it is very important to know that the qualitative efficacy of *chit shakti* that resides in *Mahabhao* and the three forms of *leela purushottam* is superlatively magnified to match the superiority of Their Blissful excellency, and so are the qualitative superiorities of *sat shakti* residing in Them.

Understand it like this. There are only two main powers: (1) *sandhini* (the almighty power), and (2) *ahladini* (the Divine love power). It is described earlier that *ahladini shakti* has four aspects, two are affiliated with almightiness and two are pure Divine love. The *sat-chit-anand* aspect of these five kinds of main Divine existences constitute as thus:

| (1) | (2) | (3) |
|---|---|---|
| *purushottam brahm*<br>(Vaikunth *lok*)<br>Lakchmi Maha Vishnu,<br>etc. | *maryada*<br>*purushottam brahm*<br>(Saket *lok*)<br>Sita Ram | *leela*<br>*purushottam brahm*<br>(Dwarika *lok*)<br>Rukmini Krishn<br>(Dwarikadhish) |
| *Sat* is the main power that appears as *sandhini shakti* in its full almighty glory.<br>❀<br>*Chit* remains as its natural quality and *anand* remains as its general quality. | *Anand* is the main power that appears as *ahladini shakti* with *sandhini* affiliation.<br>❀<br>*Sat* and *chit* remain as its natural qualities. | *Anand* is the main power that appears as *ahladini shakti* with minimal *sandhini* affiliation.<br>❀<br>*Sat* and *chit* remain as its natural qualities. |

| (4) | | (5) | |
|---|---|---|---|
| *leela purushottam brahm*<br>(Golok)<br>Radha Krishn | | *Mahabhao,*<br>the absolute supreme *brahm*<br>(Vrindaban)<br>Radha Krishn | |
| *Anand tattva* appearing as pure *ahladini shakti* in the form of *premanand,* the Divine love power.<br>❀<br>*Sat* and *chit* are its natural qualities. | | *Anand tattva* in its absoluteness as *Mahabhao.*<br>❀<br>*Sat* and *chit* are its natural qualities. | |

Now we understand that in Vaikunth abode *sandhini* power remains in its full almightiness and *anand* and *chit* qualities synonymously glorify it. In the four abodes of *ahladini* power, the *sat* and *chit* qualities naturally remain in synonymity with the qualities of their Blissful superiority. It means that, quality-wise, the *anand-sat-chit* of Vaikunth is not the same as the *anand-sat-chit* of Saket, and so on. Thus, qualitative differences do exist in these abodes which progressively magnifies the excellence of Divine lovingness in the same sequence as mentioned above.

This is the reason that the Divine mind of Shiv, Vishnu and Lakchmi, etc. cannot understand the greatness of Krishn love and the depth of His *leelas.* Thus the excellence of other Divine abodes timidly compares with the charming magnificence of Vrindaban abode.

It is seen that *leela purushottam,* Krishn, drowns in the love and beauty of Radha, but, Radha still holds Her consciousness while seeing the beauty of Krishn, because Krishn's Divine mind cannot absorb all of the affectionate charm and the sweetness of Radha's beauty which She holds in Her personality as a part of Her virtues as *Mahabhao.* That's why She is *Mahabhao,* because it is only She Who fully knows what She is and what is the depth of Her love.

## (vii) The absolute supreme *brahm* as described in the Upnishad.

*Brahm* word could be used for any gender. *"Taswahladini variyasi. Parmantarangbhuta Radha."* "The most intimate form of the main and supreme Divine power is Radha." It means that Radha is the absolute supreme *brahm* Whose other forms and powers, called *leela purushottam brahm, purushottam brahm* and *nirakar (chid) brahm,* are established and included in Her supreme personality. So, Their Blissfulness is the effulgence of Radha's personal loving Bliss.

That's why God Shiv rushed from His Divine abode (which is a part of Vaikunth abode) to Vrindaban to receive the Bliss of *maharaas* which Shree Radha gave to the *Gopis.* Also, thousands of Saints, who had received the Grace of Bhagwan Ram and Goddess Sita, waited for six million years for this occasion of *maharaas* to taste the sweetness of Radha's love.

It is like the Queen who rules the capitol, but she has granted her beloved King to rule the country. Radha is the Queen of Vrindaban. She Herself is Krishn. But, with Her Radha-form, She has designated Herself to reveal and grant the Bliss of Her loving *leelas* only, and with Her Krishn-form, along with the loving *leelas,* She has also to perform other Godly works. So, Krishn is also the governing observer of the creation of this universe which is mainly the work of His own *sandhini* power, Lakchmi and Vishnu ( नारायणोऽखिलब्रह्माण्डाधिपतिरेकोंऽश: l ). Krishn also does other almighty works but they are all related to Grace the souls in many ways.

In the *leelas* of Braj, Radha is seen only imparting Her love in various fashions, but Krishn, along with His loving plays, also killed the demons, organized Mahabharat war, gave the Gita speech to Arjun, ruled Dwarika, and delivered scriptural and devotional teachings to Uddhao. These acts of Krishn made Him famous. It also showed that almighty God *purushottam brahm* Vishnu is within Him.

Although Shree Raseshwari Radha Rani is the prime and absolute supreme *brahm*, the *para shakti*, and Krishn is the supreme *brahm*, but Krishn gained the popularity of being called the main form of *brahm*. There are three main reasons for it:

**(a) It is Radha Herself Who gave credit to Krishn by worshipping Him in Braj *leelas* or the *leelas* of Golok because the nature of 'Love' is to give, to be humble, and to serve. Radha being the prime source of Divine love, showed these qualities in its fullness in the Braj *leelas* (and, at the same time, She maintained Her originality as *Mahabhao* in the *nikunj leelas* of Braj and the *leelas* of Vrindaban).**

**(b) Krishn and other forms of God are directly involved in the creation of the universe but not Radha.** So, all the scriptures and Puranas praise the creator God, Krishn. There are also some Puranas that tell the greatness of other Goddesses and there is also Shree Sukta of the Vedas where Goddess is mentioned as *brahm*, but primarily the male form of God got the prominence.

**(c) The third reason is that the Vedas, their branches, Upnishads and Puranas are all powers of *sandhini shakti*, the *purushottam brahm*, and are thus called *paurusheya* (पौरुषेय), which means that they were revealed by *purush brahm* (the male form of *brahm*).** *Maya* is called '*prakriti*' and *brahm* is called '*purush*' in

our scriptures and Upnishads. It is a common statement that *purush* creates the universe along with *maya*. *Maya* is a power of *purush* (God) and has a feminine form. In this way, *purush brahm* remains in prominence.

Following the same traditional view, the Puranas and also the other scriptures take the liberty of describing all the forms of Goddesses as a Divine power that belongs to and resides in a *purush* form of God, like Lakchmi is *mool prakriti* of Vishnu, Durga is Vishnu-*maya* or *mool prakriti* etc. (In such contexts *prakriti* word means a prime Divine power in a feminine form that holds the power of Divine almightiness or is related to the creation.)

The Puranas, when they talk about Radha, Krishn or even *maharaas* of Vrindaban, they only refer to *leela purushottam* Krishn and Radha of Golok. They never relate to the *Mahabhao* form of Radha because they have no knowledge about that. They know the philosophical, substantial or constitutional supremacy of Radha. They may also know about the happenings of the *leelas* between Radha Krishn, *Gwalbal*, *Gopis* or other forms of God and Goddess, but they have never experienced the Blissful superiority of Radha's love of Vrindaban. It is far beyond their reach. This is the reason that their descriptions hold the superiority of *purush brahm*.

They describe the events in their own style. That's why, leaning towards the *purush* form of *brahm*, sometimes they refer to Radha as *adya prakriti* or *mool prakriti* of Krishn. But, at the same time, they also describe the supremacy of Radha upon *leela purushottam* Krishn by saying that Radha is the soul and life breath of Krishn. Krishn's life and soul is established in Radha. (कृष्णप्राणाधि-देवी । रा.उ.। प्राणाधिष्ठातृदेवी । ब्र.वै. 1/42/58) So, She is the origin of Krishn's all-greatness. **These statements automatically reveal that Radha is the absolute supreme *brahm*. This phrase, in the same way (and not vice-versa), has been used frequently in the Puranas and other scriptures and also in the Upnishad.** We can now have a quick review of the Upnishadic style of describing the Divine truth.

## (viii) The style and standard of Upnishadic descriptions.

The Upnishads are 'knowledge' to give you understanding that, (1) your soul is Divine, so you belong to God and not to this *mayic* world. (2) Only God is Bliss which your soul is desiring for. (3) So, you have to renounce your worldly attachments and divert your total attention towards God. All these facts are related to the creation of the universe which was created by God, the *purush brahm* ( स उत्तमः पुरुषः ).

**The whole concentration of the Upnishads is on renunciation and liberation from *maya* which they repeatedly describe,** so it is very normal for them to be the way they are. One more thing, they mostly use personal pronouns for God to be on the safe side because there are many forms of God. But while determining the supremacy of the form of *brahm*, they specify it only in certain Upnishads like Gopal Tapniyopnishad, Radhikopnishad, etc., not in general. We can have a glimpse of it.

(a) In the Upnishads there is a general description that *brahm* is Bliss ( आनन्दं ब्रह्म ), (b) which is further specified that He, the personal form of *brahm* ( रसो वै सः ), is the enchanting sweetness of that Bliss.

(c) The Upnishad further defines the word 'He' as the supreme *brahm* Krishn Who qualifies the word रसः, the sweetness of that Bliss ( कृष्ण एव परो देवो तं रसेत् । श्रीकृष्णो वै परमं दैवतं... यो ध्यायति रसति भजति सोऽमृतो भवति । ( गो.पू.ता. ).

(d) It again tells in the Radhikopnishad that supreme *brahm* Krishn has two eternal forms, Radha and Krishn.

" कृष्णो ह वै हरिः परमो देवः षड्विधैश्वर्य्यपरिपूर्णो भगवान् गोपीगोपसेव्यो वृन्दाऽऽराधितो वृन्दावनादिनाथः, स एक एवेश्वरः तस्य हवै द्वैतनुः ॥ "

(e) Then it describes the oneness of the two forms and the importance of Radha upon Krishn. It says,

" कृष्णेन आराध्यत इति राधा । कृष्णं समाराधयति सदेति राधिका । अस्या एव कायव्यूहरूपा गोप्यो महिष्यः श्रीश्चेति । येयं राधा यश्च कृष्णो रसाब्धिर्देहेनैकः क्रीड्नार्थं द्विधाऽभूत् ॥ "

"Her personal aides, etc. are the expansion of Her personality. Maha Lakchmi also appeared from Her. She is worshipped by Krishn and She also worships Krishn. Whatever is Radha, same is Krishn. Both are one in two forms and are the ocean of love. To reveal and to explicate the sweetness of Their loving *leelas* They are in two forms."

(f) Finally it tells the absolute supremacy of Radha as *Mahabhao* and reveals the carefully kept absolute secret of the Divine world with the admonition that this secret should never be revealed to just anyone, ( गुह्याद्गुह्यतरमप्रकाश्यं, यस्मै कस्मै न देयम् । ), and the secret is,

" एषा वै हरेः सर्वेश्वरी सर्वविद्या सनातनी कृष्णप्राणाधिदेवी चेति, विविक्ते वेदाः स्तुवन्ति, यस्या गतिं ब्रह्मभागा वदन्ति । महिमाऽस्याः स्वायुमुनिनापि कालेन वक्तुं न चोत्सहे । सैव यस्य प्रसीदति, तस्य करतलावकलितम्परमधामेति ॥ "

"Radha is the supreme Goddess of all the Divine powers, origin of all the Divine knowledges and the source of Krishn's life breath. We, the Vedas, wholeheartedly pray to Her like this. Those Saints who know Her, tell Her greatness. But even in one Brahma's lifetime (which is 311.04 trillion years) it is impossible to explain the greatness of Her total virtues. Her abode (Vrindaban) is the supreme Divine abode. It is only Her Grace that opens the doors of that abode."

" एतामवज्ञाय यः कृष्णमाराधयितुमिच्छति, स मूढतमोमूढतमश्चेति ॥ "

(g) It gives advice to souls, "Radha's name must be taken with great reverence. If anyone thinks of worshipping Krishn and ignoring Radha, he is then the most ignorant person in the world."

(h) In the end, the Radhikopnishad sings the glory of the name of Shree Raseshwari Radha Rani and says,

" अथ हैतानि नामानि गायन्ति श्रुतयः । राधा रासेश्वरी रम्या
कृष्णमन्त्राधिदेवता । सर्वाद्या सर्ववन्द्या च वृन्दावनविहारिणी ॥ "

"Glory to Raseshwari, glory to Radhey. O Vrindaban-viharini! You are the beauty and celebrity of Krishn, You are the life of Krishn *mantra*, You are the absolute origin and cause of everything Divine, and You are worshipped and adored by all the Divine dignitaries."

**Now, you yourself can see that there is a very systematic description of the Divine truth in our Upnishads. But it is not all at one place. It is scattered all over, and that's their style.** That's why a Divine personality is needed who can put them together ( आचार्यवान् पुरुषो हि वेद ), just like the scrambled parts of a mechanical wrist watch can only be correctly put together by a qualified jeweller, not by an apprentice or a man of intelligence.

Apart from the philosophical part, the Upnishads also tell about the greatness of Vrindaban abode with its detailed description, but they don't know the Blissful aspect of Divine Vrindaban. So, **Radha Herself sends Her personal aides to this earth planet who reveal this truth in their writings which is called *rasik vani* (the writings of *rasik* Saints), and that's how we come to know about the intimate charm, Bliss, lovingness, magnificence and the exciting playfulness of Radha Krishn *leelas* of Divine Vrindaban.**

## (3) The *sat-chit-anand* aspect of soul and *maya,* the creation, and the omnipresent God ( उपादान कारण ).

🌸

### (i) *Sat-chit-anand* aspect of soul and *maya*, and a brief description of Nyay, Vaisheshik, Sankhya, Yog and Poorb Mimansa.

Soul is exactly like *chit* in an infinitesimal form. It is *avyakt shaktik* like *chit*, in its pure form. Souls are of three kinds: (a) The pure souls which form a part of *nirakar jeev shakti.* (b) The pure souls having a Divine body in the Divine abodes and enjoying the Bliss of that abode. These two are called *mukt-jeev* (the souls which are beyond *maya*). (c) Then there are unlimited souls under the influence of *maya.*

The *sat* part of these souls is correct, but *chit,* being eternally influenced by *maya* (the *achit* power), is negatively distorted, and so its qualifying *anand* also becomes negatively distorted ( विकृत ).

*Maya* is *achit* (of anti-Divine nature), and *bahiranga* power (extroverted from the Divine truth). Although its existence is eternal, but its *sat* aspect is originally distorted according to its *bahiranga achit* nature. So, it perpetually cycles into a pattern of birth and death, and evolution and dissolution. There are also continuous internal changes in its physical existence during its whole span of life. **In short, it has a totally distorted existence.** It is mindless and inanimate, so, *chit* and *anand* aspect is out of the question; mountains have no mind and volcanos have no feelings. But its creation does produce anti-Divine understanding and illusive pleasure in the life of living beings, the souls. So *chit* and *anand* are completely disturbed and distorted in the field of *maya.*

The Divine *chit*, soul, having a mind and body of *maya*, enjoys the short-lived waning pleasure of this world which is always followed by neutrality, disruption, disappointment, displeasure or any other kind of unwanted situation where the person still hangs on to his future hope of being happy again which is never fulfilled to his fullest satisfaction. **This is the distorted pleasure of this world.**

The information derived through the perception of this world, which is already anti-Divine, forms an imaginary understanding in the mind which has vanity, conceit and stubbornness with limited memory, limited intelligence and limited capacity to discriminate, decide, speculate and determine the best positive move towards the achievement of its 'true happiness' whose definition it does not know. Thus, it follows its own worldly judgement while remaining attached to worldly entertainments with a firm hope of receiving its desired fulfillment that illusively haunts its emotions until death. **This is the distorted knowledge and understanding of the** *mayic* **realm.**

**Brief description of Nyay, Vaisheshik, Sankhya, Yog and Poorb Mimansa.** These five *darshan shastras* relate to renunciation and they refer to the 'self' only. They accept God as *creator* but God is not their topic of description. It's like kindergarten and preschool learning in the field of God realization. But still they hold an important aspect of our philosophy of the *mayic* creation.

**Poorv Mimansa** relates to the *yagya* and the ritual part of the Vedas describing the kind, class, outcome and consequence of such ceremonial performances. It says that such *karmas*, on their own, fructify and award celestial luxuries and make a person happy, but this happiness is only for a short period of time. That's all. It is an indirect style of teaching renunciation. It is like telling someone who is very fond of sweets to live in a sweet shop and eat as much as he can until he gets fed up with them ( ब्राह्मणो निर्वेद्मायान् नास्त्यकृत: कृतेन । ).

**Nyay and Vaisheshik** move one step further and say that *karm* is mindless, lifeless. It cannot produce its own reward or punishment which is a complexly calculated effect. So, omniscient

God helps to produce the outcome of the *karmas* of uncountable souls. God, soul and *maya* are all eternal and separate existences. God is affiliated in the creation of this world only in this sense, that He promotes the absolute and tiny atoms which, through a system of manifestation, create this world on their own. So the material power (*maya*) itself is the creator of this universe. It further tells that there are uncountable souls suffering in the world. It also tells about two substances, *atm* and *anatm* ( आत्म, अनात्म ) which means Divine and material. Through intelligent and extensive logical analysis, turn your mind from this material existence and introvert it into yourself through the practice of eightfold *yog* and *samadhi* ( अष्टांग योग ). It does not tell anything more about soul and God. It also says that previous lives' *karmas* become the destiny of this lifetime and it takes many lifetimes of practice to introvert the mind into *samadhi* (4/2/38, 41, 46, 48 न्याय).

**Sankhya** took it further and said that souls and God ( पुरुष ) are Divine and totally unattached ( निर्लिप्त ) to *mayic* creation. God enlivens the *maya*, and *maya*, on its own, creates the world ( माया उपादान कारण है ). It did not explain the Divine theory. It kept souls and God in one Divine category, the *purush*, but fully detailed the *mayic* creation, revealing all the twenty-four phases of *mayic* evolution ( मूल प्रकृति, महान्, अहंकार, पंच तन्मात्रा, पंच महाभूत, पंच ज्ञानेन्द्रिय, पंच कर्मेन्द्रिय तथा मन ).

The twenty four phases of evolution are: (1) the original *maya*, (2) its first manifestation, the *mahan*, (3) the absolutely subtle form of ego, the *ahankar*, (4 to 8) the five absolutely subtle instincts of *maya* that, later on, appear as the five elements, called *panch tanmatra*, (9 to 13) the five absolutely subtle elements (space, air, fire, water and earth) in their individual energy form called *panch mahabhoot*, (14 to 18) the five senses of perception in absolutely subtle energy forms, called *panch gyanendriya*, (19 to 23) the five physical organs of the body in absolutely subtle energy forms, called *panch karmendriya*, and (24) the subtle form of *mayic* energy, called *man*, the emotional mind.

These are all, abstract-like, extremely subtle manifestations of *maya* that happen in the same sequence as described above, and are long before the manifestation of the 'space' which we observe today.

Now, the mind of the *sankhya yogi* has to understand that, firstly it has to cross the barriers, attractions and attachments of the last twenty-two aspects of *maya* (in short, it is called the *panch kosh*, the five main layers of *maya* on the soul that includes all the twenty-two aspects). Then it has to cross the *mahan* and the original *maya* ( प्रधान, मूल प्रकृति या अव्यक्त ) and finally it has to establish itself into the pure Divine state ( २५ वां तत्त्व, पुरुष ). Then it will be liberated from all the pains of the world. It also said that the three *gunas* are not just the qualities of *maya*. They are *maya* itself. In *maha pralaya*, they remain dormant in one form ( साम्यावस्था ), and during creation, they appear in three forms as, *sattva, raj* and *tam*.

You should know that eternal peace, happiness and Bliss is the form of God, and God is not their subject. The final reach or goal of Nyay, Vaisheshik and Sankhya is total elimination of pain only ( आत्यन्तिक दु:ख निवृत्ति ). Pain is the effect of *mayic* involvement of a soul. There is not even a bit of everlasting peace or happiness in *maya* or *mayic* creation. ( न कुत्रापि कोऽपि सुखीति ॥ 6/7 ॥ ज्ञानान्मुक्ति:॥ बन्धोविपर्ययात् ॥ 3/23, 24 ॥ ध्यानं निर्विषयं मन: ॥ ध्यानधारणाभ्यास-वैराग्यादिभिस्तन्निरोध:॥ 6/25, 29 ॥ समाधिसुषुप्तिमोक्षेषु ब्रह्मरूपता ॥ 5/116 ॥ सांख्य ॥ ) It says that no one in the world could be always happy. Totally empty your mind and eliminate the attachment, attraction, liking and desires of all kinds ( निर्विषय ) through proper understanding ( धारणा ), renunciation and practice of meditation and *samadhi*, and establish it in your Divine self. This is *gyan* ( ज्ञानान्मुक्ति: ) that makes liberation (painless state) possible. Sankhya is frank and generous. It does not want to keep you in the dark. It says that if you want to have a guess about what the state of liberation is like, you already know it. It is exactly like the deep sleep ( सुषुप्ति ). So *samadhi*, liberation, and deep sleep are alike. You enter into a deep sleep-like (Divine) state forever ( ब्रह्मरूपता ). This is the state of total painlessness, the described goal of Nyay, Vaisheshik, Sankhya and also Yog.

**Yog** teaches the systematic practice of renouncing the worldly attachment and introverting the mind into the self in detail. It accepts the philosophy of Sankhya as it is. You can also say that *yog* is the practical aspect of Sankhya, as well as, Nyay and Vaisheshik. That's why it holds its importance among all the four *darshans*.

**Thus, from Poorb Mimansa to Yog Darshan, the detailed philosophy of the discardable substance *maya* and its creation, along with the intellectual procedure and the practice of its renunciation, has been described.** The most important philosophies which a soul needs to know, like the philosophy of God, His relation to the souls, His Grace and Blissfulness, and the easiest path of *bhakti* to reach Him, are explained in the last *darshan* Uttar Mimansa, the Brahm Sutra.

This is the gist of the five *darshan shastras*. Now we come back to our original topic, the omniscient God.

## (ii) The omniscient God and creation, the substance of creation *(upadan karan)* and the science of God's omnipresence.

God always resides within each and every soul. During creation He looks after the *karmas* of all the souls and, out of kindness, makes general privileges to all the souls and special privileges to the devotees according to the Divine system. He is then called *'antaryami brahm,'* the omniscient God. Apart from that He is also omnipresent in the world with all of His forms, that's how every devotee, on the complete purification of his heart, receives the Divine vision of his adored form of God.

" तदात्मानं स्वयमकुरुत ॥ " (तै. 2/7)

" ईशावास्यमिदं सर्वं यत्किंच जगत्यां जगत् ॥ " (ई. 1)

" तदनुप्रविश्य सच्च त्यच्चाभवत् । यदिदं किं च ॥ " (तै. 2/6)

" तत्तु समन्वयात् । " (ब्र.सू. 1/1/4) " पुरुष एवेदꣳ सर्वम् । " (श्वे. 3/15)

All the *Jagadgurus* have accepted that God Himself became this universe. He Himself is the cause and He Himself is the effect ( निमित्तोपादान कारण ). The Upnishad says that God has produced Himself in the form of everything, whatever is seen and observed in the universe. The Brahm Sutra says that God is omnipresent in this world, which also means that He is everything in this world.

We should think over it deeply. If God is the substance of this creation why don't the souls experience the Bliss of God, and if *maya* is the main substance of this creation how do the Saints experience only Bliss of their beloved form of God, and not the distortion of *maya* ( सर्वं खल्विदं ब्रह्म I वासुदेव: सर्वम् I सीय राम मय सब जग जानी I जित देखौं तित श्याम मयी है I ); and it is not possible to mix the two because God is only Bliss and *maya* is anti-Divine, lifeless power.

Both situations are true. This world is mundane for a soul, but for a *gyani* Saint this world is the form of *brahm;* for a Vishnu *bhakt* Saint it is the form of Vishnu; for a Ram *bhakt* Saint it is the form of Bhagwan Ram; for a *bhakt* Saint of Dwarikadhish it is the form of Vasudev and for a *rasik* Saint the same world is the form of Radha Krishn. All the *Jagadgurus* tried to explain this perplexing parable of the world in their own style. Let us try to understand it.

We have to refer to material examples: (1) Think of ice blocks in a number of shapes and colors. Temperature and color (*maya*), with the help of water, transformed itself into individual colorful solidity, but substantially it is pure colorless water (*brahm*) which is not outwardly observed, only its colorful shape is seen. (2) The fiber (*brahm*) of the thread is pure and white, but when it is spun and produced into colorful material and then to a garment, fiber is not seen, only the garment is seen (*maya*). These are just partially correct examples.

Now, think of God's omnipresent situation deeply. Suppose in a billionth section of an absolute tiny particle God is not present, then He cannot be called omnipresent. But He *is* omnipresent, and thus, His omnipresence itself shows that He Himself became everything, otherwise, He cannot be omnipresent. Just like water is omnipresent in the ice block, it means that water itself became the ice block. That much could be easily understood. But the main question still remains that, where is the creation of *maya* which binds all the souls and is experienced and perceived by all the souls? Shankaracharya said that *maya* is neither real nor fake (सदसद् विलक्षण) so it is beyond words to explain ( अनिर्वचनीय ). But we have to say something to enlighten this topic.

It's a common saying that all the bodies are made of earth and finally terminate into earth. Take an example of a seed that becomes a tree. Technically it is the soil and water that takes the form of a tree and adopts its properties. Burn any kind of tree or plant, and you will get only pure ash which is earth. It means earth is the actual substance of which the tree is made of, but you can never see or discover it by observation because you only see the properties of the tree which were in its seed, and the seed too is the form of earth which contains the properties of the tree in a subtle form. Properties means the bitter, sweet, sourness or poisonousness of its fruit, its blossoming form, style and nature, the class and kind of the tree or plant, and the shape of its leaves and bark, etc. So, you can say that pure and unadulterated earth holds these properties in the form of a seed, and also adopts the shape of these properties in the form of an evolved tree, but the soil part is not seen, neither in the seed nor in the tree, only the tree is seen.

Take another example: If you break a colored ice block you will notice that the properties of color are seen in its every piece. But the truth is that it is all pure distilled water in the shape of the ice block. The properties of color are evolved and displayed on the base of the water without affecting its initial purity.

Similarly, **God allows the *mayic* manifestation to happen on His own base.** So, virtually He Himself is the universe, but, at the same time, this universe is also the manifestation of *mayic* properties and qualities which form the mind and body of the souls.

This is the reason that *mayic* souls can only experience the *mayic* phenomena, they cannot observe the Divine omnipresence in the universe; and the Saints, whose mind and senses have become Divine with the Grace of God, can only experience the Divine aspect of this world in the form of their beloved God. They can never observe *mayic* qualities of the world because it disappears for them.

## (iii) The physical status of the qualities of *maya*.

There are two things: (1) the quality or property itself, and (2) the basic substance, or base matter, or the base in which it resides or stays. For instance, a highly scented jasmine flower has perfume when it is open. When it is in a bud state or when it is fully dried there is no perfume. When it is thrown in the rubbish and is rotted, it starts smelling bad. It means the flower contains the perfume, flower itself is not the perfume. There are certain kinds of rose flowers that have perfume and there are many that have no perfume. So, perfume is the quality and flower is the base in which it resides. The perfume could be extracted but on some base, like alcohol base, oil base or any other base.

Thus there are two separate things, quality (or virtue or property) and the base where it resides ( शक्ति एवं शक्तिमान् ).

There is another situation where both are one like camphor. Camphor itself is its perfume. The Divine powers are established in Their supreme power *prema shakti,* still they hold their individuality in a self-submissive style, and are the base of their own virtues like the second situation. **But *maya* and the qualities *sattva, raj* and *tam* are just abstract.** They don't have their own *mayic* base, that's why they are lifeless. They are sheltered in the Divine. *Maya* and the three qualities are the same thing ( अजामेकां लोहितशुक्लकृष्णाम्). It is easier to explain a situation of manifestation when we say the qualities of *maya*, but, in fact, *maya* and the *gunas* are one single thing. *Maya* means the three qualities, and the three qualities mean *maya*. When we refer to creation we say *sattva-raj-tam,* or the *gunas,* or the three qualities, and when we refer to it as a power we call it only *maya*.

So, *maya* is just an abstract character or quality which resides in God and its every phase of existence is fully dependent upon God. Its character and qualities are evolved in the form of this world on the base of God. That's why it is said that God Himself became this universe, because without Him this universe would not have existed. This form of God is called *hiranyagarbh* or *virat purush* ( हिरण्यगर्भ, विराट् पुरुष, महाविराट् ) in our scriptures. Sometimes it is called the *sagun* ( सगुण ) manifestation of God because it holds the *gunas* of *maya* along with the whole universe, and thus, in relation to that, His pure Divine form is called *nirgun*. But, primarily, *sagun brahm* means the Divine personal form of God.

**Now we know that lifeless *maya* is only an abstract existence of *sattva, raj* and *tam*.** So, initially, it appears to be like nothing ( असत् ) because it is abstract, but when it is evolved, it is a perfect truth for all the souls and, at the same time, perfectly ineffective for the Saints like a decorative dummy snake that cannot hiss, whiz or bite. For these unusual properties of *maya*, Shankaracharya called it सदसद् विलक्षण , which is like a cross between reality and non-reality.

God always remains in His own Divine glory even while acting as *hiranyagarbh*. He remains omnipresent with all of His forms and virtues in this universe as well as inside every soul. That's how a soul could channel himself to worship any form of God, whatever his mind decides, and he can also change his form of worship to Krishn devotion, anytime, without any hesitation.

# (iv) Elucidation of *advait vad,* and the *bhagwad vad* of Shankaracharya.

शंकरं शंकराचार्यं केशवं वादरायणम् । It's a famous verse saying that God Shiv descended as Shankaracharya. He came to re-establish Vedic religion in India because, in those days, the followers of Poorb Mimansa, forgetting devotion to God, were involved only in rituals and fire ceremonies with animal sacrifices with such a belief that it may take them to heaven. The followers of Jain and

Bauddh religions ( बौद्ध धर्म ), forgetting their pious and humble austerity of body and mind, become involved in criticizing our Vedas and Upnishads. The followers of Nyay and Sankhya were also involved in showing their intellectual superiority instead of practicing the prescribed form of *yog* in their books.

So, he had to formulate such a Divine theory that could infallibly cancel these wrong beliefs and practices; and thus, taking a part of the total Divine philosophy he asserted to, "ब्रह्म सत्यं जगन्मिथ्या जीवो ब्रह्मैव नापरः ", which he tried to force through his *bhashya* of the Brahm Sutra. In doing so, he had to exaggerate at most of the places to maintain his theory. (The above verse means that God is the truth and this world is illusion. You do not belong to this world. Your soul is Divine and it is *brahm* beyond doubt.)

Bauddh and Jain religions were formed to teach one single truth, that attachments and desires are the prime cause of pain. So you have to make your mind totally desireless to liberate yourself from the pains of the world. Thus, their theory and practice runs around this theme. There is no talk of God and no Divineness of the soul is described in their writings. So they are called non-Godly religions or philosophies *(nastik darshan).*

Have a glimpse of it. What we call as mind ( अन्तःकरण चतुष्टय ) in Yog Darshan, they call it soul. So, Jain religion says that soul is the size of the body which contracts when it enters a small body like a worm and expands when it enters a big body like an elephant. It is bound by its own *karmas* and is sinking in the ocean of the world with the weight of eight kinds of sinful, vainful and lustful actions *(karmas).* One has to lighten his soul from the burden of *karmas* by mental and physical penance like long term fasting (3 days to 3 months), self-restraint, strictly observing nonviolence, being humble and benevolent to every being, and doing severe penances like snatching the hair of the head, sitting on hot stone, etc. Then his soul will be lightweight and rise into the space. The Bauddh philosophy is called *shoonya vad* ( शून्यवाद ) which states that this world has emerged as an illusion from absolute nothingness. Mind also is a part of nothingness but it maintains its functional continuity by obtaining, retaining and conducting the perceived informations from the immediate present to the next present. In their theory, mind is the active live element ( चैतन्य ) that creates the senses, the world, and the body as well. They call it, (a) *antarsamudaya* and (b) *vahyasamudaya* ( अन्तर्समुदाय तथा वाह्यसमुदाय). Mind, feeling of the self, and all other pains and emotions, etc. are *antarsamudaya*; and physical body and the visual world are *vahyasamudaya*. "यत्सत् तत्क्षणिकम्" is also one of their major themes which means that everything dies every moment and a new thing is born to take its place. Yogachar Bauddh say that only *antarsamudaya* is real. The visual world is totally fake ( असत् ) and is an illusion. Their form of liberation is an absolute thoughtless state ( शून्य ), and, accordingly, they have certain procedures of technical meditation which follows strict self-restraint, humbleness, benevolence, nonviolence, and not hurting anyone by any means. Their theory is full of ( अन्योन्याश्रय दोष) self-contradictions, like the mind ( चित्त-विज्ञानस्कंध ) creates the body and the visual world, and it also stays in the body. Also, when everything dies every moment, then how could a person say that, it is the same body I am in, in which I was before? Again, nothing could be born out of nothingness ( नासतो विद्यते भाव: ). It is an axiom.

Shankaracharya gave all of them a new vision. He told that the soul is Divine and eternal and is beyond the limits of body and mind. The Upnishads and the Gita, etc. are the eternal scriptures and are the authentic authority which should be accepted and followed. They must be respected because they show us the true path of God realization. Other theories are incomplete and don't take us to God. They are only meant for partial heart purification if practiced humbly, honestly and correctly. But, if their so-called follower disrespects or even ignores God and our Vedas and *shastras* in any way, he commits a grave transgression that pollutes his mind.

It's a common practice that you don't open your heart to just anyone, and you don't show all of your precious things to just any friend. So, Shankaracharya revealed only one aspect of the Divinity which was enough to contradict their spiritual misrepresentations and make them understand their shortcomings. He toured all over India and, debating, defeating, discrediting and convincing the Bauddhas, Jains, Poorb Mimansak ritualist and Naiyaiks, etc., with his sharp-witted skillful logical oratory and the Divine influence, he completed the first part of his mission.

*Sanatan dharm* (Vedic *dharm*) has two aspects of God realization: (1) merging with the *nirakar brahm* and (2) experiencing the Divine Bliss of God in His personal form. Shankaracharya wrote his *bhashya* on the Brahm Sutra, the Upnishad and the Gita, which he used to explain only the first aspect of *sanatan dharm* in the first part of his Divine propagation.

**His *bhashya* is called the *'advait bhashya'*** which says that there was one absolute *brahm* which is *nirgun, nirakar,* and *nirvisesh*. (These terms have already been explained earlier.) *Maya* is fake, yet it stays in *brahm* and creates illusion ( विवर्त ), so it is *anirvachniya*. *Brahm* is pure *chit* (the mere Divine intellect) and *akarta* so it is not the creator of the universe. Soul is *brahm* itself which is caught up by the ignorance ( अविद्या ) caused by *maya,* and thus the same *brahm* appears in innumerable individual forms. When the ignorance is broken by the practical knowledge ( ज्ञान ) of the Vedic phrases like *aham brahmasmi,* etc., the soul loses its identity as an individual soul and resumes its originality as *brahm* which is omnipresent ( विभु ). *Maya* is fake and soul is a transitory but eternal phase of *brahm* caught up by *maya,* so, only one absolute Divine existence remains which is pure *brahm* ( चित् ). Thus it is called *advait vad* (the monistic philosophy).

One more thing you should know, that wherever Shankaracharya says *'sagun brahm'* in the *advait bhashya,* he means only *hiranyagarbh,* and not the eternal Personal form of God like Vishnu or Ram. Brahma is also a miniaturized *hiranyagarbh.* So, *sagun* word refers to: (1) Brahma, (2) *hiranyagarbh,* and (3) the Divine Personal form of God. But, generally, the *'sagun'* word is used for Personal forms of God like Vishnu, Ram, Krishn, etc. There are several kinds of devotions prescribed in the *upasana kand* of the Vedas that are related to *sagun brahm,* the *hirnayagarbh.* Their path of ascension is described as *uttarayan* or *devyan marg* that gradually reaches Brahma's abode. Those who reach Brahma's abode may receive liberation along with him after his life is finished as described in the Upnishad सयुजां सलोकतां (बृ.1/3/22) and ते ब्रह्म लोकेषु... (मुं. 3/2/6). This is called *kram-mukti* ( क्रम मुक्ति ). The Gita and the Brahm Sutra also describe this path of gradual liberation for certain *yogis, gyanis,* and ascetics.

Confusing the Divine personal form of God for *hiranyagarbh,* is the artfulness of the *advait vad* for not clarifying the situation. It is like using the term 'president in Washington, D.C., U.S.A.' and confusing it for the 'President of U.S.A.,' where the first one could only be the president of a grocery store.

Shankaracharya knew that his *advait vad,* although technically correct, was not the truthful representation of the Divine truth, but he was doing his job. After re-establishing the greatness of *sanatan dharm* in India, he decided to reveal his true form as a Krishn *bhakt* so he could compliment the inadequacy of the *advait* philosophy and establish the second aspect of *sanatan dharm.*

He wrote another book, revealing the rest of the Divine philosophy, which was his last work, the Prabodh Sudhakar, where he redefined *maya,* soul and God. He said, "*Maya* is a power of God (verses 99, 105) that creates this world with His help, and the souls are under its eternal bondage ( चिदचिद् ग्रन्थिः ). Liberation from *maya* is easily received through the *bhakti* of Krishn, Who is the supreme *brahm.*" He again says,

" जान्तु तत्र बीजं हरिभक्ता ज्ञानिनो ये स्युः । मूर्तं चैवामूर्तं द्वे एव ब्रह्मणो रूपे ॥ इत्युपनिषत्तयोर्वा द्वौ भक्तौ भगवद्-पदिष्टौ । क्लेशादक्लेशाद्धा मुक्तिः स्यादेतयोर्मध्ये ॥ " (169-170)

Here he tells the secret that the followers of *nirakar brahm* also have to obtain the Grace of a personal form of God ( द्वौ भक्तौ ) to receive liberation; however, the path of *gyan* is very difficult.

He further says,

"शुद्ध्यति हि नान्तरात्मा कृष्णपदाम्भोजभक्तिमृते ॥" (167)
" एवं कुर्वति भक्तिं कृष्णकथानुग्रहोत्पन्ना ।
समुदेति सूक्ष्मभक्तिर्यस्यां हरिरन्तराविशति ॥ " (175)

"Only Krishn devotion fully purifies the heart. A devotee should do his devotions and listen to the gracious *leelas* of Krishn with faith and love. In due course of time, a deep devotional affinity for Krishn will arise in the heart. This is the true form of *bhakti* that enriches the heart of the devotee with the sweetness of Krishn love and Krishn begins to reside in his heart." He says,

" भूतेष्वन्तर्यामी ज्ञानमयः सच्चिदानन्दः ।
प्रकृतेः परः परात्मा यदुकुलतिलकः स एवायम् ॥" (195)
" यद्यपि साकारोऽयं तथैकदेशी विभाति यदुनाथः ।
सर्वगतः सर्वात्मा तथाप्ययं सच्चिदानन्दः ॥ " (200)

"Krishn is the absolute knowledge, *sat-chit-anand brahm*, and beyond the three *gunas* of *maya*. He is the supreme form of God. He is omnipresent and resides in the heart of every soul. To Grace the souls He descended in Yadu family in His original Divine form." Further, he resolved the doubts of the intellectuals and says that Krishn appeared in Braj, lived in Braj, and played with *Brajwasis*. This all seems to be a localized happening for a common mind. But it is not. He says, "Krishn, while being seen at one place, still holds the whole universe within Himself and, simultaneously, He is omnipresent, omniscient, and omni-dweller in all the souls. He is absolute *sat,* absolute *chit* and absolute *anand*." How does it happen, is all the Divine miracle.

He is called *nirgun* because He is beyond the three *gunas* of *maya,* and He is *agochar* because He is invisible to the material eyes, but He is omnipresent in His Divine form with all of His Divine virtues. He is the form of compassion, Grace and kindness. Further he says,

"तद्द्वज्रतां पुंसां दृग्वाङ्मनसामगोचरोऽपि हरि: ।
कृपया फलत्यकस्मात्सत्यानन्दामृतेन विपुलेन ॥ " (257)

"Out of His boundless love for the devotees, whose heart, mind and soul are drowned in His loving remembrance, He appears in His absolute Divine love form and Graces them with His Divine Vision." Shankaracharya describes the beauty of Krishn for remembrance and says,

" यमुनातटनिकटस्थितवृन्दावनकानने महारम्ये ।
कल्पद्रुमतलभूमौ चरणं चरणोपरि स्थाप्य ॥
तिष्ठन्तं घननीलं स्वतेजसा भासयन्तमिह विश्वम् ।
पीताम्बर परिधानं चन्दनकर्पूरलिप्तसर्वाङ्गम् ॥ "

" आकर्णपूर्णनेत्रं कुण्डलयुगमण्डितश्रवणम् ।
मन्दस्मितमुखकमलं सुकौस्तुभोदारमणिहारम् ॥
वलयाङ्गुलीयकाद्यानुज्ज्वलयन्तं स्वलङ्कारान् ।
गलविलुलितवनमालं स्वतेजसाऽपास्तकलिकालम् ॥ "

" गुञ्जारवालिकलितं गुञ्जापुञ्जान्विते शिरसि ।
भुञ्जानं सह गोपै: कुञ्जान्तर्वर्तिनं नमत ॥
मन्दारपुष्पवासितमन्दानिलसेवितं परानन्दम् ।
मन्दाकिनीयुतपदं नमत महानन्दं महापुरुषम् ॥ " (184-189)

"O souls, if you desire to experience the supreme Divine Bliss, remember Krishn Who is sitting in a reclined pose, keeping one leg on the other under a *kadamb* tree near Kalindi river in the most beautiful Vrindaban garden. He is wearing a yellow saffron silk garment (shawl and *dhoti*). He has sandal perfume on His body which has a Divine glow that appears to be like a young rain-laden cloud with a bluish tinge. He is glorifying the whole universe with His presence."

"He is looking (at you) with His big loving eyes. He is wearing jewelled glittering earrings, *kaustubh* (jewel) necklace, and many more precious chains and necklaces. He is smiling. His Divine radiance is multiplying the glow of His ornaments. He is wearing a multicolored fragrant flower garland, called *banmala,* and His dignity is defying the effects of *kaliyug."*

Shankaracharya relates a *bal leela* of Krishn and says, "Krishn is sitting in a *kunj* with His playmates and they are eating together. All the playmates are enjoying the livelihood of the occasion. Some bumblebees, attracted with the perfume of His hair, came rambling around which are adding a new charm." Further he says, "Remember Krishn Who is the Bliss of the Divine Bliss. Goddess Ganges resides in His feet, and the breeze carrying the fragrance of the celestial flowers caresses His body. He is the supreme personality of God and Graces His devotees with Divine love."

Shankaracharya addresses the souls and says,

"कन्दर्पकोटिसुभगं वाञ्छितफलदं दयार्णवं कृष्णम्
त्यक्त्वा किमन्यविषयं नेत्रयुगं द्रष्टुमुत्सहते ॥"

"पुण्यतमामतिसरसां मनोभिरामां हरेः कथां त्यक्त्वा
श्रोतुं श्रवणद्वन्द्वं ग्राम्यं कथमादरं वहति ॥" (191-192)

"दौर्भाग्यमिन्द्रियाणां कृष्णे विषये हि शाश्वतिके ।
क्षणिकेषु पापकरणेष्वपि सज्जन्ते यदन्यविषयेषु ॥" (193)

"The beauty of Krishn defies the beauty of millions of cupids and He is so kind that He could give you anything you desire. After knowing that, who else would your eyes like to see, and what for? The *leelas* of Krishn are soul-enticing, heart-contenting and their greatness surpasses the sacredness of all the forms of devotions and meditations prescribed in the Vedas. Leaving such *leelas* and virtues of Krishn how could your ears get involved in listening to idle talks?"

In the end he says, **"It is the sheer misfortune of the senses if they are involved in futile worldly entertainments because they create the sin-improvising attachment and attitude of the mind. The best use of all the senses is to involve them in Krishn love, Krishn devotion and Krishn related activities."**

He expresses his personal feelings and says,

"सत्यपि भेदापगमे नाथ तवाहं न मामकीनस्त्वम् ।
सामुद्रो हि तरङ्गः क्वचन समुद्रो न तारङ्गः ॥"
"उदासीनः स्तब्धः सततमगुणः सङ्गरहितो
भवांस्तातः काऽतः परमिह भवेज्जीवनगतिः ॥" (244)

"O Krishn, my Lord! It is true that soul and *brahm* are substantially the same but the foremost truth is that I belong to You, I am Yours. My existence is from You and You are the Soul of my soul. It is seen in the world that ocean has the waves, waves are not the ocean."

He expresses his humble feelings and says, "*Nirakar brahm* is described as indifferent, static, virtueless and unattached to every being. O Krishn! It scares me even to think like that. If You become like that what would happen to me? I only want to love You and be with You forever."

**Shankaracharya is the same Divinity who has received *raas ras* (in *maharaas*) with the Grace of Krishn just five thousand years ago in his original form as God Shiv. How could he then keep quiet without expressing the greatness of his supreme Divine beloved Krishn. So, after completing the first part of his mission, he spent the rest of his life in Krishn-remembrance and taught the importance of Krishn devotion to the world which is the prime essence of the Brahm Sutra and the Upnishads.**

A famous verse describes the emotions of his heart. He says, "Without caring for food, just taking a little water of river Ganges, I desire to spend every moment of my life in Krishn devotion." Thus, remembering Krishn, he completed the second part of his mission and, when the time came, he ascended to his Divine abode.

"भगवति तव तीरे नीरमात्राशनोऽहम् ।
विगतविषयतृष्णा कृष्णमाराधयामि ॥"

## (v) Reconciliation of Shankaracharya's *advait vad.*

Coming back to the original topic of *advait vad* we should know that although he was not technically wrong but he did not reveal the prime truth of our scriptures in his *bhashya*. He described only the *nirakar* aspect of God for those aspirants who are interested only in liberation ( कैवल्य मोक्ष अथवा दुःख निवृत्ति ). You don't offer a big delicious meal to the one who is only interested in a little snack.

He prescribed fifteen steps of self disciplining and *yog* practices for establishing the *advait* knowledge( ब्रह्मात्मैक्य ज्ञान ) in the heart by dedicating oneself to a God realized *gyani* Saint in the Aparokchanubhuti (verses 100 to 128 and 143, 144). In the very beginning of his *bhashya* of the Brahm Sutra he described the fourfold qualities and qualifications ( विवेक, वैराग्य, षट् सम्पत्ति, मुमुक्षुत्व) of an aspirant who desires to follow the path of *gyan marg*. He also proclaimed that the path of *nirakar brahm* is very tough. On the top of that, he admonished and cautioned the followers of *gyan marg* that if they do not follow these instructions and guidelines and enter into sanctimoniousness, they will be doomed into the ditch of the *mayic* cycle of birth and death ( कुशला ब्रह्मवार्तायां वृत्तिहीनाः सुरागिणः । ते ह्यज्ञानितमा नूनं पुनरायान्ति यान्ति च ॥ ). What else could he have done to exonerate his position as a promoter of *advait vad*.

**Now check the technical part of** *advait vad*. Shankar *bhashya* says: (1) *Brahm* is single, absolute, *nirgun, nirakar, nishkriya, nirvishesh* Divine existence only. (2) Soul is the combined effect of *brahm* and *maya* called *chidabhas* ( चिदाभास ). It resumes a general identity as *brahm* after liberation, and (3) the world is fake ( संसार मिथ्या है । ).

(1) This description of *brahm* is like telling about some renowned professor of a university and saying, "O, yes, I know him very well. He has graduated from the high school in my town." Technically it is not wrong because he has also graduated from the high school, but factually he is a Doctor of Literature (D. Lit.), and

thus it is an incomplete description of him. Taking this angle of view, if you look into the *advait vad* you will find that it is only a partial description of the Divine truth.

*'Jeev shakti'* is *nirakar* and it is affiliated to *nirakar brahm*, the *chit shakti* of God. All the powers of God could be called *brahm* because they are absolute in their own dimension. So, *'jeev shakti'* could also be called *nirakar brahm* which is one single absolute power and it is *nirgun, nirakar, nishkriya* and *nirvishesh*, just like the *chit shakti*. **This is the *nirakar brahm tattva* of *advait bhashya*.**

(2) All the individual souls are the part of the same *jeev shakti*, and their feeling of 'self' is **the individuality of the pure soul permeating through *maya* and enshaping as the material mind. This is called *chidabhas*.** When this *chidabhas*, which is the veil of *maya*, is broken with the Grace of God, the Krishn *bhakt* receives a Divine personal identity and enters His Divine abode. But the *gyani* Saint loses his apparent material identity and his pure infinitesimal soul joins and remains with absolute *jeev shakti* as it is. When a hydrogen atom joins the ocean, it loses its apparent identity and it may be nicknamed to have become the ocean, because ocean itself is a collection of uncountable hydrogen atoms. Similarly, when a soul is liberated, it becomes a part of pure *jeev shakti* where an unlimited number of liberated pure souls exist as an unidentified existence, and so, the liberated soul may be said to have become *brahm* as it has merged itself into the unlimited ocean of pure *jeev shakti* (also called *brahm drav*, ब्रह्मद्रव ).

The example of the space inside an empty earthen pot and the space outside ( घटकाश, महाकाश ), and the example of the reflection of the sun in a number of water filled earthen pots ( बिम्ब, प्रतिबिम्ब), fits exactly with this situation. When the veil of *maya* is broken (the earthen pots of the example), the feeling of self, or the ego, or the individual *mayic* identity is terminated and the pure *chit* (the pure soul) remains with the unlimited pure *chit* (the *jeev shakti*).

*Jeev shakti* is bereft of Divine mind like *chid brahm* (explained earlier), so it is unaware of its 'own' existence. The liberated soul joins with it and becomes 'the same'. This is what Shankaracharya called the *brahmatva* or *bibhutva* ( ब्रह्मत्व, विभुत्व ) of a soul (the state of being *brahm* or the state of being unlimited) in the *bhashya*, where he gives the example of a river which becomes the ocean when it joins it ( यथा नद्यः मुं. 3/2/8 ). But what is the use of this *brahmatva.* When an individual (person) is dead forever, you may call him by any word you like, unlimited or double unlimited, because, neither is he going to come back to consciousness nor will he ever know that he is now qualified as *brahm,* just like receiving the Nobel prize after death.

Becoming *brahm* sounds great, but think over it, what is it worth? Suppose someone says, "I will make you the emperor of a wonderful country with peaceful inhabitants, but the condition is that, at the time of coronation, you will die forever. But don't worry, you will be buried with imperial dignity in a gold coffin. And do you know what that country is? It is Antarctica. The most peaceful land in the world where penguins live." Would you like the idea? Probably not.

(3) The third point of *advait vad* is the fakeness of the visual world. When you say, "This rose is fake," you have already accepted the existence of the fake rose. You are telling only the quality aspect of that thing, that that 'real' looking thing is not real, it is fake. Similarly when Shankaracharya said this world is fake, technically he already accepted the existence of the *mayic* world, only he rejected the deceptive pleasurableness of the world which is really fake.

Now take it from another angle. It has been explained earlier that *maya* is of two kinds: (1) the power of God that creates the world, and (2) the emotional attachment of a soul called *avidya* or *agyan* (ignorance) that causes all the problems. The second one is really fake but appears as real in practical life, and this is the most important and powerful negative force that every devotee has to deal with. When a devotee's mind is totally free from worldly attachments (यदा सर्वे प्रमुच्यन्ते कामा येऽस्य हृदिश्रिताः ।), he crosses the main *maya* easily with the Grace of God. Shankaracharya refers to this second aspect of *maya* that creates the powerful emotional (mental) world, and it is really fake.

**So, the gist is that *advait vad* does not give you anything, rather it terminates you from becoming or experiencing anything, either in this world or in the Divine world. This is the *nirakar brahmatva* of a soul. That's why Shankaracharya contradicted his own philosophy in the Prabodh Sudhakar.**

Again, the phrase *'aham brahmasmi'* (I am *brahm*) is the indication of duality, not the non-duality, and so is the phrase *'sarvam khalvidam brahm'* (this entire world is *brahm*). In these phrases *aham* and *idam* ('I' and 'this world') are the key words and *brahm* is the qualifying word, just like, "I am the king, and this entire edifice is the palace." The identity of 'I' and 'edifice' remains as a fact, and so is the individuality of a soul and the existence of this *mayic* world. Thus, the above phrases express the factual existence of soul and the world in relation to the Divine existence.

In *sutra* 2/3/43 ( अंशो नानाव्यपदेशात् ) Shankaracharya has accepted the spark-like individuality of the souls. (जीवेश्वरयोर्यथाऽग्निविस्फुलिङ्ग-योरौष्ण्यम् । अतो भेदाभेदावगमाभ्यामंशत्वावगमः । ) But, in general, he kept the theme of *advait* and, in doing so, he had to alter and twist the meaning of a lot of verses to suit his requirements, because most of the verses of the Upnishads and almost all of the verses of the Gita refer to the personal form of God.

**Take a few examples of the Upnishads.** *Gyatva devam* ( ज्ञात्वा देवम् । श्वे. 6/13 ) means, "After knowing Him (the personal form of God)." But the *bhashya* says, " देवं ज्योतिर्मयम्, after knowing God which is just the Divine light." *Jushtah...* ( जुष्टस्ततस्तेनामृतत्व-

मेति। श्वे. 1/6 ) means, "When a devotee lovingly joins his heart and mind with his Divine beloved, God, ( तेन जुष्टः ततः अमृतत्वं एति ) then he becomes Divine." But the *bhashya* says, " जुष्टः, अहं ब्रह्मास्मीति समाधानं कृत्वेत्यर्थः । When a soul absorbs himself into the thought of 'I am *brahm*,' then he is liberated." The word *jush* ( जुष् प्रीति सेवनयोः) is only meant for the loving unity of heart and mind with God, the Divine beloved. It does not mean intellectual meditation. *Paratparam...* ( परात्परं पुरुष-मुपैति ) means, "The devotee enters the Divine abode of his beloved God." But the *bhashya* says, " दिव्यं पुरुषं यथोक्तलक्षणं उपैति उपगच्छति । The soul receives the qualities of God."

**Take a few examples of the Gita.** *Mameo...* ( मामेव ये प्रपद्यन्ते । 7/14 ). Krishn Himself says, "Only those who surrender to Me are liberated from the *maya*." But the *bhashya* says, "( माम् एव ) मायाविनं स्वात्मभूतं ये प्रपद्यन्ते । Those who surrender to 'Me' which means their own 'self'." *Bhaktya...* ( भक्त्या त्वनन्यया शक्य । 11/54 ). Krishn says, "Only My selfless *bhakti* (devotion) reveals My Divine knowledge and My Divine form." But the *bhashya* says, " (ज्ञातुं) शास्त्रतो न केवलं ज्ञातुं शास्त्रतो (द्रष्टुं च) साक्षात्कर्तुं (तत्त्वेन) तत्त्वतः (प्रवेष्टुं च) मोक्षं च गन्तुं परंतप । The scriptures not only reveal the Divine knowledge, they also reveal the Divine vision of God and provide liberation." This is something which is not only twisting the meaning of it, but it is revolting, translating the word *bhakti* as 'scripture.' The most famous verse of the Gita is, *Sarva dharman...* ( सर्व धर्मान्परित्यज्य मामेकं शरणं व्रज । 18/66 ), where Krishn Himself says, "Come to Me leaving all the *dharmas*," which means leaving all the worldly ties, commitments and attachments. But the *bhashya* says just the opposite, "( माम् एकं ) सर्वभूतस्थं अहं एव इति एवं एकं ( शरणंव्रज ) न मत्तः अन्यत् अस्ति इति अवधारय इत्यर्थः ।" In general it means, "O souls, (don't go to God) consume this thought that you are God, the omnipresent."

How did Shankaracharya write this? The one who is God Shiv, form of kindness, a great devotee of Krishn and the receiver of *maharaas* Bliss. There are hundreds of reasons behind the actions of a Saint which are beyond comprehension and are related to various kinds of uncountable collective *karmas* of the souls and the existing situation of the *mayic* world. Otherwise, Ved Vyas would have written a few more *sutras* with distinct meaning like: " कृष्ण एव परब्रह्म । जीवमाया तस्य शक्त्यः । जीवोऽसंख्याः । ज्ञानगुणाश्रयः । Krishn is supreme *brahm;* soul and *maya* are Krishn's powers; souls are only *chit* and are unlimited in number, etc.," and in this way he would have greatly eliminated the probability of apparent controversies.

As a principle, *mayavad* (the materialistic philosophies, ideologies and practices in the name of God) and *bhagwad vad* (the true path and philosophy of God realization), both remain in the world. It is up to you, choose whatever you like. It so happened that *advait vad* proved to be a fertile ground for *mayavad* to grow, and thus, several fictitious ideologies developed in the name and in the style of *advait vad,* for which Shankaracharya had already admonished in his writings very strongly.

**However, the gist is** that *advait vad* is for a fully renounced ascetic who is deeply aspiring for liberation. Such a person only wishes to follow the path. He does not question, what's and why's, and the one who questions and argues, *advait vad* is not for him. So why to argue with an unqualified person. The second thing is that Shankaracharya, in his *advait bhashya,* only took a section of the total Divine philosophy, the *chit* aspect of God and especially *jeev shakti,* because it exactly fitted to his desired theme of *nirgun nirakar brahm* and soul's natural oneness with *brahm (jeev shakti)* after liberation. Accordingly, he modified the meaning of scriptural verses in the *bhashya.* But, again, he rectified it and revealed the total philosophy of soul, *maya* and God and taught Krishn devotion to the world; and when he ascended, his mind was engrossed in Krishn love.

Thus, the conflict of *advait vad* and the *Vaishnav* philosophies, which persisted in the minds of their followers for the last thousands of years, is now resolved forever.

# (4) Reconciliation of all the philosophies ( सर्व-सिद्धान्त-समन्वय ). The differential oneness of soul and God, and the oneness of Radha Krishn (अचिन्त्य भेदाभेदत्व ).

### (i) The descended Divine Personalities and the *Jagadgurus.*

There are six main philosophies of the *vedant* that were introduced by the descended Divine personalities in the last five thousand years. Shankaracharya introduced 'absolute monism,' Nimbarkacharya 'mono-dualism,' Ramanujacharya 'qualified monism,' Madhvacharya 'dualism,' Vallabhacharya 'pure monism,' and Jeev Goswami 'inconceivable mono-dualism.'

The first four Divine Personalities wrote *bhashya* (the detailed explanation) on *prasthan-trayi*: (a) the Brahm Sutra, (b) the Gita, and (c) the Upnishads. They were called the '*Jagadgurus,*' which means the Spiritual Master for the whole world. They established their *math* to continue the lineage ( सम्प्रदाय परम्परा ) of their religion. (*Math* means the holy building where an *acharya* establishes his main religious throne for the promotion of his mission, and *acharya* is such a descended Divine Personality, who introduces his philosophy of God and God realization and its related devotional practices which, later on, becomes a religion.) The tradition still continues and, up till now, the religious leaders, who sit on these thrones, are called '*Jagadgurus.*'

Vallabhacharya also wrote *bhashya* on the Brahm Sutra, explained the Gita, and established his religion, so he was called *Jagadguru.* But he himself did not establish his *math.* He only established the temple of Shree Nathji. He was a family man. His family-succession still continues. Now, there are many temples of that religion in India which are run by his descendents, called the '*Goswamis.*'

Chaitanya Mahaprabhuji, the descension of Radha Rani, assimilating the indicated theme of all the philosophies, and introducing the easiest form of devotion to Krishn through the chanting of the Divine name ( नाम संकीर्तन ), proclaimed, that the philosophy of the Bhagwatam ( सर्ववेदान्त सारं हि ), is the enriched essence of all the scriptures. His disciple, Jeev Goswami, expounded Shree Chaitanya's Divine teachings into the form of the Shat Sandarbh, which explains the detailed philosophy of soul, *maya*, God and Divine love. Mahaprabhuji did not establish his *math* or religion, but his disciples promoted his teachings in India.

Now, we will discuss, in detail, the philosophies and the teachings of these great Divine Personalities.

(1) **Shankaracharya's** philosophy is called *advait vad* (the absolute monism). The original simple *advait vad* ( यत्र वा अस्य सर्वात्मैवाभूत् तत्र केन कं पश्येत्... ) originated from God Narain. Shankaracharya gave a new touch to it. He was born in South India in May ( बैशाख शु. 5 ) in 476 B.C. which is according to the records of all the succeeding Shankaracharyas kept in Kanchi Math, South India, (where he originally lived) and also in Dwarika Math, West India. But modern historians have squeezed the date of his birth to the seventh or eighth century A.D. However, the Kanchi Math record is authentic. From God Narain to Totakacharya, Shankaracharya himself wrote the Divine lineage of *advait vad*.

"नारायणं पद्मभवं वशिष्ठं शक्तिं च तत्पुत्रपराशरं च ।
व्यासं शुकं गौडपदं महान्तं गोविन्दयोगीन्द्रमथास्य शिष्यम् ॥
श्रीशंकराचार्यमथास्य पद्मपादं च हस्तामलकं च शिष्यम् ।
तं तोटकं वार्तिककारमन्यानस्मद्गुरुन्सन्ततमानतोऽस्मि ॥"

Shankaracharya established four *math* (the religious thrones) on the four sides of India. Sringeri Math in the South, Govardhan Math in the East near Jagannath puri, Sharda Math in the West near Dwarika puri, and Jyotir Math in the North near Badarikashram. He kept Sureshwaracharya, Padmpadacharya, Hastamalkacharya and Totakacharya on these religious thrones to promote *sanatan dharm*.

(2) **Nimbarkacharya's** religion is called *dvaitadvait vad* (the mono-dualism). Its knowledge originated from Sanat Kumar. Then it came to Narad and to Nimbarkacharya. He was born in an *ashram* near Godawari river from sage Arun and Jayanti. As he grew, Naradji himself came and initiated him with Krishn *mantra*. Some devotees believe that he was born at the end of *dwapar* and some believe that he was born around the fifth century. Historians consider it to be the eleventh century. But there is no mention of Shankar's *advait vad* in his *bhashya*, which shows that he was before Shankaracharya. His *bhashya* is called '**Vedant Parijat Saurabh**.' He introduced selfless, wholehearted devotion to Radha Krishn and remembrance of Their *leelas* and virtues. He says in his Dash-shloki,

" नान्या गतिः कृष्णपदारविन्दात् संदृश्यते ब्रह्मशिवादिवन्दितात् ।
स्वभावतोऽपास्तसमस्तदोषमशेषकल्याणगुणैकराशिम् ।
व्यूहाङ्गिनं ब्रह्म परं वरेण्यं ध्यायेम कृष्णं कमलेक्षणं हरिम् ॥"
" अङ्के तु वामे वृषभानुजां मुदा विराजमानामनुरूपसौभगाम् ।
सखीसहस्रैः परिसेवितां सदा स्मरेम देवीं सकलेष्टकामदाम् ॥"

"There is no place where I can go, O Krishn! You are worshipped by Brahma and Shiv. You are my only refuge."

"I remember Krishn, Who is beyond *maya*, Who is the source of all Divine virtues, Who is supreme *brahm*, Whose lotus eyes are so loving, Who is accompanied by Balram, etc., and Who is the center of loving adoration by all."

"I remember and worship Vrishbhanu Dulari Shree Radhey Who glorifies the left side of Krishn, Who is the form of Divine love like Krishn, Who is always attended and served by thousands of *Gopis* (because She is the Queen of Vrindaban), and Who fulfills all the desires of Her devotees."

His disciple Shree Nivasacharya's commentary (**Vedant Kaustubh**) on Vedant Parijat Saurabh, Shree Shree Bhattji's **Yugal Shatak** or **Adi Vani** and Shree Harivyas Devji's **Mahavani** are the important books of *dvaitadvait* religion.

(3) **Ramanujacharya's** religion is called *vishishtadvait vad* (the qualified monism) and his *bhashya* is called **Shree Bhashya**. Its knowledge also originated from God Narain and Maha Lakchmi. Gradually it came to Yamunacharya and then to Ramanujacharya. Yamunacharya (born in 953 in Madura, South India) was the king of a small state. Once his Master, Swami Ram Mishra, asked him to come along. On the way he talked about the beauty and the kindness of God, and the futility and disappointments of this world. He took him to Shree Rangji temple and said, "This is the true wealth which is waiting for you." Since that moment, Yamunacharya left the kingship and totally devoted himself to God. Before his death he made Ramanujacharya the successor of his *math*, Shree Rangam. He wrote four books, **Stotra Ratn, Siddhi Trai, Agam Pramanya** and **Gitarth Sangrah**.

Ramanujacharya was born in South India in 1017. He was married and his wife had a worldly nature. He studied *vedant* from Yadav Prakash. Later on, he took initiation from Goshthi Purn, and then, he came to his prime spiritual Master Yamunacharya's place where he wrote his explicit *bhashya* on the Brahm Sutra and spread the message of *bhakti* in India which was his Master's last wish. He wrote more than forty books, blessed the earth planet for 120 years, and ascended to Vaikunth, where he came from, in 1137.

Ramanujacharya left his first teacher because he was not a true devotee of God, so he took initiation from Goshthi Purn. But, later on, he accepted Yamunacharya as his prime Master because his Divine status was much higher. In this way, he established this fact that a soul, desiring God's love, must dedicate himself to a *bhakt* Saint of high status who is absorbed in God's love.

In his Shree Bhashya *parishisht* he describes the qualities and feelings of a devotee and says,

" पितरं मातरं दारान् पुत्रान् बन्धून् सखीन् गुरून् ।
रत्नानि धनधान्यानि क्षेत्राणि च गृहाणि च ॥ "

" सर्वधर्मांश्च सन्त्यज्य सर्वकामांश्च साक्षरान् ।
लोकविक्रान्तचरणौ शरणं तेऽव्रजं विभो ॥ "

"O my beloved Lord! You are the controller of the whole universe, and the knower of everything that is in my heart, because You are omnipresent. I have left everyone and have come to You. Parents, spouse, children, relatives, friends and even the religious teachers and masters (who do not teach pure and selfless *bhakti*), are now things of the past. I have left my valuables, property, house and all of the attachments of the world. I have also left all the *(apar) dharmas*. I have literally left everything and have taken the refuge of Your lotus feet. Please accept me..." Further he says,

" अपारकारुण्यसौशील्यवात्सल्यौदार्यैश्वर्यसौन्दर्यमहोदधे,
निखिलजगदाधाराखिलजगत्स्वामिन्, अस्मत्स्वामिन्,
श्रीमन्नारायण अशरणशरण्य अनन्यशरणं त्वत्पदारविन्दयुगलं
शरणमहं प्रपद्ये ॥ ' शरणागतोऽस्मि तवास्मि दास ' इति
वक्तारं मां तारय ॥ "

"O refuge of destitutes! O ocean of unlimited kindness, gentleness, affection, generosity, opulence and Divine beauty! You are the Master, Lord, and Soul of the whole universe, and all of us. O Shree Narain! You are the protector of all who wholeheartedly love You. I take refuge in Your lotus feet."

"My heart is yelling that I am only Yours; I am Your eternal servant and You are my only refuge. Please help me, save me, and relieve me from this cosmic ocean of *maya.*"

These words represent the depth of devotional surrender and dedication in *bhakti* or *prapatti* which he introduced to the world.

(4) **Madhvacharya's** religion is called *dvait vad* (the dualism). Its knowledge is believed to have originated from Brahma, but Madhvacharya did not mention any lineage of his previous *acharyas*. So, *dvait vad* got its fame along with Madhvacharya's

name. He was born in South India near Udipi in a highly learned *brahman* family in the early thirteenth century, and, in fact, **all the Jagadgurus were born in pious, learned** *brahman* **families.**

He took the order of *sanyas* when he was eleven, studied *vedant,* travelled to Badrikashram where he met Ved Vyas who asked him to promote *Vaishnavism.* He wrote more than thirty books including *bhashya* on the Brahm Sutra and the Gita in about thirty years of his lifetime, established the deities of Radha Krishn and Sita Ram, etc. in Udipi, visited many places in India and established the greatness of *bhakti* (devotion). He called for his main disciple Padmnabh to take his place before his death, and thus, spending more than eighty years on this earth planet, teaching *bhakti* to the souls, he left the world. At the end of his *bhashya* he wrote a verse that tells his total philosophy:

" श्रीमन्मध्वमते हरि: परतर: सत्यं जगत्तत्त्वतो
भेदो जीवगणा हरेरनुचरा नीचोच्चभावं गता: ।
मुक्तिर्नैजसुखानुभूतिरमला भक्तिश्च तत्साधनं
ह्यक्षादित्रितयं प्रमाणमखिलाम्नायैकवेद्यो हरि: ॥ "

He says, "Shree Hari, Vishnu, is the main personality of *brahm.* This world is a fact (not illusion). Soul and God are totally different. Souls are eternally subordinate to God. There is always a classification of status (lower or higher) among the souls even in the liberated state. Liberation is defined as the personal experience of the Divine Bliss. Selfless, singleminded devotion to the personal form of God is the means of liberation. **Perception, surmisation and Divine documentation**s are the only ( प्रत्यक्ष, अनुमान, शब्द ) means of achieving a decision; and all the Vedas and *shastras* indicate towards the attainment of the personal form of God."

(5) **Vallabhacharya's** religion is called *shuddhadvait vad* (the pure monism) or the *pushti marg*, and his *bhashya* is called Anu Bhashya. He was born in Champaranya village of Raipur (M.P.) India in 1478 on the eleventh waning moon of Vaishakh month according to the lunar calendar. *Shuddhadvait vad* started from

God Rudra (Shiv) so it is also called Rudra *sampradaya*. This knowledge came to Vishnu Swami, then to Gyan Dev, to Nath Dev, and then, gradually to Vallabhacharya.

Vallabhacharya introduced loving devotion to Bal Krishn. There is a statement in the Bhagwatam, "पोषणं तदनुग्रहः ।" (2/10/4) which means that it is the Grace and kindness of Krishn on all of His devotees that fosters, develops and stabilizes the devotional feelings in their heart, so it is called *'poshan'* or *'pushti.'* That's how Vallabhacharya called his path the *pushti marg*.

In his very young age he went to Kashi to study scriptures from Madhvendra Puri and he was well versed in it by eleven when he decided to go to Vrindaban. After living sometime in Vrindaban he went out touring the holy places of India. He reached Vijaynagar where he quietened the intellectual scholars by his Divine wisdom and was greeted by the king and the learned people by the title of *Vaishnavacharya*. Then he went to Ujjain. After touring some more places he came back to Vrindaban and, at the age of twenty-eight, he entered into married life. He wrote **Anu Bhashya** and many other books out of which **Subodhini, Tattvarth Deep Nibandh** (1. Shastrarth Prakran, 2. Sarvnirnaya Prakran, 3. Bhagwatarth Prakran), and **Shodashgranth** are most important.

Vallabhacharya established a temple of Shree Nathji in Govardhan and introduced a very elaborate system of Deity worship. He lived there. Surdas, Kumbhandas and other Saints used to sing *leela* songs in the temple every morning and evening. The last few years of his life he lived in Kashi. Glorifying the earth planet for 52 years, once, when he was taking bath in the river, a big bright light appeared near him and, along with that light, in front of hundreds of people in 1530, he ascended and disappeared in the sky.

He had two sons. Goswami Gopi Nathji was more introverted in Krishn devotion and Goswami Vitthal Nathji was more learned and was more popular. So he took the throne of his father. Vitthal

Nathji (who was called Goswamiji) carried on the tradition. He had seven sons. So, later on, seven temples of *pushti marg* were established to accommodate the seven Goswamis. Out of which four temples are in Braj.

Vallabhacharya says,

" एकं शास्त्रं देवकीपुत्रगीतमेको देवो देवकीपुत्र एव ।
मन्त्रोऽप्येकस्तस्य नामानि यानि कर्माप्येकं तस्य देवस्य सेवा ॥ ४ ॥ "

"There is only one scripture to be studied, the Gita, which is the song of the son of Devki, Shree Krishn. He is the only God to be worshipped. His names are the only true *mantras*, and only His devotion and service is the best action a soul could do." He further says that,

" वेदाः श्रीकृष्णवाक्यानि व्याससूत्राणि चैव हि ।
समाधिभाषा व्यासस्य प्रमाणं तच्चतुष्टयम् ॥ ७ ॥
उत्तरं पूर्वसन्देहवारकं परिकीर्तितम् ।
अविरुद्धं तु यत्तस्य प्रमाणं तच्च नान्यथा ।
एतद्विरुद्धं यत्सर्वं न तन्मानं कथञ्चन ॥ ८ ॥ " (शास्त्रार्थ प्रकरण)

"The Vedas (the Upnishads), the words of Krishn Himself (the Gita), the Brahm Sutra, and the Bhagwatam which is called the ecstatic statements ( समाधि भाषा ) of Ved Vyas, are the four main scriptures that reveal the Divine truth. Out of the four, the Bhagwatam is the final authority. (The description of the form of God is much more clear in the Gita as compared to the Upnishads, and the ascension of a *yogi* up to *brahm lok* is better described in the Brahm Sutra than the Gita, but the Bhagwatam clearly describes everything in detail.) So, whatever is in these four scriptures, should be accepted, not the others. If any clarification is needed, the statement of the Bhagwatam should be taken as final."

The following is called the *brahm sambandh mantra* in *pushti marg:*

"सहस्रपरिवत्सरमितकालजातकृष्णवियोगजनितताप-
क्लेशानन्दतिरोभावोऽहं भगवते कृष्णाय देहेन्द्रियप्राणान्तः-
करणानि तद्धर्माश्च दारागारपुत्राप्तवित्तेहापराणि आत्मना
सह समर्पयामि । दासोऽहं श्रीकृष्ण तवास्मि । दासोऽहं
श्रीकृष्ण तवास्मि । दासोऽहं श्रीकृष्ण तवास्मि ॥ "

*(brahm sambandh mantra)*

It is believed that, with the will of Krishn, Vallabhacharya introduced the *brahm sambandh mantra* for the *Vaishnavas* which is a guideline of dedication to be sincerely followed. *'Brahm sambandh'* means establishing and recognizing the relationship between you and your Divine beloved Krishn. It says,

"O beloved Krishn! I suffered to extremes in this world since uncountable lifetimes because I had forgotten You. So my heart is totally devoid of happiness. (Now I realize my mistake.) I totally submit all that belongs to me including my soul to You. Body, senses, life, heart and mind along with their attachments, family, house, children and all of my belongings are for Your service. O Krishn! I am your eternal servant. I belong to You. I am Yours, I am Yours, I am Yours."

Vallabhacharya called *'pushti marg'* to this form of dedication and devotion, and for other forms of practices like, *karm, gyan,* devotion and worship to the almighty forms of God, he called *'maryada marg.'*

(6) **Shree Chaitanya Mahaprabhu,** who was the descension of Radha Herself, came to show us the simple and easy form of true *bhakti* that easily reveals the Bliss of Golok and Divine Vrindaban. His philosophy is called *achintya bhedabhed vad* (the inconceivable mono-dualism), which was written by his disciple Jeev Goswami. Shree Mahaprabhuji appeared on the Holi day in West Bengal (Navadweep) in 1485 and ascended to Golok in 1533. Thus, Gracing the earth planet for 48 years, he established the magnificence of *bhakti* in such a way that gave a deep unforgettable impression in the heart of every *Vaishnav* devotee (*Vaishnav* is a general term for the worshipper of Bhagwan Vishnu or Ram or

Krishn). He said that Krishn is supreme *brahm* and the Bhagwatam is the explanation of the Brahm Sutra so no further explanation is needed. But, for the devotees, how to attain that Krishn Bliss, he explained all the aspects of devotion in eight verses called the 'Shikchashtak'.

His disciples Roop, Sanatan and Jeev Goswami, etc., wrote a number of books which are the guidelines for every devotee desiring God realization. Philosophy, *leela,* the devotional aspect, all of them are in these books. For reference: **Shat Sandarbh** *(achintya bhedabhed vad),* **Kram Sandarbh** ( क्रम संदर्भ ) of the Bhagwatam and **Gopal Champu** by Jeev Goswami, **Govind Bhashya** on the Brahm Sutra by Vidya Bhushan. **Chaitanya Charitamrit** and **Govind Leelamritam** by Krishndas Kaviraj. **Chaitanya Chandramrit, Sangeet Madhao** and **Vrindaban Mahimamritam** by Prabodhanand Saraswati. **Brihad Bhagwatamrit** by Sanatan Goswami, and **Bhakti Rasamrit Sindhu, Ujjwalneelmani, Hansdoot, Uddhao Sandesh, Lalit Madhao, Vidagdh Madhao,** etc. by Roop Goswami, and many more books.

## (ii) The common theme as accepted by all the four *Jagadgurus* and also by Jeev Goswami.

(1) Souls are unlimited, infinitesimal individuals of two kinds, free from *maya,* and under the bondage of *maya.* They are pure *chit.* The phrase *'tattvamasi'* expresses substantial oneness. It expresses duality of soul and *brahm.* The *chit* aspect of soul is substantially the same as of *chid brahm.* A God realized Saint experiences the same kind, class and amount of absolute Divine Bliss as his beloved God experiences in that particular Divine abode. For example: the Bliss of Vishnu and a Vishnu *bhakt* Saint is the same.

(2) *Maya* is a lifeless, mindless, and *trigunatmak* eternal entity that resides in God, and evolves with the help of God in the form of this universe. God is both, the cause and the effect in this creation, but He remains totally unaffected from the qualities of *maya* ( निमित्तोपादान कारण, अविकृत ).

(3) *Maya* and souls, both are subordinate existences. But souls have eternal intimate relationship with God, so they naturally desire to serve their beloved God.

(4) To be in the abode of your beloved God, to be near Him, and to be near Him and to serve Him in any way in His Divine abode, is the goal of devotion. This is liberation from *maya* and the experience of the Divine Bliss as said by the phrase *'raso vai sah.'*

(5) God is one ( अद्वितीय ). He has many powers and virtues that have their own characteristics but they exist in total oneness in a self-submissive manner in the supreme personality of God ( स्वगत भेदाभेद ). The main form of God is *sagun sakar* in which His *nirgun nirakar* form resides. He is gracious and kind. Singleminded *bhakti* with full dedication and humbleness is the means of experiencing His Grace, that opens the door of His Divine vision ( तस्मिन्दृष्टे: परावरे । मयि दृष्टेऽखिलात्मनि । ), eliminates the *mayic* bondage and reveals the Divine abode of your beloved God.

## (iii) Their differences in describing the states of *brahm* and the revelation of Bliss.

There are some philosophical differences in the *bhashyas* of the *Jagadgurus* that relate to determining the situation of soul and *maya* in relation to God. But the general devotional theme of *bhakti* still remains unaffected, which is the only most important thing for a devotee.

**Ramanujacharya** says that soul and *maya* are the affiliates of *brahm* ( चिदचित् विशिष्ट ब्रह्म ). They are the 'body' and *brahm* is the 'Soul' in both states, creation and absolute dissolution ( स्थूल तथा सूक्ष्मावस्था युक्त चिदचित् शरीर विशिष्ट ब्रह्म). In absolute dissolution, soul stays with a subtle veil of *maya* ( कारण शरीर एवं आनन्दमय कोष ). He also says that *chit* soul is not knowledgeable itself; soul *receives* the knowledge. So, knowledge is required to be given, and to be received ( ज्ञान सापेक्ष है ).

**Nimbarkacharya** says soul and *maya* are the powers ( शक्ति ) of God ( शक्तिमान् ). Soul is a fraction of God ( अंश ) so there is a duality, but God is the integral Divinity of the souls ( अंशी ) so there is also non-duality between soul and God ( दैताद्वैत ).

He says that *brahm* is the base ( शक्तिमान् ) of all the Divine powers ( शक्ति ) like *sandhini, ahladini,* etc. All the powers have their own Divine qualities, so they are different, yet they are all established in the same *brahm.* So *brahm* and the Divine powers, both are fully one, that's why it is called *dvaitadvait vad.*

**Madhvacharya** says that soul, *maya* and God are totally different. Vishnu *tattva* is totally independent ( स्वतंत्र तत्त्व ), and soul and *maya* are totally dependent ( अस्वतंत्र तत्त्व ). Ignorance is also as stable as the Divine knowledge, because without the Divine knowledge ( ज्ञान ), ignorance ( अज्ञान ) can never be broken. He stresses on five dualities: (1) God to soul, (2) God to *maya* and the *mayic* world, (3) soul to soul, (4) soul to *maya* and the *mayic* world, and (5) the duality of every aspect, part and fraction of this creation from one to another. He said soul is totally different than God, so it is a totally separate power ( द्वैत ). He strongly advocated the duality, so his philosophy is called *dvait vad.*

**Vallabhacharya said that *brahm* is the source of all the dharmas, and holds simultaneous contradictory situations. So brahm is 'sarva dharm samanvit' and 'viruddha dharmashrai'** ( सर्वधर्मसमन्वित एवं विरुद्धधर्माश्रिय ). He strongly stressed on the substantial purity and equality of soul with *brahm,* that's why his philosophy is called *shuddhadvait vad.*

**Jeev Goswami** further improved the theory of soul and *maya.* He said that all the unlimited numbers of souls collectively form one single substance which is called the *jeev shakti* of God Krishn. It is unlimited and consists of unlimited numbers of infinitesimal souls. He also said that along with *maya, kal* (the time) and *karm* (the unlimited *karmas* of unlimited souls) are also eternal which help the creation. So, (a) God, (b) soul, (c) *kal,* (d) *karm* and (e) *maya,* are all in this creation. Soul is neutral, and *maya* is the extroverted power of Krishn ( बहिरंगा शक्ति ).

He also defined the functions of *sandhini* and *ahladini shakti*. He said that the situation of total self-submissive unity ( अभेद ) and the qualitative differentiality (भेद) of the powers of Krishn, is subtle and distinct at the same time, and it is beyond human comprehension.

He said that *shakti* ( शक्ति, the power) cannot stay on its own without *shaktiman* ( शक्तिमान्, the basic substance or the base in which the power resides), and *shaktiman* cannot represent itself without *shakti*. **Nimbarkacharya** and **Vallabhacharya** also refer to this aspect of *shakti* and *shaktiman*. Jeev Goswami further expounds this philosophy and says that this situation is beyond words to explain and also beyond comprehension ( अचिन्त्य ), so his philosophy is called *achintya bhedabhed*.

Jeev Goswami also designates *mayic* souls ( मायाबद्ध ) as *vibhinnansh* ( विभिन्नांश, separate power), and other Divine powers as *swansh* ( स्वांश, personal powers). There is also another term used in this respect: *tatastha shakti* ( तटस्था, indifferent power), and *antaranga shakti* ( अन्तरंगा, internal or personal power).

It is said that God adopts the form of this world ( परिणाम ), still He remains unaffected with the qualities of *maya* ( अविकृत ). This is called *avikrit parinam vad* ( अविकृत परिणाम वाद ). Ramanujacharya, Vallabhacharya and Nimbarkacharya accept it as it is. But Jeev Goswami further says that God always stays the same ( अविकृत ) and in His own Divine glory. He does not transform Himself, only *maya* expands and evolves itself on the base of God. Shankaracharya's theory is called *vivart vad* ( विवर्त वाद ), which means only illusion.

**Nimbarkacharya** describes the four states of *brahm*: (a) अचिन्त्यानन्तस्वगतसौख्यसुधासिंधु । The full exposure of Divine love virtues in which He is engrossed (He means Radha Krishn). (b) जगदीश्वर । The state of almightiness, the creator God. (c) मुक्त-बद्ध जीव । All the souls, and (d) भगवन्मय जगत् । this world which is the transformation of *brahm*. **Ramanujacharya** tells it in this way:

पुरुषोत्तम, चित्, अचित् । (a) the personality of *brahm*, Maha Vishnu or Narain, (b) the souls and (c) the *maya*. **Madhvacharya** divides the total existence in two sections: स्वतंत्र and अस्वतंत्र ( जीव, जगत् ). (a) The independent Divinity (Maha Vishnu), and (b) the dependent existence (of soul and *mayic* world). It is also called *swatantraswatantra vad*. Soul is live ( चेतन ) and *maya* is lifeless ( अचेतन ). **Vallabhacharya** says that only Krishn is the supreme adorable form of God ( पूर्ण ब्रह्म ), and **Jeev Goswami** also says that Krishn is the supreme *brahm*.

### The revelation of Bliss.

**Ramanujacharya** revealed the Bliss of *dasya bhao* of Maha Vishnu and also added the devotion of Bhagwan Ram and Krishn in his religion. **Madhvacharya** revealed the Bliss of *dasya bhao* of Maha Vishnu but he also gave importance to the devotion of Ram and Krishn. **Nimbarkacharya** revealed the Bliss of Radha Krishn. **Vallabhacharya** introduced devotion to Krishn with mainly *sakhya* and *vatsalya bhao*, and **Chaitanya Mahaprabhuji** introduced mainly *madhurya bhao* of Krishn along with all other *bhao*.

## (iv) The reconciled truth.

If you keep in mind these basic facts that God is *viruddh dharmashrai*, *sarva dharm samanvit* and He is the subject of Divine experience, you will find that there is no real controversy. All of the different opinions of the *Jagadgurus* described above are the descriptions of the Divine truth from different angles as we have already explained in this chapter and the previous chapter.

Soul and *maya* are two amazing existences that subordinately reside in God. *Maya* is subordinate because it is lifeless, and souls are subordinate because they are under the bondage of *maya* and are unlimited in number so they need to be controlled. Soul (collectively) is a power ( शक्ति ), which is affiliated ( विशेषण ) to *chid brahm*, and it is the same as *chid brahm* in nature and quality ( अभेद ). But, *chit* is a single inseparable power of *sat-chit-anand brahm,* so there is total oneness between *chit shakti* and supreme *brahm,* whereas the souls are not in that category. They are individual, infinitesimal, and unlimited in number. Thus, there always remains the difference ( भेद, द्वैत ) between a soul and God. But it is the unlimited kindness of God ( पुष्टि, कृपा, अनुग्रह ) that He awards His own personal power to the dedicated singleminded devotee ( प्रपत्ति, शरणागति, भक्ति, सेवा, उपासना ), and makes him equally Blissful as Himself.

*Maya* is also a power ( शक्ति ) that is affiliated ( विशेषण ) to *chid brahm.* God has a nature of being the same in all the situations. Just like: algae grows on the water but the water of the pond remains the same. So, *maya* evolves and expands according to its own nature on the base of God, and God remains the same. He does not 'become' omnipresent, He is naturally omnipresent, all the time, whether it is *maha pralaya* or creation. But it appears that God has adopted the form of this creation because of the *mayic* evolution. That's why the phrase *avikrit parinam* is used. God is the omnipresent Soul of all the souls in all the situations, creation or no creation.

As regards the description of the goal of devotion, you should know that all the *Jagadgurus* had descended on the earth planet from certain Divine abodes. Thus they described the greatness of the Divine abode, the Divine relationship, and the class of *bhao* according to their own Divine status. It's all very natural. (The sequence of the Divine abodes, their Blissful superiority, and the form of God in that abode, has already been described earlier.)

---

समस्त भगवतशक्तियां प्रेमशक्ति के अनुगत हैं एवं श्रीकृष्ण प्रेमस्वरूप हैं अतः श्रीकृष्ण पूर्णतम ब्रह्म हैं । महाभाव उस प्रेम की वह परिपूर्णतमावस्था है जहाँ कृष्णतत्त्व अपने ही स्वरसानन्द में लीन हो जाता है, फिर भी महाभावस्वरूपिणी राधा अपनी मुस्कान से वृन्दाबन की लीलाओं को प्रकाशित करती रहती हैं । अतः राधा परिपूर्णतम ब्रह्म हैं ।

## (v) Oneness of Radha and Krishn and the *bhedabhed* situation. Radha is the absolute supreme *brahm* and *Mahabhao*.

God has unimaginable varieties of Bliss, love, beauty and magnificence. We will give you some more facts of the Divine world to form and improve your devotional faith in Radha Krishn.

**All the Divine powers and all the almighty forms of God are established in *ahladini shakti* and *ahladini shakti* is established in *prema shakti* which is Krishn Himself. So Krishn is the supreme form of *brahm*. *Mahabhao* is such an infinite absoluteness of the culminating sweetness of *prema shakti*, where Krishn *tattva* drowns in the ocean of its own lusciousness. Still Radha, the *Mahabhao*, keeps on glorifying the leelas of Vrindaban with Her loving smile. So, Radha is the absolute supreme form of *brahm*.**

This state of *bhedabhed* of Radha Krishn is absolutely beyond comprehension, beyond question and beyond intellect. Beyond intellect situations of the Divine world may only be understood to some extent at a very high state of *divine-love-consciousness*, and that too with the Grace of a *rasik* Saint.

Radha Krishn have two kinds of powers, **(1) dependent** ( आश्रित) and **(2) personal** ( स्वरूप ). Dependent powers are two, soul and *maya*, and personal powers are many in *sat-chit-anand* form.

Among **personal powers**, (a) one is the **prime** power ( प्रमुख ) which is *prema shakti* (the Divine love power), and (b) the others are **self-submissive** ( अनुगत ) powers which include all the Divine powers that are related to Vaikunth, Saket and Dwarika abodes.

Radha and Krishn Both are forms of 'Divine love' power and also hold the 'Divine love' power within. Their pure Divine love *leelas* are seen in Golok and Vrindaban only.

Thus there are three states of *bhedabhed*, (a) the *bhedabhed* of soul and God, (b) the *bhedabhed* of *swaroop shakti* and Krishn, and (c) the *bhedabhed* of Radha Krishn. The *bhedabhed* status of soul and God is somewhat easy to understand because there is a distinct difference, but the *bhedabhed* of the Divine powers *(swaroop shakti)* and Krishn is very very difficult to intellectually conceive; and the *bhedabhed* of Radha Krishn and Their *leelas* may not even be assumable at a very high state of devotion *(bhakti)*. But by then, you don't intellectually desire to know anything, you remain engrossed in Divine love. That's why Jeev Goswami called it *achintya-bhedabhed*.

The *leela* Bliss of Radha Krishn is of four kinds: *nibhrit nikunj ras, nikunj ras* of Vrindaban, *nikunj ras* of Golok, and *braj ras*. *Nikunj ras* is again of three kinds, Radha prominence, Krishn prominence, and Both.

## (vi) The secret of *shakti shaktiman* (*brahm* and its powers) and the oneness of Radha Krishn.

One thing more, you must know that *shakti* and *shaktiman* can never be separate. They only appear in two forms, just like *shaktiman* prominence Vishnu and *shakti* prominence Lakchmi, but Both are in Both and Both remain in Both. This situation is only up to *prema shakti*, the *Prime* Divine power that assimilates all other Divine powers. Beyond that, the situation is different, and it is the dimension of Golok and Vrindaban where *shakti* and *shaktiman* become one (like the sweetness of a candy).

"रसो यः परमानन्द एक एव द्विधा सदा ।
श्रीराधाकृष्णरूपाभ्यां तस्यै तस्मै नमो नमः ॥" (पद्म. पु.)
"एकं ज्योतिर्द्विधाभिन्नं राधामाधवरूपकम् ॥" (ब्रह्माण्ड पु.)

The absolute supreme *brahm* Radha Herself is both, *shakti* and *shaktiman*. She is the absolute absolute Bliss. The Padm Puran and Brahmand Puran say that this Bliss ( रसः ) is Radha and Krishn, one in two forms. So, They are absolutely one ( अभिन्न ). "येयं राधा यश्च कृष्णः ।" The Upnishad says that whatever is Radha, same is Krishn and whatever is Krishn, same is Radha.

The Upnishad further says, "क्रीडनार्थं." It means, to express, to experience and to give that Bliss, Radha Herself became Krishn, or you can say that **Radha eternally has two forms, one as Radha and the other as Krishn, where Both are** *shakti* **and Both are** *shaktiman.* **That's how Both are exactly one and the same.**

Without the female and male form the intimate love cannot be revealed or experienced; so both forms are necessary. Thus, Radha and Krishn reveal, experience and give all kinds of *dasya, sakhya, vatsalya* and *madhurya* love in Golok. In Vrindaban, They reveal the supreme *madhurya* love, where Radha holds the main prominence. This is all *leela ras* which is desired by Lakchmi and Shiv.

The male and female form of Divinity is in every abode. But, in the abodes of almighty forms of God, the female form represents *shakti* and the male form represents the *shaktiman* form of *brahm,* although Both are in Both.

Thus, taking the theme and the philosophy of more than four hundred scriptures, the total philosophy of soul, *maya*, creation, God (*brahm*), His eternal omnipresent personality, His almighty forms, Divine love forms and Their abodes, and also the form of supreme *brahm* (Krishn) and absolute supreme *brahm* (Radha), including the philosophies of all the *Jagadgurus* with reconciliations, are described.

The producer and knower of all the scriptures, Ved Vyas, says, " सा विद्या तन्मतिर्यया । The outcome and the immediate effect of learning and understanding is to start loving (Radha) Krishn immediately." If it hasn't happened, try it again, and again, and again, until you begin to desire God in your life, because it is the desired aim of all the scriptures. **Otherwise all the wisdom is in vain, and all the efforts are futile.**

Uddhao, who was the foremost scholar, *Gyani* and *Yogi* during the time of Krishn, when he went to Braj and learned that the Divine euphoric joy he was experiencing was almost nothing as compared to the *nikunj ras* (Divine love) that Radha could give, he felt overwhelmed. He desired ( चरणरेणुजुषामहम् ) to adore the footdust of those *Gopis* whose every breath was for the service of Radha Rani and who were so loving to Her. **He could not find words to praise the greatness of Radha, so he turned towards the *Gopis* and said,**

"वन्दे नन्दव्रजस्त्रीणां पादरेणुमभीक्ष्णशः । 
यासां हरिकथोद्गीतं पुनाति भुवनत्रयम् ॥ " (भा.10.47.63)

"I adore and worship to the footdust of those *Gopis* of Braj whose songs of selfless love for Krishn sanctifies the whole world."

# 5.
## Characteristics of
## *Karm, Gyan, Yog,* and *Bhakti.*

### (1) *Karm.*

#### Good *karmas.*

Good *karmas* (actions) are of two kinds: (a) doing good actions in general, like doing good to others, charity, social service, religious worship and religious fasting, etc., and (b) observing Vedic rituals like, ***sandhya, agnihotra, yagya,*** etc. They are daily or occasional, small or large ceremonies done in a strictly prescribed manner with the utterance of Vedic verses. There are also many kinds of Vedic fire ceremonies, from very small to very extensive. They are all Vedic rituals.

**Both kinds of *karmas* are finished after they fructify** and appear as worldly luxuries and comfort in the next lifetime. The period, kind, and class of such a comfort is determined according to the kind, class, sincerity, and the amount of *karmas* done in the past life. One should not think that sincerely helping the poor and serving mankind will reveal God's abode. Only pure selfless *bhakti* reveals God's abode. Good deeds could only reveal the celestial abodes where the doer of good deeds enjoys *mayic* luxury for a limited period of time, and then comes back on this earth planet.

" आब्रह्मभुवनाल्लोका: पुनरावर्तिनोऽर्जुन ।
मामुपेत्य तु कौन्तेय पुनर्जन्म न विद्यते ॥ " (गी. 8/16)

" ते तं भुक्त्वा स्वर्गलोकं विशालं क्षीणे पुण्ये मर्त्यलोकं विशन्ति ।
एवं त्रयीधर्ममनुप्रपन्ना गतागतं कामकामा लभन्ते ॥ " (गी. 9/21)

" यं यं वापि स्मरन्भावं त्यजत्यन्ते कलेवरम् ।
तं तमेवैति कौन्तेय सदा तद्भावभावित: ॥ " (गी. 8/6)

" अनेकचित्तविभ्रान्ता मोहजालसमावृता: ।
प्रसक्ता: कामभोगेषु पतन्ति नरकेऽशुचौ ॥ " (गी. 16/16)

Krishn says in the Gita, "The one who has already realized
God in this lifetime goes to God's abode after death, others are
born according to their state of consciousness before death, (good,
bad, selfish, devilish or devotional) into the similar situations in
the world, either as a human being or a being of lower species. The
confused ideologists who neglect pure devotion to God, enter into
darkness because of their transgressions and material attachments."

## Limitations of Vedic rituals.

There are mainly four kinds of Vedic rituals: (1) *Nitya karm.* It
relates to the daily morning and evening prayer type of ritual. (2)
*Naimittic karm.* It is done occasionally. It is like observing a Vedic
ceremony before entering a new house (*grah pravesh*) or giving name
to a baby child (*nam karn*), etc. (3) *Prayaschittya karm.* It is the
observance of penance with Vedic worship for the redemption of
any sinful deed already committed. (4) *Kamya karm.* It is conducted
by reciting Vedic *mantras* in a prescribed manner and performing a
Vedic fire ceremony, called *yagya,* by placing on the ground one or
more (up to a hundred thousand) fire chambers, for throwing the
offering to the gods into it, and with a desire to fulfill a personal
wish. *Kamya* means any kind of *mayic* desire.

The first three, in general, are religious Vedic formalities, and
come in the category of good deeds. The fourth one is extensively
detailed in the ritual part of the Vedas and the Poorv Mimansa.

There are many kinds of *kamya karm,* and they all involve fire ceremony called *yagya* (the word *yagya* is often misspelled as *yagna* by many writers). There are very strict rules for its observance.

स्वरतो वर्णतो वा मिथ्या प्रयुक्तो यजमानं हि नस्ति ॥
षडभि: सम्पद्यते धर्म: ॥

It means that if all of the ritualistic requirements are not fulfilled without any compromise, the consequence of the *yagya* may be disastrous; if it is fulfilled, only then it may have positive results. In this age, it is extremely difficult to fulfill all the requirements as prescribed in the Vedas.

For instance, the first requirement is that the *brahman* priest, who is conducting the *yagya,* must be religious minded, pious, celibate and must recite each and every accent of every alphabet of the *mantra* exactly according to the rules of the Vedic grammar. This is *very* difficult to find. Even in Varanasi, which is the main center of literal scriptural wisdom and a prime place for Sanskrit education in India, there would be only some scholars who could pronounce Vedic *mantras* in an exacting manner.

The produce and the materials used in *yagya* must also be pure and pious, and must be bought from the money which is earned truthfully and through honest means. Similarly, there are many more ritualistic requirements still to be fulfilled.

Considering these barriers, the Ramayanam says, " कलि नहिं योग न यज्ञ न ज्ञाना । In this age of *kaliyug, yagya, gyan* and *yog* are not possible, so they are restricted and *bhakti* is advised." But people are people, they don't go after the truth, they go after the showiness, and they do whatever they like to do without considering the consequence.

## Limitations of *karmas.*

Good *karmas,* done with any kind of material motivation, are finished after they fructify as good luck or good destiny in the next lifetime.

There is also a provision of doing good deeds selflessly without any worldly motivation, which is for heart purification. The practice of *varnashram dharm* also comes in this category ( न्यासस्य गतयोऽमलाः । भा. ).

Ved Vyas says,

"तावत्कर्माणि कुर्वीत न निर्विद्येत यावता ।
मत्कथाश्रवणादौ वा श्रद्धा यावन्न जायते ॥ " ( भा. 11/20/9 )

"Do good *karmas* until pure renunciation or a true desire to listen to the *leelas* of Krishn arises in the heart." When a deep desire to find God appears in the heart, the motivation of the mind is changed and the person desires to spend most of his time in devotion to God. His previous commitments of good deeds etc. are automatically redeemed and their practices are no longer required to be done, because he is devoting all of his time in the remembrance and devotion *(bhakti)* to his beloved God. The social and celestial commitments of a soul mentioned in certain scriptures ( ऋणानि त्रीण्यपाकृत्य ) are only for such a person who is not doing selfless devotion to God. The Bhagwatam says ( देवर्षिभूताप्तनृणां... भा. 11/15/41 ) that such words of the Manu Smriti etc. do not apply for a selfless Krishn devotee. It is just like that boy who has left the school and has taken admission into the university.

## (2) *Gyan.*

### *Gyan* and *agyan.*

Although the word *gyan* literally means understanding of the Divine truth of soul and God relationship, which is also a basic requirement of *bhakti*, but the term *'gyan'* and *'gyan marg'* is generally used for impersonal God where a person believes that his soul and God *(brahm)* are same. It is also called the *advait gyan*.

### How is it obtained?

*Sat-asat vivek* (truth and non-truth discrimination) is called *gyan*. Truth is God, and non-truth is *maya*, the world. "You belong to God only, your soul is Divine *brahm,* you don't belong to *maya,* so, terminate all the attachments of the world immediately." This kind of firm 'understanding' is called *gyan* (ज्ञान ), and the opposite to it is called *agyan* (अज्ञान, ignorance). It is practiced in two ways: (a) the expansion of your own soul is the omnipresent absolute *brahm,* or (b) the absolute *brahm* is your own soul. Soul is Divine, but the human mind is an eternal product of *maya* so it naturally likes material luxuries and happiness, and, accordingly, it forms its firm opinion that this material world is the field of happiness. **This ignorance of the human mind is also eternal which is extremely hard to break because of its substantial oneness with the *mayic* world around it.**

To reverse this ignorant understanding, a person has to do a lot of thinking, determining, deciding, and extensive practice to establish *gyan* in his mind. Such an intellectual practice is called *swadhyay* ( स्वाध्याय ). Certain Upnishads like Mandookya, Yog-shikha, Sanyas, Jabal Darshan etc. are the main source of such knowledge. Written in a traditional philosophical terminology and logic, there are also many other books on this topic (like Vivek Chudamani, Panchadashi, Yog Vashishth etc.) whose main theme is the same as explained above.

The result of *swadhyay* is renunciation and the existence of only one desire in the mind, the liberation. If it is not happening, there is something wrong. There are two sides of the same mind, intellectual and emotional. Intellectual part of the mind governs the emotional part. Normally, such practitioners are emotionally attached in the world in some way, but if they are open-minded, they may accept their mistakes, and such an understanding may result into deeper renunciation. **But if the ignorance of self-accepted knowledgeability has gone deeper into the intellect, the intellect will resist to accept its own ignorance.**

For such people the Muktikopnishad relates a phrase, " शास्त्रवासनयापि च ," which means that the literal study of *advait* philosophy and the scriptures, with a desire to accumulate more intellectual information, is a kind of intellectual material attachment. It must be avoided. **The effect of *gyan* is *vairagya* which means detachment from all kinds of worldly attractions and attachments, and the effect of *vairagya* is the dawn of a deep desire in the humble heart to meet God. If this is not happening, it is only an intellectual indulgence, and it is a still deeper form of ignorance *(agyan)*.**

In this state of confused consciousness, which is mostly found in the followers of impersonal God, the person begins to believe that he has received *gyan* although he is in ignorance. This is called *pandit maninah* (पंडितमानिनः) in Sanskrit. This situation creates similar *sanskars* in the mind, which deepens the ignorance of the intellect even further in a self-multiplying manner. For that state of mind, it is said, " ज्ञानलव दुर्विदग्धं तं ब्रह्मापि न रंजयति ." It means that even the creator god, Brahma, will fail to give him some devotional understanding because the person is not willing to accept his ignorance out of his stubborn vanity. This is a very pitiable and hopeless situation of ignorance.

## Gyan marg.

The *advait gyan* is of two kinds, literal and practical ( परोक्ष तथा अपरोक्ष ). We have a definite system of how to follow this path.

" श्रवणं तु गुरोः पूर्वकं मननं तदनंतरम् ।
निदिध्यासनमेवेदं पूर्णबोधस्य कारणम् ॥ " (शुकरहस्योपनिषद्)

"This 'knowledge' (*gyan*, ज्ञान) has to be properly received (*shravan* श्रवण) from a *gyani* Saint (not just buying a book on *vedant*, reading it or learning it from a teacher who knows Sanskrit, and starting to believe himself a *gyani*). Then conceiving that 'knowledge' in the mind by continuous remembrance of it (*manan* मनन ). Then practicing it (according to the Yog Darshan) until the mind synonymously adopts the 'form' of that knowledge ( निदिध्यासन ). Now it is practical knowledge (बोध)." Practice of holding the *gyan* in the mind is called *nididhyasan*.

I will give you one example of *shravan* from Mandookyopnishad and you yourself will know how difficult *gyan marg* is. It says,

" अयमात्मा ब्रह्म ॥ 2 ॥ नान्तःप्रज्ञं न बहिष्प्रज्ञं नोभयतःप्रज्ञ न प्रज्ञानघनं न प्रज्ञं नाप्रज्ञम् । अव्यवहार्यमग्राह्यमलक्षणमचिन्त्यं स आत्मा स विज्ञेयः ॥ 7 ॥ "

"You have to understand, conceive, and practically experience the *atm tattva* which is the real 'you' and which is *brahm*, and which is neither knowledge ( प्रज्ञम् ) nor anti-knowledge, neither knowledge inside, nor knowledge outside, nor both, and it is not even the form of knowledge. (It is such an existence which is not even known, understood or identified by its own self.) It is beyond every known and unknown examples of existences in the world ( अलक्षण ), so it is impossible to imagine it ( अचिन्त्य ); and it is beyond any kind of communication, association, revelation or manifestation ( अव्यवहार्य ), so it is impossible to 'conceive' it in the mind, even in its purest state ( अग्राह्य )."

If you seriously start imagining *brahm* on these guidelines, you may develop an imaginary self-conceited vanity of knowingness, because *brahm* is "unimaginable"; and if you really force yourself to start practicing such an unimaginable theory, you may soon need a psychiatrist to treat you for confused (self) identity, because the *advait brahm* is "inconceivable."

For these reasons, Shankaracharya has described fifteen steps of *nididhyasan* in the Aparokchanubhuti. The first twelve are for disciplining oneself into pure *sattvic* living, controlling the emotions of the mind, observing the futility and illusiveness of worldly happiness, renouncing all the attachments and attractions of the world, and absorbing oneself into pure Divine thoughts. The last three (*dharna*, *dhyan* and *samadhi*) are for introverting the mind into a complete thoughtless pious state called *nirvikalp samadhi*. The purest state of such a *samadhi* is the final stage of *gyan*, the practical understanding of the pure 'self.' This stage has many names, *gyan, vigyan, atm-gyan, bodh*, etc.

The stage of *atm-gyan* is, in fact, not the true knowledge of the soul, because the Divine soul is beyond intellect. What happens is, that the mind, when it is fully purified, receives the reflection of the soul which is a very pleasant euphoric feeling of an unknown limit that surpasses the material pleasurableness. This experience of the intellect is called *atm-gyan*. But the pure mind of the *gyani* still holds all the seeds of material attachments which may sprout anytime with the material association and the force of negative *sanskars* of his past lives. Thus, *gyan marg* is not a complete path of liberation.

## The limitations of *gyan marg*.

Pure **literal** *gyan* removes the basic ignorance and inclines the person into the practice of *gyan marg*. The **practical** *gyan* (पूर्णबोध) also introduces the pure *sattvic* state of the self (mind) and then its function is finished, just like liquid soap cleans the dirt of the material and finishes itself. **So, practical *gyan* practically removes the ignorant attachments of the world and leaves the person in a pure state of the mind. It does not unite the soul with God** ( कैवल्यं सात्विकं प्रोक्तम् ।).

Thus, *karm* (good deed) could provide material or celestial happiness or renunciation of a certain limit, and *gyan* could provide the highest class of renunciation and the purity of the mind only. The basic mind always has all of its *mayic* defilements and weaknesses. So, an *atm-gyani* may again fall in the mire of *mayic* attractions, because his mind still contains all the unlimited ( संचित ) *karmas* of his unlimited past lives. He is not yet liberated.

# (3) *Yog.*

## *Yog* and Yog Darshan.

The Yog Darshan, written by sage Patanjali, is the main authentic scripture on the philosophy and the practical teachings for obtaining a perfect thoughtless state of the *sattvic* mind called *nirvikalp samadhi*. This kind of practice is called *yog* and its practitioner is called a *yogi*. There are some more books on *yog* but they are like the affiliates of the Yog Darshan. There are some Upnishads like the Yog Shikhopnishad but they all follow similar guidelines of practice and understanding as it is in the Yog Darshan.

*Yog*, in fact, is the practical side of *gyan*. That's why the Upnishad says,

" योगहीनं कथं ज्ञानं मोक्षदं भवतीह भो: ।
योगोऽपि ज्ञानहीनस्तु न क्षमो मोक्षकर्मणि
तस्माज्ज्ञानं च योगं च मुमुक्षुर्दृढमभ्यसेत् ॥ " (यो.शि. 1/13)

It means that the person desiring *kaivalya mokch* (the kind of liberation that joins a soul with the impersonal aspect of God) must follow both, the *gyan* and the *yog*. Without *yog, gyan* cannot be fully established in the heart, and without *gyan, yogic* attainments may develop a deep desire of ruling and enjoying the world which is pure *agyan*. Thus both are the compensating factors to each other, just like the two wings of a bird that flies and dives into the ocean of *kaivalya mokch* (in short it is called *mokch*). In this verse the word *gyan* means the intellectual correct understanding of the *advait vedant*.

**The above verse does not prescribe *mokch* through *gyan* and *yog*, it only implies.** Understand it by an example: suppose a person desires to get a Master's degree (like a *gyani* desires for *mokch*) and has enrolled himself in the college, but he never properly attended the classes and never properly studied. This is just *gyan* (knowledge) without practice. The second person is not keen at all to attend the classes of the college but, to feed his intellectual desire of learning, he studied the full course at home (like a *yogi* who desires to experience *yogic* miracles and transcendences). This is practical *yog*. None of them singly are able to receive the degree. A person has to have both, desire to get the degree and to attend the college to complete the study, only then he can appear in the examination.

One more thing, if for any reason, he fails to appear or fails to do it right at the last moment, he won't get the degree because a degree is not just a piece of paper to be bought, it is a certified 'gift' from the college administration (this is the Grace of God which will be explained ahead). But it is implied that when a person has a desire to pass the examination (the *gyan*), and he has properly studied the course (the *yog)*, he may pass. Why can't he certainly pass the examination? The Yog Darshan itself is the answer.

The final goal of the Yog Darshan is only to receive a state of the mind where, in its very pure state, it assimilates its natural understanding of the 'truth' in the state of *nirvikalp samadhi* and remains there. It is called *swaroop pratishtha* or *swaroop nishtha* ( स्वरूप प्रतिष्ठा, स्वरूप निष्ठा ). Truth means the Divineness of the soul. The *yogi,* while practicing *nirvikalp samadhi,* after crossing the illusive and distracting effects of *mayic gunas, sattva, raj* and *tam* (which appear as emotions, attachments, and the attractions of the world) has to cross the restrictions of the five elements, and then he has to merge his conscious 'self,' the *ahankar* ( अहंकार ), into the totally pure state of *sattva gun.* This is called the state of *'niranjan'* ( निरंजन ) or the *'triputi vilaya'* ( त्रिपुटी विलय ). In this stage, the knower (pure mind), the knowledge (of the Divineness of the soul), and the blissful experience (of the closeness of the soul with the mind), all the three are merged into an unconscious like pure state of *mayic sattva.*

This is *'kaivalya'* of the Yog Darshan which is the end of the *yogic* practices and the final limit of *yogic* attainments as said in its very last *sutra,*

" पुरुषार्थशून्यानां गणानां प्रतिप्रसवः कैवल्यं
स्वरूपप्रतिष्ठा वा चितिशक्तिरिति ॥ " (4/34)

It means that many lifetimes of regular, continuous, sincere, and faithful practice of *gyan* and *yog,* without falling and being attached in the world, may elevate a *yogi* up to the final stage of *yog* called *kaivalya.*

Now we know that the *yogi* does not cross the ocean of *maya,* he only stays in pure *sattva* for which the Bhagwatam says, "कैवल्यं सात्त्विकं प्रोक्तम् ।, the *kaivalya* state of a *yogi* is only *sattvic.*"

The first set of blockages (called *avaran*), which a *yogi* has to cross during the practice of *nirvikalp samadhi*, are the five subtle elements of earth, water, fire, air and space.

(**The states of *nirvikalp samadhi.***) The first *nirvikalp samadhi* happens when the *yogi* crosses the subtle earth element of *maya.* Just like before entering deep sleep you pass through a dream or a dreamy state. Similarly, before entering into *nirvikalp samadhi* (commonly called *samadhi*), the *yogi* passes through a conscious visual state of the subconscious mind, called *dhyan,* or *sabeej samadhi* ( ध्यान, सबीज समाधि ) in *yogic* terms.

*Samadhi* (also called *nirbeej samadhi*) is a no-thought state ( शून्यमिव समाधिः ॥ 3/3 ) like deep sleep. But the state of *dhyan* or *sabeej samadhi* is the main state of *sattvic* experiences that qualify the quality and state of the *samadhi.* Imagine a *pond,* in the desert, in a grassy land, in a grassy land with some wild flowers, in an ordinary garden, or in a beautiful garden. Pond is of the same kind, but its value and desirability is assessed according to its surroundings. Thus, the act of diving in the pond (*samadhi*) is the same, but the joy of walking to the pond (*dhyan*) is different according to its surroundings.

Similarly, there are many kinds and classes of pre-*samadhi* experiences that determine the particular state of the *yogic samadhi.* A *yogi* devotee has to practice *samadhi* strictly under the direct guidance of a *yogi* Saint, who knows the state of his disciple's *samadhi* and, accordingly, he gives further instructions what to do.

The Yog Darshan, in general, explains the kind of *siddhis* (amazing *yogic*-psychic-powers) which a *yogi* receives during the practice of *samadhi.* But it does not specify that, at what stage what kind of *siddhi* is received. At one place in its Vibhuti Pad it says,

" स्थूलस्वरूपसूक्ष्मान्वयार्थवत्त्वसंयमाद् भूतजयः ॥ 44 ॥ The *yogi* has to engross his mind during the *dhyan* state into the (a) perceptible form ( स्थूल स्वरूप ), (b) perceptible quality ( गुण स्वरूप ), (c) subtle form ( सूक्ष्म स्वरूप ), (d) consolidated form ( पंचीकरण स्वरूप, अर्थवत्त्व ) of all the subtle elements (earth, water, fire, air and space) of *maya,* and (e) the independent form ( स्वतंत्र स्वरूप, अन्वय ). Then he gains control over them."

These are the practical and subtle states of *samadhi* that need not to be intellectually understood. That's why sage Patanjali did not describe it in detail. However, it can be said that there are six main states of *samadhi*, out of which five are gradually received when the *yogi* crosses the layers of the five subtle elements of *maya*.

After that, the *yogi* has to cross the *mayic* layer of *ahankar* (the ego, or the conscious 'self'), which is the toughest one. It is also called the *anandmaya kosh.* This is the final limit of *yogic* attainment and this is the sixth and the purest state of *nirvikalp samadhi.* (Certain scriptures on *advait* philosophy tell about the seven stages of '*gyan*,' सप्त ज्ञान भूमिका . The first one of these is the state of total renunciation and the perfection of the first six aspects of the eightfold *yog.* The other six stages of *gyan* somewhat correspond to the six states of *nirvikalp samadhi.* The last one of them is called the *turiya* stage, तुरीयावस्था.)

There are still two more *avaran* ( आवरण ), *mahat-tattva* ( महत्तत्त्व) and the original *prakriti-tattva* ( प्रकृति तत्त्व अथवा मूल प्रकृति ) to cross, which is only possible with the Grace of God. (*Mahat-tattva* is the very first aspect of the evolution of *maya* before this universe came into being.) In this way, there are eight layers (*avaran*) of *maya* to cross. They are the subtle forms of the existence of *mayic* (1) earth, (2) water, (3) fire, (4) air, (5) space; (6) the subtle ego (*ahankar*), (7) *mahat-tattva*, and (8) *prakriti tattva* (the original cosmic power or the original *maya* itself).

In short, we can say that the function of *gyan* is only to remove *agyan* and the limit of *yog* is to obtain *nirvikalp samadhi* (thoughtless transcendence) of the highest kind of *sattva gun.* Both leave their practitioner on the way, they don't take him to God. Moreover, their practice is extremely difficult for an ordinary person. See for yourself through its verses *(the sutras).*

## Practical difficulties of *gyan* and *yog.*

**(1) Severity of the practice.** "अथ योगानुशासनम्।" (1/1). This is the very first *sutra* of the Yog Darshan telling the strictness of the *yogic* rules to be followed. It says that the discipline of *yog* practice is thus commanded, " योगश्चित्तवृत्तिनिरोधः । " (1/2). *Yog* means to completely quieten the fickleness of the mind. "दृष्टानुश्रविकविषयवितृष्णस्य वशीकारसंज्ञा वैराग्यम् ॥" (1/15). Totally renouncing the desires and the attachments of all the perceived and heard about things of the mundane, psychic, and celestial world is called *vairagya* (the class of renunciation which is required in *yog*). " यमनियमासनप्राणायाम- प्रत्याहारधारणाध्यानसमाधयोऽष्टावङ्गानि ॥ " (2/29). There are eight main steps of *yog* practice with many subdivisions.

The very first step, *yam*, is described as, " अहिंसासत्यास्तेय- ब्रह्मचर्यापरिग्रहा यमाः ॥ " (2/30). The person desiring to follow the path of *yog* must have *vairagya* (as explained above) and must observe nonviolence, physically and mentally. He should not get angry and he should avoid the situations that cause anger. He should not steal or think of stealing anything in any style. Not even stealthily looking to a pretty girl because he has to observe all the rules of physical and mental celibacy. He should be truthful to his practice and to his Master and must not collect, possess or accumulate worldly assets, property or things in excess of his bare requirements to maintain his body.

These are the first basic requirements. They are like the admission fee to enroll oneself into the college of *yog.* Then there are six more steps to reach up to *dhyan* ( ध्यान ), the pure *sattvic* form of meditation as described by Patanjali.

To reach the last one, the *samadhi* ( शुद्ध निर्विकल्प समाधि ), it takes a number of lifetimes of continuous practice without falling or fooling around in worldly entertainments because there are six major layers of *mayic* blockages to cross (explained earlier). The Yog Sutra says that many lifetimes of faithful and continuous practice ( स तु दीर्घकालनैरन्तर्यसत्कारा-सेवितो दृढभूमिः ॥ 1/14 ) reveals the very pure form of *samadhi* which is recognized by the attainment of the eight supreme *yogic* powers ( ततोऽणिमादिप्रादुर्भावः ॥ 3/45).

Further, the *sutra* says, " स्थान्युपनिमन्त्रणे सङ्गस्मयाकरणं पुनरनिष्टप्रसङ्गात् ॥ (3/51). Even at the last and top most state of *samadhi,* if the *yogi* rejoices and involves himself in the enjoyment of celestial luxuries on the invitation of a celestial god, the *yogi* may fall back into the world and lose his *yogic* height, because (तासामनादित्वं चाशिषो नित्यत्वात् ॥ 4/10) the desire to enjoy the world stays very deep in the heart and it is eternal." The desire to receive self-appreciation is still deeper which becomes the main cause of a *yogi's* downfall.

The Yogshikhopnishad also describes the extreme difficulties and hardships of *yog.* It says,

" ज्ञानं तु जन्मनैकेन योगादेव प्रजायते ॥
पश्चाज्जन्मान्तरशतैर्योगादेव विमुच्यते ॥ " (यो.शि. 1/55)

**"It takes many lifetimes of continuous practice of *yogic* disciplines to establish *gyan* (the stable understanding of the illusiveness of *mayic* happiness and the Divineness of the true self) in the mind. Further, it takes hundreds of lifetimes of continuous practice of *samadhi* to enable a *yogi* to receive liberation." You can imagine the unimaginable rigidness of the unbroken renunciation and practice of *samadhi* for life after life without being attracted in any of the *mayic* fascinations. This is *yog.* If you still wish to practice, it is your option.**

**(2) Unimaginability.** Followers of the path of *gyan* and *yog* are the believers of the impersonal form of God. We have a personality, so we can only think of a personal relationship, not impersonal. We can never even assume anything of a total formless existence, because all of our imaginations are based on five kinds of perceptions which have some kind of form. For instance: even formless things like space, light, darkness or a radiant energy like gamma rays also have some kind of subtle form, and *nirakar brahm* is not like that. So whatever we will imagine, will not be *brahm.*

Thus we can't even create a true *dharna,* which is an intellectual conception of *nirakar brahm* before starting the impersonal meditation. *Dharna* means intellectually trying to conceive the unity of your soul (which is also *nirakar* and beyond the field of the mind) with the omnipresent *brahm.* It is almost impossible to start creating *(brahm) dharna* if you have even a bit of worldly attachment in your heart.

**(3) The adversity of the five *kosh.*** The *karmas* of a person, his ignorance, and his attachment in the world ( कर्म, अज्ञान, आसक्ति ) are all eternal, but they are not for eternity. They can be eliminated. The ignorance and the attachment has to be gradually eliminated by the *yogi* himself through *gyan* and *yog,* and, to ensure *mokch,* the uncountable *karmas* of uncountable past lifetimes are removed by the Grace of God.

In the *advait* path, *rasaswadan* ( रसास्वादन ) is totally prohibited. *Rasaswadan* means to relish or to enjoy. There is no joy in the illusive *mayic* appearance, so there is nothing to enjoy, and there is no bliss anywhere in the manifestations of the three *gunas* (*sattva, raj, tam*) of *maya* so there is nothing to relish.

Thus, a *yogi* or *gyani* has to eliminate not only the desire of enjoyment or liking of something in the world, but also the feeling of any kind of enjoyment which he already receives through his senses. He has to do it by diverting his mind towards soul-*brahm* unity. Not only that, he also has to avoid the enjoyments of the deep and exciting *sattvic* euphoria of *anandmaya kosh* that emerges as a pure *sattvic* experience during the practice of *samadhi* and at the highest level of heart purification. It happens prior to the *niranjan* state of *yogic* attainment. These are very extensive philosophies of the practical aspects of *gyan* and *yog* which we have described in a mini-nutshell.

*Annmaya, pranmaya, manomaya, vigyanmaya,* and *anandmaya* are the five *kosh*. *Kosh* means sheath. It refers to obstructions or the layers of *mayic* manifestations on the soul. The first two are **gross physical** and **subtle physical** layers and are related to the conscious state and the dream state of the mind. The last three are the deeper states of the mind: (a) *man,* (b) *buddhi* and (c) *ahankar ( ahankar* **and** *man, ahankar* **and** *buddhi* and just *ahankar).* The first one (of the last three) is related to the deep desire for sense gratification. These desires, in a subtle form, go deeper up to the unconscious layer of the mind. The second one is related to the deep desire for intellectual gratification (like self praise, etc.). It goes still deeper up to fully unconscious layer of the mind. Up till now the *yogi* has crossed the obstacles of four *kosh* which corresponds to the five subtle layers of five elements. The last one, the *anandmaya kosh,* is *ahankar,* the pure *sattvic* 'ego' or 'self' which is very close to the soul. When a *yogi* reaches this stage of *yogic* evolution, a blissful outburst of *sattvic* euphoria overpowers his mind, a part of which is experienced in the awakened state and, in its fullness, it is experienced in the *dhyan* state. But the *yogi* is not supposed to stop and enjoy it, because he has to cross this layer *(kosh)* also.

So, now we know that there is no such word as 'enjoyment' in the dictionary of *yog* and *gyan,* and that makes it further difficult to practice dry meditation and renunciation. Still if someone wants to follow this path out of whim, or ignorance, or because of past *sanskars* of *yog,* or any other reason, our *acharyas* have laid these conditions: (1) acquire complete renunciation ( पूर्ण वैराग्य ), physical and mental both, (2) find a *yogi* Saint of that class ( श्रोत्रिय ब्रह्मनिष्ठ तथा योगनिष्ठ ), and (3) then practice *yog* and *gyan* strictly under his guidance while living near him ( सान्निध्य ).

**(4) The unprotectiveness.** The biggest drawback of this path is the absence of Divine protection. The formless *nirakar brahm* has no apparent Divine virtues because **all the Divine virtues refer to the Divine personality of God,** like His kindness, His Grace, His beauty, His absolute knowledge, etc. So, the *nirakar brahm* can neither Grace nor protect its devotee in any way, nor can it appear in his pure mind.

That's why a *gyani* or *yogi* has to submit himself to a personal form of God, during or at the final stage of his *advait* practice of *samadhi*, to receive *mokch* with His Grace. For this very reason, the Yog Darshan, at three places, suggests to meditate upon a personal form of God; and **Jagadguru Shankaracharya also tells a *yogi* to surrender to a God realized Spiritual Master and a personal form of God, in the Aparokchanubhuti.**

## *Yog* is incomplete without *bhakti*.

The Yogshikhopnishad says, " भक्तिगम्यं परं तत्त्वमन्तर्लीनेन चेतसा । (2/23). The supreme Divine truth is attainable through *bhakti*."

(Vyas *bhashya* व्यास भाष्य)

" ईश्वरप्रणिधानाद्वा ॥ २३ ॥ प्रणिधानाद्भक्तिविशेषादावर्जित ईश्वरस्तमनुगृह्णात्यभिध्यानमात्रेण ॥ तदभिध्यानमात्रादपि योगिन आसन्नतमः समाधिलाभः समाधिफलं च भवतीति ॥ पुरुषविशेष ईश्वरः ॥ २४ ॥ न च तत्समानमैश्वर्यमस्ति । तस्माद्यस्य साम्यातिशयैर्विनिर्मुक्तमैश्वर्यं स एवेश्वरः । स च पुरुषविशेष इति ॥ तज्जपस्तदर्थभावनम् ॥ २८ ॥ प्रणवाभिधेयस्य चेश्वरस्य भावनम् । "

**Vyas *bhashya* on the Yog Darshan** is the most authentic explanation of *yog sutras*. It says in *sutra* 23 of *samadhipad* that submission *(bhakti)* to *Ishwar*, the supreme God (while practicing *samadhi*), facilitates and ensures the achievement of *nirvikalp samadhi* ( समाधि लाभ ), and also ensures the Divine attainment, the liberation ( समाधि फल ), which is not possible without His Grace.

Further, in *sutra* 24, it defines the word *'Ishwar'* (God) and says, "No one equals to His almightiness. No one could be equal to Him and no one could be greater than Him. He is the only supreme almighty God. He is *purushottam*." (The Divine personal form of God is called *purushottam*.)

By using the phrase ' साम्यातिशयैर्विनिर्मुक्तम्,' Ved Vyasji is indicating that the *'Ishwar'* word is for 'Krishn,' because he has used the same phrase in the Bhagwatam (2/4/14) for describing Krishn's supremacy.

In *sutra* 28, Ved Vyas says, "According to *yogic* principles, a *yogi*, while assimilating the Divine theme of *'pranav'* in his mind ( अभिधेय ), should affectionately remember ( भावना ) God Krishn, because He is the indicated Divineness of *pranav*." The Gita also tells the same thing in the verse, " ओमित्येकाक्षरं ब्रह्म... I " (8/13). The gist is that the Yog Darshan also prescribes devotion *(bhakti)* to Krishn, because the practice of *yog* is extremely difficult and is not protected by the Grace of God.

Shankaracharya says that ( जटिलो मुण्डी लुञ्छितकेशः काषायाम्बर बहुकृतवेषः...I ) worldly desires are so deep that they keep on haunting the mind of even those ascetics who have physically renounced the world. That's why the Yog Darshan prescribes the first five steps of eightfold *(ashtang) yog* for the practice of total renunciation before starting *dhyan* (meditation). Failing to which, if a person willfully tries this path, he will develop a kind of self-accepted hypocritical superiority of himself, which will be ingrained in his intellect; and for this situation Bhagwan Shankaracharya again says,

" कुशला ब्रह्मवार्तायां वृत्तिहीनाः सुरागिणः ।
ते ह्यज्ञानतमा नूनं पुनरायान्ति यान्ति च ॥ " (अपरोक्षानुभूति)
" अहं ब्रह्मास्मि कर्ता च भोक्ता चास्मीति ये विदुः ।
ते नष्टा ज्ञानकर्मभ्यां नास्तिकाः स्युर्न संशयः ॥ " (शं.)

"Those who have material attachments and ambitions of any kind and yet talk of *vedant* and *gyan,* will never cross the cycle of birth and death, because they are totally mindless and are still in deep ignorance, and have not acquired *brahmi vritti.*" *Brahmi vritti* means observing the whole universe as *nirakar brahm* and not acknowledging any joy or happiness in the world.

Krishn says in the Gita that the path of *gyan* is the most painful path ( क्लेशोऽधिकतरः I अव्यक्ता हि गतिर्दुःखम् I ), whereas the path of *bhakti* *(divine-love-consciousness)* is easy and simple. He says, "I am easily attainable with *bhakti* ( तस्याहं सुलभः पार्थ I ) and also My true devotees are protected by Me ( न मे भक्तः प्रणश्यति I )."

Ved Vyas says in the Bhagwatam,

" येऽन्येऽरविन्दाक्ष विमुक्तमानि-
नस्त्वय्यस्तभावादविशुद्धबुद्धयः ।
आरुह्य कृच्छ्रेण परं पदं ततः
पतन्त्यधोऽनादृतयुष्मदङ्घ्रयः ॥ " (भा. 10/2/32)

"Diverting their minds with utmost difficulty from *mayic* attractions, the few *yogis* who reach the final stage of *yog* after crossing the five *koshas* begin to believe that they have crossed the ocean of *maya*. But they are mistaken, because they are still under the bondage of *maya*. For this mistake, during the period of past bad *sanskars*, they may be attracted to *mayic* luxury which will make them fall back into the field of worldly attachments. A *yogi* has to know that the *mayic* ocean can only be crossed with the Grace of Krishn." **Thus we know that the practices of *karm*, *gyan and yog* are only for heart purification and are within the field of *maya*.**

## *Hath yog* and Tantra books.

*Hath yog* is a physical practice of purifying and controlling the physical functions of the body, the nervous system, and the flow of the subtle oxygen (*pran vayu*) that runs into the veins and the arteries of the whole body. It is a subsidiary of Patanjali Yog Darshan and consists of 84 *yog* postures, 24 deeply and subtly effective postures (*mudras*), 8 kinds of breathing exercises, 3 blocking procedures (*bandh*), and 6 cleaning procedures (*shat karm*). *Mool bandh* (one of the 3 blocking procedures) and the lotus posture is used in evolving a subtle psychic energy, called the *kundalini*, through meditation, which is dormantly sitting near the tail bone at the lower end of a nonphysical energy-nerve, *brahm nadi*, which is the life giver of *chitra* and *sushumna nadi*. It is all *hath yog*. Even a worldly person with *mayic* ambitions can practice it. But its true application is for rising higher in *yog* which is described earlier. This is the total *hath yog*.

There are certain books in Sanskrit language called the Tantra books. They emphasize on *mantra* worship with strict disciplinary formulative practice. Some of them involve *hath-yog*-type meditation also. Their *mantras* are related to a personal form of God. There are many kinds and classes of these books. Some of them also teach pure *bhakti,* but all of their practices are formulative and disciplinary, not affectional.

They are like: sitting in a proper pose, repeating a Sanskrit *mantra* for a certain length of time or for a certain number of times, and, in the end (also in the beginning), worshipping the God of that *mantra* with certain verses of worship. Also, offering flower, fruit and food in a prescribed manner. Sometimes the person has to make a promise in his mind as to how many times he is going to repeat that *mantra,* say 125, 250 or 500 thousand times or one million times along with other formalities... During that period he is supposed to maintain celibacy, have restricted diet, and observe silence, etc. This kind of practice is called *anusthan* which means disciplinary worship with some kind of desire, material or Divine.

Not being the prime topic of this book, *karm, yog, gyan,* and *tantra,* etc. are briefly described just to comparatively evaluate the simplicity, potency and the Divine graciousness of *bhakti* which unites a soul with God in His loving personal form.

## *(4) Bhakti.*

### Definition of devotional *bhakti.*

Affinity with God is *bhakti.* Affinity is not any kind of action or intellectual decision or its application. It is a feeling of sweet relationship with Radha Krishn that dawns in the heart, lives in the heart and evolves in the heart. When this affinity is for a material being, it is called *moh* (worldly attachment in ignorance), and when it is for a personal form of God it is called *bhakti.* *Bhakti* also means total dedication to God with a humble desire to receive His Grace for Divine experience. This is pure or selfless (*nishkam*) *bhakti*. It is a devotion from the heart for your Divine beloved God.

## Kinds of *bhakti.*

There are three kinds of *bhakti:* (a) selfless, (as described above), (b) selfish (*sakam*), and (c) affiliated with *karm* or *gyan*. Those who follow *bhakti* are called *bhakt* or devotee.

*Sakam bhakti.* There are some people who, because of their past good *sanskars,* have some affinity for God, but when they have any trouble they ask God for help. Involved in worldly attachments, they don't know the importance of God realization. Thus, their affinity slowly dies in ignorance as they get older. Normally, people are only selfish, they are not a true devotee. According to our religious history, a *sakam bhakt* (selfish devotee) is the one who is both, *bhakt* and *sakam* (having a specific worldly desire). Like *bhakt* Dhruv, who desired to become a great king, and, with this desire, he devoted every breath of his life for God realization until he visualized Him. It means asking for something from God with 100% faith in Him only, like Dropadi, etc.

God fulfills every desire of His *bhakt,* either worldly or Divine, but first the devotee has to visualize Him. When God realization happens, He is standing in front of you, so you can ask anything from Him. If you wish you can even ask Him to make you Brahma, and He will make you Brahma of some planetary system. But then you will be designated as a *sakam bhakt* in the Divine abode and you will join with that class of Saints.

*Bhakti* **affiliated with** *gyan* **or** *karm,* **etc.** Desiring liberation (*kaivalya mokch,* कैवल्य मोक्ष ) is literally not a worldly desire, but again, it is not a very good Divine desire, because liberation eliminates the possibility of experiencing *prem ras* (Divine love). Once a soul is liberated, it is merged in *nirakar brahm* forever. So, *rasik* Saints of *Vrindaban* have advised the souls to eliminate all kinds of *mayic* desires including the desire of *mokch*. A devotee should only desire to receive selfless Divine love (*premanand*) of Radha Krishn because this is the supreme blissful experience of the Divine realm.

As explained earlier, *yog* takes a soul up to the final limit of *sattva gun* and reveals the true closeness of the soul (the real self). This stage is called *atm-gyan* or *turiya* stage. The unlimited *karmas* of the past unlimited lives (*sanchit karm*) and the *mayic* veil ( चिज्जड़ग्रंथि ) are still there. The *yogi* then has to humbly submit himself to the supreme God (any personal form of God) to receive His Grace that could terminate the bondage of *karmas* and terminate the *mayic* veil. This humble surrender with a desire to receive His Grace, is *bhakti*. This could be done either while practicing *yog* or at the final stage of *yog*.

The Gita explains this situation. It says,

" ब्रह्मभूतः प्रसन्नात्मा न शोचति न काङ्क्षति ।
समः सर्वेषु भूतेषु मद्भक्तिं लभते पराम् ॥
भक्तया मामभिजानाति यावान्यश्चास्मि तत्त्वतः ।
ततो मां तत्त्वतो ज्ञात्वा विशते तदनन्तरम् ॥ " (गी. 18/54, 55)

It means that *yog* reveals the pure 'self' and *bhakti* reveals God.

**Practically it thus happens:** After crossing the *anandmaya kosh*, the Grace of God is transmitted through a *yogi* Saint (a Divine personality) into the heart of his disciple (the *yogi* devotee). The *yogi* devotee is already experiencing the Divine reflection of his soul in close proximity in his pure mind. When the Grace of God (through his spiritual Master, the Saint) enters his mind, his bondages are broken. Now he experiences the truth of soul's eternal and substantial Divine unity and similarity with *nirakar brahm* (*chid-brahm*, चिद्ब्रह्म ). This is the '*aham brahmasmi*' (अहं ब्रह्मास्मि) state, the experience of soul-*brahm*-substantial-oneness. Instantly he enters into *brahm-turiya* or *brahm-leen* state which is a Divine state of total unconsciousness. Then he comes to the surface. The *aham* (pure ego) merges into *brahm* and only *brahmasmi* is left which further shapes up as इदं सर्वं ब्रह्म which means 'all of this is *brahm.*' He is now seeing the whole world as the expansion of *brahm* (*sarvam khalvidam brahm,* सर्वं खल्विदं ब्रह्म।). This all happens within seconds. **This is the secret of the Upnishadic statement 'aham brahmasmi.' This is experienced only once, not even twice.**

A well known example of this kind is Totakacharya who was Graced by his Master Jagadguru Shankaracharya. This is the Divine state of a *gyani/yogi* Saint. Now *leshavidya* ( लेशाविद्या, the minimal presence of pure and *sattvic mayic* mind) is still left, which remains until the end of the existing fate or destiny of that *yogi* Saint. **The period of *leshavidya*, which is after receiving *brahm gyan* and before the time of death, is the only opportunity when a *gyani* Saint experiences *brahmanand,* and that is also on the ground of his *sattvic* mind.** He is then called *jeevanmukt* ( जीवनमुक्त ). At the time of death, the *leshavidya* is also terminated and his mindless soul joins with the *jeev-shakti* of *chid brahm.* His personal identity is terminated, and just the soul is left. He is now called *videhmukt* ( विदेहमुक्त ). Without any kind of Blissful experience, his soul remains in a totally neutral state forever. This is *kaivalya mokch.*

Now, those who are involved in Vedic rituals, *hath yog,* other *sattvic* practices, austerity, or any kind of religious formality or disciplinary repetitions of *mantras* (*anusthan*), etc., can also selflessly submit their good deeds to Krishn and start doing pure *bhakti* that will take them up to God realization.

## Why only *bhakti* reveals God?

The answer is simple. These practices are *sattvic.* So, on their own, they can only elevate a person up to *sattvic lokas* (celestial abodes), not to God ( योगस्य तपसश्चैव न्यासस्य गतयोऽमला: । महर्जनस्तप: सत्यं भक्तियोगस्य मद्गति: ॥ भा. 11/24/14). Although the practice of doing *bhakti,* like chanting, meditating, worshipping a Deity, etc., is also *sattvic* but the feeling in *bhakti* which is 'affinity' or 'humble submission' to his beloved God, is not an action. It is a recognition of his sweet relationship with Krishn.  So it directly relates to God Krishn Who is beyond *maya*.  That is why *bhakti* is called *nirgun*. " सात्विकं सुखमात्मोत्थं । निर्गुणं मदपाश्रयम् ॥ " (भा. 11/25/29).  It is very simple to understand, that God realization or Grace of God is absolute, and there cannot be absolute or unlimited quantity of continuous *sattvic* actions with no negativity.  There is only one way.  Just ask Him with full 100% faith in Him and He will bestow His Grace upon you.  This faith, love, remembrance, asking and humbleness is *bhakti*.

When you have faith in someone, you begin to like him.  When you like him more, you begin to love him.  When you love him, you like to serve him.  When you serve him you become humble and like to be near him, and all of that ends up into deep affinity. **A true affinity has no demands and no requisites.  There is only one desire to love him and to serve him and to make him happy, because you feel happy in his happiness.  Such feelings for Radha Krishn is *bhakti* ( तत् सुखे सुखित्वम् ).**

## Everything is received from *bhakti*.

Bhagwan Ved Vyas says,

" अन्तः शुद्धिः बहिः शुद्धिः तपः शान्त्यादयस्तथा ।
अमी गुणाः प्रपद्यन्ते हरिसेवाभिकामिनाम् ॥ " (गरुड़)

" यत् कर्मभिर्यत्तपसा ज्ञानवैराग्यतश्च यत् ।
योगेन दानधर्मेण श्रेयोभिरितरैरपि ॥ " (भा. 11/20/32)

" सर्वं मद्भक्तियोगेन मद्भक्तो लभतेऽञ्जसा ।
स्वर्गापवर्गं मद्धाम कथंचिद्यदि वाञ्छति ॥ " (भा. 11/20/33)

" यद् दुर्लभं यदप्राप्यं मनसो यन्न गोचरम् ।
तदप्यप्रार्थितो ध्यातो ददाति मधुसूदनः ॥ " (भक्ति सं. 98, गरुड़ 178)

It means, "A *bhakt* devotee receives everything through *bhakti*.  Purification of the heart, physical purity, the outcome of all kinds of *sattvic* austerity (without doing austerity), and all kinds of *sattvic* attainments and experiences are easily received through *bhakti*."

Krishn says that the outcome of all kinds of devotional asceticism and selfless Vedic rituals, the outcome of *yogic* practices, the outcome of *sattvic* charity and social work, the outcome of any kind and any amount of religious practice, or any kind of good work or Godly work *(dharm)* whatever it could be, is all received through *bhakti*. He further says that the *sattvic* virtues like, renunciation, detachment from worldly attractions and attachments, and practical knowledge of soul's eternal relationship with Krishn *(gyan, vairagya)* etc., are all the natural outcome of *bhakti*.

"Whatever a *bhakt* (devotee) desires," Shree Krishn says, "He receives everything with My Grace upon God realization. The monarchship of this world, the seat of Indra (the king of gods), the seat of Brahma (the creator), the absolute liberation *(mokch)*, or My Divine abode, Golok or Vrindaban, is all received through *bhakti*." *Anjasa* ( अंजसा ) means that it is all received very easily through *bhakti*.

The fourth verse says, "Through *bhakti* you receive all of that, (a) whatever is very rare to achieve *(durlabh,* दुर्लभ ), (b) whatever is impossible to achieve by any practice *(apprapya,* अप्राप्य ), and (c) whatever is impossible even to imagine. This is all given by Radha Krishn to His devotee."

(a) Four things are rare to achieve in this world: (1) the human birth in such a situation where teachings of God may be available ( मानव देह ), (2) to receive the true path of *bhakti* *(divine-love-consciousness)* from a *bhakt* Saint ( साधना मार्ग ), (3) to be able to ignore worldly attractions and reduce worldly attachments ( वैराग्य ), and (4) to establish one's mind in the remembrance of Krishn name and feel affinity for Him ( भाव भक्ति ). They are all attained through *bhakti*.

(b) Two things are impossible to achieve by any kind of practice. They are: (1) liberation, and (2) access to the Divine abode of almighty God. Both are attained through *bhakti*.

(c) **Ved Vyas says that a Krishn *bhakt* also receives such things which are even beyond imagination. What are they?** They are: (1) experiencing the ever-increasing and ever-new love of Radha Krishn, (2) experiencing Their relational proximity, and (3) experiencing Radha Krishn's personal love and desire to serve Their *bhaktas* of Golok and Vrindaban abode. All three together are called '*rag*,' or Radha Krishn love, or Divine love or *ras* or *Vrindaban* Bliss. This is also received through *bhakti*.

A soul could think of a state of no pain forever. This is the liberation of *gyanis* and *yogis*. There are some very happy moments in a person's life. He can thus imagine a state of absolute happiness, absolute bliss and absolute beauty of a non-ending character. This is the Bliss of the Divine abode of the almighty forms of God, Vaikunth. The supreme God of Vaikunth, Maha Vishnu is the creator of the whole universe with unlimited clusters of galaxies and He is only a fraction of Krishn's power.

" महाविराड् महाविष्णुः त्वं तस्य जनकः विभो ॥ "
" विष्णुर्महान् स इह यस्य कलाविशेषो
गोविन्दमादिपुरुषं तमहं भजामि ॥ " (ब्र.सं. 48)

In this way, if you seriously try to think you will discover that Krishn's Divine greatness is beyond imagination, and that Krishn could become a personal friend of yours in Divine Golok and behave like an obedient friend, is also beyond imagination. Not only that, His relational closeness could be experienced in such an absolute proximity in the heart where it is hard to find the demarcation line between you and Krishn, Whose fraternal love, in that absolute proximity, is increasing and increasing every moment, and will keep on increasing the same way forever, and you will be experiencing all of that in your heart and with every pore of your body, and your absolute experiencing ability will also absolutely increase to experience the ever-increasing, ever-new, ever-charming, and ever-exciting beauty, sweetness, charm, love, excitement and relational friendliness of your Divine beloved

Krishn, and your Krishn remains with you all the time and desires to serve you by giving you His limitless love, affection, caring and protection all the time, forever.

**Every aspect of such a 'love' is beyond, beyond imagination. But that is not the end of it.** In all the respects, it limitlessly further deepens, sweetens, and enriches up to the maternal relationship like mother Yashoda, and then up to the *Gopis'* relationship. Furthermore, there are many classes of *Gopis* in Divine Vrindaban who are closer and closer to Radha, the Queen of Vrindaban, Who is the 'life' of Krishn ( प्राणाधिष्ठात्री सा देवी ). **You can become any one of these and live with Radha and Krishn in Golok or Divine Vrindaban forever, only through *bhakti*.**

Carefully read these lines over and over again and you will find that your mind has accepted and understood the greatness, the sweetness and the simplicity of *bhakti,* and your heart is now desiring the love of Radha Krishn. 🙈🙈🙈

# 6.
## Detailed Explanation of *Bhakti.*

## (1) *Bhakti* (Divine and devotional).

### Devotional *bhakti* and Divine *bhakti*.

"भक्त्या संजातया भक्त्या विभ्रत्युत्पुलकां तनुम् ।" (भा. 11/3/31) Ved Vyas says, "*bhakti* reveals *Bhakti.*" It means devotional *bhakti* reveals the Divine *Bhakti.* The same thing is said as भज्यते इति भक्ति: । भजनं भक्ति: । Affinity and submission to a personal form of God is devotional *bhakti*, and a Divine state, where a Saint naturally loves Radha Krishn is Divine *bhakti.* Devotional *bhakti,* devotional love, *seva* or devotion is the same thing. The natural state of *Bhakti* is Divine and it is a Divine power. In the devotional stage the devotee tries to develop the feeling of love and longing for his Divine beloved Radha Krishn and he wants to spend most of his time in Their loving remembrance to feel Their closeness. When this devotional *bhakti* is one hundred percent complete, the Grace of Radha Krishn reveals the Divine *Bhakti.*

### Everyone has recommended the path of *bhakti* for God realization.

Krishn Himself says,

"यथाग्निः सुसमृद्धार्चिः करोत्येधांसि भस्मसात् ।
तथा मद्विषया भक्तिरुद्धवैनांसि कृत्स्नशः ॥" (भा. 11/14/19)

"भक्त्याहमेकया ग्राह्यः श्रद्धयाऽऽत्मा प्रियः सताम् ।
भक्तिः पुनाति मन्निष्ठा श्वपाकानपि सम्भवात् ॥" (भा. 11/14/21)

" कथं विना रोमहर्षं द्रवता वा चेतसा विना ।
विनाऽऽनन्दाश्रुकलया शुध्येद् भक्त्या विनाऽऽशयः ॥" (भा. 11/14/23)

"यथाग्निना हेममलं जहाति ध्मातं पुनः स्वं भजते च रूपम् । आत्मा
च कर्मानुशयं विधूय मद्भक्तियोगेन भजत्यथो माम् ॥" (भा. 11/14/25)

" यथा यथात्मा परिमृज्यतेऽसौ मत्पुण्यगाथाश्रवणाभिधानैः । तथा तथा
पश्यति वस्तु सूक्ष्मं चक्षुर्यथैवाञ्जनसम्प्रयुक्तम् ॥" (भा. 11/14/26)

"भक्त्या त्वनन्यया शक्य अहमेवंविधोऽर्जुन ।
ज्ञातुं द्रष्टुं च तत्त्वेन प्रवेष्टुं च परन्तप ॥" (गी. 11/54)

"सर्वगुह्यतमं भूयः शृणु मे परमं वचः ।
इष्टोऽसि मे दृढमिति ततो वक्ष्यामि ते हितम् ॥" (गी. 18/64)

"मन्मना भव मद्भक्तो मद्याजी मां नमस्कुरु ।
मामेवैष्यसि सत्यं ते प्रतिजाने प्रियोऽसि मे ॥" (गी. 18/65)

"क्षिप्रं भवति धर्मात्मा शश्वच्छान्तिं निगच्छति ।
कौन्तेय प्रति जानीहि न मे भक्तः प्रणश्यति ॥" (गी. 9/31)

The above verses tell that, only through the loving devotion, the *mayic* impurities of the heart are burnt in a considerably very short time, the devotee feels closer and closer to Krishn, and, in the end, he receives the Divine vision and Divine love of Krishn. **This is the topmost secret of the secrets of the Divine realm, that only *bhakti* reveals God, in any form, a devotee desires.**

"ज्ञात्वाज्ञात्वाथ ये वै मां यावान् यश्चास्मि यादृशः ।
भजन्त्यनन्यभावेन ते मे भक्ततमा मताः ॥" (भा. 11/11/33)

Krishn further says, "My devotee does not have to study the intellectual philosophies of the *vedant* or the Upnishads. He only has to learn and understand the devotional philosophy which is needed to maintain and develop his devotional faith and love in Me. Anyone who loves Me becomes very dear to Me."

Even those great Saints, who represented the path of *gyan,* advised in their writings to follow the path of *bhakti.* **Shankaracharya**, the promoter of *advait* philosophy, **Patanjali**, the writer of Yog Darshan, **Kapil**, the producer of Sankhya Darshan, and even the four eternal *Gyanis,* **Sankadik**, said that *bhakti* is the easiest path to terminate the bondage of *maya,* so you should surrender to God. The only best thing to do in your life is to immediately submit your heart and mind to God and do *bhakti,* because the *karmic* and *mayic* layers of bondages, which even the greatest *yogis* and *gyanis* cannot break, simple hearted devotees of Krishn easily cross with His Grace. So, O souls of the world, it is My personal advice that you must worship Krishn.

" मोक्षकारणसामग्र्यां भक्तिरेव गरीयसि ॥ " (शं.)

" ईश्वर प्रणिधानाद्वा ॥ " (यो.द.)

" एतवानेव लोकेऽस्मिन् पुंसां निःश्रेयसोदयः ।
तीव्रेण भक्तियोगेन मनो मय्यर्पितं स्थिरम् ॥ " (भा. 3/25/44)

" यत्पादपङ्कजपलाशविलासभक्त्या कर्माशयं ग्रथितमुद्ग्रथयन्ति सन्तः ।
तद्वन्न रिक्तमतयो यतयोऽपि रुद्धस्रोतोगणास्तमरणं भज वासुदेवम् ॥ "
(भा. 4/22/39)

## (2) Kinds of *karmas, karm yog,* kinds of *sanyas,* and four kinds of desires.

**The four classes of *karmas.***

There are four classes of *karmas:* (1) neutral *karm,* (2) bad *karm,* (3) good *karm,* and (4) devotional *karm.* In our scriptures, thoughts and actions, both are considered *karm.*

**(1) Neutral *karm* or neutral deed:** Actions related to our daily living without any good or bad motivation like eating, sleeping, walking, working in the office, etc., are neutral *karmas*.

**(2) Bad *karm* or sin or bad deed:** They are of two kinds, (a) general sinful actions, and (b) spiritual transgressions. **General sinful actions**, as we all know, are hurting or harming anyone in any form, breaking the social or moral law, and stealing, lying or cheating etc.

**Spiritual transgressions:** Spiritual transgression is much more devastating than a social sin or crime. It pollutes the doers mind immediately. In general, disrespecting or even disregarding Radha Krishn (or any personal form of God), His Divine love, His Divine abode, His associates of the Divine abode, His Divine names, His *leelas* and His devotees is called "spiritual transgression." Also, when a person acting as a spiritual teacher, in the pretense of promoting religion or Vedic *dharm*, enjoys his pride of being a teacher, and enjoys worldly comforts offered by his followers, he is committing a greater transgression. It is like a policeman, who is supposed to prevent crime, gets involved in unlawful activities.

The transgressions of a sanctimonious teacher are also transferred to his followers, because of their faithfulness and sincerity towards their teacher. You should not get confused with the idea that 'sincere faith and dedication' will always give positive results. **Sincerity, faith, and dedication, are only the joining factors, that allow you to receive the inner qualities of the person who you are attached to.** (More explanation is on page 252.) So, the faithful follower of such a teacher commits similar transgressions.

Another kind of transgression, which such ambitious people commit, is to wrongly translate our scriptures, changing their meanings to their own likings, and writing and speaking incorrect philosophy of true *bhakti* (devotion). This is, in fact, a very grave continuous transgression, because everyone who reads or follows them is misguided. Puranas tell about the hellish punishments for such transgressions, but the attachment to short-lived-material-popularity hardens their hearts to such an extent that the admonition of our *shastras* don't even bother them.

Disrespecting the forms of God (other than the one a person worships), disregarding the *acharyas* (other than the one a person likes), rejecting *bhakti* and introducing a style of worship of one's own liking, introducing an intellectual technique of meditation and calling it *raj yog* or *gyan yog* or *bhakti yog* etc., are all the outcome of an ignorant, discontented or a deceitful mind. When they are willfully done, they become transgressions.

Nityanand was the descension of Balram, so devotees called him *'prabhu'*. Our descended Masters of Vrindaban, in whose name religions are formed, are called *'acharyas'*, and their family descendents are called *'goswamis'*. Ambitiously using these titles with one's own name is as grave a transgression as disrespecting the Grace of Krishn, because it is a religious misrepresentation. Associating with a transgressor is also a transgression.

Disregarding His kindness and Grace is also a serious transgression. Once I casually asked a person, "Why did you miss the *satsang*?" He immediately replied, "How could I have come without His Grace?" I have seen people say such things quite often, when it relates to God. But the dilemma is that they don't make such a plea in their worldly life. They don't say the same thing to their boss when they are late at work, because there is a fear of being fired. Such a mentality of throwing your mistake or carelessness on God is a direct disregard to His Grace, and it is a direct transgression that shows the craftiness of your mind and the ungratefulness of your heart. Because, you are blaming the One Who has always Graced you, and is still Gracing you...

For a religious teacher, showiness of such a godliness to his followers and admirers which he is not, is a religious misrepresentation, and it becomes a transgression. There are many who have made it a business, but there are some who sometimes recognize their mistake.

"न शिष्याननुबध्नीत ग्रन्थान्नैवाभ्यसेद् बहून् ।
न व्याख्यामुपयुञ्जीत नारम्भानारभेत् क्वचित् ॥" (भा. 7/13/8, ना. परि. 5/22)

The Bhagwatam clearly admonishes that, before God realization, a true devotee of God (Krishn) must not make disciples, must not enter into a hobby of learning the philosophies of various scriptures as an intellectual indulgence, must not do preaching to gain and enjoy his popularity, and he must not involve himself in any kind of religious or nonreligious project that distracts him from his devotion.

Sometimes it happens that a soul, longing for the vision of God, begins to wholeheartedly remember God. But still, all the worldly desires are dormantly held in his heart. His devotional attitude attracts the religious public and he may thus start preaching Gita, Bhagwat or Ramayanam etc. He may be believing that he is helping people, or distributing the Divine name to people, but, in fact, it is his own material mind ( मायासक्त मन ) which is bluffing his intellect ( बुद्धि ) and making him enjoy the sweetness of his popularity, in the pretense of religion.

If this situation goes on, a time comes when his conscience is hardened with such transgressions and his devotional receptivity is fully blocked. But, before it happens, the person must think over it deeply and very carefully, and try to correct his mistakes.

Nothing is too late to start. **This human life is the only chance to receive the Divine loving association of your sole loving Krishn and Radha, and to be with Them in Their Divine abode Vrindaban forever.** So, this life should not be wasted in the alluring excitements of self-praise, affectionate devotees and popularity, which is just for a short time, and it is followed by a long dark destiny of *karmic* consequences.

Social sins pollute the mind and create bad destiny in the next lifetime. Spiritual transgressions pollute the mind, block the devotional receptivity of the heart as well as the mind, and create negative *sanskars* (or bad *sanskars*) that hinder or block the devotional experiences of affinity, love and longing for your beloved God, in this lifetime, and also in the next lifetime.

**(3) Good *karm* or good deed, also called *apar dharm* or *dharm*:** We all know what a good deed is, like honestly helping others, giving any kind of *sattvic* charity, and observing truthfulness in everyday living, etc. Apart from that, all kinds of religious rituals and activities, worshipping formalities and devotion to God and Goddess with a desire to receive His Grace for family well-being and material gain of any kind are also called good deed.

**(4) Devotional *karm* or devotional action:** It is also called *par dharm* (explained in Chapter 2).

## What is *karm yog* and *karm sanyas*?

When a person has decided that only God realization is the prime aim of his life, but he has a family commitment, so, while doing his duties in the world, without being attached to them and their consequences, he continues his unbroken devotion to Krishn; it is then called the *karm yog*. Doing *karm* in the world, and *yog* (unity) with Krishn, is *karm yog*.

The Gita defines *karm yog* as thus, " कर्मण्येवाधिकारस्ते मा फलेषु कदाचन । " (2/47), and " तस्मात्सर्वेषु कालेषु मामनुस्मर युध्य च । " (8/7). Krishn says, "O Arjun! You have to do *karm* without being attached to its consequence. Your duty is only to do the *karmas*, their outcome is not in your hands, so don't be grieved or greedy on its failure or success." The second thing He says, "O Arjun! You must remember Me all the time and then do your duties." **Thus, both requirements have to be fulfilled: (a) remembering Krishn all the time (*sarveshu kaleshu* means 24 hours), and (b) doing all the *karmas* without any attachment. Then it becomes the *karm yog* of the Gita, otherwise not.**

You first think about the result, and then you do things. You never do such things which you are sure to fail. You would not even open your eyes if you know that there is an ugly scene in front of you. Again, how could your remembrance remain unbroken during sleep, and how could your mind do two things simultaneously, remembering Krishn and working in the office? Both situations appear to be impossible. People read, teach, preach, memorize, give talks about the Gita and *karm yog*, write books and open Gita centers, but they fail to truly reconcile the above situations, because the Gita is a precise practical Divine knowledge, not a hypothetical description.

Now understand the secret of *karm yog* which is a simple practical fact. ***Karm yog* is a combination of: (a) decision, (b) desire, (c) understanding, and (d) devotion.** Decision to realize God in this lifetime, and thus making it the primary aim of your life, is the first step of *karm yog.* When the decision is firm, you naturally desire and long to visualize your beloved God. Increasing your love and longing and sincerely desiring Him is the second step. Then comes the correct understanding of the devotional philosophy and your relationship with Radha Krishn. Only then you start doing your devotions correctly while living in the world. **The first two things you have to do on your own, and the last steps are explained in detail in this book.**

Some pious hearted people think that sincerely doing good work in the society and helping others is also *karm yog* and it will please Krishn; and some people, at the end of the day, say a brief prayer, "O Krishn I offer my whole day's good and bad actions at Your lotus feet," and they think that they have done *karm yog.* These are all self-deceptions. The first person's deeds are classified as 'good *karm*' not 'devotional *karm*,' which are governed by the general *karmic* rules of the Divine government. The second one's few minutes of prayer could be considered as devotion, the rest is only good or bad *karm.* You should know that only that period of time is classified as devotion which is directly spent in the loving remembrance or meditation of your beloved God. One should clearly understand that only sincere devotion (*bhakti*) to God, with a desire to receive His love and vision, activates the Grace of God. Apart from that, all kinds of good deeds, and all the practices that relate to *gyan* and *yog,* are totally governed by the *karmic* laws of *maya*. They do not relate to the power of God's Grace.

All the four aspects are required to qualify it as *karm yog*, which, when done correctly, produces such positive results that it really stays 24 hours in the heart. Hundreds of our devotees experience it in their daily life.

*Sanyas* and *karm sanyas* is the same thing. The one who takes *sanyas* lives singly and devotes all of his time in devotion to God and service to the Divine mission. *Sanyas* literally means to leave all worldly attachments and to live in the world for the service and the attainment of God. The devotional part in *sanyas* is the same as in *karm yog*.

**Kinds of** *sanyas***:** There are mainly two kinds of s*anyas,* Vedic *sanyas* which is also called *advait sanyas,* and *Vaishnav sanyas. Vaishnav sanyas* could be taken by a person of any caste or nationality who is a renounced and wholehearted devotee of Vishnu, Ram or Krishn. Normally they wear orange or white or peach colored material. Their old name is changed, either fully or partially, and their new name is like Haridas, Hari Sharan, Ramdas, or Shyam Dasi, Gyaneshwari, Uma Devi, etc.

## Vedic or *advait sanyas.*

The mention of *sanyas* in the Upnishad tells about the merits of a *sanyasi.* (The one who takes *sanyas* is called *sanyasi.)* The four orders of life as described in our scriptures are: (a) The educational period while observing full celibacy. It is called *brahmacharya.* (b) Then, entering into married life, not to be drowned in lust and luxury, but to experience the futility of worldly happiness while observing social and religious duties along with devotion to God. It is called *grihasth.* (c) Afterwards, leaving the family and worldly activities, leading a partially renounced life with the spouse, and trying to spend most of the time in devotion to God and devotional service. This is called *vanaprasth.* (d) The fourth and the highest order of life is *sanyas.* All of these orders of life have their own disciplines, and also, certain Vedic rituals are prescribed to observe which are categorized as 'good *karm*.' Devotion to God is prescribed in all the stages of life.

The Upnishad says, " यदहरेव विरजेत्तदहरेव प्रव्रजेत् । " (जा.). "There is no age restriction for taking *sanyas*. Whenever a person deeply begins to long for God and the true renunciation rises and stabilizes in the heart, he can take *sanyas*."

Sanyasopnishad defines the renunciation as thus " दृष्टानुश्रविकविषयवैतृष्ण्यमेत्य प्राक्पुण्यकर्मविशेषात्संन्यस्तः स वैराग्यसंन्यासी । " (सन्यासोपनिषत् 1-13). "Leaving the attachment of all the perceived and non-perceived *mayic* entertainments, and relinquishing, (a) the desire of physical comfort, (b) the study of scriptures for intellectual indulgence, and (c) the desire to receive name, fame and recognition in the material world, is called *vairagya* (renunciation), which a *sanyasi* is supposed to have."

Shankaracharya rejuvenated the Vedic system of *sanyas*. He made definite rules and regulations and strict disciplines related to devotion and renunciation for a *sanyasi*. Accordingly, only a male, born in an Indian *brahman* family, single, fully renounced, of sound mind and desiring only God in his life, can take Vedic *sanyas*, no one else. He is distinguished by his new name that ends with the word '*anand*' and is followed by the second name (surname), '*Saraswati*' or '*Teerth*' or '*Ashram*,' like, Prabodhanand Saraswati, Krishnanand Teerth, etc. There is an offshoot of Vedic *sanyas*, called *dashnami*, where people of other caste can also take *sanyas*, but not women. Their surnames are *giri, puri, bharti, ban, aranya, parbat*, or *sagar*. Out of all the ten surnames, *Saraswati* is more prestigious. These *sanyasis* wear peach or orange colored material.

Shankaracharya also established four spiritual seats called *math* on the four sides of India, and wrote the **Mathamnaya** describing the merits and qualifications of the *sanyasis* sitting on those seats that hold the title of Jagadguru Shankaracharya.

Although definite conditions and qualifications have been laid down by our great masters for taking *sanyas,* still there are many ambitious people who become *sanyasi* and add the best reverential words of the dictionary to their names, to gain popularity in the religious community. I have been to *ardh kumbh mela* (the largest religious fair in India) at Allahabad this year (1995), and was surprised to see such exploitations in abundance where people used 'freely picked titles' with their names, like: *anant shree vibhushit, akhand-bhumandal-acharya, prabhupad, jagadguru, beetrag, shrotriya brahmnishth, maharishi, paramhans, paribrajakacharya, peethadhishwar, saraswati, sad guru, guru mata, guru deo,* etc., etc. However, the discipline of true *sanyas* is explained here, so that the general public may also understand the truth about *sanyas.*

**Thus, a true *sanyasi,* devoting his life for the realization of God's love, is called *karm sanyasi* or *sanyasi.***

## Four kinds of desires related to God.

There are three qualities of *maya* residing in every heart, *sattvagun* (pious), *rajogun* (selfish) and *tamogun* (negative or evil). Each *gun* resides in all the three *gunas* in certain limits. Thus, *sattvagun* has a touch of *tamogun* and *rajogun*; *rajogun* has a touch of *sattvagun* and *tamogun;* and *tamogun* has a touch of *sattvagun* and *rajogun*. People in *tamogun* are involved in bad *karmas*. People in *rajogun* are involved in their own personal selfish activities. People in *sattvagun* do good *karmas* and are inclined towards God. Those who worship God have four kinds of desires related to their existing *mayic* qualities of the mind: (1) *sattva-tam,* (2) *sattva-raj,* (3) *sattva-sattva* and (4) *gunateet sattva* (सत्व-तम, सत्व-रज, सत्व-सत्व, तथा गुणातीत) .

The first one relates to those historical demons who worshipped God with a desire to rule and terrorize both worlds, celestial and material, like Ravan, Kumbhkaran, Bhasmasur, etc. The other three are related to the devotees of this world.

Wholeheartedly and faithfully doing devotion to God but having a worldly desire like Dhruv and Dropadi (they desired worldly kingdom and self protection from God). This is the second kind. Desiring liberation or vision of an almighty form of God, to eliminate the material bondage, is the third one; and desiring nothing for himself, just selflessly loving his Divine beloved God, is the fourth and the highest one. (The word *gunateet* literally means beyond the field of *maya*.) In the words of the Gita, "त्रैगुण्यविषया वेदा निस्त्रैगुण्यो भवार्जुन I " which means, not desiring anything of this *mayic* world, but desiring the Divine love of Krishn only.

After God realization every devotee enters the Divine abode of his worshipped form of God and enjoys absolute Bliss, but his relational proximity with God varies according to his previous devotional attitudes. In every Divine abode there are some Saints who are close to God in His personal service, some are less close, some only enjoy the Bliss of the abode, some have more freedom to see God any time, and some have less freedom of that kind. Thus, there are many kinds of Divine variations which correspond to the devotee's style and kind of devotion, and the degree of worldly desires or selflessness, during the devotional period.

## (3) The progressive description of *bhakti* in our scriptures. Your relationship with Krishn and *gopi bhao*. Form of God realization in *raganuga* tradition, *bhao bhakti*, and *sattvic bhao*.

꙰

**The form of *bhakti* and the form of Divine realization as described in, (a) the Upnishads and the Puranas, (b) the Brahm Sutra, (c) the Gita, (d) the Bhagwatam and (e) the *rasik vanis*.**

The practice of *bhakti* for any kind of Divine attainment is the same, and that is total submission of heart and mind with faith, love, and humbleness to the lotus feet of your beloved form of God. But, the class of *bhakti* and its resultant Divine experience is qualified by the desired Divine aim and the form of God which a devotee desires to attain.

Now we will briefly describe **the Divine approach of our major scriptures. Our Hindu philosophy of God is so extensive that it can never be described in a few volumes of writings. So we have different groups of scriptures describing a particular aspect of God and God realization.** As explained earlier, (1) liberation, (2) Bliss of almightiness, and (3) Divine love are the main aspects of Divine attainment.

**(a) The Upnishads** tell the total philosophy of God, and **the Puranas** tell a little more about Radha Krishn and Vrindaban. But mainly they tell about the liberation and the almighty abodes of God. **(b) The Brahm Sutra** tells the philosophical part of soul, *maya* and God, and explains almost the same as the Upnishads. One more thing it tells: that a Saint enjoys exactly the same amount and quality of Divine Bliss as God Himself. **(c) The Gita** tells the total philosophy of the Upnishads in short, and in a precise manner. It also tells about *gyan* and liberation. But the main theme of the Gita is, " सर्वधर्मान्परित्यज्य मामेकं शरणं व्रज ।," which relates to selfless devotion to Krishn. It does not tell which form of Krishn to worship.

The first listeners of all of these scriptures were the souls desiring Divine happiness, but the first listener of the Bhagwatam was a God realized Saint, absorbed in absolute Divine transcendence. Thus, **(d) the Bhagwatam** starts from what is beyond *nirakar brahm* and almighty God. It also incorporates the philosophies of all other scriptures (the Upnishads, the Puranas, the Brahm Sutra and the Gita).

" सर्ववेदान्तसारं हि श्रीभागवतमिष्यते । " (भा. 12/13/15) Ved Vyas says that the philosophies of all the scriptures (related to soul, *maya*, God, God realization, descensions of God, and various forms of God) are described in the Bhagwatam. The supreme power of

God is Divine love (the *ahladini* power), and thus, God, in His absolute beauty and supreme Divine love form, is Krishn, Who did the *maharaas*. This form of Divine love is beyond *brahmanand* and beyond the Bliss of almighty God. This is the main topic of the Bhagwatam. Once you dip yourself in the Bliss of Krishn, Who enticed the hearts of all the *Gopis* with the sound of His flute, you would never like even to think of other forms of Godly Blissfulness.

(e) There is still one thing that Bhagwatam did not openly describe, and it is the personality of Radha Rani which is the prime life-force and the essence of the total Divine existence. This is described in the **rasik vani** which reveals the *leelas* of Radha Krishn.

Thus we see that, in a progressive manner, the Upnishads, the Brahm Sutra and the Puranas take us up to liberation and the Bliss of the almighty form of God; the Gita, assimilating their theme, takes us further up to the Bliss of Divine love mixed with Divine almightiness; and the Bhagwatam, incorporating all the theories of all the scriptures, further takes us up to the pure form of Divine love, the abode of Radha Krishn. The writings of *rasik* Saints, expounding the Divine love theory of the Bhagwatam, further explain the topmost Bliss of Radha Krishn of Divine Vrindaban, which any soul could receive through selfless devotion and with Their Grace.

## What is the form of selfless *bhakti*?

There is one thing very peculiar in the Divine world. You have to have 100% faith and dedication to enter any kind and class of Divine attainment, be it the liberation (like deep sleep) or the Bliss of almighty God, or the topmost Divine Bliss of Radha Krishn which is beyond the conception of the creator Brahma. It is like a jeweller announcing the SALE of every item in his shop for only $100. It could be either a glittering fake stone necklace, or an elegant gold necklace, or a 15 carat blue diamond necklace with 5 carat solitaire Kashmir sapphire.

When everything is of the same price why not decide for the best. Our great Masters have explained everything. Now the choice is yours. But they still suggest that it is wise to go for the best, which is the Bliss of Divine Vrindaban.

Roop Goswami says, to achieve the supreme goal of your life and to receive the association of Radha Krishn, you should follow the loving pattern of *Brajwasis* and devote your life for Krishn devotion. He says,

" अन्याभिलाषिताशून्यं ज्ञानकर्माद्यनावृतम् ।
आनुकूल्येन कृष्णानुशीलनं भक्तिरुत्तमा ॥ "

(भ.र.सिं. 1/1/13, पूर्व भाग, प्रथम लहरी)

"Devotion should be pure and selfless. The devotee should not be desiring anything of the *mayic* world from Krishn, not even asking for liberation from Him, not affiliating with any kind of Vedic ritualistic practices, not associating with any kind of *yogic* meditation, and not getting involved with any kind of other spiritual practices. He should only love Radha Krishn and drown his heart and mind in the loving relational remembrance of Radha Krishn." The Bhagwatam also says the same thing, ( अहैतुक्यव्यवहिता या भक्ति: पुरुषोत्तमे ॥ भा. 3/29/12).

## Your relation with Krishn.

As explained earlier, **a soul has three types of relations with God: (1)** substantial oneness, **(2)** constitutional unity, being a fraction of God's power like a drop of the ocean, and **(3)** relational affinity, being loved by God.

These relations give rise to a stable state of such an experience in the Divine world that corresponds to the type of relational concept a devotee has formed in his mind during his devotional period. **The first one** is the *advait* concept of *gyanis* and *yogis* who think of God and soul as one substantial identity. So, it is like a relation with no relation. **The second one** is called *shant bhao* which is like a subject to his gracious king, a kind of dignitary relationship. It is seen in Vaikunth.

**The third type** is a loving relationship with your supreme Divine beloved (God) which is the main form of soul and God relationship, appreciated by all the *rasik* Saints. **There are mainly five kinds of such relationships**, *dasya bhao, sakhya bhao, vatsalya bhao, samanjasa bhao* and *madhurya* or *gopi bhao* (previously explained in the third section of Chapter 2). *Dasya bhao* is popular in Saket *lok* and *samanjasa* in Dwarika. *Sakhya, vatsalya* and *madhurya* are the three main *bhao* in Golok.

In practical devotional life a devotee humbly surrenders to Radha Krishn to receive Their Grace. He may decide in his mind as to what he wants to become in the Divine abode, whether he wants to become a *Gwalbal* of Krishn, or mother of Krishn, or a *Gopi* in Golok or Vrindaban. But, in day to day devotion, only one *bhao* of servitude remains predominant up to God realization.

**What is *gopi bhao* devotion?** All the *Gopis* adore Radha Krishn as their own soul, but some lean towards Krishn's side, some towards Radha's side, and some love Both equally. This gives a new charm in the *leelas* of Golok and Vrindaban, and also gives you the privilege of how to adore Radha Krishn, according to your personal preference.

**The true love of a devotee for Radha or Krishn is beyond the physical boundaries. It is directly related to your soul.** Take an example: a mother is longing to meet her son, and a wife her husband. Both come home and meet after a long time. While they are meeting, a moment comes when the mother, while embracing her son, loses her bodily feeling and her heart feels a soft, contenting bliss in which she drowns for a second. The same thing happens to the wife. In spite of physical relational differences there is something that is commonly experienced by both. It is a heart to heart relationship, beyond physical relations. Radha is the Soul of your soul. Krishn is the Soul of your soul. So a devotee's feeling of relationship with Radha Krishn is called soul relationship, which is beyond any form of known relationship in the world. It is beyond compare. Their love slowly enters and impregnates your heart and soul as your loving devotion increases.

Thus, loving Radha Krishn with a desire to personally serve Them as a *Gopi,* and to participate in all the *leelas* of Divine Vrindaban, is devotion with *gopi bhao.*

## What is remembrance?

The name of Radha Krishn, Their beauty, *leelas* and virtues, Their abode and Their *rasik* Saints, are all one ( नाम, रूप, लीला, गुण, धाम, जन ). Engross your mind in any of them. Thinking of Their *leelas* and virtues, singing Their name and the *leelas,* remembering (in your mind) any chanting of Radha Krishn's name and *leelas,* meditating on Their smiling face and body, mentally imagining or visualizing any of Their *leelas,* feeling the presence of Radha Krishn very close to your body, believing that you are sitting or living in the real abode of Radha Rani (the Barsana dham), is remembrance. Such a remembrance, when followed by a feeling of true humbleness, fills your eyes with tears of love that takes you deeper into your heart and brings Radha or Krishn or Both closer to you. These feelings are called '*bhao.*'

(**Procedure of remembrance for a Westerner who has never thought of a form of God.**) Radha Rani is very kind. She has already revealed Her Divine name and virtues in the world which are the means of remembrance. If you have any kind of reservation in conceiving the personal form of God, just remember in your mind the name of Radha Krishn, and chant or listen to the chanting of Their Divine names. **While remembering or listening to the chanting of the names you must try to feel and recognize the presence of the Divine Grace and kindness of Radha Krishn.** Lovingly conceiving the name and the virtues of Radha Krishn will naturally bring Their form in your heart and you may begin to feel Their personal closeness in due course of time ( सुमिरय नाम रूप बिनु देखे । आवत हृदय सनेह बिसेखे ॥ ).

## Stages of devotional *bhakti.*

Chaitanya Mahaprabhuji, in the Shikchashtak, explained the seven stages of *bhakti* in the verse, "चेतो दर्पण मार्जनम् ।" His disciple

Roop Goswami simplified it into three stages, *sadhana, bhao* and *prem.* Further he describes the qualities of a devotee. He says, " उत्तमो मध्यमश्चैव कनिष्ठश्चेति स त्रिधा । " (भ.र.सिं. 1/2/16).

"The best devotee is the one who has full faith in Krishn and his Master, and he fully understands the devotional philosophy (like, the value of human life, importance of God realization, the superiority of Radha Krishn love, the greatness of *bhakti,* etc.). The one who has faith in Krishn and his Master but his understanding about the path is incomplete, comes in the ordinary class of devotees. The one whose faith and understanding both are unstable, his progress on this path also remains unstable, and thus, he comes in the lowest class of the devotees."

Correct understanding and firm faith, both are equally important for a steady progress in devotion. Krishn says,

" मय्येव मन आधत्स्व मयि बुद्धिं निवेशय । " (गी. 12/8)

"Engross your heart in Me and establish your mind in Me." Faith stays in the mind and love stays in the heart. Faith is more important, because if faith is shaken, devotional love slowly begins to fade ( संशयात्मा विनश्यति ), and when faith is strong, devotion automatically develops ( न मे भक्तः प्रणश्यति ). **Faith is the dominating aspect of devotion and it is subject to correct understanding that stays in the intellect, and love is the outcome of positive faith and understanding that purifies both, the heart and mind, and further elevates the feelings of love for Radha Krishn.**

That is why Krishn says that a devotee whose heart is drawn towards Me (out of his past devotional *karmas*) should also do effort to improve his 'understanding' in order to stabilize his 'faith,' and to have a firm determination to realize Divine love in this lifetime; and the devotee who has understood this fact should wholeheartedly do the devotion.

Roop Goswami says in the Bhakti Rasamrit Sindhu, " सा भक्तिः साधनं भावः प्रेमा चेति त्रिधोदिता । " (1/2/1). "Such a selfless devotee slowly rises from his initial *'sadhana'* stage to *'bhao'* stage, and then to the ultimate *'prem'* state."

The first stage of *bhakti* is called **'sadhana bhakti.'** In this stage a devotee is trying to bring Radha Krishn into his life. He tries to meditate on Krishn, and someone else appears in his thoughts. He tries to think of some *leela,* and a worldly scene overtakes it. One should know that everything takes time in the beginning. A child takes a year's learning to start walking. A young boy takes many months to learn the simple alphabet. So, why to be disheartened? You must continue your regular devotions with faith and dedication. This is the sign of correct understanding. It will slowly reduce the fickleness of your mind and, after some time, you will begin to feel the closeness of Radha Krishn.

## The form of devotion, *bhao bhakti* and *prema bhakti.*

It is already described at various places but you can again understand it like this, that simply worshipping, chanting, repeating a name, or reciting holy verses is not classified as devotion or *bhakti,* it is only a good deed. **A firm decision, to receive the Divine vision and love of Radha Krishn, is to be made in the mind.** After such a decision and understanding, when a devotee faithfully and lovingly remembers Radha Krishn, sings Their name, listens to the chanting, meditates on Their form and *leelas,* worships and decorates the Deity, does *arti* and homage or does any kind of service that relates to Radha Krishn, it is then classified as devotion *(bhakti).*

In one sentence you can say that selfless loving submission to Radha Krishn with a desire to serve Them and to love Them (as *Brajwasis* did), and to be one of Their loving associates in the Divine abode, is called *raganuga bhakti,* or divine love devotion, or *divine-love-consciousness.* Such a *bhakti* gives rise to *'bhao bhakti,'* and the devotee begins to feel a natural longing for Radha Krishn. At the **final stage of *bhao bhakti*,** the devotee reaches a stage of extreme longing when even a second's delay in the Divine vision of Krishn or Radha or Both (as a devotee's feelings would be) appears to be unbearably very, very long, as described by Shree Chaitanya Mahaprabhu in the Shikchashtak,

" युगायितं निमेषेण चक्षुषा प्रावृषायितम् ।
शून्यायितं जगत्सर्वं गोविन्द विरहेण मे ॥ "

Then, with the Divine Grace of Radha Krishn and his Master, the devotee receives the Divine power and his whole personality is Divinized. He receives the Divine vision of Radha Krishn, and the Divine love he now experiences is called *'prema bhakti.'*

## What is God realization in the *raganuga* tradition?

A devotee of the *raganuga* tradition, desiring the Bliss of Divine Vrindaban, receives the Grace of Shree Raseshwari Radha Rani and Krishn. At the moment of God realization, when he receives the Divine power, his material subtle body, mind and senses along with all kinds of *karmas* and the existing fate are totally terminated, and, simultaneously, they are replaced with the Divine body, mind and senses of pure Divine love substance with which Vrindaban abode is made of. Vrindaban abode is the personal expansion of Radha's own personality.

It means, the devotee Saint sees the beauty of Radha Krishn with the eyes of Radha, and experiences the love of Radha Krishn with the heart and mind of Radha. Radha, Krishn, Vrindaban, Divine love, all the loving *leelas,* and all the Saints of Divine Vrindaban are the same. In such a state of total oneness, the absoluteness of the experiences of Divine love ascribed to an infinitesimal individual (Devotee) soul, by the Grace of Radha Krishn, is a Divine marvel on its own, whose greatness is even beyond the imagination of Maha Lakchmi and Brahma.

The Devotee Saint enjoys the Bliss of *maharaas* and the *leelas* of Radha Krishn in Divine Vrindaban with a progressively self-multiplying sweetness of every vision, forever. This is *premanand* or *prema bhakti* or Divine *bhakti* of Radha Krishn.

But, to experience that, you have to do something, and that is to keep increasing the depth of your *bhao bhakti*.

## Describing the indications of *bhao bhakti*.

Roop Goswami in the Bhakti Rasamrit Sindhu says,

" क्षान्तिरव्यर्थकालत्वं विरक्तिर्मानशून्यता ।
आशाबन्ध: समुत्कण्ठा नामगाने सदा रुचि: ॥
आसक्तिस्तद्गुणाख्याने प्रीतिस्तद्वसतिस्थले ।
इत्यादयोऽनुभावा: स्यु: जातभावाङ्कुरे जने ॥ " (1/3/25-26)

It means, that the devotee whose field of worldly attachments are submerged in the loving attachment of Radha Krishn, enters into *bhao bhakti*. It shows up in his daily life. The indications are as thus:

(a) The agitation and anxiety of the mind reduces and gradually subsides. He feels calm even in adverse situations ( क्षान्ति: ).

(b) He does not waste time in idle talks. He tries to remember Radha Krishn all the time, because he understands the value of time, the value of human life and the importance of God realization in this very lifetime ( अव्यर्थ कालत्वम् ).

(c) His heart feels more affinity for Radha Krishn and less for worldly things because he has understood the transitory and disappointing nature of worldly happiness ( विरक्ति: ).

(d) He feels a little uncomfortable when someone praises him. He knows that great *rasik* Saints are really praiseworthy and also the other devotees, not him, because he maintains his humbleness ( मानशून्यता ).

(e) He believes that someday Radha Krishn will surely appear before him, because he feels Their closeness in his day to day life, and that closeness keeps on gradually increasing according to his devotional progress ( आशाबन्ध: ).

(f) Devotional and loving excitement ( समुत्कण्ठा ) takes place in his heart and mind instead of general agitation, anxiety and disappointment. His devotional excitement is not the build up of his thoughts or thinking. It is natural. For instance: he is sleeping or remembering some *leela.* Suddenly he feels that Radha has come, or Krishn came and touched him. Such an experience really excites him. He looks around and sees nothing, still he 'feels' that Radha or Krishn or Both were there. It is a kind of devotional hallucination of *bhao bhakti.* One should be very careful in understanding this feature that such symptoms may also arise in a weak mind which is only partly devotional. In that case it is not a symptom of *bhao bhakti.* It could be an aberration of the mind. One should know that devotion is done with a healthy and sound mind.

(g) His heart is always singing the name of Radha Krishn very quietly. Whenever he gets the opportunity, he chants the name in his mind or out loud. He feels an appeasing sweet thrill in singing Radhey name or Krishn name, because he feels the oneness of Radha name with the personality of Radha, and Krishn name with the personality of Krishn ( नामगाने सदा रुचि: ).

(h) He feels very much attached to each and every virtue of Radha and of Krishn (depending upon the devotional preference of a devotee). He listens, describes, remembers, and talks about the virtues of Radha and Krishn and feels a growing contentment in his heart ( आसक्तिस्तद्गुणाख्याने ).

For instance: a *Gopi* inquisitively asks other *Gopis,* who were sitting and talking, "Dear friends! Could you tell me one thing, why does Krishn have a dark complexion when His father Nand Baba and mother Yashoda both have fair complexion?" One *Gopi* leans her head to one side resting on her hand, thinks a little, and says, "Don't you know that our sweet naughty Krishn is always absorbed in our eyes which are decorated with collyrium, that's why His beautiful complexion grew dark."

कजरारी आँखियान में बस्यो रहत दिन रात ।
प्रीतम प्यारो हे सखी ताते श्यामल गात ॥

Other *Gopis* listened, and liked the idea with a big nod. One *Gopi* was still thinking. She said, "Yes, that's right, but there is one thing that rejoices me the most, and that is, when Krishn loses His naughtiness in the presence of our Radhey, and I see His eyes slowly drooping into Her love..." *Gopis* were ever absorbed in such loving talks of Radha and Krishn.

(i) He feels real affinity with the Divine abode of Radha Krishn where They live, and the Braj where They lived. The name 'Vrindaban' becomes as pleasing as Radha Krishn, because the beauty, love and charm of Vrindaban is synonymous to Radha, and the exciting factor of Vrindaban is synonymous to Krishn. Barsana dham and Braj, where They lived just recently, only 5,000 years ago, and the places of Braj where They played, spent evenings with *Gwalbals* and *Gopis* and rejoiced *Brajwasis* with Their presence, all of them still represent the presence of Radha Krishn for such a devotee ( प्रीतिस्तद्व्रसतिस्थले ) who has fully devoted his life for the realization of Radha Krishn love.

These indications of *'bhao'* gradually develop and slowly enter the depths of the heart and mind of the devotee. As they enter, they further purify the heart and, simultaneously, reveal more of such experiences and feelings of love and affinity. The devotee, crossing all the layers of *bhao bhakti*, finally enters into a state of total heart purification where his longing to meet Radha Krishn and the excitement to visualize Them reaches the climax and all the experiences of *bhao* are visually materialized in an absolute pure *sattvic* form. The material bondage is then broken, *(Jeevatv) mayic*-soulhood is terminated, never to be repeated again, for which the Ved says, " न स पुनरावर्तते, " and the *vedant* says, " अनावृत्ति शब्दात् अनावृत्ति शब्दात्," and the whole new dimension of Divine love, Radha Krishn and Vrindaban is revealed to him forever. The materiality of the *mayic* world disappears ( आकाशकुसुमवत् ) without a trace, and there remains an eternal omnipresent existence of Vrindaban *leelas* of Raseshwari Krishn.

## Physical indications of *bhao.*

" स्वल्पमात्राश्रुपुलकादय: ।
स्तम्भ: स्वेदोथरोमाञ्चस्वरभेदोऽथवेपथु: ।
वैवर्ण्यमश्रुप्रलय: इत्यष्टौ सात्विका: स्मृता: ॥ " (भ.र.सि.)

Roop Goswami describes the physical indications in *bhao bhakti.* He says that in the beginning of *bhao bhakti*, a devotee feels a little melting of his heart during devotion. His eyes become wet and his heart feels a little thrill. Such feelings, during devotion, indicate that the devotee has begun to feel some affinity for Radha Krishn.

As the feeling of affinity deepens, further physical expressions appear during remembrance. They are: stillness of the body for some time, perspiration, rising of goose pimples, change of the tone of voice during chanting, shaking of the body, change of facial look, fainting and tears. They are called *sattvic bhao*, the **devotional expressions**. These expressions are the outcome of the feelings of closeness with Radha Krishn during chanting, remembrance and meditation. Tears and thrill are common. Other expressions appear at the higher stages of *bhao bhakti.*

## Divine expressions of a Saint.

The above expressions also appear in Saints and then they are called **Divine expressions.** There are many classes and kinds of all of these expressions which are related to the hundreds of ecstatic stages of Divine love as experienced by the *rasik* Saints. You may have heard a word *samadhi* (ecstasy) which is a state of absorbment of the mind. It is only of two kinds in a *gyani* Saint: *brahm gyan* and *brahm-leen* state. But, there are primarily sixteen kinds of *samadhi* in Divine love, which are further classified according to the relational closeness of a Saint with his Divine beloved Radha Krishn. There could be a whole book on this very topic if I have to write all of them, but it is enough for us to know that all of the Divine love stages are exceptionally marvelous, and sweet, and unbelievably incredible, which are experienced by a Saint who has adored and worshipped Radha Krishn with the *raganuga* style of devotion. Now I give you one example of Divine expressions.

Vilvamangal, who was a great *rasik* Saint of Vrindaban, said many verses in his early days during his ecstatic walk towards the land of Vrindaban. He says,

"हे देव, हे दयित, हे भुवनैकबन्धो,
हे कृष्ण, हे चपल, हे करुणैकसिन्धो ।
हे नाथ, हे रमण, हे नयनाभिराम,
हा हा कदनुभविितासि पदं दृशोर्मे ॥ " (कृष्ण कर्णामृत)

In this verse, he is addressing Krishn in many ways which relate to his inner state of Divine love. Here is a brief description of his ecstatic experiences:

Constantly remaining in various states of Divine love ecstasy, Vilvamangal feels a sweet pain of love for his beloved Krishn. Tears come from his eyes and he says, **"O Lord!** (Why don't You show me Your sweet face?)." His feeling of separation increases and Krishn appears in front of him, smiling. He feels a deep thrill in his heart. Krishn, his love for Krishn, and his own being, merge into a kind of endless feeling of Krishn love and he says, **"O life of my heart and the consort of my soul!** (You are so great; who can imagine Your graciousness?) **You are the sweetest friend of every soul."**

Now he is experiencing a deep love of Krishn in his whole body. Goose pimples appear and his excitement increases. It has almost crossed the border line of his conscious forbearance before he drowns into deep unconscious ecstasy. Suddenly, he again sees Krishn, standing in a style, and mischievously looking towards him as if He is going to pour all of His love into his heart. Vilvamangal says, **"O Krishn, O my naughty Krishn, O ocean of** kindness." He could not say any more. Feeling an extreme affection for Krishn, he tries to say something more in His praise, but, the tone of his voice changes and his throat chokes with the feeling of excessive love. He could only say, **"O Soul of my soul, (You are so great)."** Now he feels the presence of Krishn, with all of His intimate loving sweetness, very close to his heart and soul, and he whispers, **"O Sweetheart."**

The form of Krishn, which he was seeing in front of him, disappears. He feels a kind of inseparable separation. His hands and legs tremble, body perspires and mind feels an intense longing. Krishn again appears in an ever-new charm and beauty. The vision of Krishn, after an intense longing, extends an extensively contenting appeasingness to his heart, soul, mind and eyes. His body becomes still for some time in total ecstasy. He regains consciousness, and says, **"O charm of my eyes."**

The beauty of Krishn is so charming and so great that his conscious mind could not take it. It drowns into it. Before drowning, he deeply desires Him and says with a deep sigh, **"When will I see Your lotus feet again?,"** and saying so, he faints with a feeling of overpowering love of Krishn.

It all happened in a short while. He was so overwhelmed with the sweet excitement of the various forms of ecstasies of love and longing at the same time that he could say only a few words. But these few words of the verse are the true representations of his inner feelings and experience whose blissfulness is beyond any examples known to the world.

## What should be the ultimate devotional goal?

Considering all the facts and the statements of our scriptures and the *rasik* Saints, it is best to desire for the experience of Divine love of Radha Krishn of Divine Vrindaban, which is desired and praised by all the Divine personalities.

(4) All the Divine powers are dedicated to Radha Krishn. Fallacies that create confusion, and the ignorance and pride that block the Grace of Krishn. Explaining 'ये यथा मां प्रपद्यन्ते.'

✿

## All the forms of God are dedicated to Radha Krishn.

" राधिकांशो लक्ष्मीदुर्गाविजयादिशक्तिरिति । तस्याद्या प्रकृती राधिका नित्या निर्गुणा सर्वालंकारशोभिता प्रसन्नाशेषलावण्यसुन्दरी अस्यांशाद् बहवो विष्णुरुद्रादयो भवन्ति ॥ " (राधोपनिषत्)

" नारायणोऽखिलब्रह्माण्डाधिपतिरेकोंऽश: । " (राधिकोपनिषत्)

" कृष्णो द्विधारूपो बभूव स: । वामार्धांगो महादेव: । " (दे.भा. 9/2/82)

It means that all the almighty forms of Goddesses emanate from Radha, and Vishnu and Shiv emanate from Krishn. They are all powers of Radha Krishn, so naturally They are dedicated to Radha Krishn.

" दिव्यं वर्षसहस्रं च तपस्तप्त्वा हिमाचले । दुर्गा च तत्पदं (राधा पदं) ध्यात्वा सर्वपूज्या बभूव ह ॥ सरस्वती तपस्तप्त्वा पर्वते गंधमादने । लक्षवर्षं च दिव्यं च सर्ववंद्या बभूव सा ॥ लक्ष्मीर्युगशतं दिव्यं तपस्तप्त्वा च पुष्करे । सर्वसंपत्प्रदात्री च जाता देवीनिषेवणात् ॥ सावित्री मलये तप्त्वा पूज्या वंद्या बभूव सा । षष्ठिवर्षसहस्रं च दिव्यं ध्यात्वा च तत्पदम् ॥ शतमन्वन्तरं तप्तं शंकरेण पुरा विभो । शतमन्वंतरं चेदं ब्रह्मा शक्ति जजाप ह । शतमन्वन्तरं विष्णुस्तप्त्वा पाता बभूव ह ॥ "

(दे.भा. 9/8/101-106)

The Devi Bhagwatam says, "**Goddess Durga**, the lion rider, became very famous in the Divine world by worshipping Radha in deep engrossment. **Goddess Saraswati** deeply worshipped Radha on Gandmadan hill in the Himalayas for a hundred thousand celestial years and became famous. **Maha Lakchmi**, in deep meditation, worshipped Radha in Pushkar for a hundred *mahayugas* and became an important Goddess among others Who could impart all the boons to Her devotees. **Goddess Savitri,** absorbed in the thoughts of Radha, worshipped Her at Malaya Hill for sixty thousand celestial years. **God Shiv, Brahma, and also Maha Vishnu worshipped Her for seven thousand one hundred** *mahayugas* and received the ability to create and protect the universe." One celestial day equals our one year, and one *mahayuga* equals 4.32 million years of this earth planet. **These lines reveal one very important thing that all of these forms of God and Goddess receive Their Divine ability from Radha Rani.**

The Bhagwatam says,

" यद्वाञ्छया श्रील्ललनाचरत्तपो विहाय कामान् सुचिरं धृतव्रता । "

"With the desire of receiving the footdust of the *Gopis* of Braj, Goddess Lakchmi worshipped Radha Krishn for a very long time." There are hundreds of such references in our scriptures. The indications of the period of worship is to give the reader an importance of Radha Krishn's greatness. For a common person, it is very difficult to worship even a few hours a day. So, when a person reads that God Shiv austerely worshipped all the time in full engrossment (this is called '*tap*' in Sanskrit) for **thirty thousand million years,** he may assumingly calculate the greatness of this event in his limited mind. But the fact is, that all the forms of God and Goddess are adoringly self-submissive to Radha Krishn in a natural way since eternity, because Their forms and powers are naturally established in the personality of Radha Krishn.

This kind of natural adoration is lovingly revealed in a description in the beginning of the Samrahasyopnishad. " रमारमणो वैकुण्ठे नारायणः स्वयं ध्यानापन्नोऽभवत् । तदा लक्ष्मी: पप्रच्छ । किं ध्यायसि ? किं जपसि ? परं कौतूहलं मे मनसि वर्तते । त्वत्तः परं कोदेवः ? को लोक: ? यस्य त्वं ध्यायसे । " In the Vaikunth abode, Maha Lakchmi observed that Maha Vishnu is all the time absorbed in some thought. When He is alone He closes His eyes and goes inside. She became very curious so She asked, "My Dear, would You mind telling Me who is in Your thoughts all the time. Who do You meditate upon? I am very eager to know if there is anyone who is greater that You?"

Maha Vishnu then describes in detail the absolute supremacy of Radha Krishn love, the greatness of Vrindaban abode, and the indescribable sweetness of the Bliss of *maharaas* which is beyond the reach of the devotee Saints of Brahm *lok*, Shiv *lok* or even Vaikunth *lok*. " ब्रह्मलोके स्थिता रुद्रलोके स्थिता इमां लीलां न जानन्ति । मम भक्ताः बहवः सन्ति तेऽपीमां लीलां न जानन्ति । "

After Bhagwan Ram's marriage, during His descension period, when Goddess Sita was leaving for Ayodhya, Her maids at Her father's house felt an unbearable pang of separation. **Goddess Sita** then Graced those maidens and told them to take birth in Braj where they will receive the Bliss of *maharaas* by Radha Krishn.

**Goddess Parvati** (Gauri) always desired to join *maharaas*, and all the time She remembered Radha. Just like some people in the world have personal secrets which they don't tell to anyone, **Parvati** and **Shiv** also have a very personal secret which They don't reveal to the Saints of Vaikunth abode; and that is the name of Radha Krishn which They hold in Their hearts as a Divine treasure. So, when Parvati heard the special sound of the flute, which was an indication that Krishn is going to do *maharaas*, She rushed to Vrindaban and, with the Grace of Shree Radha, She joined the group of the *Gopis*.

**God Shiv** also came to Braj, His heart was longing to see Radha Krishn. For a long time He was waiting for this opportunity to experience the Bliss of *maharaas* and now the time had come. He entered the woodlands of Vrindaban, quickly assumed the form of a *Gopi*, and came to Radha.

" पुरा महर्षयः सर्वे दण्डकारण्यवासिनः ।
ते सर्वे स्त्रीत्वमापन्नाः समुद्भूताश्च गोकुले ॥ " (पद्म. उत्तर खण्ड)

"सच्चिदानन्दलक्षणं रामचन्द्रं दृष्ट्वा सर्वाङ्गसुन्दरं मुनयो वनवासिनो विस्मिता बभूवुः । तं होचुर्नोऽवद्यमवतारान्वै गण्यन्ते आलिङ्गामो भवन्तमिति । भवान्तरे कृष्णावतारे यूयं गोपिका भूत्वा मामालिङ्गथ ।" (कृष्णोपनिषत्)

It means, that all the sages of Dandak forest in central India, who were doing devotional austerity, saw Bhagwan Ram during His descension period and desired to experience His intimate Divine love. Bhagwan Ram, knowing their wish, told them to wait until the appearance of Krishn, because that class of Divine love (*premanand*) only Krishn can give. Later on they all took birth as *Gopis* in Braj and they were Graced by Radha Krishn.

At the time of the descension of Radha, as well as Krishn, and also at the time of the ascension of Radha and Krishn, Shiv, Brahma and Indra etc. came, showed Their dedication and sang homage.

## Can the devotion to an almighty form of God be changed to Krishn devotion?

Sometimes some people, who worship some form of God or Goddess, ask if they may add Krishn devotion to their existing pattern of worship.

You should know that worship or devotion to God is for receiving His love and vision, not for family prosperity. Material gain and loss, and good and bad destiny, is the outcome of your past lives' good and bad actions. They cannot be undone. The most important thing is that whatever Shiv, Durga, Vishnu, etc. can give to His devotee, Krishn can do better than that, and, on the top of that, He can give you His Divine love which enticed the heart of all the *Gopis* and *Brajwasis*. "सर्वं मद्भक्तियोगेन मद्भक्तो लभतेऽञ्जसा ।" (Bhagwatam). So, why not just become a single-minded devotee of Radha Krishn?

It is quite obvious that worshipping Krishn selflessly is going upward, because all the forms of God (Shiv, Vishnu, etc.) are established in the personality of Krishn, and all the forms of

Goddess are in Radha. Thus, a person, practicing any kind of religion or devotion to any form of God, can replace his devotion with the devotion to Radha Krishn. The Bhagwatam says, **"Other forms of God are naturally rejoiced with the devotion to Radha Krishn."**

" यथा तरोर्मूलनिषेचनेन तृप्यन्ति तत्स्कन्धभुजोपशाखाः ।
प्राणोपहाराच्च यथेन्द्रियाणां तथैव सर्वार्हणमच्युतेज्या ॥ " (भा. 4/31/14)

Still if a person has some hesitation, he can take his time to understand this truth. There is a simple way to overcome this situation. Just sincerely request for help from your God or Goddess (whoever you worship) that your desire to worship Radha Krishn be fulfilled...

Those who are involved in observing Vedic rituals, those who are practicing *yog*, those *sanyasis* who are following *advait marg*, and those hermits and ascetics who are doing some kind of pious austerity, can also replace their existing practices with pure Radha Krishn devotion and experience the Bliss of Their name and *leelas*, which is the true requisite of their soul.

## Can every Saint or every form of God enlighten a devotee with Vrindaban Bliss?

After reading the whole philosophy, still sometimes, some people ask such naive questions. The fact is that every form of God has His own specific name, form, abode and Divine Blissfulness. One should know that God realization means realizing a specific form and Bliss of God. So it is very obvious that, not any Saint, but only *that* Saint who himself has received the Grace of Radha Krishn and is absorbed in Their love, can teach the correct form of Krishn devotion to a devotee; and, on complete heart purification, he can impart his Divine Grace that will reveal the vision of Radha Krishn. A Saint makes his devotee Divinely like himself. Thus a *gyani* Saint can only impart *gyan* to his devotee, a Vishnu *bhakt* Saint can only impart the vision of Bhagwan Vishnu to his devotee, and so on. Saint is synonymous to the form of God he has realized. So, for the same reason, if a person comes to a Krishn *bhakt* and desires the vision of Shiv, the Krishn *bhakt* Saint will advise him to go to some Shiv *bhakt* Saint, because only Radha and Krishn reside in his heart and only Their devotion he can teach.

There is one exception. If a devotee has evolved himself to such a height that he could communicate with the form of God (he is worshipping) in his meditation; and if he really desires from Him to receive Radha Krishn love. Then, that form of God or Goddess may direct the devotee to go to a certain *rasik* Saint and become his disciple wholeheartedly.

You should know that no other Divine form of God or Saint can reveal and impart the Bliss of Divine Vrindaban, except Radha Krishn and a *rasik* Saint. (A *rasik* Saint is the one who has received the Grace of Radha Krishn and is always absorbed in Their love.) So it is only up to you. You have to make up your mind and decide if you really desire to enrich and fulfill your life with the love of Radha Krishn by wholeheartedly accepting and following the devotional guidelines of *raganuga* devotion.

## Explaining some of the existing fallacies.

There is a common fallacy prevailing in the world for hundreds of years which is damaging the Divine truth. It is: ' सब एक ही तो है । All forms of God are same,' 'all is same,' 'paths are many, goal is one,' 'all the worshipers go to the same place,' etc., etc. Those who say such things, either they have no real definition of the Divine goal, or they are referring to liberation and the impersonal aspect of God. In both ways they impair the Divine truth of our scriptures.

**The path to God is one and only one, not many; and that is *bhakti*, the loving devotion to God.** The other practices like, austerity, fasting, rituals, various forms of good deeds, techniques of meditation, *yog* practices, etc., are all the preparatory or preliminary processes of heart purification. They are not the main path (already explained earlier). Although God is one, but He has many forms, names and Divine abodes with specific Blissful characteristic that specifies the class of Blissfulness of a particular form and abode of God; and that is the main topic of the explanations of all the *Jagadgurus* whose philosophies are distinguished as *vishishtadvait, shuddhadvait, dvaitadvait, dvait,* and *achintya-bhedabhed* (explained earlier).

Those who talk like this that *all is same,* why don't they just boil all the veggies together, and boil all the grains together, and eat, when all the veggies and all the grains are substantially the same? No, they don't do such a thing, because they are very concerned about their material comfort, not God realization. People are very picky about everything in their life, like, dresses, shoes, car, house, food, and even a simple thing like tea and coffee (black, white, less cream, more cream, no sugar, less sugar, more sugar, etc.), but when it comes to God, they repeat the same slogan *'all is same.'*

It shows only two things: (1) either their worshipping etiquette is customary, just to gain the blessings of any God for family protection and well-being, or (2) they are ignorantly following this pattern of thought, but they may be really wanting to find God's love. The first category of people are materialistic. They should improve their understanding that human life is for God realization. The second category of people may be *sattvic,* but they are misguided by the existing ideologies and fallacies. They have to correct their misunderstanding and proceed on the correct path of *bhakti.*

Thus we see how the wrong concepts of our devotional philosophy are being introduced in the public by ignorant teachers and preachers, that harm the innocent followers of God and hamper their devotional progress. **You should know that it is very important to have correct understanding of the devotional truth. Only then you can proceed on the correct path to God. Misconception about** the forms of God will always mislead you. People say 'faith is God.' Wrong. It should be 'faith *in* God.'

A person, holding on to his ancestor's heirloom and faithfully believing it to be of gold and ruby, when he goes to a pawn shop in extreme urgency of money, gets only a few tokens because it was made of gold filled brass and garnets. His whole life's faith went down the drain. **So, faith at the wrong spot will not give you right results. Similarly, having no faith in the right thing will also make you a loser, because you lose something very special which you could have gained by having faith in it.**

**Thus, correct faith in a correct place gives correct results in this world and also in the Divine world. Faith is the binding factor. Whoever you are attached with, you develop a synonymity to the qualities of that personality.** So, faith and attachment in Radha Krishn and Their devotee Saints will bring you closer to Radha Krishn, and wrong faith due to ignorance will distract you. Ignorance is always misleading. That is why we are incorporating all the necessary devotional informations in this book.

## Ignorance, fallacious beliefs, and pride, that block the Grace of Krishn.

**Ignorance is of three kinds:** It is related to the people of *tamogun, rajogun* and *sattvagun.* Ignorance in *tamoguni* people makes them mean, selfish and vainful, and they have no fear of God. Ignorance in *rajoguni* people makes them worldly, and they are always looking for things of self-interest. Sometimes they have a little fear of God, but whenever they worship God they do it with a hope that God will give them material prosperity and happiness.

Ignorance in *sattvaguni* people appears as misconception or misunderstanding, and incorrect or incomplete understanding of the Divine truth, with a mild, subtle or gross vanity of knowingness. From normal *sattvic* people to even highly evolved souls fall in this misconceptional ignorance, and often, for their whole life, they remain in such an ignorance, because they believe that whatever they believe is right. The same theory "श्रद्धावान् लभते ज्ञानम्" applies in all the stages, that a 'humble' mind is open to learning, not a presumptuous one.

Misconception normally relates to impersonal ideologies. Jagadguru Shankaracharya has himself said in the Aprokchanubhuti that those, whose minds are not absorbed in the Bliss of *brahm* (God) and they intellectually talk like, '*nirakar brahm* becomes *sakar*, everything is *brahm*,' etc., are in absolute *agyanvad* ( अज्ञानवाद ) which means total ignorance. When Chaitanya Mahaprabhu visited Kashi, on his way to Vrindaban, and saw people talking like this, he called them *mayavadis* ( मायावादी ) which means mentally materialistic and intellectually showing their pride of knowingness. The idea that *nirakar brahm* becomes *sakar* is as false as a fairy tale. God does not become anything new. All the forms of God and His prime descensions are eternal and have Their own eternal Divine abode. Certain almighty forms of God like Vishnu, Shiv, Durga, etc. descend in the celestial space of each *brahmand* which becomes like a branch office of Vaikunth. When one *brahmand* is dissolved, that branch office is closed. It again opens up when a new *brahmand* is created. Bhagwan Ram and Krishn also descend on this earth plane, from time to time, for a short period. In this way, to Grace the souls, there are unlimited number of descensions and ascensions of God happening all the time in the unlimited number of *brahmandas*, in this endless universe. All the forms of God are omnipresent, so, there is no problem for God to do so. But all the original and eternal Divine abodes like Vaikunth, Golok, Vrindaban, etc. always remain eternally the same and unchanged.

**All the forms of God including His impersonal form, called** ***chid-brahm* ( चिद्ब्रह्म ), are eternal.** ***Maya* is, in fact, a *nirakar* lifeless power of God that assumes a *sakar* shape of this world along with its celestial gods and goddesses, and then again, it goes back to its *nirakar* state in *maha pralaya* (the totally dissolved state of this universe). So, it is *maya* and the celestial gods and goddesses that become *sakar* from *nirakar*, and then back to *nirakar*.**

This world is a *mayic* creation, so always such non-Godly (*mayavadi*) fallacies and ideologies remain in the society. Although it is so clearly written in our scriptures that the *nirakar* form of God is established in His *sakar* form ( ब्रह्मणो हि प्रतिष्ठाऽहम् । ), still it is seen that sometimes even great scholars and highly evolved *sattvic* souls, ignorantly or mistakenly, fall for such fallacious ideas that hamper their spiritual progress.

A highly learned *sanyasi* of Kashi, who had a great reputation, when he spoke on *maharaas* or Krishn *leela,* he felt a thrill in his heart which people saw as tears coming from his eyes. But, for himself, he worshipped the symbolic form of a Goddess *(Shree Yantra)* which is affiliated to the almightiness of God, and, praying to the celestial gods, he held wrong impersonalistic beliefs in his mind which is evident from his writings.

" नमोऽस्तु रुद्रेन्द्रयमानिलेभ्यः । ...तथापि भक्तिरसायनकारास्तु अद्वैतसिद्धान्तानुसारिणः । ...निर्गुणस्यापि सगुणत्वाद्युपपत्तिः । "

A world renowned and truly renounced *yogi* from South India, who expired in 1950 and had attained considerable heights in *yog,* told about the sweetness of the transcendental sound of the flute in one of his speeches. But he never desired to receive the Grace of the Divine flute player, Krishn, Who could have elevated his spiritual experiences by unlimited times. A renowned orator on *vedant* from Madras who was greatly respected by the intellectuals all over the world, and who himself was a seeker of Truth, never thought of believing the words of God, the Gita, where Krishn Himself says, that if someone wishes only liberation, He can give it very easily; but the person has to selflessly surrender himself to Me.

What could be the reason of such a mishap, except the subtle vanity of knowingness that he is right, and thus, knowingly or naively, not believing in the *Vaishnav* philosophies of selfless devotion to Radha Krishn, which is introduced by the supreme Divine Spiritual Master Krishn Himself ( कृष्णं वन्दे जगद्गुरुम् as said in the prologue of the Gita).

Once, at the end of a general speech when I invited devotional questions, a person asked me if a Spiritual Master is necessary for God realization. I asked him to think carefully and tell me if he has learned anything in his life without the help of someone or something. He thought for a minute and said, "No."

It is true that in every *kaliyug* sanctimoniousness grows in abundance, but that is the outcome of your society which is getting more and more materialistic every day. There are millions who worship God, but, out of them, how many truly and wholeheartedly desire to see God in their lifetime? Maybe a few.

Selfish, prejudiced and arrogant people cannot enter the path to God, because it is a path of humbleness. There is everything in the society in various forms, from evil to good and from good to Divine. Whatever is the quality of your mind, your actions follow the same direction. The branches of prominent religions have adopted worldliness in many ways and flocks of people are following it. Do the followers come to find God? No, they don't want God in the true sense. They want either the blessings of God for their health, wealth and material happiness, or they are interested in vanity elevating impersonal practices, psychic elevations, receiving fame by following a religious group or society, pridefully following certain religious fantasies, and practicing fallacious faiths, etc.

This is all the effect of *kaliyug.* But, you have to be sincere if you really desire God. Vanity of *Vaishnavism* or vanity of being a renounced *sanyasi,* degrades the soul and entices him into deeper materialism. You should know that the Bliss of God cannot be experienced by vanity elevating practices. It could only be experienced by practicing love, faith, sincerity and humbleness dedicated to your soul-beloved God in His personal form, as explained in His own words in the Gita and the Bhagwatam.

**Radha and Krishn are the Supreme Divine Master. Directly surrender to Them. Try to be sincere and humble and develop a**

longing for Them.  Then you will see for yourself how much Grace They have already showered upon you.

Now we understand that renunciation, practice and devotion are the helping factors.  The most important thing is the correct understanding.  Whatever you understand, you develop a similar faith in your mind, and wherever is your faith, you receive similar results.  So, **to have faith in Radha Krishn you have to understand the superiority of Vrindaban Bliss, only then you can proceed on the path of** *raganuga bhakti.*

" ये यथा मां प्रपद्यन्ते तांस्तथैव भजाम्यहम् ॥ " **Krishn has no desire of His own.  Whatever style of love and dedication you offer to Him, He will make it Divine and give it to you.**

A person working in a big company under the immediate boss, does not directly know about the supreme boss, the proprietor of that firm, whose main office is in another country.  Technically he is working for the supreme boss, but apparently he is being paid by the immediate boss (on behalf of the supreme boss).  Similarly, all the *bhaktas* (devotees) of every class and kind are technically related to Krishn, but the Grace of Krishn they receive, is in *that* form of God which they have conceived in their heart.

Take it like this: all the almighty forms of God and Goddess are established in *ahladini* power, and *ahladini* power is established in *Mahabhao* or Radha Krishn.  It is thus the expansion of Radha Krishn's Grace which is seen and found in all the Divine abodes, and in all the forms of God and Goddess. A devotee is worshipping God Shiv.  He receives Shiv's vision and enters His abode.  It could be said that: (a) Shiv has Graced him and given him His Divine abode, or (b) Krishn has Graced him in the form of God Shiv and awarded him Shiv's abode according to his faith and dedication to that form of God.  So, apparently, he has received Shiv's Grace, but, constitutionally, that Divine Grace originated from Krishn.

This is what Krishn says in the Gita," ये यथा मां प्रपद्यन्ते तांस्तथैव भजाम्यहम् । ". It means that, on complete purification of the heart, He serves and awards (भजामि) Divine experience to every devotee according to his conception and the quality of dedication during his devotional period ( यथा प्रपद्यन्ते ).

Conception means the form of God a devotee desires to attain, like Vishnu, Shiv, Durga, Ram, Krishn or *nirakar*, etc., and the quality of dedication means the quality of selflessness in devotion. It means, if he only desires to love Him and receive His love, or he has combined feelings of enjoying *mayic* luxuries (mundane, celestial, or Brahm *lok*) and also receiving His vision. **Krishn has no personal preference. He is the giver. Whatever is the conception and quality of your dedication and devotion, He will give it to you.**

If you only wish for liberation, He will give you liberation without any Blissful experience. If you desire for worldly kingship, celestial kingship or the seat of the creator Brahma, He will give you that also. But when you enter the Divine abode your classification of Divine Blissfulness will not be the same as other selfless devotee Saints of that abode, because your selflessness was blemished by your worldly desires from God during the devotional period.

If you desire for Vaikunth Bliss (the *bhagwadanand*), He will give you that. If you desire for Saket or Dwarika Bliss (*premanand* mixed with the almightiness), He will give you that. If you want pure *premanand* which is desired by Brahma and Uddhao, Krishn will also give you that kind of love which *Brajwasis* had, and if you still desire for the highest form of *premanand*, Radha Krishn will give you the love of *madhurya bhao* of Braj (Golok) which is longed for and desired by Shiv and the supreme Goddess of Vaikunth, Maha Lakchmi. There is still one more, the ultimate experience of *madhurya bhao* of Divine Vrindaban. It is Graced by Radha Rani.

You must know that the devotional requirement of all of the above mentioned Divine attainments is the same. So why not desire for the Vrindaban Bliss where Raseshwari Radha Rani, along with Krishn, personally cares for each and every Devotee Saint and gives Her maximum love which everyone in Divine Vrindaban experiences with every pore of his Divine body.

## " नष्टो मोह: स्मृतिर्लब्धा ..." The light of true Divine knowledge has now dissipated the darkness of ignorance.

The open-minded devotee, who carefully reads, studies and understands the Divine knowledge revealed in this book, gains an insight. He begins to realize the depth of ignorance he was in, and, at the same time, a deep desire to meet Radha Krishn rises in his heart. Correct knowledge or correct understanding ( ज्ञान ) dissipates the ignorance ( अज्ञान ), induces the feeling of renunciation ( वैराग्य ), and develops a longing for his true Divine beloved, Radha Krishn, in his heart. All the three happen simultaneously, not in a progressive sequence.

**So, lack of longing means lack of understanding. In that case, study it again, and try to understand your soul relationship with Radha Krishn. They were with you since eternity but you overlooked Their Grace because of your material attachments. This world never gave you stable happiness, but still you kept running after the mirage of material hope. They are your true friends indeed, in need, in distress, and in prosperity, but you never stretched your hands to Them so They could hold you tight and not let you fall in the world. They are the Soul of your soul and the life of your heart; then how could you forget Them even for a second?**

The moment a devotee understands these facts, he realizes that his heart is softening. The more he understands, the more humble he becomes. His moistened eyes begin to desire for Their vision, and his heart says:

O Radhey! Come to me and be with me all the time. Please don't leave me alone in this world. You know that only You are mine and only Your lotus feet are my refuge.

O my soul loving Radhey! Your name is the treasure of my heart and Your kindness is the consolance of my soul. My only desire is to love You, to be near You and to do whatever You want me to do.

O Queen of Vrindaban! When will You show me Your Divine Vrindaban. I am longing for the day when I will become Your loving *Gopi* forever.

The devotee also feels the Grace of Krishn and these feelings appear in his heart:

O my beloved Krishn! Now I realize that You always waited for me with Your open arms to embrace, but my sinful heart did not let me come to You. It's uncountable lifetimes that I have been away from You.

O form of kindness Shree Krishn! Who can know You without Your Grace? O ocean of love! Your love is my only desire and Your service is my only wish. You are the Soul of my soul and You are the life of my life. You are the joy of my heart and the liveliness of my mind.

O Krishn! This *maya* has deceived me for so long. Now I want only You and Radha in my life. Please fill my heart with Your love and longing, and make me Your own forever.

That is the luckiest day of the soul when such feelings adorn his heart and he decides to devote his whole life in the loving devotion of Radha Krishn. Now he needs further guidance of how to proceed on this path of *raganuga* devotion and how to overcome the practical difficulties that come on the way.

# 7.
# The Practical Side of *Raganuga* Devotion.

## (1) Procedures and obstacles.

### How to proceed on this path?

Relational feeling, meditation and remembrance, devotional discipline, internal remembrance, and confidence are the five main aspects of devotion.

(1) **Relational feeling.** A devotee should always every moment remember his soul relationship with Radha Krishn, as described in the fourth and sixth chapter, and feel affinity. The more you will remember, the more you will feel closer to Them. This remembrance is like the life force of all other aspects of devotion, so it is of first importance.

(2) **Meditation and remembrance.** Meditation in *raganuga* devotion is not a physical disciplinary act of concentration in the brain area. Meditation means: (a) feeling the Divine presence of Radha Krishn or your Master near you. You can also feel Their touch or the perfume of Their body or the perfume of the garland They are wearing. (b) You should try to visualize in your imagination any *leela* of Braj or Vrindaban or Barsana where you are either an observer or a participant in that *leela*. You can be

very close to Radha Rani or Krishn in the *leela* or be in the crowd, as you prefer. (c) Name of Radha is Radha Herself, and name of Krishn is Krishn Himself. So, while doing the chanting, or while listening to a chant, or while remembering a chant in your mind, you should feel the synonymity of the Blissful sweetness of Radha Krishn with the name, and, at the same time, think of any *leela,* or feel and imagine the presence of Radha Krishn near you. Radha name is as sweet as Radha. Feel an affinity with the name along with Radha Krishn. (Concentration or meditation in any part of the forehead area is a *yogic* technique, and meditation in the heart is related to the methodical forms of worship and devotion called *vaidhi bhakti* or *anushthan.* These are not done in this path.) (d) While remembering Radha Krishn, bring your 'self' down to your heart area, feel love, affinity and longing for Radha or Krishn or Both in your heart, and then feel Their presence near you. While thinking of Their form think of Their full youthful form.

(3) **Devotional discipline.** (a) Devotion should be done regularly, twice every day for at least half an hour. If you're living at one of our centers, join morning and evening devotional meetings. At home, you should do your devotion in the morning and in the evening (at your own convenient time). Start from half an hour at a time. You can increase this time up to an hour later on. **Devotion** means doing or listening to a chanting, or remembering any name of Radha Krishn along with meditation and relational feeling as explained above. Apart from morning and evening devotion you should also do five to ten minutes meditation before and after your sleep. Right before you are going to sleep (either while lying in your bed or sitting in your bed), think of some of your favorite chanting in your mind, engross yourself into it, and then sleep. Do the same thing in the morning when you wake up from sleep, then go to freshen up.

(4) **Internal remembrance.** In fact, internal remembrance is a kind of Divine Grace of a *rasik* Saint, but, as a preliminary course, you can try to think of any simple chanting in your mind most of

the time in 24 hours, and try to feel the presence of Radha Krishn near you.

(5) **Confidence** in meeting with Radha Krishn in this lifetime, **faith** in the graciousness and the kindness of your Master, and **joyfulness** in doing devotions, are also very important factors. **The moment you will have full faith that 'Radha' name is Radha Herself, She will appear in front of you. Believe me, it is true.**

All of these five aspects are important for a steady progress in your devotion. Some devotees prefer to think of Krishn more than Radha, some prefer Radha, and some like Both equally. They are all correct. There are all kinds of *Gopis* in Vrindaban.

There are no progressively changing methods of devotion in this path like the other paths of *yog,* etc. The same name, same chanting and same remembrance of *leela,* form, and name will take you up to the final limit of heart purification. Of course, the experience of your closeness with Radha Krishn, the depth of Their love, longing and affinity in your heart, the experience of emptiness and fakeness of *mayic* entertainments, and the vividness of the Divine Grace, will gradually increase as you proceed on this path.

## Obstacles of the path.

There are certain obstacles of the path which a devotee has to cross wisely.

(1) **Bad *sanskars.*** *Sanskar* means conditioned reflex of past *karmas.* Bad *sanskar* means bad *karmas* of the past life that appear in this lifetime as bad destiny. Bad destiny is of two kinds: (a) **physical**, like, physical, social, family or monetary damage and (b) **spiritual**, like, such bad feelings which internally hamper your faith and dedication and slow down your devotion. They are like the high hills and the ditches on the path of devotion. From a few hours to a few days or months they prolong, and appear from time to time. (There are also good *sanskars* in life which are just the opposite.) When such bad *sanskars* come, you have to be more

careful. You should not let any negative thought stay in your mind. Have positive thinking. **Do your devotions regularly without fail, hold on to Radha Krishn and your Master, and be careful not to commit any spiritual transgressions. Bad days will pass, and good days will follow.**

(2) **Sensual attraction.** If you are married, keep your marital entertainments in moderation, do your devotions and increase your affinity for Radha Krishn. If you are single, and you want to remain single, and you have a deep desire to find God, you have a better chance to experience Divine love. But you must keep yourself away from the attraction of the opposite sex. Even among the devotees, try to be totally aloof from such situations, and keep yourself busy in your remembrance. Ved Vyas says,

"स्त्रीणां स्त्रीसंगिनां संगं त्यक्त्वा दूरत आत्मवान् । " (भा. 11/14/29)

**"The devotee, who has devoted his life for Krishn realization, must keep himself away from the associations of lustful people and from the attraction of the opposite sex." Because, if such an attraction turns into an emotional friendship of any limit, it instantly defaults the dedication and the sincerity of relational affinity with Radha Krishn.**

(3) **Fault finding.** People, also devotees, have a nature of not looking into their own faults but to recognize the faults of others. This habit must be avoided because, as soon as a devotee looks into the faults of other devotees, he, unknowingly, increases his subtle vanity that hampers his humbleness to that extent and, at the same time, his mind stops seeing its own fault, and thus, they are not reduced or removed. Instead, if he tries to see his own faults, his devotional humbleness will increase and his faults will slowly begin to disappear from his mind. It is the best attitude of a devotee to notice good qualities of other devotees and recognize his own faults and mistakes, and try to correct them.

Saints actions are Divine. They cannot be judged by material reasonings. They are only meant to Grace a soul; still, sometimes, some devotees feel critical to some extent about certain behavior of their own Master. If such ideas persist in the mind, this could be disastrous for devotion. Because, it is the constant flow of the loving Grace of the Divine Master which is felt as *bhao* (affinity) for Radha Krishn in the heart of the devotee, on the basis of his continuous love and dedication for his Master. So, when the sincerity of dedication is affected with adverse thoughts, the flow of Grace is affected and, consequently, the feeling of *bhao* is affected. If the devotee is dumb enough to persist on in his meaningless contradictory thoughts, he may enter into a kind of stressful and prejudicial mental state of unjoyousness. If it further persists for a long time, he may lose his devotional *bhao* and he may fall to any extent. It is thus wise to immediately repair and correct his thoughts and feelings by positive thinking.

A *rasik* Saint already has the Grace of Radha. He does not personally need anything for himself. If he is living in the world, it is only to Grace the souls. **If he accepts your service of any kind, it is only to Grace you. If he loves you or yells at you for any reason, it is also only to Grace you. Your ignorant mind may not understand some of his behavior, because they are beyond material logic, still they are only gracious and are the form of kindness.** His every move is the act of his inner kindness which can be clearly seen at the higher stages of *divine-love-consciousness*, but, at the lower stages of *bhao,* it should be taken and understood with faith. So, it is imperative for a devotee to have positive devotional thoughts all the time to ensure steady devotional progress in his life. **Remember the moments of love and kindness your Master has showered upon you. Even if he has lovingly placed his hand just once on your head, it is enough to remember his Grace and kindness, and be engrossed in the loving feelings of your beloved Master, for your whole life.**

4) **Pride, prejudicialness, inferiority complex, and personality problems.** Every soul has an inborn nature of pridefulness. But a

devotee has to overcome this weakness by maintaining devotional humbleness.

Humbleness cannot be imposed by mere thinking. It is also a natural quality of every soul which is related to *sattvagun,* and pridefulness is related to *rajogun* which is more predominant in a common person's life. All the three *gunas* remain in a person's heart and mind all the time, but, at one time, one of them remains predominant. In a worldly person, *rajogun* stays all the time in his mind and *sattvagun* appears very little. In a true devotee's mind, *sattvagun* stays most of the time and *rajogun* appears for a short time. There are varying degrees, intensities, and lengths of *sattvagun* and *rajogun* appearing in a person's mind that qualify his worldliness or his devotional consciousness.

At a higher stage, love, longing, affinity (*bhao*), and humbleness naturally reside in the heart of a devotee because they are the various forms of the same blissful flow of Radha Krishn love. But, in the beginning, before reaching that stage, a devotee has to carefully maintain these feelings by observing all the aspects of devotion.

Personal pride is sometimes very strong. Once a devotee was strongly told by his Master about his mistake which he repeatedly committed. The devotee, instead of correcting his mistake, felt personally offended, began to think negatively in his prideful mind, and thus, ruined his devotional life. Imagine, a soul has been unlimited times rebuked, insulted and corporally punished by worldly people in uncountable lifetimes; but he could not tolerate the kind admonition of a father-like Master which was for his own good. This is just the vainful pride of a person which is one of the strongest enemies of *bhakti.*

So, a devotee should be very careful not to let his humble mind sneak out into the *rajoguni* field of pridefulness. **You should know that a true Master showers his Grace upon all the souls in general, whoever comes to him. But, when a soul accepts him as** his Divine guide on the path to God, the Master begins to think about the devotee's spiritual welfare, and, in taking care of the devotee's devotional progress, the Master has to be strict at times, because souls are prone to be careless by nature since uncountable lifetimes. Whatever a Master does for his devotees is only out of his gracious kindness, otherwise why should a self-complacent personality, whose mind is drowned in Radha's love, even look towards any soul of this world?

**Prejudicialness and inferiority complex directly hits your devotion and causes discomfort to your Master.** Sometimes, to some people, it happens that after doing a lot of effort, positive results are not experienced in life, and the person becomes frustrated and prejudiced. He should know that such things are the outcome of his own bad *sanskars* and bad *karmas* of past life, which he himself has created. He should have patience. ( नीके दिन जब आइहैं फिरत न लागी बार l ) There is always moonlight after dark nights. Bad *sanskars* have a limit. When they finish, good days will come and glorify your days.

Some devotees, when they feel low, begin to think that they cannot do enough service, they are not intelligent enough to do right things, they are not very useful, they are not as good as other devotees are, etc., etc. Such feelings of inferiority complex must be avoided. They are the enemy of *bhakti.*

You should know that any kind of feeling of dejection or any kind of prejudicialness or any kind of depressing thought defaults the devotional flow and creates discomfort to your Master. Therefore, such feelings must be avoided. When you have given yourself in the hands of Radha Rani, Krishn and your beloved Master, then why to worry. Just feel blessed that you have found the path of *raganuga bhakti* (which thousands of other seekers of God are still searching for) and improve your personal weaknesses.

A few devotees have such personality problems that they cannot adjust with others. They should know that **forgiveness and doing** something good for other devotees has a very comforting effect in the heart. Try it. Everyone does everything for himself, if you do something good for others, it is quite consoling and, at the same time, it improves your humbleness which is the foundation of *bhakti*.

The most important thing to understand, is the preciousness of *bhao bhakti* and the Grace of your Master. This should not be sacrificed for trifling materiality and the mundaneness of one's own personal nature, weakness or ignorance.

(5) **Wrong association.** Association is of two kinds: physical, (the people you associate with), and mental (the literature you read or study). Try to avoid the association of such people who create conflict in your path of devotion even though they may be your friends or relatives. If it is unavoidable due to any reason, then, firmly and very politely, tell the person that this is your personal choice and that he or she should not bother to interfere with your spiritual way of life.

Mental association is all up to you. Read such spiritual books that help build your faith and devotion. Books on other topics like, rituals, *yog*, *vedant*, austerity, etc., are written with an entirely different point of view which deters from the style of *raganuga* devotion, so they should be avoided.

"सा विद्या तन्मतिर्यया" Whatever association (physical or mental) creates or may create a conflict, is to be avoided. It is called wrong association, and whatever association improves your dedication and feeling of love and longing for Radha Krishn, is to be honored, because it is good association.

These are the main obstacles on the path of devotion. **An intelligent devotee foresees the consequence of these adversities and, thus, wisely overcomes them when they come.**

There is one more thing. A devotee has to be careful not to associate in any form with any kind of *mayavadi* publications and propagations which are in abundance in the world.

## What is *mayavad?*

There are only two directions, towards *maya* and towards God. The first one is *mayavad,* and the second one is *bhagwadvad.* Although all the materialistic activities that induce material attachment are called *mayavad,* but this term mainly refers to such organizations which appear to be Godly (because they talk about *vedant, yog,* Gita, Bhagwatam, Upnishad etc.) but their effect is the stimulation of subtle vanity and pridefulness in the followers. The reason is that their promoters have worldly ambitions to gain popularity in the world. In the name of God they take you away from God. In the name of *bhakti* they introduce only formality, and in the name of *gyan* (knowledge) they induce only *agyan* (intellectual indulgence). How? It is very easy to understand.

Up till now you have already learned that *bhakti* is the only path to God and *bhakti* means the feeling of affinity which is experienced on the base of humbleness and relational closeness with your beloved form of God. Thus, (a) **humbleness,** (b) **affinity** and (c) **relational closeness** are the devotional elements that take you to God.

(a) **Pridefulness** of being a *Vaishnav* or a *sanyasi* or any such thing instead of humbleness, (b) mere **worshipping formalities** instead of true affinity, and (c) **worldly attachment** instead of the feeling of relational closeness with your beloved God, will take you away from God. Because: (a) **Vanity or pridefulness** tends towards showing the person's own significance, and his disregarding and criticizing mentality becomes a grave transgression (explained in Chapter 5). (b) All the **worshipping formalities** without true affinity and love for God are only good *karmas,* not devotion (explained in Chapter 5), and (c) **worldly attachment** along with religious practices of *jap,* meditation, *arti,* worship, fasting, recitation of Gita, Bhagwatam, Ramayanam, etc., without relational attachment with God, will either carry a worldly desire from God, or it will be a hypocritical demonstration to show his assumed religiousness in the public. In this way, all of these activities will form transgressional sanctimonious *sanskars* in the mind of the doer which may pollute his mind. So this is all *mayavad.*

Now it is clear. Don't go for the self-proclaimed credit of the promoter or teacher. Don't consider whether he is a *sanyasi* or a *Vaishnav* or anything else. Don't even think whether he is talking about the Gita or the Bhagwatam or promoting or representing any Hindu religion. Just look into him personally. If he is teaching pure devotion *(bhakti)* as described in the beginning of this chapter, and his followers and disciples have these virtues (humbleness, affinity, relational feeling and closeness with their adored form of God), that is correct. If not, then that is not a true spiritual mission; and if pridefulness, mere devotional formality, mechanical repetition of name, observing rituals, and no affinity or true relational feeling with Radha Krishn is seen, it is a pure *mayavadi* organization. It is a universal truth that a disciple is the reflection of his Master, and a follower receives the qualities of his teacher. When you are faithfully attached with someone, your attachment becomes a channel to receive the qualities of that person whatever he is in his heart (not whatever he says or does).

For the same reason, a dedicated devotee receives *bhao bhakti* from his *rasik* Saint Master, but the dedicated devotee of a sanctimonious teacher receives only a *rajoguni* feeling of self-superiority instead of Radha Krishn affinity, because his ambitious master or teacher is internally enjoying the delight of his ambitiousness through his religious propagations.

There are many organizations whose promoters have formulated their own ideology. Some of them take a few verses from our scriptures (which is of their own choice) and, in the pretense of Vedic philosophy, they promote their own concept. There are still some more who, disregarding our great *acharyas* and their teachings, create their own theory and create a new *mantra* and popularize their own belief. Such materialistic missions and organizations are always in abundance in every *kaliyug,* so it is nothing abnormal if they are in abundance nowadays. Our scriptures have already predicted about such happenings in *kaliyug*. ( दंभिन्ह निज मति कल्पि करि प्रगट किये बहु पंथ ॥ मारग सोइ जा कहँ जोइ भावा । पंडित सोइ जो गाल बजावा ॥ जो कर दम्भ सो बड़ आचारी ॥ सब नर कल्पित करहिं अचारा । जाइ न बरनि अनीति अपारा ॥ रामायण )

There is one more thing, that these *mayavadi* organizations have large followings and plenty of resources, because their ideology is soothing to egoistic and material minded people and boon seeking individuals whose field of attachment is not God, but their own personal world.

Remember this formula that **pride takes you away from God and humbleness brings you closer to God.** Singlemindedness in devotion ( अनन्यता ), affinity for your soul beloved God with relational feeling ( अनुराग ), and devotional humbleness ( दीनता ), is called *bhakti.* If it is not found in a religious organization, and religious showiness, or a showiness of worshipping acts and a feeling of self-superiority is there, then it is only *mayavad,* nicely wrapped in a fancy religious wrapper.

The ninth chapter tells about the fifteen important fallacies which are the product of ignorance. Read them carefully and keep them in mind. Now you have an instant measure of checking the authenticity of a spiritual path or a spiritual organization. If you find these fallacies in someone's literature or speeches, you should know that he is ignorant of scriptural and devotional truth. You will be surprised to discover that, beyond your expectations, a great number of them will fall in the same category. But truth is truth. **A true devotee should remain indifferent to them. He should not argue with them.** You must know that a God realized Saint does not make mistakes. Even the writings of less educated Saints like Meera Bai etc. reveal true devotional secrets.

**The Divineness of a Divine personality's words.** Mainly there are three kinds of people in the world: Saints, true devotees, and worldly people. **It is a general rule, that the action, behavior, writing and speech of a person imbues the quality of his inner personality** (Divine, devotional or materialistic). Accordingly the

Divine writings of *rasik* Saints have great devotional value because they represent the Divine love of Radha Krishn. All the *leela* songs (called *pad*) which they wrote, are like *mantras* for a devotee of Radha Krishn.

You should know that words on their own don't produce the effect, but the imbued energy and the force which is behind it, produces its effect on the mind of the one who uses it. For instance: a Saint of Vrindaban *bhao* is singing or writing a *leela* song. While doing so he is actually seeing the *leela* of Radha Krishn. So, each and every word of that writing is imbued with Divine love, which, when used by a devotee for his devotion, produces pure devotional effects on his mind. Another person, desiring his popularity, also writes a similar song about Radha Krishn, but the words of his song contain materialistic characteristics only, because the writer is an ambitious material being.

Take another example of a very popular chanting, "Radhey Rani ki jai, Maharani ki jai..." A Saint also sings the same chant with his heart filled with the Divine love of Shree Radhey. A true devotee of Radha Krishn sings that chant with a deep loving desire to visualize Their Divine form. A religious and honest professional, with better music and voice, sings it with a desire to sell it (in a cassette form) and make money out of it, and an ambitious religious teacher, with an ambition of getting immediate popularity, sings it to influence the audience.

Suppose, a recording of the chant is made of all the four kinds of people and is available for listening. The first two have devotional value as they are filled with love and longing for Radha Krishn. If you listen to such chants and speeches, your heart and mind will be gradually purified and your devotional qualities will increase. The third one may be pleasing to the ears but it has no devotional value, because the voice behind it had no devotional attitude. The fourth one has negative effects imbued in it because it contains the sanctimoniousness of the singer's heart. If you regularly listen to the chant or speech of such a person, **your**

material attachments will stabilize instead of being reduced and a consciousness of self-superiority will develop in your heart that you are better than others. Such a practice will increase the impurity of the mind, harden the heart more and more, and a time may come when your heart and mind may become totally unreceptive to correct devotional advice.

You must know that true devotion softens the heart, improves humbleness, and fills your heart with the true longing for Radha Krishn that increases your confidence and brings Them closer to you. **It is thus advised that the chantings, speeches and reading material etc., whatever you use to uplift your devotion and dedication, must be imbued with pure devotional attributes.**

## (2) Bliss of the name and Grace.

### How to experience the bliss of the name, and how to experience affinity for Radha Krishn?

Name is blissful, but its blissfulness remains hidden unless it is experienced. For example, Saints say that Radha's vision and 'Radha' name is equally blissful. It means, the loving experience you could have by seeing Radha is the same as saying 'Radha.'

There is nothing in the world like this, otherwise you would say 'pizza' and the full flavored taste of pizza would appear in your mouth. In this world, words are just the sounds to indicate a situation, object or a living thing, created and improved and collected in the dictionary by the people of a particular country as their civilization progressively evolved and their scientific and technical knowledge advanced. But, in the Divine world, the 'name' is a Divine power, and thus, the 'name' and 'form' are synonymously one and eternal.

Now the question is, how to experience the bliss or the sweetness of the Divine name? This could only happen when you develop a true relational affinity with Radha Krishn. Only then you could feel the loving sweetness in the remembrance of Their name, *leelas* and virtues.

It is seen that even after doing conventional devotions for a long time according to the system of the existing Krishn religions, people do not experience the real relational affinity with Radha Krishn. The Bhakti Rasayan answers this question. It says,

"प्रथमं महतां सेवां तद्यापात्रता ततः ।
श्रद्धाथतेषान्धर्मेषु ततो हरिगुणश्रुतिः ॥ 34 ॥"
"ततो रत्यङ्कुरोत्पत्तिस्स्वरूपाधिगतिस्ततः ।
प्रेमवृद्धिः परानन्दे तस्याथ स्फुरणन्ततः ॥ 35 ॥"

Other scriptures also say,

"भक्तिस्तु भगवद्भक्तसंगेन परिजायते ।
सत्संगः प्राप्यते पुम्भिः सुकृतैः पूर्वसंचितैः ॥" (वृहन्नारदीय पु.)
"आदौ श्रद्धा ततो साधुसंगोऽथ भजनक्रिया ।" (रूप गोस्वामी)
"रे मन रसिकन संग बिनु रंच न उपजै प्रेम ।
या रस को साधन यहै और करौ जनि नेम ॥" (ध्रुव दास)
"सतां प्रसंगात्... तज्जोषणादाश्वपवर्गवर्त्मनि
श्रद्धारतिर्भक्तिरनुक्रमिष्यति ॥" (भा.)
"नाम्नामकारि बहुधा निजसर्वशक्तिः
तत्रार्पिता नियमतः स्मरणे न कालः ।
एतादृशी तव कृपा भगवन्ममापि-
दुर्दैवमीदृशमिहाजनि नानुरागः ॥" (गौ. महा.)
"यस्य देवे परा भक्तिर्यथा देवे तथा गुरौ ॥" (श्वे. 6/23)
"प्रणिपातेन परिप्रश्नेन सेवया । उपदेक्ष्यंति... ॥" (गी.)
"प्रथम सुने भागवत भक्त मुख भगवत वाणी ।
द्वितीय अराधे भक्ति व्यास नव भांति बखानी ॥
तृतीय करे गुरु सेवन होय सर्वज्ञ रसीलो ।
चौथे होय विरक्त बसै बनराज रसीलो ॥
पांचे भूलै देह सुधि तब छठी भावना रास की ।
सातें पावै रीति रस श्रीस्वामी हरिदास की ॥" (स्वामी हरिदास)

In general, it means that a devotee, who is deeply desiring to receive the vision of Radha Krishn, receives such an affinity called *bhao* or *bhao bhakti* with the Grace of a *rasik* Saint, not from his own doings. Bhakti Rasayan analyzes this situation and says that first you should have a deep desire to meet Radha Krishn. Then faithfully accept the discipleship and be in the service of a *rasik* saint. Then, with his Grace, experience *bhao*. This is the sequence. All the scriptures said the same thing in their own words.

Mahaprabhuji indicates the obstinacy of past and present lives' spiritual transgressions of a devotee by the word '*durdaio*' (misfortune) in the Shikchashtak, which blocks his heart from experiencing the relational closeness (*bhao*) with Radha Krishn (the detail of spiritual transgressions is in Chapter 6). This is the reason why a devotee, on his own, cannot undo his own misfortune (*durdaio*). He needs Divine help, and that's what Radha Rani provides in the form of a living Saint on this earth whose Grace opens up the heart of a selfless and truly dedicated devotee, and the devotee begins to feel devotional affinity.

The Grace of Shree Raseshwari Radha Rani is always available. It is up to you to be wholeheartedly desiring for Her Grace with firm determination and hope. Then it is not very long when a Saint will come into your life; and, if you intelligently dedicate yourself and join your heart and mind in faith and confidence with him, his Grace will automatically flow into your heart. Just like, when you join the wiring of your house with the mains you get the electricity, but not before that, even if the main power line is very close to your house. **Faith and dedication are the joining factors, and doubt or confusion or faithlessness of any extent are the prohibiting factors.** Thus, when you join your heart and mind with the heart of the Saint, his Grace enters your heart. So, your experiences of *bhao* are, in fact, the transmuted Grace of your Master. How much the Grace is received, depends upon many factors, like: the devotee's past *sanskars* (good and bad), present state of devotion, dedication, servitude, humbleness, worldly attachments, personal commitments, the way of his living, his associations and worldly affiliations, etc.

## What is Grace?

God Himself is Grace. He is the form of Bliss, Knowledge and Grace. All these three together are the personality of God. It is the power of Grace that, (a) makes a Saint equal to God in experiencing the Divine Bliss of that abode, (b) makes the descension of Ram and Krishn to happen ( मुख्यं तस्य हि कारुण्यम् ), (c) sends eternal Saints on the earth planet to help and guide the souls to God, (d) creates the universe and enlivens the souls, (e) reveals the Vedas and the scriptures, (f) makes other occasional descensions of God to happen, like Ved Vyas etc., (g) reveals the Divine vision and Divine love of God to a devotee on complete purification of his heart, and much more.

In Chapter 4, it is explained that the absolute supreme personality of *brahm* is Radha, the *Mahabhao*, Whose other form is Krishn. Thus Radha Krishn are the absolute form of Grace and absolute form of *guru tattva*. So it is said, कृष्णं वन्दे जगद्गुरुम् , "salutations to *Jagadguru* (the supreme spiritual Master of the world) Krishn." The Divine power that reveals God to a soul is called *Guru tattva* which is just a gracious act of the power of Grace. Thus, Gracing a soul with *bhao bhakti* in his devotional period by a Saint, and, at the end, Gracing him with the Divine Vision, is the act of '*guru tattva*'. The power of Grace and *guru tattva* is the same which is greatly praised in all the scriptures. Saints represent the Grace and Bliss of God on the earth planet, so they are also called '*guru*' or the 'form' of Grace. ( सबै संत गुरुदेव हैं व्यास हिये परतीति । )

The Grace of Krishn is the glory of Radha's Grace, and the Grace of Radha Krishn glorifies the other forms of God and Their abodes, but the superiority and the powerfulness of the power of Grace relates to the sequence of the Blissful superiority of the forms of God and Their abodes.

Ved Vyas revealed this deep secret with a Divine act so that a common man can also understand the superiority of various forms of Divine Grace. He enlivened two verses of the Bhagwatam with the Grace of Krishn of Golok and asked one of his disciples to go and sing them where his son Shukdeo was lying in impermeable Divine (*brahm-leen*) *samadhi* for a number of years. The disciple went to Shukdeo, sang the verses, and he was astonished to see that the sound of the (Divinely Graced) verses intervened the Divine *samadhi* of Shukdeo and he opened his eyes. The reason was, that the Blissful graciousness of the verses (of Krishn virtues) was much superior to the Divine Blissfulness of the *samadhi* which he already had. It was like replacing the raw candy which was in his mouth with the finest Swiss chocolate.

The Divine Bliss and Grace is one kind of power with its two aspects, and it always relates to a personal form of God. Its introducing aspect is called 'Grace' and its experiencing aspect is called 'Bliss'. Bliss also includes the Divine knowledge. For instance: the Grace of Vishnu reveals the Bliss of Vaikunth, or you can say that Vishnu Graces His devotees with His Divine knowledge, vision and Bliss. Similarly, the Grace of Bhagwan Ram reveals the Bliss and Knowledge of Saket; the Grace of Dwarikadhish reveals the Bliss and knowledge of Dwarika abode, and so on. The personality of God is a particular form of Grace, Bliss and knowledge (कृपा, आनन्द, ज्ञान। चिदानन्दमय देह तुम्हारी।), and His abode is the expansion of His own personality which has the same class of Divine Blissfulness. This is the reason that an almighty form of God cannot reveal the Bliss and knowledge of the Divine love form of God to a soul. So, God Vishnu can only reveal the Bliss of His own abode Vaikunth, not of Saket or any other abode, and so on.

Similarly, a Shiv *Bhakt* (Saint) can Grace his devotee only with the Bliss of Shiv, a Vishnu *Bhakt* with the Bliss of Vishnu, and a Krishn *Bhakt* with the Bliss of Krishn. But when a highly evolved Shiv devotee or a Vishnu devotee or the devotee of any other form of God or Goddess faithfully comes in contact with a Krishn *Bhakt*, his devotional feelings are automatically elevated.

So, from his own experience, he could see the superiority of Krishn love. Roop Goswami says,

"तत्र गीतादिषूक्तानां चतुर्णमधिकारिणाम् ।
मध्ये यस्मिन् भगवतः कृपा स्यात्तत्प्रियस्य वा ॥
स क्षीणतत्तदभावः स्याच्छुद्धभक्त्यधिकारवान् ।
यथेभः शौनकादिश्च ध्रुवः स च चतुःसनः ॥ " (भ.र.सिं. 1/2/21-22)

"The devotee who singlemindedly and wholeheartedly worships God with some kind of worldly desire in his heart (like *Bhakt* Dhruv), when he comes in contact with a *rasik* Saint and receives his Grace, his previous form of devotion fades out, and in its place, remains pure Krishn devotion. Even a *gyani* Saint, who is absorbed in (*brahmanand*) the Bliss of the impersonal form of God, when he luckily encounters a *rasik* Saint and receives his Grace, his experience of *brahmanand* disappears, and in its place, remains the loving experience of Krishn Bliss. The same thing happens to *gyani* Saints and the other devotees of God when they happen to come to Braj (during the descension period) and receive the direct Grace of Radha Krishn."

# (3) Receiving Grace.

## How does a Saint impart his Grace?

Saint is a living form of Divine Bliss and Grace of that form of God which he has attained. So, receiving the blessings or Grace of a Saint is not a just a customary act as people normally think. You have to deserve to receive it.

A long time ago, when I first started to give discourses on *divine-love-consciousness*, I was still unaware of local worldly customs because I had remained introverted for almost my whole life in the thoughts of God. Once, in Bombay, I was sitting alone on the beach when a young couple suddenly appeared and produced a young baby in front of me, which they carried in a basket, and requested me to bless the child. I didn't know what to do. I just casually asked, "What kind of blessing do you want, do you want your child to become a Krishn devotee or a *sanyasi* or what?" The father hastily said, "No, no, no, nothing of that kind, please just place your hand on his head, that's all." I did so, he felt happy, and left immediately. I came back to where I stayed and told about the little incident to my devotees. They said, "People believe that if a Saint places his hand on the child, it will bring prosperity in his life."

It is a fact that the majority of people don't want God, they only want blessings for their material prosperity. It took me a few years to understand the nature and the behavior of worldly people. The insincerity of their promises, the deceitfulness of their friendliness, and the sanctimoniousness of their worship to God were all alien to me, because I was used to trusting what a person confessed.

However, you should know that the blessings of a Saint are only for the devotional upliftment of a devotee, and those blessings come from his heart. But you have to qualify yourself to receive his blessings and Grace.

" एवंव्रत: स्वप्रियनामकीर्त्या जातानुरागो द्रुतचित्त उच्चै: ।
हसत्यथो रोदिति रौति गायत्युन्मादवन्नृत्यति लोकबाह्य: ॥
वाग् गद्गदा द्रवते यस्य चित्तं रुदत्यभीक्ष्णं हसति क्वचिच्च ।
विलज्ज उद्गायति नृत्यते च मद्भक्तियुक्तो भुवनं पुनाति ॥ " (भा. 11/14/24)

The Bhagwatam says, "The Divine expressions of *bhao* in the ecstatic state of Divine love are seen in a Saint, from time to time, while talking about Radha or Krishn, or chanting, listening, and telling the virtues, names and *leelas* of Radha Krishn. Sometimes he has tears in his eyes, sometimes he smiles, sometimes he laughs, sometimes he feels separation and sometimes he feels very close to Radha Krishn, sometimes he is still, sometimes he faints, sometimes he loudly or softly says Radhey Radhey or Krishn Krishn, and sometimes he ecstatically dances. Such a Saint sanctifies the place where he lives, and glorifies the whole world."

Such a Saint Graces the souls in many ways.

**(1) By his presence.** It is a common axiom that everything has a radiation. A human being has three kinds of radiations: (a) bodily radiation, (b) brain waves, and (c) mental quality (*sattva, raj, tam* or devotional). A Saint has Divine radiation from his whole being that makes the surroundings Divinely virtuous which could be felt by any faithful and open hearted devotee to the extent of his own devotional receptivity.

**(2) Speech.** There are always sanctimoniously oriented religious missions in the world that misguide the souls and corrupt the true Divine teachings by introducing their own system of faith; and there are also true Divine missions that truly guide the souls to God. There is a cycle of four *yugas* called, *satyug, tretayug, dwaparyug* and *kaliyug.* In *satyug,* such worldly missions are very few and the Divine missions are in abundance. In *tretayug,* the number of worldly missions increase. In *dwaparyug*, it comes to fifty-fifty, and in *kaliyug* (the present age), the worldly missions grow in abundance, leaving a few Divine missions. This fact has already been explained by Ved Vyas in the Padm Puran.

"न हि वैष्णवता कुत्र सम्प्रदायपुरस्सराः ।
एवं प्रलयतां प्राप्तो वस्तुसारः स्थले स्थले ॥ " (पद्म पुराण)

**A Saint re-establishes the Divine truth of *bhakti* and shows the correct path to God through his speeches and writings.**

**(3) Instructions.** When a soul understands the importance of God realization, comes to a Saint and accepts him as his Divine guardian, the Saint explains to him the 'procedure of devotion' and also keeps on giving him personal and devotional instructions, from time to time, for his spiritual welfare. This is all his Grace. Every instruction of a Saint follows his Grace.

**(4) By accepting service.** Service is done in three ways, physical, mental and monetary (तन, मन, धन). Dedication and doing devotion is called mental service. Service is the direct means of receiving the Grace of your Master, and, 'following the advice and instructions of the Master' is the best service which a devotee could do ( आज्ञा सम न सुसाहिब सेवा ).

Dedication, devotion, physically doing some service in the *ashram,* and monetarily serving the *ashram* and the Divine mission of your Master, are all forms of service. **A *rasik* Saint does not personally need anything for himself because he is directly under the care of Sarveshwari Radha Rani and Krishn, but he accepts the services of his devotees because they are the tokens of their love. This loving offering automatically attracts the Grace of the Master.**

(5) **Blessings.** Blessings of a Saint are mainly of four kinds: **general, occasional, personal and special**. In general, he blesses all the souls who come into his contact, by his presence and teachings. Sometimes if some soul wants some guidance in his existing style of religious practice, he explains the Divine truth to him. Sometimes someone wants to do some voluntary service or donation for his mission, which he accepts. These kinds of occasional instances of Grace are also seen.

Grace or blessing of a Saint is the same thing. It is his gracious affectionate feeling for a soul or a devotee which is called the 'blessing'. Generally a Saint thinks good for all the souls. But, when a person firmly and faithfully joins his heart and mind with the heart of the Saint and desires to receive the love of Radha Krishn, he then becomes a devotee. All such devotees are like children of their Spiritual Father in a big spiritual family, so he personally cares for them.

**According to the faith and love of a devotee for his Master, the Master also thinks of him lovingly which becomes a Divine boon for the devotee, because the loving thoughts of a Saint contain Blissful Divine power that reaches the heart of the devotee as the Divine blessings of his Master.**

A Master keeps on blessing his devotees all the time, and a devotee could receive such Divine blessings while being anywhere in the world. Distance makes no difference. So it is up to you how much you keep your Master happy by your humble love for him, and how much you receive his favor, Grace and blessings, and how much you win his confidence in you.

At the final stage of heart purification, your Divine *rasik* Master will specially Grace you with the Love and Vision of Radha Krishn. This final and special Grace is called '*prem dan*' that reveals the Divine *prema bhakti*, the Bliss of the *raas ras* of Divine Vrindaban.

## Devotion and service.

In the early stages of devotion, all three kinds of services (as described above) play the most important part of devotion. For instance: (a) All the efforts and physical and mental involvements, that took place in earning that money which you offered for the *ashram* or for the promotion of *divine-love-consciousness,* becomes pure devotion. (b) All the physical services you do for the *ashram* or for the promotion of *divine-love-consciousness,* are also counted as pure devotion in the Divine records.

Except for a highly evolved devotee, it is very difficult to do chanting, remembrance or meditation for a long time. The rest of the twenty-four hours you have to spend in such a way that they should not create worldly *sanskars* in the mind. So, this is the only way to maintain the devotional credit most of the time, to involve yourself in any kind of physical or monetary service which equals to your regular devotions.

One more thing, when you are doing such service that directly involves the working of the mission, you also attract the direct attention of your Master which is in your favor. So, those who understand the value of service, they make it the prime aim of their life. **Service quickly purifies the heart, brings you closer to your beloved Master and Radha Krishn,** and releases your worldly attachments which are the prime obstacles of selfless devotion.

There are a few suggestions to make the service more valuable and effective. While doing any kind of service you should frequently keep on remembering your Master or Radha Krishn close to you even for a short period of time, maybe a few seconds or a few minutes. Also, service is not a job to do, it is devotion. Any kind of service is just devotion. It stabilizes your humbleness.

In return of our services what we receive is beyond words to explain. We have a material body and mind. If a Saint accepts our services and rewards it with *bhao bhakti,* what could be better than that. There is nothing in the whole of the universe that compares to the Grace of a Saint. This is only the Grace of the Master that shines in the heart of a devotee as the blissful experience of Radha Krishn love.

# (4) Devotional theory at a glance.

🦚

## Summarizing the practical form of devotion.

There are six main things to remember and to observe: (1) Maintain the feeling of your eternal relationship with Radha Krishn as a deep affinity in your heart, all the time ( धारणा ). (2) Do your regular devotions without fail ( साधना ). (3) Keep your mind devotionally absorbed and remember Radha, Krishn, or your Master (singly or any combination) always near you (समाहितावस्था). (4) Recognize the Grace of your Master, that whatever devotional experience you have received is all because of his Grace and kindness ( कृपानुभव ). (5) Keep yourself away from all kinds of wrong associations (कुसंग त्याग), and (6) have faith in the gracious kindness of your Divine beloved and eternal friend Radha Krishn and your Master, and never let any kind of disappointing thoughts enter your mind ( विश्वास ). **Why to worry when you've given your hand in the hands of Radha Krishn.**

**While doing your regular devotion,** the first thing you should do is to feel that you are sitting in the Divine abode of Raseshwari Radha Rani and Krishn, and there you are chanting or remembering Their name and seeing Their *leelas*. Keep your eyes closed (or open as you prefer) during devotion, recognize the feeling of love and affinity in your heart, feel the presence of Radha or Krishn or Both near you, try to keep yourself unaware of the disturbances of the surroundings if any, and engross yourself in devotion. That is how regular devotion should be done.

**'The name Radhey is Radha Herself ,' and so is Krishn. If you just realize this truth, it is enough to explode your feelings of love for Her and to really feel Her presence in front of you...**

A *rasik* Saint says,

" अनाराध्य राधापदाम्भोजयुग्ममनासेव्य वृन्दाटवीं तत्पदाङ्कम् ।
असंभाष्य तद्भावगंभीरचित्तान् कथं श्यामसिन्धोरसस्यावगाहः ॥ "

"If you have not adored the loving lotus feet of Shree Radha, if your heart and mind does not reside in Vrindaban which was ornamented by the footprints of Raseshwari Radha Rani during *maharaas* while dancing with Krishn, and if you have not served and received the Grace of such *rasik* Saints of Braj whose heart is the abode of Shree Radhey; how could you taste the blissful lusciousness of the ocean of Krishn love, which is the glory of Radha's own personality?"

# 8.
# Kinds, Classes and Nature of Saints.

## (1) The prominent Divine Personalities.

God and Saints are Divine and so are Their definitions. We are going to write simple historical facts and the general nature of Saints that would enable a faithful person to understand the qualities of a Saint.

### The prominent Divine Personalities of the last three thousand years.

In the last three thousand years the most prominent Saints were the five *acharyas* (Shankaracharya, Nimbarkacharya, Ramanujacharya, Madhvacharya, and Vallabhacharya), Chaitanya Mahaprabhu and his main disciples Roop, Sanatan, and Jeev Goswami, and also Swami Haridas and Hit Harivansh. Shree Chaitanya Mahaprabhu who was the descension of Radha Herself, appeared to establish the discipline of divine-love-devotion (*bhakti*), so he acted like a Krishn devotee. The other Saints were the descended eternal Saints. Apart from that, there were hundreds of Saints during that period, glorifying the various parts of India, like, Goswami Tulsidas, Guru Nanak, Tukaram, Narsi Mehta, Meera Bai, Vishnu Swami, etc.

# (2) General nature and behavior of Saints.

## General nature.

All of these Saints lived like a normal person. They remained absorbed in the love of their Beloved God. They were never in the habit of showing cheap miracles or showing their self-superiority, always remained humble, never introduced a new *mantra* or a new form of God or a new concept of God, and never gave a secret *mantra* or a secret initiation to a devotee; rather they said that every name of God is equally Divine and potent. The most important thing is that they never introduced their own theory of God. They followed the guidelines of our eternal scriptures: the Upnishads, the Gita and the Bhagwatam. Even Chaitanya Mahaprabhu, the descension of God, followed the guidelines of the Bhagwatam in teaching the form and devotion to Krishn.

## They introduced *bhakti* (*divine-love-consciousness*).

The philosophical description of soul, *maya,* God, Bhagwan, Krishn *tattva,* and *bhakti tattva,* etc., is extensively explained in the writings of the main *acharyas* in a traditional style, but their devotional teachings are very simple and similar.

Shankaracharya says, *'tawaham,'* "O Krishn! I am Yours. Please make me Your own and Grace me with Your love." Ramanujacharya says that *'prapatti'* introduces the Grace of God. *Prapatti* means total submission of heart and mind to serve Him and to be with Him in His Divine abode. Madhvacharya says the same thing, to fully surrender to God and do *bhakti* because He is the only one who is truly yours. Vallabhacharya's introduction of *'pushti,'* Nimbarkacharya's 'devotional meditation of serving Radha Krishn (अष्टयाम सेवा),' Hit Harivansh and Haridas Swami's 'remembrance' of Radha Krishn's *nikunj leelas* with a desire to become an associate in Their Divine *leelas,* and Chaitanya Mahaprabhuji's emphasis on the 'chanting of Krishn name' while meditating on His form and *leelas* with love and longing, are all various procedures and styles of doing *'bhakti,'* which **ISDL introduces as *'divine-love-consciousness.'***

## They did not teach *yogic* style techniques of meditation which are done in the forehead area.

These great Masters never introduced such techniques of meditation, either in general or to their disciples. Technical meditations are based on intellectual thinking in a contemplating, beholding or observing manner, and they can only be good enough for temporary peace of mind or reducing some stress of modern living.

Techniques relate to the *mayic* field only. They never even touch the Divine field, and the most authentic evidence of this statement is the Yog Sutra itself which describes that the procedure of *samadhi* is only to purify the heart.

*Brahm* realization of a *yogi* happens only when he faithfully surrenders to a personal form of God. That is why our historical *Gyanis* emphasized on surrendering to God along with the practice of *samadhi*. The most renowned *Yogi* Shankaracharya opens his heart and says that without devotion to Krishn, the heart cannot be fully purified (शुद्ध्यति हि नान्तरात्मा कृष्णपदाम्भोजभक्तिमृते ।).

## They showed the path of *bhakti* only to their adored form of God. They did not teach rituals or *mantras* for family prosperity.

One should know that the personality of a true Saint is synonymous to the Blissful form of God he has attained, although he gives respect to all the forms of God. So he teaches devotion to that form of God which is in his heart. That's why when Meera Bai was asked to worship Goddess Gauri by her family members, she said that she did not know anything or anyone except her Giridhar Gopal Krishn.

All of our historical Saints propagated and taught the devotion of the same form of God they had attained. For instance: A person, desiring to visualize God Shiv, goes to Tulsidasji and requests him to show the path to God Shiv. Tulsidasji, a devotee of Bhagwan Ram, would say that he can only teach him the *bhakti* of Bhagwan Ram. Suppose that person goes to Vrindaban to Swami Haridas and asks the same thing. Haridasji would say, "My child! The love of Radha Krishn has fascinated my heart so much that I don't see anything but the *leelas* of Radha Krishn. I can only bless you with Their love. I have nothing else." Now the person has only two choices, either he finds a Shiv *bhakt* Saint or he accepts Krishn devotion.

So we see that a Saint shows the path of *bhakti* to his own adored form of God only. He does not give *mantras* of every form of God to worship. It does not mean that multiform devotion to God cannot be done. It could be done, but, in that case, that devotion will be classified as 'good deed' not *bhakti*. *Bhakti* is always singleminded (अनन्याश्चिन्तयन्तो माम्).

A Saint does not teach or involve himself in any kind of rituals or any type of fortune telling activities. He teaches pure *bhakti*.

**There is a definite universal Divine system of: (a) submission, service and devotion of a devotee, and (b) receiving the Grace of God through a Saint. Divine experiences cannot be randomly obtained. One has to follow the Divine rules if he desires to experience God's love.**

## How did they initiate?

The actual word is '*deekcha*' ( दीक्षा ). The nearest word in English is initiation. *Dikcha* literally means to impart devotional feelings (or experiences) in the heart of the devotee disciple. The procedure is very simple: (1) dedication of the devotee, (2) acceptance by the Saint, and then (3) the Saint teaches the method of devotional remembrance.

Take an example: A devotee comes to Chaitanya Mahaprabhu, dedicates himself, asks for Divine guidance and desires to become his disciple. Mahaprabhuji, seeing his sincere desire to find Krishn,

internally accepts his request, and teaches him how to remember Krishn's name in his heart all the time and how to do the chanting. That's all.

**This is called initiation.** Nothing much happened outwardly. The devotee did not receive any secret word, or a secret name, or a secret *mantra* from Mahaprabhuji. The same name and form of Radha Krishn, which he already knew, was again told to him in a systematic manner with Divine blessings. **But internally there was a big difference. The devotee received the Divine blessings of Mahaprabhuji which was very special to him. It changed his life. He received devotional feelings in his heart instantly when he was taught the procedure of devotion.** It is like an orphan, who already had a place to live and food to eat, has now found a home where he can call someone his 'father' who personally cares for him.

When a Saint gives devotional instructions, he includes his Grace with it which is instantly experienced by the disciple as a kind of affinity for Radha Krishn.

## (3) Kinds and classes of Saints.

### Kinds of Saints.

In every abode of God there are such Saints who are with God since eternity. They are called 'eternal associates' of God *(nitya siddha mahapurush)*. Then there are such Saints who were ordinary souls at one time, but, after understanding the importance of God realization, did *bhakti,* purified their heart, and, with the Divine Grace of God and the Master, they became Saints and entered the Divine abode. These Saints are called 'general associates' of God *(sadhan siddha mahapurush)*. Both kinds of Saints are unlimited in number, and are in all the abodes of all the forms of God.

Sometimes, with God's will, certain eternal associates descend on the earth planet to show the path to God and to establish *divine-love-consciousness (bhakti)* in the world. All the *acharyas* were the descended associates (Saints). Some souls, who receive God realization, also live here for some time. Thus, both kinds of Saints live on the earth planet and help the souls in following the path to God.

There are many categories of Saints in every Divine abode. The discrimination of their categories depends upon the closeness of their service in the Divine abode. It is all described in our scriptures.

## Classes of Saints.

There are two main classes of Saints, *gyani* Saints and *bhakt* Saints. *Gyani* Saints are those who have attained *nirakar brahm* (the formless aspect of God). The theory of Saints and God is very extensive, but, for our general understanding, we should know that *bhakt* Saints are those who adore a personal form of God. *Bhakt* Saints are of two kinds, *bhakt* Saints and *rasik* Saints. Worshippers of almighty forms of God (like Vishnu, Shiv, Durga, etc.) are called *bhakt* Saints, and those who worship Divine love forms of God are called *rasik* Saints. Thus the *rasik* Saints of Vrindaban who revealed the topmost secret of the Upnishads, the *leelas* of Radha Krishn, and showed us the path of *raganuga bhakti*, are of the highest kind.

## (4) Recognition.

## Recognition of a Saint.

A Saint cannot be recognized through intellectual application, because the Divine qualities of a Saint are hidden inside his personality and his outer appearance is like a normal person. **Just like a mother is recognized with the eyes of a son, a Saint could be recognized with the eyes of such an open-minded devotee who is**

longing to find God and desiring to meet a Divine guardian (Saint)
who could show him the path of Divine love.

Normally people's minds are not fair or equitable. They have
created their own theory about God, Saint and devotion as they
have read in various books which have confused their minds. This
situation creates difficulty in finding the right path. But, the
descriptions in this chapter will give an open-minded person enough
understanding, so that he can recognize his Divine guide and
proceed on the path to God.

**The most important thing is that a true Spiritual Master
(Saint) comes into the life of a devotee with the Grace of God
which is activated by his sincere yearning for Him.** It means you
cannot go around the world looking for a Saint who can Grace you
with God's vision. **The procedure is like this:** (1) The person
desiring God's love must increase his longing for God on his own.
(2) He should then keep desiring from God that He should send
one of His Saints in his life. (3) Then, with the Grace of God, the
faithful devotee will find some Saint, who he may recognize to
some extent on the basis of his selfless and sincere longing for
God's vision.

## Who could be your Divine Guide?

A soul earnestly desiring for the vision of God attracts His
Grace and it is very likely that he may find a true Divine guide
(Saint), but it is also possible that his humble ignorance, out of his
naiveness, may develop faith for a person of sanctimoniously
refined behavior. This situation will ruin his devotional progress
and stimulate his hidden (and inherent) pridefulness. Considering
this hazard, Vallabhacharya ordains,

" कृष्णसेवापरं वीक्ष्य दम्भादिरहितं नरम् ।
श्रीभागवततत्त्वज्ञं भजेज्जिज्ञासुरादरात् ॥ " (सर्वनिर्णय प्रकरण 227)

"A devotee, aspiring for Krishn love, should dedicate himself
only to such a Krishn *bhakt* Saint who has conceived the theme

and Bliss of the Bhagwatam in his heart and who is deeply absorbed in (Radha) Krishn love, not just ceremoniously acting to be a *Vaishnav.* When you find such a Saint, serve him and adore him wholeheartedly. His Grace will sprout the love of Radha Krishn in your heart."

' सेवापरम् *seva param*' word in this verse refers to the Divine state of Krishn love. '*Seva*' means *bhakti* ( भज् सेवायां धातु ), 'Krishn *seva*' means the Divine *bhakti* (भजनं भक्ति:) of Krishn. So, 'Krishn *seva param*' does not only mean the worship of Krishn's Deity as some people translate, it means such a *bhakt* Saint who has attained the Divine love of Krishn, and who is absorbed in the service of his Divine beloved Krishn. It means, the one who is absorbed in Krishn love. ' वीक्ष्य *veekchya*' word means 'having observed,' which is not possible for a material mind to observe the Divineness of a Saint. But one thing is possible. A *rasik* Saint holds the infinite love of Radha Krishn in his heart all the time. Sometimes it happens that such a love overwhelms his consciousness which physically shows up as 'Divine expressions' (explained in Chapter 6). That could be observed by the humble and faithful eyes of a devotee, and if the devotee closely associates with such a Saint, his faithful heart may also feel the warmth of Radha Krishn love just by being near him. This is what Vallabhacharya means by कृष्णसेवापरं वीक्ष्य .

The term " दम्भादि रहितं नरम् " explains that the devotee must be careful not to involve himself with any of the *mayavadi* preachers and their ideologies. He should keep himself away from such people whose hearts are bereft of Krishn love, but they put on a *Vaishnav*-like or a *bhakt*-like appearance. They may talk about the Gita and the Bhagwatam, but all of their misleading and sanctimonious behavior becomes spiritual transgression which throws them into the *mayic* darkness after death, and the same thing happens to their faithful followers because they also commit transgressions by following them. ( मामप्राप्यैव कौन्तेय ततो यान्त्यधमां गतिम् । गी. ॥ ततो भूय इव ते तमो य उ सम्भूल्या<sub>ः</sub> रता: । ईश. ॥ ) Goswami Tulsidas relates this situation and says, " गुरु शिष अन्ध बधिर कर लेखा । एक न सुनइ एक नहिं देखा ॥ " It means that such a person, who exploits the faith of innocent God-fearing people, is so much *blinded* with his own transgressions and profane vanity that he is not observing his own dark destiny. Also, his followers are so *deaf* that they don't listen or heed to the correct teaching of selfless loving devotion to Radha Krishn, because their minds are conditioned with wrong beliefs. They blindly follow him, and thus, enter into deep *mayic* darkness. The Upnishad paraphrases this as " अन्धेनैव नीयमाना यथान्धा: ! " which tells in a story form, that an ambitious and clever blind person lied to other blind people and told them to follow him. He pretended to have gained the eyesight. All the unintelligent blind people faithfully followed him and ended up into a deep ditch, because their leader was also blind.

Ramanujacharya openly asserted to this fact that a seeker of God's love must surrender only to such a Saint who is absorbed in God's love. He further advised that an aspirant of God's love may humbly leave his previous *gurus* if any, who do not teach selfless devotion to God, or who are not deeply engrossed in God's love, or whose association does not sprout the true humble affinity for your beloved God and reduce your worldly attachments. Ramanujacharya himself practiced this theme in his life and, respectfully detaching himself from his first Master, accepted Yamunacharya as his prime Master, surrendered to him and delivered the message of selfless loving devotion to God to the world.

Chaitanya Mahaprabhuji says ( ...तत्राग्रहो नापर: ) that you should desire for the highest form of Krishn love which is seen in Divine Vrindaban, and you should not associate with any of such teachings, preachings, writings, and philosophies, including their teachers and preachers, who do not teach pure and selfless loving devotion to Radha Krishn (called *raganuga bhakti).*

The Bhagwatam describes these facts very beautifully in one verse,

" सतां प्रसङ्गान्मम वीर्यसंविदो भवन्ति हृत्कर्णरसायना: कथा: ।
तज्जोषणादाश्वपवर्गवर्त्मनि श्रद्धा रतिर्भक्तिरनुक्रमिष्यति ॥ " (भा. 3/25/25)

It means that when a *rasik* Saint, whose personality is a living form of Krishn love, describes the *leelas* of Radha Krishn, it attracts the heart of such listeners who desire for the vision of the personal form of God, because the name and the *leelas* of Radha Krishn are imbued with the power of Divine love.

Again, when that devotee's heart and mind is convinced that this is the path for which his soul was longing since eternity, he desires to serve and surrender to that Saint and desires to remain in his Divine care. Then, the Saint accepts him as his disciple, shows him the path of *bhakti,* and thus, a loving spiritual relationship is formed (तज्जोषणात्), uniting the heart of the devotee with the heart of the Saint, his Divine father, where Radha Krishn are already residing.

Then, with the blessings and Grace of that Saint, the devotee experiences *bhao bhakti.* His bad *sanskars* (negative conditioned reflexes of past lives' bad *karmas*) are reduced. (श्रद्धारतिभक्तिरनुक्र-मिष्यति ।) The degree of his worldly detachment, feeling of the closeness and faith in meeting with Radha Krishn, and the experience of the sweetness of Divine name and the *leelas,* are gradually increased.

This is the luckiest day for the soul when he finds the true path. **Thousands have found, why can't you be one of them?**

# 9.

## Summarizing the Philosophy of Soul, *Maya*, God, the Blissful Superiority of the Divine Abodes, and the Fallacies that Block the Path to Krishn.

❀

### (1). Soul, *maya* and God.

The simultaneous mono-dualistic existence of various forms of God in a self-submissive nature is beyond the understanding of the material intellect, because the material world along with the mind is a product of *maya*, and God is Divine.

**The *maya* physically exists as time and space energy and has 'positive' (*sattva*), 'negative' (*tam*), and 'self attractive' (*raj*) qualities seen in every aspect of material creation which develops a constant state of 'motion' and 'change' in a gradual degrading manner with its resultant 'death' that instantly promotes 'rebirth' to keep the situation even, and thus keeping the cycle of birth and death moving along with the ongoing movements of 'time' in its own endless 'space.'** This is the theory and secret of material existence in a nutshell which modern physicists are still trying to probe.

It is true that God cannot be fully understood with material intellect ( यो बुद्धेः परतः), but it is also true that, according to the writings and the experiences of our great Masters, His Blissfulness, Kindness, Graciousness and the Blissful superiority of one 'form' to 'another,' can definitely be understood by a faithful aspirant of God's love to an extent that he can surely proceed on his devotional path, and that is what we have described in this book.

"मूर्तं चैवामूर्तं द्वे एव ब्रह्मणो रूपे ।" (प्र. सु.)

It means that God has personal form and also a formless *(nirakar)* or impersonal form. The word *moortam* has come first which indicates the prominence of the personal form. The Gita further explains that the impersonal *(nirakar)* form is subordinately established in the personal form of God.

*Vaishnav acharyas* further expounded this theory and said that God has a power called *jeev shakti* which is *nirakar* (formless). All the souls (which are unlimited in number), either liberated ones or non-liberated ones, are part of the same *jeev shakti.* This is the *'nirakar* state*'* where pure Divine souls of the *gyani* Saints remain. It is called the state of absolute liberation *(kaivalya mokch)* or total termination of the feeling of 'self.' This *nirakar* state is affiliated to *nirakar (chid) brahm* which is just a Divine existence. It does not have Divine virtues like Kindness and Graciousness, etc., that is why a *gyani* has to surrender to a personal form of God to receive liberation through His Grace. The Gita says that the path of *gyan* or *nirakar brahm* is extremely difficult ( क्लेशोऽधिकतरः... ) and the path of devotion to a personal form of God is easy and simple (भक्त्या त्वनन्यया शक्य...).

The main personal forms of God are: Krishn, Ram, Vishnu, Shiv and Goddess Durga. Vishnu, Shiv and Durga's Divine abode is called Vaikunth, Bhagwan Ram's abode is Saket, and Bhagwan Krishn's abode is Dwarika, Golok and Divine Vrindaban. The forms of Ganesh, Kartikeya, and Maha Kali are included in Shiv's personality. Vishnu, Shiv and Durga, etc. are called the almighty forms of God. Krishn and Ram are the Divine love forms, whereas Krishn is the supreme form of Divine love and Radha is the life and soul of Krishn. She is the Queen of Divine Vrindaban. That's why all other forms of God and Goddess, subjectively or self-submissively, reside in the personality of Radha Krishn.

This secret has been revealed in the Gita in the verse,

"ये यथा मां प्रपद्यन्ते तांस्तथैव भजाम्यहम् ।"

That's why the Devi Bhagwatam, the Bhagwatam, the Brahm Sanhita, Nimbarkacharya, Vallabhacharya, and the descension of Radha, Chaitanya Mahaprabhu and his disciples, and all the *acharyas* (great Masters) of Vrindaban have established this truth that the sweetness of the Divine love of Radha Krishn exceeds the blissfulness of all other forms of God, although the devotional limit of purifying the heart is the same for the attainment of any form of God. It is like a jeweler who says that everything in his shop costs $200 whether you buy a steel watch, or a gold watch, or even a Rolex diamond watch. It is your own free will whatever you choose, but the price is the same.

Divine is Divine, and the qualification for its attainment is the same, because every situation of the Divine realm is unlimited. Still there are qualitative differences in the exceeding lusciousness of the Divine Bliss which is experienced in the form of ever-new and ever-increasing sweetness of Radha Krishn love by all the *Gopis* and *Brajwasis*. **There is nothing in the Divine world that could compare with the sweetness of the love of Radha Krishn.**

## (2). General concept of God and His Divine abodes.

GOD IS EQUALLY OMNIPRESENT WITH ALL OF HIS FORMS AND ABODES

| (1)<br>VAIKUNTH | (2)<br>SAKET | (3)<br>DWARIKA | (4)<br>GOLOK | (5)<br>VRINDABAN |
|---|---|---|---|---|
| LAKCHMI VISHNU<br>PARVATI SHIVA<br>DURGA | SITA RAM | RUKMINI KRISHN | RADHA KRISHN | RADHA KRISHN |

*Nirakar brahm* is also omnipresent and is affiliated to all the forms of God.

All the personal forms of God along with the impersonal aspect are equally omnipresent in the universe. All the forms of God are eternal and absolute. Their abodes are also eternal and absolute. The Divine name of God, His form, and His abode are all one. All forms of God have a particular style, taste and sweetness of unlimited Bliss so They have their own Divine dimension. Still They are all various forms of one single God, because "the absolute" cannot be divided. This is called "the simultaneous mono-dualistic existence of the Divine (God)." How does it exist, is beyond the intellectual comprehension of the material mind. But a soul, desiring God's vision, can faithfully adore any form of God.

The omnipresent Divine abodes, from Vaikunth to Divine Vrindaban, exist in their own Divine dimension. The sequence of abodes as illustrated above relates to their exceeding superiority of Divine Blissfulness where Vrindaban abode reveals the highest Blissful experience of the Divine realm.

## (3). Soul is eternally related to God.

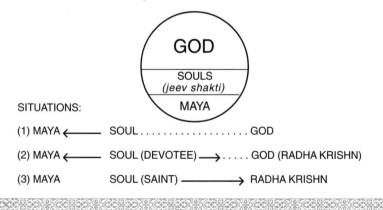

The relationship of a soul to God is eternal, firm and natural, which could be forgotten but not broken.

The word 'God' is like the word 'color' which could only be recognized and obtained when you describe the name, like 'blue color,' or 'green color,' etc. Similarly the relationship with God is recognized and becomes evident only when a person develops faith in a particular form of God which has a proper name, like, God Krishn, God Shiv, etc.

The personality of an individual is formed of body, mind and soul, where soul is related to God but mind and body are related to *maya*, that's why mind is naturally attracted to *mayic* creations. The livening power in your body is the soul, and that is the real 'you.'

Mind is an eternal affiliate, and body is a transitory affiliate to the soul which dies and reincarnates. Mind is eternal, so the *karmas* and its *sanskars* are also eternal (*anadi*). Mind is an eternal form of *maya*. On its own, it does not know about the soul's relationship to God, and it always recognizes and enjoys the objects of the *mayic* world and its *mayic* relations through the perception of the material world. This state of mind is called *agyan* (अज्ञान, the ignorance). **This is situation number (1).**

The *mayic* creation has its own inherent nature. The world is made of positive and negative elements, and this situation is experienced as mental and physical happiness and painfulness by a person in the world. This situation is everlasting without any modification.

So, the mind has to be taught the truth about your true relationship with God. When the mind really understands this truth, which is called *gyan* (ज्ञान, the knowledge), and the person whole-heartedly begins to worship God in His personal form (say Radha Krishn), his worldly ties are loosened, because his heart and mind is now tied up in love with Radha Krishn, Who is, in fact, his true and eternal Divine beloved. **This is situation number (2).**

Situation number (3) is the state of ultimate submission of the heart and mind to Radha Krishn when, with Their Grace, the devotee visualizes Their Divine form and the *mayic* bondage is completely broken. Now he experiences the intimate love of his eternal relationship with Radha Krishn forever, and forever.

## (4). The power of Grace influencing the destiny of certain souls.

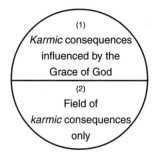

(1) Only wholehearted devotion to a personal form of God *(bhakti),* **where the prime aim of life is to receive the vision or love of God,** is related to the Grace of God.

Consequence. The devotee, either selflessly or non-selflessly worshipping Radha Krishn or any other form of God (like *Gopis*, Arjun or Dhruv), when he wholeheartedly desires God, he receives the Grace of God to some extent. Only at a very high stage of *divine-love-consciousness* one can keep his mind engrossed 24 hours in devotion. Influenced by worldly emotions, devotees also do some good and bad actions. Still, because of his dedication to God, his present devotion and future rebirth is positively influenced by the Grace of God, and his beloved God provides all the relatively possible facilities for his progress towards God realization.

(2) Those who do devotion to God, (a) with worldly desires, or (b) for any kind of material gain, or (c) as a family custom, or (d) as a general likeness to all the forms of God, and those,

(a) who do intellectual meditation of any kind, or (b) practice *yog* according to the Yog Darshan of sage Patanjali, or (c) practice any kind of mental or physical technique for meditation or concentration, also those, who (a) study *vedant* and Upnishad to gain and maintain the knowledge of self and *brahm* (called *gyan marg*), or (b) practice any form of meditation related to the impersonal aspect of God, or (c) do any kind of good action or good deed, they are all governed by the general *karmic* laws of the *mayic* realm. Their actions do not relate to the power of Grace. **God's Grace is activated only when a devotee wholeheartedly desires God for His vision and love.**

**Consequence.** All kinds of good deeds, *yog* practices and devotion to God, with material desires, are related only to the *sattvic* quality of *maya*. So its follower always remains in the *mayic* realm. Their actions are fructified according to its good and bad quality, and their rebirth is controlled according to the state of their emotional consciousness before death.

## (5). A comparative study of the personal and impersonal existence of God.

OMNIPRESENT GOD IN THE UNIVERSE

1.
The Personal
form of God
(sakar brahm)

2.
The impersonal
aspect of God
(nirakar brahm)

**Omnipresence:**
(1) The *sakar brahm*, say Radha Krishn, are omnipresent. One should not question, 'How a personal form could be omnipresent?' A material body is always spot existent, and the Divine body of God is always omnipresent. It is an axiom. It is a Divine miracle, beyond the understanding of human intellect.

(2) The *nirakar brahm* is also omnipresent.

**Divine virtues:**
(1) The *sakar brahm* is kind, Gracious, form of Divine Bliss and Divine beauty, omniscient, and has many other Divine virtues.

(2) The *nirakar brahm*, according to Shankaracharya's description of *advait* philosophy, has no such virtues. It is simply a Divine existence. It has no Graciousness or kindness and, even if it has some Blissfulness, it is absolutely non-experienceable after liberation.

**Conceivability:**
(1) Out of kindness and Grace, Radha Krishn descended on the earth planet 5,000 years ago. All the Saints, with Divine mind and eyes, saw Their boundless Divine beauty, experienced Their limitless Divine love and described in their writings which became the guidelines for the devotees of the world to

remember Their form and name. There are many deities and pictures of Radha Krishn and Their *leelas* which are available for devotional remembrance and meditation.

(2) *Nirakar brahm* has no such facility. It cannot be illustrated or portrayed in any of the five kinds of perceivable styles because it has no form. Light, darkness, void, and space, do not resemble the formless form of *brahm*. It cannot be imagined as electrical, mechanical or any kind of radiant energy, etc. It has no proper name, and it is beyond all the perceptible forms known to the mind. **It means if someone tries to imagine or conceive *nirakar brahm*, he will only conceive an aspect of *mayic* existence.** That's why Shankaracharya, in the Brahm Sutra, laid the condition of total renunciation of worldly attachments, as a preliminary requirement, for a follower of this path.

**Devotional convenience:**

(1) All the perceptible ways like singing, chanting, decorating, visualizing, smelling the perfume and eating sweet *prasad*, could be used in devotion to Radha Krishn, externally as well as internally, while lovingly remembering Their name and *leelas*.

(2) For a devotee of *nirakar brahm*, each and every perception and its enjoyment is *mayic*, so it should be avoided during meditation, both, externally and internally. Thus, it is extremely difficult to neutralize the mind with all the thoughts and enter into *nirakar samadhi* (a total thoughtless state of ecstasy of a very pure kind).

That's why our *acharyas* advised the path of *bhakti* for everyone in this age.

**Form of liberation:**

(1) After the termination of the *mayic* bondage, a Radha Krishn *bhakt* enters the Divine Vrindaban, lives near Radha Krishn, and experiences the ever-new sweetness of the same 'love'

which Krishn has for Radha and Radha has for Krishn and which the *Gopis* of Vrindaban always experience.

(2)    For a follower of *nirakar brahm*, at the termination of the *mayic* bondage, his own personal identity is also terminated. His *nirakar* soul joins the *jeev shakti* of God and stays there in a kind of total-deep-sleep-state forever, never to wake up. This is called *kaivalya mokch*. Roop Goswami has said,

" भुक्तिमुक्तिस्पृहा यावत् पिशाची हृदि वर्तते ।
तावद् भक्तिसुखस्यात्र कथमभ्युदयो भवेत् ॥ " (भ.र.सिं. 1/2/22)

"As long as the desire for the attainments of material luxuries and *kaivalya mokch* resides in the heart, the sweetness and Bliss of *bhakti* cannot be tasted."                    ☸☸☸

## (6). The kinds of *samadhi*.

Ecstacy; total absorption of the mind; or a thoughtless state of the mind. It is of two kinds, devotional and Divine.

1(a).    Devotional *samadhi* of a *yogi* relates to the pious (*sattvic*) quality of *maya*, and, (b). of a *bhakt* relates to the pious *bhao* state of the *bhakti* where his mind drowns in the feeling of loving affinity of his beloved God. The quality and the class of the *samadhi* of a *yogi* or a *bhakt* devotee corresponds to the selflessness and the state of his devotional evolution on the path of God realization.

2(a).    The Divine *samadhi* of a *Yogi* or *Gyani* is primarily of only one kind because it relates to one single formless (*nirakar*) and non-virtuous *brahm*. There are two forms of this *samadhi*. First one is called *sahaj samadhi* (सहज समाधि) which is the awakened state of the mind with natural Divine engrossment, and the second one is called *samadhi* or *nirvikalp samadhi* or *brahmleen samadhi* (समाधि, निर्विकल्प समाधि, ब्रह्मलीन समाधि) which is the fully unconscious state of the mind in total Divine engrossment. There is also a variation of *sahaj samadhi* when there is a partial consciousness. It is also called *samadhi*, or *dyanavastha* (ध्यानावस्था), in which the *yogi* Saint remains in a meditative state, bodily unconscious and mentally conscious where he could see or hear anything of his own liking. (b). The *samadhi* of a *bhakt* Saint is of many kinds and forms. The most fascinating ecstacies happen in the field of Divine love of Radha Krishn. For instance: a *rasik* Saint of *gopi bhao* experiences four kinds of *samadhis* in all the four states of his Divine mind (conscious जाग्रत, subconscious स्वप्र, unconscious सुषुप्ति, and fully unconscious तुरीय), and all of these sixteen kinds of *samadhis* are multifold and imbued with the amazing delight of ever-new charm of Radha Krishn *leelas*.

## (7). The most valuable theory of our Upnishads is the qualitative Blissfulness of self-submissive powers and forms of God.

| GOD OR *BHAGWAN* OR *POORN BRAHM* | |
|---|---|
| *ahladini shakti* or *prema shakti* (the Divine love power) | *sandhini shakti* or *aishwarya shakti* (the almighty power) |
| The Divine dimension of *premanand* | The Divine dimension of *bhagwadanand* |
| Radha Krishn the Supreme Divine love form | Lakchmi Vishnu<br><br>Parvati–Kali Shiv–Ganesh, Kartikeya<br><br>Durga–Nav Durga etc. |
| Vrindaban, Golok  Dwarika, Saket | Vaikunth |

" स्थूलं सूक्ष्मं कारणं ब्रह्मतुर्ये श्रीवैकुण्ठ द्वारका जन्मभूमि: ।
कृष्णस्याथो गोष्ठवृन्दावनन्तत् गोप्याक्रीडं धाम वृन्दावनान्त: ॥ " (1/8)

" राधाकृष्णविलासपूर्णसुचमत्कारं महामाधुरीम् ,
सारस्फारचमत्कृतिं हरिरसोत्कर्षस्य काष्ठा पराम् ।
दिव्यं स्वाद्यरसैकरम्यसुभगाशेषं न शेषादिभि:,
सेशैर्गम्यगुणौघपारमनिशं संस्तौमि वृन्दावनम् ॥ " (1/4)

" सर्वानन्दरसैकविन्दु-परमानन्दाम्बुधिस्यन्दनं,
सर्वश्रिर्यवनं श्रियोऽपि हृदयाक्ष्याकर्षणश्रीभरम् ।

शुद्धानन्दरसैकसारसुचमत्कारैकधाराकरं,
सौरभ्योज्ज्वलताच्छतामसृणतामाधुर्यवत्तरमद्भुतम् ॥ " (4/101)

" श्रीराधायाः शिञ्जन्मणिनूपुरपादविन्यासान् ।
सप्रेम तत्र तत्र स्मृत्योदश्रा वसन्ति तद्धने धन्याः ॥ " (4/91)

**Prabodhanand Saraswati**, in the **Vrindaban Mahimamritam**, while relating the progressive subtleness of the Divine Bliss of *nirakar brahm,* Vaikunth, Dwarika, Gokul (Golok) and Vrindaban, says that Vrindaban is such an abode where, "The amazing *leela* Bliss of Radha Krishn reaches its absolute charm and sweetness. This Divine and everlasting Bliss is experienced (by the *Gopis*) in a limitlessly ever-increasing style. Even the almighty God *(ishwar)* Vishnu finds it impossible to describe its greatness. I adore and worship Vrindaban." Further he says,

"Vrindaban is such an ocean of unlimited Bliss, whose one drop includes the sweetness and charm of all other Divine abodes. It excites the heart and eyes of Maha Lakchmi (but She cannot receive it). This pure Divine love is abundantly poured in Divine Vrindaban (by Shree Raseshwari Radha Rani and Krishn). Its loving perfume, refineness, Divine purity, and heart touching sweetness exceeds the excellence of any description."

"Those who live in Vrindaban (the abode of Radha), feel Her closeness, hear the sound of Her anklets in their imagination as if She is walking around, and desire to see Her. They are the luckiest souls in the world."

The essence of the Divine knowledge and the substance of the Upnishads, is the description of the Divine Bliss whose absolute essence is called *nikunj ras,* as described by the *acharyas* of Vrindaban.

The qualitative superiority of the sweetness of absolute Bliss of various Divine abodes, which are also absolute in themselves, is difficult to intellectually understand. But, for a devotee, desiring

God realization, the statements of our *acharyas* and the scriptures are enough to form a firm faith in the predominating excellence of the intimate sweetness of Radha Krishn love which is called the *nikunj ras* of Divine Vrindaban.

The Upnishad says that God has many powers. Out of these two are main. His supreme power is *ahladini shakti* (also called *prema shakti*), the Divine love power. Another main power is **sandhini shakti (also called *aishwarya shakti*), the almighty power, which is self-submissively established in *ahladini* power. The absolute supreme form of the *ahladini shakti* is Radha** ( परमान्तरङ्गभूता) Whose other form is Krishn. Thus Both are one.

The Chaitanya Charitamrit, the Shat Sandarbh and other writings of our *acharyas* explain it in detail. They say that 'the almighty power,' which is established in Radha Krishn, has many forms like Vishnu, Shiv, etc. They are the forms of the almighty power. Although they have Their separate abodes but they are all called Vaikunth abode and their Bliss is called *bhagwadanand*.

All the forms of God and Goddess of the Vaikunth abode are a fraction of the power of Radha Krishn ( विष्णुर्महान्स इह यस्य कलाविशेष: ). So, these forms are said to be self-submissively residing in Radha Krishn. It means, for instance, Krishn can act as Vishnu (as He did while killing the demons and Kans) but Vishnu can not become Krishn. Also, all the Goddesses worship Radha.

**The expansion of Radha Krishn's own personality:** The two abodes, Saket and *Dwarika* are the expansion of *ahladini shakti* where the Divine love (*premanand*) has a touch of *sandhini shakti*, the almightiness. This situation partly obscures the exciting sweetness of pure Divine love. That's why the Saints, who had the vision of Bhagwan Ram, during His descension period, again came as *Gopis* to experience the Bliss of Radha Krishn love, and the chief queen of Dwarika, Rukmini, desired for the Grace of Radha.

Radha Krishn represent Themselves as Sita Ram in Saket abode. Krishn is Dwarikadhish in Dwarika abode and Rukmini is the manifestation of *sandhini shakti* (Lakchmi) in the realm of *ahladini shakti*.

The Divine Vrindaban and Golok, reveals the full bloom sweetness of Divine love which is called *nikunj ras* and *braj ras*. The Chaitanya Charitamrit says that the essence of the *ahladini* power is called *prem ras* (Divine love), and the absoluteness of all the aspects of *prem ras* is called *Mahabhao,* and that is Radha Herself. Golok abode represents both *braj ras* and *nikunj ras* whereas Vrindaban represents only *nikunj ras*. *Nikunj ras* is the supreme form of *braj ras*.

A few examples may give a better understanding:

| (1) | (2) | (3) |
|---|---|---|
| Vaikunth | Saket, Dwarika | Golok, Vrindaban |
| Bliss of almightiness *(bhagwadanand)* | Divine love mixed with almightiness *(aishwarya mishrit premanand)* | Pure Divine love *(vishudha premanand)* |

Just like, one dollar, ten dollar and one hundred dollar bills (of U.S.A.) appear the same but there is a difference in their merit because of their varying preciousness;

just like, cologne, regular perfume, and a concentrated perfume, of the same kind, looks similar, but there is great difference in the depth, intensity and the desirability of its fragrance;

just like, a child feels happy when he sees his father, but his playfulness is fully restricted because his father is sitting in his office where he is the boss. In an evening party the child's playfulness is less restricted. But, at home, the child can freely and lovingly play with his father the way he likes;

similarly, there are qualitative differences in the advanced excellence of the Divine Bliss in the Divine abodes as illustrated above.

## (8). Dispelling fifteen most important fallacies that have misled simple-hearted devotees for centuries.

(1) Misrepresenting the Divine personality of Krishn by using a misleading word 'incarnation' for His 'descension' ( अवतार ). (Detailed explanation on pages 358.)

(2) कृष्ण word is pronounced as 'Krishn' not 'Krishna.' Whoever introduced it, was totally unaware of the Sanskrit pronunciation and also the language, because the latter ( कृष्णा ) means Radha, not Krishn. 'A' suffix ( टाप प्रत्यय ) makes certain words feminine. So we see, how these misleading concepts and words get started by some educated naive people, and others (that also include religious teachers, writers, scholars, and philosophers, etc.) keep following it blindly for hundreds of years, without even confirming its authenticity.

Similarly, there are so many such words which are incorrectly spelled and pronounced for centuries, like Rama, Arjuna, Lakchmana, yoga, jnana, etc.

(3) Another fallacy is, that God Vishnu descended as Krishn. Someone started and others began to follow this wrong concept without even caring to look into the Bhagwatam or the Garg Sanhita where this event is described. In fact, Krishn Himself descended as Krishn. Vishnu is a subordinate power so He naturally comes along within the body of Krishn whenever He descends to the earth planet. (Detailed explanation on page 79.)

(4) "See God in everyone," is also a leading fallacy, very commonly told by many spiritual preachers. Is it possible in practical life to do it? Could you see God in your wife when she is yelling at you, or your office boss when he is angry at you for no reason, or a burglar entering your home with a gun in his hand? Probably not. Then why such impractical statements are being told and listened to without caring? Just traditional blind faith. Such fancy statements and imaginations could be the product of a

very impractical mind that has never done any devotion seriously.

The Gita says, " वासुदेवः सर्वमिति स महात्मा सुदुर्लभः । ". A God realized Saint sees the whole world as his beloved God, not a devotee. This is the state of God realization. A devotee does not go around seeing God everywhere, rather **he conceives God in his heart and mind**. " मय्येव मन आधत्स्व मयि बुद्धिं निवेषय । " The Gita says that a devotee should engross his heart and mind in the loving 'remembrance' of Krishn's name, form, *leelas* and virtues.

**In daily life, a devotee must try to feel the presence of his beloved God, in His personal form, near him (not imagining the energy of God in every object). If you feel the presence of God near you and you know that He is looking at you, you cannot do anything wrong. So, a Saint *sees* the Divine form of God in the world and a devotee *conceives* the devotional form of his beloved God in his heart and mind and tries to feel His presence near him.**

(5) The most devastating fallacy that was started by some ignorant impersonalists, is that 'all the forms of God are the same,' or '*nirakar brahm* becomes *sakar.*' Just think over it that the originator of *advait vad,* Shankaracharya himself, who was God Shiv, adores Krishn and advises souls to worship Krishn because it is only Krishn devotion that fully purifies the heart; and a person calling himself a devotee of God or a follower of Shankaracharya crosses his own supreme Master's words. (Detailed explanation on pages 103, 250, 253.)

(6) Another *mayavadi* ideology is, "It *(brahm)* is in everything. It's the same that speaks from within you. You are soul *(atma)* and soul is not the doer of any action. It's just your senses that are involved in action, etc., etc." Such ideas elevate vanity, kill humbleness and the fear of God (that He will punish you for your wrong doings), and encourage free material indulgence. Shankaracharya has already admonished such confused *advaitvadis* for such behavior. (Detailed explanation of *gyan* and *gyan marg,* page 194.)

(7) A common saying that 'the goal is one and paths are many,' is also an impersonalistic belief. God is one. It is correct. But His abodes are many. (a) *Chid brahm* (the *nirakar brahm*), (b) Vaikunth, (c) Saket, (d) Dwarika, (e) Golok, and (f) Vrindaban are the main Divine abodes. How can they all be one? The fact is that *the path is one, and only one,* and it is *bhakti*. But the Divine goals (abodes) are many, and all of them are absolute and unlimited. Shankaracharya said, "द्वौभक्तौ भगदुपदिष्टौ (170)." It means, *"Bhakti* reveals the true Divine knowledge of *nirakar brahm* and eliminates *maya."* Thus there is only one path, *bhakti*, to reach any abode or any form of God. (Detailed explanation of *bhakti marg* is in Chapter 5 and 6 and page 250.)

(8) People are seen, saying, "Oh, he is very lucky. God has showered His Grace upon him. First he only had a small shop, now he owns a factory." Money is purely a material thing, and God is Divine. You must know that **God's Grace showers Divine wealth, not material.** Material wealth and facility is the outcome of your own past goods deeds. It's true that God can give you anything. He can give you the seat of Brahma, Indra, or make you the most wealthy person of the world, but only after God realization, not before that; and then you wouldn't be attached to it. (Detailed explanation on the philosophy of *karm* is in Chapter 5.)

(9) Some people believe that if you live a pious life and keep doing devotions for your whole life, you will reach God after death. It is not so. Whatever you and your *karmas* are before death, you are reborn accordingly. **You have to realize God in the existing lifetime before death (** इह चेदशकद् बोद्धुं प्राक्शरीरस्यविस्रस:। तत: सर्गेषु लोकेषु शरीरत्वाय कल्पते ॥ कठ. **), only then you enter His Divine abode, otherwise not.** Death is simply the end of the existing destiny of *karmas* ( प्रारब्ध ), and birth is the beginning of a new destiny of past lives' *karmas*. So, a Saint goes to the Divine abode, and a devotee is reborn as a devotee. When a devotee becomes a Saint with the Grace of God and his Master, then the whole world becomes the Divine abode for him and, after his physical death, he enters the Divine abode of his beloved God forever.

(10) An adamant belief among the *advaitvadis* is that conditioning the intellect with the firm thought of soul and *brahm* unity, through the repeated study of *vedant* books ( स्वाध्याय ), will give them liberation after death. The truth still remains the same. One should know that 'intellect' itself is the bondage. Whatever you and your *karmas* are in this lifetime before death, you are reborn accordingly. The *gyan* ( ज्ञान ) that liberates a soul is the practical *gyan* which is subjected to total heart purification through eightfold *yog,* and the Grace of God. (Detailed explanation on *gyan marg* is in Chapter 5.)

(11) Once a man told me that his grandfather, in his old age, went to Kashi (a holy town in India) and lived there until death, as it is said that whoever dies in Kashi, is liberated. He also said, "My father, before death, called for all the family members, said good-bye, and told us that he was going to leave the world. He was saying all the names of God, suddenly he hiccupped and died." The man was really curious to know if his father went to Vaikunth or not. These are common beliefs of the religious society.

Think over it deeply. Just dying in a particular place cannot liberate a soul from the eternal bondage of *maya*, otherwise criminals also can go there in their old age, die, and get liberated. There must be some secret behind it, and the secret is that a devotee has to experience the Divineness of that holy place (Kashi, Haridwar, Prayag, Ayodhya, Braj, etc.) which is only possible with the Grace of God. Then, when he dies in the Divinely experienced holy place, he goes to that Divine abode, because the Grace of God had already Divinized him before death.

The second thing is uttering the name right before death. Think over the exact time of death. Generally people think that when the person stopped perceiving, he is dead. No, he is not. First the body stops functioning, then senses stop perceiving, then heart stops beating, and afterwards brainwaves stop. This stage is called death in the medical science, but the soul is still there and the person is not completely dead. At this point the soul's subtle mind becomes clairvoyant for a short while and he sees where is he going to reincarnate. When the exact death time arrives, the soul along with the mind is forced to leave the body. This is the procedure of death.

Leaving the body, without going through all these procedures, is only possible when he and his mind have become Divine, which means when he has become a Saint. So we see that his voice and thinking stopped long before the actual time of his death.

Such instances only indicate the devotional piousness of the heart. According to the Gita ( शुचीनां श्रीमतां गेहे... ), such a soul reincarnates in a pious well-to-do religious family where he further continues his devotion.

(12) A very fallacious story that amused me when I heard it the very first time is, that the *Vaishnav* religious mark on the forehead ( तिलक ) and a thin wooden bead chain of a holy plant on the neck ( कण्ठी ) scares the god of death ( यमराज ) so he does not come close to that person. Instead, the pious gods come and take him to God's abode at the time of death. I wonder how people could believe such senseless and illogical stories. Those who tell such stories are absolutely ignorant of devotional procedures.

(13) Some people, before going to bed, think of Krishn for a few minutes and say, "O Lord! I offer You all of my good and bad deeds of today. Please forgive me and redeem me from their consequences," and go to sleep, believing that their *karmas* are nullified. If a few words of prayer could cancel the *karmic* consequences, then why bother saying it every day. Just say it once a year, or once in 10-15-20 years, or just once before death. The truth is, that these are just intellectual deceptions. **Each and every *karm* is recorded and kept, and it never finishes until it becomes your destiny ( प्रारब्ध ).** There are rules and regulations in the Divine government. Accumulated *karmas* ( संचित कर्म ), which are unlimited, are only finished after God realization ( क्षीयन्ते चास्य कर्माणि तस्मिन् दृष्टे: परावरे । ). The bad destinies of this lifetime could

be redeemed to a certain extent by a Saint, but the percentage of redemption will depend upon your selfless devotion, faith, dedication and service ( संत दरस जिमि पातक टरई । ). The effect of bad *karmas* and transgressions of this lifetime could be reduced to a certain extent by humble devotional repentance, and confession to your Divine Master requesting him for forgiveness. These are the general rules.

As regards devotional actions, you should know that only those moments are considered devotion when you are actually remembering God and that also without any worldly desire. For instance: you are sitting in *satsang* and your mind is, (1) wandering in your office, house, business, friends, family and kitchen etc., (2) emotionally involved in the thoughts of love and enmity in the world, and (3) for some time it comes back and listens to the *satsang* and chanting carefully. In a short period of time you created thousands of *karmas*. The *karmas* of the first category are neutral *karmas* having no good or bad outcomes. The *karmas* of the second category are *rajoguni* and *tamoguni karmas*, which means worldly *karmas* and bad *karmas*. Only the third category of *karmas* may be called devotional *karmas* if they are done selflessly. Every thought is counted as *karm.*

(14) Many people, having a religious faith, follow a certain routine of worship as advised by someone. For instance: a person recites one chapter of the Gita, does sixteen or any number of rounds of *jap,* and does some more recitation followed by prayer and some worshipping formalities of the deities who are all placed together on a small holy altar. All of that he does every day in the morning before breakfast and believes that he is doing *karm yog* of the Gita. (*Jap* means repeating God's name and counting it by holding a bead chain in the hand and mechanically sliding its beads with the fingers with every name you repeat.)

**The truth is still the same as described before. Only those moments are counted as *karm yog* in which your mind was sincerely meditating upon the form of God to receive His vision**

**and love, and not for any kind of material gain.** The other time which is spent in *jap*, recitation and worshipping etc. is only categorized as 'normal good deed', not devotion; and the rest of the daytime activities of that person are regular good or bad actions.

The 'name' that redeems the sins and reveals the Bliss of God ( मेटत कठिन कुअंक भाल के । ) is the one which is taken singlemindedly and wholeheartedly with unbroken faith and confidence in your beloved God. When this faith becomes full one hundred percent ( जासु नाम सुमिरत इक बारा । उतरहिं नर भवसिन्धु अपारा ॥ ), and the devotee says, "O, Krishn! Please come. It's a very, very long time I have been away from You. Now this separation is drowning my soul..." The next moment Krishn appears in front of him in His absolute Divine love glory.

(15) There is also a great confusion in the general public about the 'vision' of God. Sometimes some pious people receive a vision of God in their dream or in a hallucination-like state, and then they begin to believe that after death they will go to God's abode. They should know that such experiences are only the indications of past good *sanskars* and that they should humbly devote their life for God realization instead of forming a pride of having a vision. Let us think over it carefully. Visions are of two kinds: (1) Divine and (2) devotional.

**The Divine vision** happens only on complete heart purification and with the Grace of a Saint. *Mayic* bondage is terminated, *karmas* are finished, mind and senses are Divinized, the beloved form of God appears in front of the devotee in absolute Divine glory, *maya* disappears, and the whole world instantaneously becomes the form of the Divine. This all happens simultaneously. After that, it remains the same until he leaves this world and enters the Divine abode. It's like a blind person receiving eyesight when darkness disappears and light remains. You should know that only Divine vision reveals the Divine abode, not the devotional visions.

**The devotional vision** happens in four ways: (1) dream, (2) devotional hallucination, (3) meditation and (4) sometimes visual perception. On the path of *yog*, vision of any form of God or a historical Saint during pre-*samadhi* state is only a transitory reflection of his past good *sanskars* and does not have much *sattvic* value as compared to the visions on the path of *bhakti*.

In *bhakti marg* (for a selfless devotee of Radha Krishn), visions represent *bhao* and they are directly connected with Radha Krishn. That's why it is said that Radha Krishn truly reside in the heart of Their devotee in the form of *bhao*. At higher stages of *bhao bhakti*, visions happen in many forms of varying intensities and in many ways as described above. Sometimes, due to a very good *sanskar*, an extraordinary visionary experience also happens. But they are all devotional experiences. A devotee should not consider himself important because he has had a vision or he is having visions. He should maintain his humbleness and improve his love and longing for Radha Krishn until he receives Their final Grace and vision.

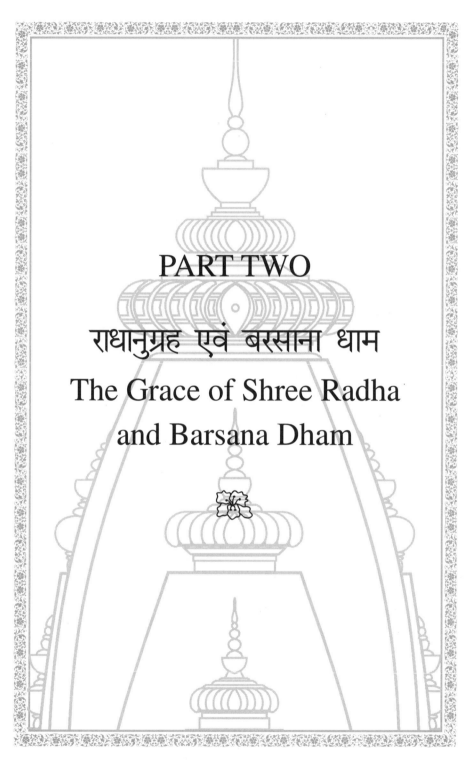

# PART TWO

## राधानुग्रह एवं बरसाना धाम

## The Grace of Shree Radha
## and Barsana Dham

# 1.
# Formation of Barsana Dham.

## The appearance of Radha Rani.

Shree Radhikaji descended on the earth planet in India 5,000 years ago and stayed more than 100 years in Her original Divine form in Barsana village in Braj. Mathura district is called Braj. At the time of Her appearance sage Narad, God Shiv and Brahma, etc. came to have the vision of Shree Radha Rani. She appeared in Her full Divine love glory.

The appearance of Shree Raseshwari Radha Rani was not just a Divine incidence. It was pre-planned in the Divine world with every detail. The absolute supreme Divinity of the entire Divine kingdom and the Queen of Divine Vrindaban was going to appear, so it had to be properly organized. Millions of Saints of Golok and Divine Vrindaban gradually descended in Braj preparing for Her arrival, and thus, making it a total Divine society with Divine surroundings.

Before Her appearance all the good omens were seen in Braj. Birds twittered with joy 'Radhey Radhey...' and animals chuckled. Celestial gods and goddesses sang the glory of Shree Radhey and God Shiv swooned in Her ecstatic love. Sage Naradji began to dance and the creator Brahma could not find a word to praise his own luck as Radha Herself was descending in this world. Every *Brajwasi* was anxiously waiting for Her appearance.

In such a Divinely joyous atmosphere Radha descends and appears in Braj as the daughter of King Vrishbhanu. Kirti, Her mother, sees Radha in Her full grown Divine beauty. That's how Radha appeared.

Krishn also descended 5,000 years ago in His full Divine glory. He stayed twelve years in Braj, then He went to Mathura, and then to Dwarika. There are many places, called *leelasthali,* in Braj which are of significant importance, but Barsana and Vrindaban are the most important places in Braj. The reason is that Radha lived all the time in Barsana and Radha Krishn revealed the Bliss of *maharaas* in Vrindaban on the Sharad Poornima night.

## Radha Krishn and Divine love.

The Upnishad says,

"कृष्णेन आराध्यत इति राधा ।" (रा. उ.)

It means Krishn worships Radha, because Radha is the soul of Krishn. Radha also worships Krishn, because Krishn is the beloved of Radha.

"येयं राधा यश्च कृष्ण: ।"

Radha and Krishn Both are one. Both adore and worship each other because Both are like the two flames of the same fire of supreme Divine love (रसाब्धिर्देहेनैक: क्रीडनार्थं द्विधाभूत्).

Radha is called *Mahabhao,* the absolute supreme bloom of Divine love. The same power is in two forms, Radha and Krishn, or you can say that Radha Herself is Krishn. They worship each other. Still, Radha is the prime absolute form of supreme Divine love power.

Shukdeo Paramhans said in the Bhagwatam, " योगमायामुपाश्रित:," which means that Krishn, before doing *maharaas,* asked Radha to

Radha Kund gardens and back of Shree Raseshwari Radha Rani Temple

give Her consent to do *maharaas*. Radha permitted, Krishn called for the *Gopis,* and *maharaas* started.

*Maharaas* is the Divine dance of Radha Krishn along with unlimited number of *Gopis* when Krishn multiplied Himself in unlimited forms of Krishn. This Divine *leela* happened once when Krishn was in Braj on the Sharad Poornima night. **Thus we find, that the excelling charm of Radha's personality, in all the playful acts *(leelas)* of Radha Krishn and the *Gopis,* is seen in the writings of all the great Masters of Vrindaban. Radha Rani is called Raseshwari, Nikunj Viharini, Vrindaban Viharini, Vrindaban-adhishwari, and many more such names.**

Shree Raseshwari Radha Rani distributed the nectar of Divine love to all the *Gopis* and *Brajwasis* (the people of Braj) throughout Her stay in Barsana, then She ascended to Her Divine abode, Vrindaban, along with Krishn. The sweetness of such Divine love surpasses the Blissfulness of all other forms of God, that's why the Vishnu *bhaktas* became Krishn *bhaktas* when Chaitanya Mahaprabhu visited South India. Also, the *Gyanis,* forgetting their Divine transcendence *(samadhi),* became absorbed in Krishn love which was, in fact, the glory of Radha.

## Barsana and nearby *leela* places in Braj (India).

Barsana village is the abode of Radha Rani in Braj. It is situated near a small hill, and, on top of the hill, there is a temple of Radha Rani. The surrounding villages near Barsana are the villages of the eight personal aides of Radha: Lalita, Vishakha, Indulekha, Tungvidya, Rangdevi, Sudevi, Champaklata and Chitra. The Gahvar woodland, which was a blossoming natural garden in those days, is on the outskirts of Barsana. There are holy ponds near Barsana called Prem Sarovar, Piri Pokhar and Gahvar Kund or Radha Kund. Also there is a place called Vilasgarh on a nearby hill which was Radha's garden mansion. There are also some *raas mandals* (a circular cemented or paved area in the woodlands) in the vicinity of Barsana. Devotees believe that Radha Krishn and the *Gopis* come and do *raas* in the night on these *raas mandals.*

When Chaitanya Mahaprabhuji visited Braj, he stayed one night at a place near Govardhan hill where chanting of Radha Krishn name went on for the whole night. This place is called Shyam Kuti. Govardhan hill is about fourteen miles from Barsana, and Vrindaban is further twelve miles away from Govardhan. Govardhan hill is famous for the childhood *leelas* of Krishn and His playmates.

All of these places are worshipped by the devotees. People visiting these places remember the *leelas* of Radha Krishn related to those places. It is believed, and also experienced by the evolved devotees, that those *leelas* are still happening, and Radha Krishn still play in those places.

Out of hundreds of holy places of India, Braj is most important. In fact, the whole of Braj is such a Divine nucleus that it attracts all kinds of God-loving people from all over India.

## Barsana Dham in the U.S.A.

The Grace of Shree Radha Rani inspired the heart of Shree Swamiji and he thought of creating something very special for the people of the West where they could have similar benefits as if they were actually in Vrindaban or Barsana in India. It was not just like buying a piece of land and constructing an edifice on it. It had to be the revelation of Radha's Grace, as all of our holy places in India are either related to a descension of God or a great historical Saint lived there whose Divine presence made it holy (तीर्थी कुर्वन्ति तीर्थानि).

In 1988, during the annual Intensive, Shree Swamiji announced that we could have Barsana Dham in the U.S.A. The devotees were thrilled with this news and, according to the guidance of Shree Swamiji, they started looking for a suitable property. Shree Swamiji personally went to many places and saw a number of properties in Pennsylvania, upstate New York, New Jersey, Washington D.C., Virginia, Maryland, Northern California, etc. None of the properties were really suitable according to the Divine dream of Shree Swamiji to create Barsana Dham. We were looking for a scenic wooded area with a stream and harvestable land.

One of our devotees found such a property in Austin, Texas, and thus, we purchased it in 1990. It was named Barsana Dham. There were some houses and a 130 year old stone building on the property, all in a very run down condition. We fully renovated the stone building, built houses, a large kitchen and dining hall, and we moved in. We had our first Intensive in Barsana Dham in October, 1991.

In 1991 Shree Swamiji graciously revealed the most important *leela* places of Braj in Barsana Dham. The site for Shree Raseshwari Radha Rani Temple and Ashram was decided. Vilasgarh, Prem Sarovar, Shyam Kuti and Govardhan hill were established. The stream that runs across the property was named Kalindi (the Yamuna river of Vrindaban), the hill was named Barsana hill, Radha Kund, Man Mandir and Mor Kuti were also located. These are the important places of *nikunj leelas* of Radha Krishn.

Shree Swamiji personally planned and designed Shree Raseshwari Radha Rani Temple and Ashram complex which includes Radha Kund at the back of the temple and Maharaas Mandal.

On the Sharad Poornima day of October, 1992, we celebrated the foundation laying ceremony of Shree Raseshwari Radha Rani Temple. **Shree Swamiji had personally brought the holy waters of all the important ponds of Braj along with the water of Yamuna river. He also brought the holy dust (soil) of Barsana, Vrindaban, and Govardhan collected from very special *leela* places. All of this was laid in the center of the temple foundation by Shree Swamiji himself. It was something very special that happened in the Divine history of America which was beyond words. Devotees felt a great surge of Divine energy around the foundation area. Afterwards, some devotees used to go over there and sit for hours, feeling the presence of Radha Krishn.**

Sharad Poornima is the day when Radha Krishn descended the Divine Vrindaban in Braj and revealed the Divine Bliss of *maharaas*. That's why Shree Swamiji chose that particular day for laying the foundation of the temple, and, in this way, Vrindaban and Barsana (the Divine abodes of Radha Krishn) were both established in this Barsana Dham.

It is only the Grace of Radha Rani that Shree Swamiji has revealed and established this Barsana Dham in its true form where sincere devotees of God could feel blessed in the same way as they feel when they visit Braj, the land of Radha Krishn, in India.

The physical appearance of Barsana Dham is greatly reminiscent of Braj (Barsana) in India, so it becomes very easy for the devotees of Radha Krishn to remember Their *leelas* at this place.

Holy places of Barsana Dham.

Foundation Laying Ceremony of Shree Raseshwari Radha Rani Temple, October 11, 1992.

# 2.
## Shree Raseshwari Radha Rani Temple.

### Shree Radha Rani Temple in India.

Mostly, there are temples of Radha and Krishn. Some temples are of Krishn alone. There are only two temples of Radha Rani in the whole of Braj in India. One is in Barsana village, which is the main one, and the other one (which is a very small temple of Radha Rani) is in Man Sarovar, a small village on the other side of the river Yamuna.

A few hundred years ago there was a great Saint, Goswami Bhattji Maharaj, who lived in Barsana village. Once, in a vivid Divine dream, he saw a Deity of Radha Rani buried on the Barsana hill nearby his hut. He told this to the villagers. They came. The Deity was recovered from the ground and kept in his hut on an altar. For him the Deity was Radha Rani Herself, but for the visitors it was simply a Deity. After Shree Bhattji expired, a temple was constructed on the hill and the Deity of Shree Radha along with another Deity of Krishn was established in the temple.

### Our ancient temples and the modern trend of temples.

Our ancient temples like Govind Deoji, Bihariji, Radha Raman, Radha Vallabh, Gopinathji, Madan Mohan and Srinathji were established by our great *acharyas* (*rasik* Saints). The followers of those *acharyas* devotionally visualized Radha Krishn in those Deities while having *darshan*. **When a devotee respectfully comes to the temple and faithfully sees God in the Deity, it is called** *darshan*. So the purpose of the temple was to lovingly remember Radha Krishn and to feel Their closeness.

As time went on, temples and monasteries grew rich, the loving aspect of the devotion receded, religious practices remained as ritualistic formalities, and materialism began to pervade. Thus, in the last few hundred years, the temples, that were constructed by religious and wealthy individuals, were mostly like a monument of their religious pride. They became a place of tourist attraction and boon-seeking religious people of the world. People mostly go to these places to see the beauty and the massiveness of the temple building, not to selflessly adore God through the Deity.

## We have to bring back the originality.

The Grace of Shree Radha Rani appeared in the heart of Shree Swamiji and he visualized Barsana Dham and Shree Raseshwari Radha Rani Temple. Later on, the vivid Divine dream of Shree Swamiji took its shape, and thus, Barsana Dham and Shree Raseshwari Radha Rani Temple came into being. In this way, the Divine originality of our ancient temple tradition of our great Masters of Braj was re-established.

## Shree Raseshwari Radha Rani Temple in the U.S.A.

"सर्वाः शरत्काव्यकथारसाश्रयाः । " "शरदोत्फुल्ल मल्लिका: । " (भा.) When Shree Radha Rani distributed the Bliss of *maharaas* to Her loving *Gopis*, the atmosphere of the whole of Vrindaban was perfumed with the scent of the flowers of all the seasons that bloomed together to intensify the charm of the full moon night of the Sharad Poornima. The breeze was fragrant, the sky was clear with some scattered clouds, and the weather was pleasant. Our Swamiji incorporated all the feelings of these writings of the Bhagwatam and produced it in the form of Shree Raseshwari Radha Rani Temple.

Thus, this is the only Temple in the world that has been constructed in consideration with all the aspects of the devotional feelings of a devotee and so it has become a place of pilgrimage for millions of devotees living in the Western world. It is constructed under the full guidance of Shree Swamiji and it follows the Divine guidelines of the Radhikopnishad, Gopal Tapniyopnishad, Devi Bhagwatam, Bhagwatam, and the writings of great Masters of Vrindaban.

Radha Rani has hundreds of names. Raseshwari is one of Her most important names. It comes from Radhikopnishad. **'Raseshwari' name signifies the absolute sovereignty of Radha's excelling blissful charm, beauty, love, graciousness, and kindness** which encourages a devotee to feel that he can also receive the Divine Grace of Radha Rani, and become one of the Divine associates of Radha Krishn in Divine Vrindaban where he can enjoy the ever-new and ever-increasing Divine love ( दिव्य प्रेम रस ) forever.

The Temple is designed in such a way that it captures the heart of a devotee and his mind feels a devotional excitement where he finds his beloved (God) Radha Krishn closer to his heart. On both sides of the shrine there are large glass windows overlooking the hill, and the native flowers. It appears as if the shrine is situated in a blossoming garden of a beautiful hilly area under the early morning sky where a fragrant breeze is caressing the Temple of Shree Radha Rani. The devotee, while sitting in the spacious *satsang* (meditation) hall in front of the shrine, could naturally feel the devotional energy and the spiritual serenity which was found in the ancient *ashrams* of our Vrindaban Saints. The devotee feels that he is, in fact, sitting in a true *leela* place of Braj in India.

## Temple architecture.

Shree Raseshwari Radha Rani Temple and Ashram complex, along with the formation of the Deities, are all designed according to Shree Swamiji's vision. He personally explained every detail to the architects. It is an excellent achievement of North Indian, South Indian, ancient, and modern styles of architecture. The floral patterns on the entrance doors, the entrance of the shrine, and the style of columns are marvelous. There are 84 columns and five levels in the building. The shrine and the *satsang* hall are together. The graceful Radha Kund and the Maharaas Mandal, which has 64 columns, are also part of the Temple complex. The Temple guest rooms have speaker facility, so the guests can listen to the chantings and the programs happening in the Temple. Every room has a scenic view of Barsana Dham.

This is Barsana Dham and Shree Raseshwari Radha Rani Temple where devotees and visitors feel relaxed and experience the opening of their heart.

## Divine messages of our scriptures as depicted in the main hall.

The present religious systems and the preachings of nowadays are so confusing that people do not know what is original, authentic and true. They remain confused about the forms of God and the path of God realization and don't know what to do.

A very unique and important feature of the Temple *satsang* hall is that it depicts the essence of the entire *Bhartiya* philosophy, so that a visitor can actually see it all at one place, and decide and determine the devotional goal of his life. The most important themes of all the important scriptures are described in a continuous panel on all the four sides of the hall under the realistic depiction of the sky with some clouds. The theme of the Gita is on the east side, the Upnishads on the west side, the Bhagwatam towards the shrine side, and the Puranas and the Ramayanam is on the north side towards the main entrance. Along with the writings, extraordinarily beautiful and devotional pictures of Radha, Krishn, and Radha Krishn also glorify the panels of the hall. In this way the Temple hall itself stands as a source of Divine knowledge that relates to all the important aspects of devotion.

## The Deity Establishment Ceremony (1995), as seen and experienced.

5,000 years ago... the world felt the Divine breeze on the Sharad Poornima night when the absolute Divine love power, Shree Raseshwari Radha Rani, revealed Her Divine love form in *maharaas* in Braj, in India. On the Sharad Poornima of October 8, 1995, She has especially glorified the earth planet once again with the manifestation of Her Divine Grace at Barsana Dham.

As the *Brajwasis* rejoiced when Shree Radha appeared in Braj 5,000 years ago, devotees from around the world joyously made their journey to Barsana Dham for Sharad Poornima, 1995, to witness Her appearance in the form of Her Deity, in the newly completed Shree Raseshwari Radha Rani Temple.

The Deity Establishment Ceremony, *moorti pratishtha mahotsav,* of Shree Raseshwari Radha Rani began on October 6th with recitations from the Vedas. On October 7th, throughout the day, international Spiritual leaders *(mahatmas)* delivered inspiring discourses about the Divine significance of Shree Raseshwari Radha Rani and the path of *raganuga bhakti (divine-love-consciousness)* that Shree Swamiji is teaching to the world.

During the evening program of devotional chanting, the devotees, dignitaries and *mahatmas* experienced an extraordinary Bliss and Grace in the remembrance of the Divine names of Radha Krishn. In the anticipation of the next day's ceremony, many devotees spent almost the whole night celebrating and garlanding the Temple, and those who were able to sleep, dreamed of the celebrations of the next day.

The morning of Sharad Poornima, October 8, 1995, began with the grand chariot procession (**Rath Yatra**), where the three foot Deity of Shree Raseshwari Radha Rani, wearing all the jewelry, rode a beautiful chariot, that was decorated with roses and marigolds grown at Barsana Dham. The devotees, their hearts thrilled with the first *darshan*, chanted, played musical instruments, and danced as they followed the chariot along the procession route. Shree Swamiji did the first *arti* at the Temple entrance and then all the guest *mahatmas* did the *arti*. The procession started. Meera Devi, Ranjana Devi, Gyaneshwari Devi and some other devotees were sitting on the chariot and chanting Radhey name. The overjoyed crowd of devotees, dancing and singing Radhey name, walked along with the chariot. The procession passed through Barsana Dham's East side gate, traveled along the main road in front of Barsana Dham, and re-entered from the main gate. All along the procession of Shree Raseshwari Radha Rani flowers were showered from the sky. It was like the celestial gods and goddesses overjoyously showering hundreds of thousands of flowers on Radha Rani as a sign of their deep gratitude for Her. During the procession, four times *arti* and worship was done by the devotee families of Barsana Dham.

Shree Swamiji himself led the procession to the Temple. The procession stopped at the main entrance of the Temple. Flowers were still being showered from the sky (from the helicopter), and the devotees, who were standing on the roof of the portico, were also showering flowers on Radha Rani and the dancing crowd of the *mahatmas* and the devotees.

The scene and the atmosphere was beyond words to explain. Everyone was enchanted with the devotional delight and was chanting Radhey name. Someone was dancing, someone swaying, someone rocking, someone clapping, someone quietly meditating with closed eyes and someone was admiringly watching the happening. The most incredible scene was that all the guest *mahatmas* were singing Radhey name and dancing hand in hand with Shree Swamiji.

That was something, which was never seen before, or expected by anyone who was there. The ground was covered with the flowers and the *mahatmas* were dancing amidst the showering flowers with their hearts filled with the joy of the Gracious celebrations of Shree Raseshwari Radha Rani. After some time, the chariot of Radha

Rani was moved to a safer place and the crowd then gathered in the Temple hall.

The long awaited moment had come, and Shree Swamiji was now going to reveal the *vision* of Radha Rani. Shree Swamiji entered inside the main Temple, and after a few minutes he came out. The *'Darshan'* was now open. Guest *mahatmas* had the first *darshan*, then all the devotees. What the devotees and *mahatmas* experienced during that time surpassed all of their expectations. It was something so great in their lives that cannot be described. We could only say that we had a glimpse of the meaning of the word *'balihar.'*

Shree Swamiji, on the request of devotees, graced the occasion and delivered a speech, first in English then in Hindi, describing the secret of Raseshwari name. He also said that the prime aim of all the religions is to experience the blissfulness of God which is Divine and undivided. He explained that the religious diversities may automatically disappear if (keeping aside the ritualistic and cultural differences) people begin to desire to experience that undivided love of God.

After that we had lunch break (*prasad*). The whole *ashram* was flooded with the devotees. There were more than nine hundred cars parked in Barsana Dham. Apart from the main hall, people were also watching the program on TV while sitting on the verandah and the tent which was especially arranged to hold the exceeding crowd of the devotees. In the afternoon, from 3:30 p.m., programs again started. Dignitaries and special guests reflected on the greatness of the event through their messages of sincere best wishes and appreciation of the Temple. Many well wishers who were unable to attend, sent their messages through letters which were read out.

The notable ones were the messages from the President and Vice President of the U.S.A., former President of India, Ambassador of India, the Mayor of Austin, Jagadguru Shree Shankaracharya Swamigal of Kancheepuram Math, Jagadguru Shree Shankaracharya Bharti Tirth Swamiji Maharaj of Sringeri Math, the Temple presidents and many other Hindu organizations of India and the U.S.A. etc.

A beautiful cultural program from the professionals of Houston, Dallas, San Antonio and Austin area, which went on for more than two hours, expressed deep devotional feelings as they performed devotional dances and songs. At the end of the program, the *maharaas leela* was enacted by the Barsana Dham devotees. Some devotees felt that they were actually witnessing the Divine event.

**The saying in India** न भूतो न भविष्यति **came true.** It means an event which is Divinely so special that nothing like it has ever occurred in the past, and is so unique and extraordinary that it is not likely to happen soon in the near future. Those who attended these celebrations would call the Deity Establishment Ceremony of Shree Raseshwari Radha Rani as the Divine benevolence of Shree Swamiji. Established for the first time in the West, this is something that will be remembered forever in the spiritual history of the world.

The dawn of the Divine energy, with the establishment of the Deity of Shree Raseshwari Radha Rani at Barsana Dham, will introduce harmony and peace in the world. The Deity represents the presence of Shree Raseshwari Radha Rani on the land of the U.S.A., and Barsana Dham represents the Divine abode of Radha Krishn. We decided to have *Rath Yatra Celebrations* every year on Sharad Poornima day.

## Nikunj darshan.

The most loving *leelas* of Radha Krishn were performed in the *kunj* and the woodlands of Braj. (*Kunj* is a beautiful secluded area where blossoming trees, flowering bushes, creepers and perfumed flowers grow together to create such a sheltered and shaded setting where Radha, Krishn and *Gopis* could sit and play and dance. *Kunj* and *nikunj* are the same thing.) *Rasik* Saints have described thousands of *nikunj leelas* where Radha Krishn sat on a swing or a flower decorated throne, and the *Gopis* sang, danced, played, did *arti* or anything to please Them.

Deity Establishment Ceremony, October 7 - 8, 1995.
(Showering flowers on the Temple.)

Deity Establishment Ceremony, October 7 - 8, 1995.
(Above: First *darshan* of the Deity. Below: Discourses by renowned *mahatmas*.)

Five hundred years ago, when our *acharyas* established temples of Radha Krishn, the situation was different. They did not visualize the Deity as if it was made of stone. They visualized it as Divine Radha Krishn, and so they advised the devotees to meditatingly feel the presence of Radha Krishn in the Deity.

In this way the 'Deity worship,' as introduced by our great *acharyas*, was a form of loving adoration to your soul-beloved Radha Krishn, where a devotee, sitting in front of the Deity and believing the Divine presence of Radha Krishn in it, tried to heighten his feelings of love and longing for Radha Krishn through chanting meditations while remembering Their *nikunj leelas*. Thus, for such a devotional practice, not just a ritualistically worshipped statue on a fancy altar, but a beautiful *nikunj darshan* of the Deity was necessary.

In those days, the *leela* places of Vrindaban, Barsana, Govardhan etc. were flowering woodlands. So, the temple, surrounded by the woodland and the flower plants around it, gave enough inspiration to the devotees to think of the *nikunj leelas* of Radha Krishn.

Now, with the excessive increase of population, trees have been cut down and the natural surroundings are destroyed. Thousands of temples have been constructed in the last hundreds of years, but they do not represent the *nikunj* view at all which is an important factor in forming the devotional imagination of Radha Krishn *leelas*.

Considering all these devotional aspects, Shree Swamiji decided to manifest something unique that could reveal the real *nikunj darshan* of Radha Krishn; and so the beautification of the shrine and the realistic depiction of a most beautiful *nikunj* was created by the skilled professionals. **Thus, this is the first Temple in the world that represents the true devotional view of *nikunj* *leelas* which is the essence of the Bhagwatam.**

Another important thing is the formation of the Deities which represents the real truth of Vrindaban Bliss as described in the Radhikopnishad and other scriptures.

"परमान्तरङ्गभूता राधा ॥"
"कृष्णेन आराध्यत इति राधा ॥"
"एकं ज्योतिर्द्विधाभिन्नं राधामाधवरूपकम् ॥"
"प्राणाधिष्ठात्री सा देवी ॥"

*Mahabhao*-Radha Herself is Krishn of Divine Vrindaban, and, Radha and Krishn Both reveal the Bliss of *maharaas* which is called Vrindaban Bliss. To describe this Divine secret, Shree Swamiji has established the main Deity of Shree Raseshwari Radha Rani ( महाभावस्वरूपा राधा ) and next to it are the Deities of Radha Krishn in *raas* pose. So our Temple represents both aspects of Radha *bhao*, Raseshwari Radha Rani as *Mahabhao* and Raseshwari Radha Rani as Radha Krishn. That's why it is called Shree Raseshwari Radha Rani Temple.

As soon as a person enters the shrine hall, he sees Shree Raseshwari Krishn in a *nikunj* under the morning sky where a blossoming *kadamb* tree is glorifying the space, and many kinds of flowers are blooming near a stream. On both sides of the main shrine are huge glass windows overlooking Radha Kund, Radha Kund gardens, Maharaas Mandal, Barsana hill and the fields of natural wildflowers that beautify Barsana Dham.

Devotees, while doing devotions, can feel that they are really sitting in Divine Vrindaban or Divine Barsana Dham in a *nikunj* under the open sky and are having *darshan* of Radha Krishn.

## Visitors.

Every day a number of visitors come to see the Temple of Shree Raseshwari Radha Rani and Barsana Dham. They experience a peaceful serenity as soon as they enter the gate. They feel devotional happiness in the atmospheres of Barsana Dham wherever they go, as if the whole of Barsana Dham is a Godly land, something above this material phenomenon. They desire to come back to Barsana Dham again. A few people have reported a very unusual experience. They said that while driving on the highway when they passed alongside Barsana Dham, they felt very peaceful in their heart. Such experiences signify the divinity of Barsana Dham.

Above: Morning *satsang* and *darshan* of Radha Rani.
Below: Shree Swamiji.

# 3.
# A Brief Biography of Shree Swamiji.

## His early days and taking *sanyas*.

His Divinity Swami Prakashanand Saraswati, lovingly called Shree Swamiji by his devotees, was born in January, 1929 on *saphala ekadashi*, the eleventh moon night (that falls in December or the first week of January, according to the lunar calendar) in a religious and respectable Brahman family of Ayodhya, India. In his childhood once he heard the story of Radha Krishn, *Gopis* and *maharaas*. It stuck to his heart. Since then he longed for Radha Krishn and desired to go to Vrindaban where They did *maharaas*.

Keeping his devotional feelings deep in his heart, Shree Swamiji continued his formal studies. At the age of twenty-one, in 1950, he renounced the world and went to Joshimath in the Himalayas and then in 1951 he took the order of *sanyas*. Seeing his esteem of renunciation and deep feeling of God consciousness, in 1952, he was offered to be the successor of Jagadguru Shankaracharya of Joshimath which is one of the most renowned

Over a number of years living near Shree Swamiji the devotees learned a lot about his kindness, caring and Graciousness and also about his natural deep love for Radha Rani. During that time sometimes Shree Swamiji revealed some of the events and incidents of his life which were collected by the devotees and are now systematically put together so that other devotees could also receive inspiration and guidance in their devotional life.

Meera Devi, Priya Dasi

religious thrones of India. He very politely refused by saying, "My final desire is to go to Vrindaban. I have given my life for the service of Radha Rani, so I cannot live forever in Allahabad."

Following the strict discipline of *sanyas*, he lived in the Himalayas (Joshimath, Badrinath, Rishikesh, and Haridwar, etc.), the forests of Amarkantak, near the Narbada river, Allahabad, and Kashi etc., for about four years.

Amarkantak is the origin of the river Narbada. For about six months he travelled and remained nearby Narbada in the dense forests of central India, which stretches up to hundreds of miles and is inhabited by tigers and leopards whose sparkling eyes in the night pierce the dense darkness of the jungle. He went up to Onkareshwar Mahadeo and then returned to Allahabad.

Later on Shree Swamiji went to Badrinath (Himalayas) in 1953. He met a *yogi* Saint who lived in a cave very close to the Badrinath Temple near the natural spring of hot water. Mostly he remained absorbed in his natural *brahm-gyan* state. At that time the *yogi* had only one friend, our Swamiji. They both met and talked about Divine matters quite often. The local people liked the *yogi*. But the other *sanyasis,* who lived there to gain their own popularity, rebuked him. The pilgrims used to go to these other *sanyasis*. **See the world of *kaliyug*, where even the religious people don't recognize the Divine reality, they go after the materiality, wrapped in a fancy religious outfit.**

Once someone told Swamiji about Swargarohan hill where King Yudhishthir was escorted to the celestial abode in a celestial chariot. Swamiji thought of going over there out of curiosity. Normally people don't go there because the journey is rough, no village nearby, no food or water available on the way, and no proper tracks to proceed. Just indications of hills are there to follow. It becomes inaccessible and very dangerous after the first snowfall which could happen any time in October.

It was the month of October when Shree Swamiji went towards that hill. He was never alone. He vividly felt the presence of God near him. He walked for three days and it took again three days to walk back, enjoying the sereneness of the places that he came across, he walked through the dangerous track. He had one blanket and a pot *(kamandal)* of water, which he used for five, six days.

Shree Swamiji stayed in Badrinath for more than a month. Afterwards he came to Haridwar, and then to Allahabad. From there he went to Kashi.

## Shree Swamiji in Braj.

Until then he had travelled and seen enough of hills, mountains, ancient temples, holy places, jungles and dense forests where wild beasts, like lions and tigers freely roamed around. He went to those places, prior to going to Vrindaban, for one reason that, no such thought be left in his mind that he has not seen such places of India, because he wanted to spend all of his devotional life in Braj.

Shree Swamiji now decided to go to Vrindaban to fulfill his long awaited desire to be in the abode of Radha. It was the early winter of 1954 when he started for Vrindaban. When he entered the lands of Vrindaban he felt at home, just like someone returns home after a long journey. He was excited to reach Vrindaban. He stayed in an *ashram.*

There is a place in Vrindaban called Seva Kunj which was almost the center of *maharaas* where Radha Krishn and *Gopis* danced together. There is a very small temple there, surrounded by dense native bushes, and is enclosed by a high boundary wall. It is totally secluded in the night, no one lives there, but Shree Swamiji stayed three nights over there without telling anyone.

In those days, in a temple in Vrindaban, beautiful *raas leela* was being played in the night. In the day time, Shree Swamiji normally went out to see various places and temples of Vrindaban, and in the night he started going to see that *raas leela* which was played by a local party. *Raas leela* is a kind of stage show where the *leelas* of Radha Krishn, *Gopis* and *Brajwasis*, based on the songs and writings of the *rasik* Saints of Vrindaban, are played. The crowns and the costumes of Radha Krishn and *Gopis* are exquisite.

It was winter time. There was a little problem. The *raas leela* used to finish around 11:00 p.m. and the *ashram* gate was closed at 10:00 p.m. Although the *ashram* people were very polite to Swamiji, but he did not want to disturb them in the night. So, every night he stayed out near a pond under a tree, and at 6:00 a.m., when the gate of the *ashram* opened, he sneaked in. No one ever knew, because, if they had known, they would never have let him stay outside in the shivering cold of November.

Time went on. After one month, Shree Swamiji desired to go to Barsana, his most loving place, the abode of Radha Rani. He arrived at Barsana. It was evening time. He went to the main Radha Rani Temple. He had nothing for the whole day. After the late evening *arti* at 9:00 p.m., the priest of the temple gave him some *prasad* to eat. The temple doors were being closed, so he had to go out.

Swamiji knew nothing about the vicinity. The night was cold and dark. (The temple is on the hilltop and is surrounded by the jungle of native trees.) He simply moved out into the jungle. He could not go much further because the ground was very uneven. Somehow he spent the night in the jungle. He was exposed to excessive cold and got sick. There was no medical aid available.

Next morning he walked around and found a run-down deserted temple called Man Mandir on the other side of the Barsana hill, which is about half a mile away from the main temple. The temple had a few rooms with only walls and roof, no doors to shut and had broken floors where rodents had made holes and two snakes were living. He liked the place as he could live there uninterrupted by the people. He started living there.

That was the time when he felt the personal Grace of Shree Radha. Shree Swamiji says, "Radha Rani was my Divine Guide, Master, Beloved, Friend, companion and everything for me. Practically, I lived under Her Grace all the time." On the Makar Sankranti of 1955, Shree Swamiji visited Allahabad where he received the Grace of Shree Kripalu Mahaprabhu, the supreme Divine descension of this age, and then he went to Pratapgarh with him for some time. Afterwards he came back to Barsana. Drowned in Radha's love he lived in Barsana for many years. He also lived in other isolated *leela* places of Govardhan and Kamban.

In this way, for almost sixteen years he lived in Barsana, Govardhan, Kamban, Charan Pahari, Shyam Kuti, Man Sarovar, Bhandir Ban and many other places in Braj. He lived in Barsana for about twelve years. Devotees, who met Shree Swamiji at that time, always found him absorbed in Radha Krishn love. The scriptural secrets were naturally revealed to him. Sometimes when he read the Ras Panchadhyayi he felt that the verses of the Bhagwatam became alive for him. Later on, with the Grace of Shree Radha, Swamiji started giving discourses on *divine-love-consciousness*. During the last part of his stay in Barsana, sometimes, for a short time, he went out to spread the message of Divine love and then came back to Barsana.

## He decided to spread the message of *divine-love-consciousness* and formed the International Society of Divine Love.

In early 1971 he decided to spread the message of Radha Rani in an organized way. He had a few faithful devotees who built a small *ashram* for him in Vrindaban. He made a tour of India, went to many towns, and, on a special request from his devotees, in December, 1972 he went to Hong Kong. From Hong Kong he went to Singapore, Indonesia, Fiji, New Zealand, etc. His first book, Towards the Love Divine, was published in 1974. In those days Shree Swamiji stayed sometime in India and sometime in Fiji and New Zealand.

Once, when he was in New Zealand, a devotee came to Swamiji and asked his advice as to which book (in English) he should read to know more about Krishn. Swamiji had no idea about that so he asked him to bring some books for perusal which he did. To his dismay, Shree Swamiji found that none of them were philosophically correct. Some were biased, and most of them failed to accept the Divine supremacy of Krishn's descension. Shree Swamiji told the devotee that they were no good as philosophy books but if he liked he could read them just like a story book.

Shree Swamiji then decided to expound the philosophy of Radha Krishn devotion in detail through his writings and speeches.

In order to spread the Divine message of Shree Radha Rani, he founded the International Society of Divine Love in 1975 in India. Later on in 1976 he went to England, U.S.A., and back to New Zealand, and India.

In 1978 he formed the Society in New Zealand and, at the same time, he established an *ashram* in Remuera, Auckland. Since then Shree Swamiji has travelled around the world many times. In 1981 he formed the International Society of Divine Love in the U.S.A. and established an *ashram* in Philadelphia in 1984.

## His Divine vision about Barsana Dham in the U.S.A.

In 1988 Shree Swamiji told about his Divine vision of creating Barsana Dham in the U.S.A. Devotees were extremely happy to hear this news. They looked around for a suitable property in many states. They found it in Austin, and 200 acres of scenic land with a hill and a stream were bought in 1990. It was named Barsana Dham by Shree Swamiji. After establishing Barsana Dham, Shree Swamiji started spending most of his time in the U.S.A.

The International Society of Divine Love (India) has built a large *ashram* on ten acres of beautiful land in Vrindaban as its international center and named it 'Jagadguru Dham.' It has 30 guest rooms, and it is a very beautiful *ashram* in Vrindaban.

Shree Swamiji also decided to have an *ashram* in Barsana (India), in the actual descension place of Radha Rani. We already had twelve acres of land there so, on January 14, 1992, ISDL (India) celebrated the foundation laying function of the Barsana *ashram* and named it 'Rangeeli Mahal' which means 'the Palace of Radha Rani.'

Shree Swamiji's whole life is a Divine benevolence. There is an extensive collection of his speeches and his writings on the philosophy and the practical aspects of God realization in the form of books and audio/video cassettes. He has given their publishing rights to the Society.

## His extreme renunciation and absorbment in the love of Shree Radhey.

Devotees know that a major part of his conscious mind always remains absorbed in the love of Radha Krishn even while talking, lecturing, or dealing with the people of the world. He totally avoids irrelevant talks, but we have seen that he pays full attention to a soul who truly desires to receive Krishn love.

When he was living in the isolated *leela* places in Braj (India), practically he kept nothing with him. There are hundreds of *leela* places of Radha Krishn in Braj where small structures like an old temple without doors, or a pond, or a *raas mandal*, or just one or two rooms without doors (all in a very run-down condition), are still there. These places are outside the villages of Braj. Only certain important places are properly maintained, the others are not. Our Swamiji lived in those places where no one cared to visit.

When he was living in Barsana, the other devotees who lived in or around Barsana, suggested many times to at least make a small place for his living, as they all had something of their own to live in. But Shree Swamiji said that, the whole of Braj is Radha's abode where we all live; so he never made even a single room for himself. Even now, when the Society owns millions worth of properties, he lives a very simple life.

The style of his living in those days was an example of devotion, dedication and renunciation. Eating very little and absorbed in Radha's love, he established the discipline of a true renounced devotee of Radha Krishn. Once, in an isolated place in Govardhan, absorbed in the Bliss of Radha Krishn *leelas*, he remained for thirty days without any food, he only had water two or three times a day. There was a well nearby in the bushes where villagers came to fetch water morning and evening. He just went over there and had some water. There could be rarely a few who could maintain such a renunciation. Even those, who deeply long for the vision of Krishn, do need protection, a proper place to live, and food to eat.

## His whole life is a Divine charity.

Considering the physical difficulties of the devotees, Shree Swamiji decided to have such a place where the dedicated souls, who have left worldly desires and have only one desire to receive the Grace of Radha Krishn, could live and do their devotions. He then established three main *ashrams*: Vrindaban (India), Barsana (India), and Austin (U.S.A.). The ancient *ashrams* of our great Masters were also established on the same principles.

Thousands of souls have been Graced by Shree Swamiji and their minds have been established in pure devotion to Radha Krishn. They have found Divine refuge in him. Shree Swamiji's association opens up the heart of a true seeker of God's love, and he discovers that he has really found someone, for whom his soul was longing to be with for a long time.

## Affection for his devotees.

Swamiji is a friend of every soul. He is always humble. He says that he is a devotee of Radha Rani. He can only guide you to find Radha Krishn love. You may call him your Divine guide, Divine friend, Divine father or Divine mother whatever you wish. He has great affection for his devotees and he cares for them very much. Most of his devotees feel that he is always with them even if he is not physically present.

When Shree Swamiji speaks, his teachings go deep into the heart, and the warmth of his love develops a desire in the listener's heart to meet Radha Krishn, the supreme Divine beloved of every soul. It is hard to turn one's own mind away from the attractions of the world and bring it into the loving remembrance of Radha Krishn, but, with the Grace of Shree Swamiji, it becomes easy for a dedicated soul.

This is what the Bhagwatam describes, that the association of such a *bhakt* Saint reduces worldly attachments and develops a desire to receive Krishn love ( सतां प्रसङ्गान्मम वीर्यसंविदो भवन्ति... ).

There are many kinds of ecstatic states in Krishn love. One of them is called 'conscious ecstasy,' which means, that a person is physically conscious yet, simultaneously, his heart and mind is drowned in Krishn love which is a natural all-time state of his inner consciousness.

Shree Swamiji's state of 'conscious ecstasy' is quite evident. In 1976 when he was touring England, a leading physicist of London, C. Maxwell Cade, writer of The Awakened Mind, witnessed the ecstatic state of Shree Swamiji in the first meeting. Dr. Cade was doing psychobiological research (for the previous eight years) on meditation, and the altered states of the consciousness of the mind. He writes, "Those who have close contact with His Divinity know that he remains continually in his Divine love transcendence. In other words, he has attained to that level of consciousness at which he is in the higher reaches of meditation, and in everyday waking consciousness at the same time. This corresponds to *yogic sahaj samadhi,* or what Carl Jung termed *the Transcendent Function.*" He says that he believes it to be the state beyond the Awakened Mind. Further he says that his 'fifth state' research opened up for him with another visit of Swami Prakashanand Saraswati. He expresses his amazement and says, "He had not seen anyone who could equal Shree Swamiji's feat of touching a number of subjects on the head and immediately raising their pattern of consciousness by two levels, from the ordinary waking state into the advanced fifth state. In at least one of these subjects, the higher state persisted for three days and was an unforgettable experience."

Shree Swamiji is one of the few great Saints of the world who has attained the highest form of God's love, yet he is humble and forgiving. Although he teaches devotion to Radha Krishn, he has regard for all the religions and all the Saints who have shown the true path of devotion to God. He is so absorbed in Radha's love that he has no time for irrelevant or argumentative talks.

## His knowledge about the Divine science of the scriptures is unequalled.

His description of the Divine philosophy holds the authenticity of its Divine originality. He can expound any spiritual topic with such a clarity as if he is describing a visual account. His scriptural understanding is unequaled, and his Divine approach is unquestioned. He is the first person who has bridged the long-lived gap between religion and the modern science and has scientifically brought them together which is evident in his book, The Sixth Dimension.

To understand the secret of our scriptures, a devotional heart longing for God's vision and a true Saint's guidance is compulsory, not only academic learning. In the last hundreds of years, most of the books written about Krishn in the English language were misleading. Some of them were written by prominent spiritual leaders of India. They all made one grave mistake of describing Krishn as an 'incarnation' which cancels the supremacy of Krishn's *omnipresent absolute Divine love form* described in the Upnishads, the Gita, the Bhagwatam, the other Puranas and the Brahm Sanhita, etc.

Shree Swamiji dispelled this fallacy by enlightening us with the knowledge that **the absolute supreme *brahm*, Krishn, Himself descended on the earth planet 5,000 years ago in His original absolute Divine form. His descension was called *'avatar'* which literally means 'to descend.'**

Many more such religious fallacies, which obstruct the devotional growth of an individual, have been removed by revealing the real truth of our scriptures by Shree Swamiji, in his writings and speeches.

## Speeches on *prasthan trayi* (the Upnishads, the Gita and the Brahm Sutra) and systematically revealing the history of 5,000 years and back.

Our ancient *acharyas,* the *Jagadgurus*, wrote detailed explanations called the *bhashya* on *prasthan trayi,* which is: the Brahm Sutra, the Upnishads and the Gita. They are all in Sanskrit language and in great logical detail, unintelligible to a simple devotee. Shree Swamiji, not only explained all of them in a simple understandable style, but also reconciled them, and removed the literal differences of their writings, which were causing intellectual frictions among the followers of those religions.

**Individually explaining the Brahm Sutra, the Upnishads and the Gita *(prasthan trayi)* in his speeches, in full detail (which have been videotaped), Shree Swamiji also revealed the actual history of India of the last 5,000 years.** This is all in his speeches. This is the area where historians have made mistakes in determining the period of events. Our Indian calendar started in 57 B.C., which also tells the beginning of *kaliyug* as 3102 B.C. Emperor Yudhishthir reigned 36 years, and in the thirty seventh year, (in 3102 B.C.), Krishn ascended to His Divine abode which was the beginning of *kaliyug*. Thus the Mahabharat war had happened in 3139 B.C.

The Bhagwatam was first said by Shukdeo to Parikchit thirty years later in *kaliyug*. It means **the Bhagwatam was produced by Ved Vyas sometime before 3072 B.C., and all the four Vedas and the Upnishads were reproduced earlier than the Bhagwatam. The Bhagwatam is also our history book written by such a descended Divine personality, Ved Vyas, who knew all about past, present and future *(trikalagya)*. He predicted our history in detail with the names of the kings and their period of reign, up to around 320 B.C., and the beauty is that it all happened as predicted. Since 320 B.C. and up to today, the main events of our history are already known to us. Thus, from 3139 B.C. to today we have a systematic account of our history, which Shree Swamiji has described in his speeches on the Upnishads.**

The Bhagwatam goes prior to that. It tells, in brief, the total history of India and the earth planet, called *manvantar katha*. It goes as far as 155.52 trillion years back, when the creator Brahma, after receiving the Vedic knowledge from Krishn (during his meditation called *parabhiddhyan)*, revealed the Vedas to the sages of India, for the very first time. That was the period when our planetary system was originally created.

Scientists know about the partial death of the sun when it becomes a dwarf. This is also described in our scriptures, with precise calculations, that it had happened to our sun 18,000 times up until now, and a similar situation of our existing sun will again happen in 2,347 million years when it will have consumed all of its fuel.

Thus we know that the division of periods, cycles of time, and the account of our history, is systematically described in our scriptures. This has all been explained by Shree Swamiji in his speeches and in his writings.

His books are unique examples of his exceeding knowledge related to the science of the material and the Divine dimensions. His Divine greatness is remarkable. He is so simple that he is the friend of every soul desiring God realization. It is a joy to be in his presence. The warmth of his love melts the hearts of the audience and his closeness opens the path to God. His personality is like a fire of God's love. Just come to him with sincere faith and receive it. **There is nothing in the world that could equal to what he has already given to us.**

# 4.
# International Society of Divine Love (ISDL).

ISDL was founded by His Divinity Swami Prakashanand Saraswati (Shree Swamiji), a great Saint from Vrindaban (India), who spent his whole life in loving devotion to Radha Krishn.

In his very childhood, he saw the agony of the world and, to his dismay, he found people sleeping in ignorance and constantly planning to enjoy the short-lived happiness of this world, not thinking about God Who is total Bliss, and not caring to come out of this cosmic ocean of pains and disappointments. There were very few who wanted God, but the varying theories and the stories of different religions made it hard to choose the right path to God and to check its authenticity.

Considering these difficulties and to provide the right path to the true seekers of God's love, Shree Swamiji established the International Society of Divine Love. Its aims are: (a) to introduce the true philosophy of our scriptures (the Gita, the Upnishads, the Bhagwatam, etc.) in the world, and (b) to provide invaluable Divine charity in the form of practical guidance to the devotees, sincerely desiring to receive the vision and love of God.

Up to 1994, we have published six books in the U.S.A.: (1) Towards the Love Divine, (2) Philosophy of Divine Love, (3) The

Shikchashtak, (4) Biographies of Rasik Saints, (5) The Sixth Dimension, and (6) The Path to God (a revised edition). These books explain the philosophy and the devotional truth of our scriptures. Apart from that, we have video and audio speeches of Shree Swamiji on the Gita (146 speeches), the Upnishads (36 speeches), and the Brahm Sutra (108 speeches). Furthermore, there are more than 200 audio and video speeches on general topics, such as: the truth of the world, *mayic* phenomena, God the almighty, God Krishn, Krishn devotion, Krishn *leelas*, etc.

For the practical guidance of the devotional path, the teachers of our Society, who have taken *sanyas* in the *raganuga* tradition of Krishn devotion, give lectures around the world, organize weekend Intensives, and teach devotion to Radha Krishn.

ISDL was first founded in Vrindaban, India, the descension place of Krishn, in 1975. In 1978 Shree Swamiji founded the Society in New Zealand and established an *ashram* in Auckland. Shree Swamiji then came to the U.S.A. and founded the International Society of Divine Love in 1981. In 1990 ISDL bought 200 acres of property in Austin, Texas, which became the main center of ISDL. This is our Barsana Dham.

ISDL has many centers in the U.S.A. All the centers have services *(satsang)* on every Sunday and Wednesday for the general public. Shree Swamiji's speeches are frequently viewed on local cable television channels around the U.S.A. We also have *satsang* every morning and evening at all the centers and *ashrams* for the devotees who live there.

Divali celebrations.
(Above: Lights and fireworks. Below: Evening *satsang*.)

Above: Holi celebration.  Below: Janmashtmi celebration.

# 5.

# General Teachings
of Shree Swamiji.

The teachings of His Divinity Swami Prakashanand Saraswati relate to ancient Hindu scriptures like, the Gita, the Bhagwatam and the Upnishads. After taking *sanyas*, Shree Swamiji studied both, *advait vedant* and *Vaishnav darshans,* and also visualized their secrets during his devotions to Radha Krishn. From childhood, his inclination was towards Radha Krishn, so he followed the path of *bhakti*. He spent a major part of his life in secluded devotion to Radha Krishn in Braj. It was the Grace of Shree Radha that he started preaching the path of *raganuga* devotion that takes a soul to Radha Krishn, the ultimate goal of life.

## General philosophy.

The world is attractive and the human mind is ignorant, so it falls for that attraction, develops attachment, and becomes sentimentally or emotionally involved. This involvement induces a person to cross social rules that becomes sin. Sinful *karmas* and their consequences create such a destiny that inflicts physical and mental pain, discomforts and disappointments in life.

The universe has a law of *karmas* categorized as 'good' and 'bad.' If you do good actions you get better comfort in the next life, and if you do bad actions you receive more discomfort and pain in the next life. The choice is yours.

There is also omnipresent gracious God in this universe Who is willing to help you. If you don't want to be governed by the *karmic* laws of the material world, release your worldly attachments and transfer them to God. When your love and attachment is 100% towards God, He will reveal His Divine form to you, and then you will be Blissful like Him and will live with Him in His Divine abode forever ( तद्विष्णोः परमं पदं सदा पश्यन्ति सूरयः । न स पुनरावर्तते । ).

There are two classes of souls: (1) those souls who are under the bondage of *karmas* and live in this universe, and (2) those who are above the bondage of *karmas*, have Divine body, and are living in the Divine world of their beloved form of God. There are unlimited number of souls in both worlds, material and Divine.

The forms of God and Their Divine abodes are known to us through our scriptures, and the teachings and writings of our great Masters. The style and the practice of the path to God is also revealed through our scriptures (like the Gita, the Bhagwatam and the Upnishads), and the teachings and writings of our great Masters.

A Saint or a Master means that he has experienced a particular form of God (every form of God is absolute), like Krishn *bhakt*, Ram *bhakt*, Vishnu *bhakt*, etc. Thus, according to his own experience, he teaches that style of devotion to God. Sometimes certain eternal Saints, with the will of God, descend to the earth planet from the Divine world and teach the path to God. Every Divine world has a proper name like Vrindaban, Golok, Dwarika, Saket and Vaikunth. The abode of Radha Krishn is called Vrindaban and Golok which reveals the highest sweetness of Divine love.

# What is Hinduism or *Sanatan Dharm*?

Sometimes people ask what is Hinduism or *Sanatan Dharm*? We can say that *Sanatan Dharm* or Hinduism is a complete science of Divine immortality revealed by the supreme God Himself. In fact, the word Hindu is not the original word. In our scriptures India is called 'Bharatvarsh,' and this planetary system along with the celestial worlds is called *'brahmand.'* Around the 14th century, instead of Bharatvarsh, people started calling it 'Hindusthan' and its residents were called the 'Hindus.' Later on the British again changed its name and called it 'India.' The word 'Hindu' and 'India' gained so much popularity that they became commonly spoken words. **Thus, *Bhartiya* philosophy and religion is now called Hinduism, or Hindu philosophy, or Hindu religion.** *Sanatan* means eternal and *dharm* means religion. Thus *Sanatan Dharm* means the eternal universal religion which is now called Hindu religion.

Although Hinduism has both aspects, Spiritual and social, but Hindu religion is specially known in the world for its Spiritual wealth, not to be found anywhere else, because it reveals the complete science of soul, *maya*, God and God realization. **Hinduism teaches loving devotion *(bhakti)* to supreme God (in His various forms) for the whole world.**

The Divine energy that unites a human being with the supreme God is called *bhakti* or *'divine-love-consciousness'* which is the heart of Hindu religion. Our main Divine scriptures are: (1) the Upnishads (Vedas), (2) the Gita and (3) the Bhagwatam. The Gita is the short and simplified account of all the Upnishads. The Bhagwatam tells more about the devotional aspects and the supremacy of Krishn Bliss along with the theories of the Gita and the Upnishads. The Bhagwatam is also our Divine history book. It tells, in detail, about the creation of the universe along with our planetary system with exact time divisions.

Our scriptures originate directly from God so they are eternal. The Vedas (Upnishads) are produced by the creator Brahma on the earth planet, in the very beginning of human civilization. From time to time, an eternal Saint called Ved Vyas reproduces all the scriptures without any alterations. This is the beauty of our scriptures that they remain the same in all the ages on this earth planet. Accordingly, around 3100 B.C., all of our scriptures were reproduced by Ved Vyas and are available now in their original form.

We have six main devotional procedures in our Hindu religion describing the dedication and worship to **the six main forms of the same one single God. They are: (1) God Krishn, (2) God Ram, (3) God Vishnu, (4) God Shiv, (5) Goddess Durga, and dedication to (6) the impersonal form of God.**

(1) Our scriptures like the Gita, the Upnishads and the Bhagwatam are all eternal and protected by God Himself, and (2) the supreme God never incarnates, He descends (*avatar*) and ascends. **These two basic facts are the heart of Hindu religion. If one does not understand this truth, he is very naive and ignorant.**

Devotion to supreme God Lord Krishn (or Radha Krishn) is one of the major branches of Hindu religion followed by a majority of the people of India. The International Society of Divine Love, Barsana Dham, teaches the same authentic and original form of worship to Radha Krishn. This form of devotional worship (although eternal) gained popularity since the latest descension of the same supreme God Lord Krishn around 3200 B.C. Out of His kindness, He Himself came to the earth planet, appeared in Mathura district in His original Divine form, lived in India for more than 100 years and revealed the knowledge of the Gita for the good of mankind.

We teach loving devotion to God in the form of Radha Krishn called *raganuga bhakti* or *divine-love-consciousness*. We use the original (scriptural) Divine names of Radha Krishn for chanting and remembrance. We welcome everyone who sincerely loves God and desires to visualize His Divine form.

# What is *avatar*?

*Avatar* means 'descension.' It is used for God. Sometimes an eternal Saint also comes on the earth planet with the will of God to specially establish *'bhakti'* in the world. Suppose Radha says, "Dear Chitra! Go to Braj, re-establish the *raganuga bhakti* and guide the souls," and Chitra comes to this world as a Saint. Then that Saint may be called the descension of *Gopi* Chitra.

**The descension of God, on the earth planet, is always in His Godly glory and in His eternal Divine form,** but human beings do not recognize His Divineness because they have material mind. Only Saints see Him in His absolute Divine glory and in His eternal Divine form. There are mainly three kinds of descensions: *poornavatar, anshavatar* and *gunavatar.*

*Poornavatar* is only two, Krishn and Ram, and it happens at a scheduled time over and over again. Between the two descensions of Krishn or Ram, there is a minimum gap of at least 18 million years. Sometimes God descends to execute a particular job. He is then called **anshavatar.** Just like Ved Vyas especially descended to reproduce all the scriptures 5,000 years ago. So, you may call Ved Vyas as a great Saint, or a descended Saint, or a descension of God.

*Gunavatar* is a permanent descension of all the almighty forms of God in the celestial space. Out of them, two are main, Shiv and Vishnu. Positive *(sattva)* and negative *(tam),* are the two main forces of eightfold *maya*: earth, water, fire, air, space, emotional and intellectual mind and ego.

" भूमिरापोऽनलो वायु: खं मनो बुद्धिरेव च ।
अहंकार इतीयं मे भिन्ना प्रकृतिरष्टधा ॥ " (The Gita)

God Vishnu is affiliated with the positive force and God Shiv with the negative force of *maya.* The cosmic power *maya* is totally inanimate, it needs a Divine touch to keep it working. Thus these almighty forms of God stay as *gunavatar* in every *brahmand,* as Governor Administrators of the *brahmand.*

Parvati, Kali, Ganesh and Kartikeya are affiliated with Shiv, and Lakchmi is affiliated with Vishnu. Durga, along with Her other affiliates, also stays in the *brahmand.* An individual world, that consists of sun, moon, earth with human beings and a planetary system, is called *brahmand.* Every *brahmand* also has a Divine creator called Brahma. There are unlimited number of *brahmandas* in this endless universe.

Bhagwan Krishn is also called ***premavatar*** because He comes to give Divine love. *Prem* word means Divine love. When Krishn went to Dwarika, He was then called Dwarikadhish. All kinds of *avatars* are described in the Bhagwatam and in other scriptures.

## Radha Krishn descend in Their original Divine form on the earth planet.

It may appear unbelievable but it is true that, in the twentieth century, the majority of English publications on Krishn philosophy and His *leelas* written by renowned writers, scholars, spiritual leaders, teachers and preachers, etc. have given misconceptions about Krishn's Divine personality.

The basic fact of our scriptures is, that Divine is always Divine, and material is always material. God has Divine body which is omnipresent. How can the supreme God have a body of human flesh and blood which is totally material? It is absolutely unscientific, illogical and impossible. Then, how did these writers use such a wrong word 'incarnation' for Krishn's *avatar*, when there is already a word 'descension' which is equivalent to the Sanskrit word *'avatar'* (अवतरणं इति अवतारः), which means to descend from the Divine abode into the material world?

Radha Krishn descend on the earth planet in Their original Divine form, from time to time, to reveal the Vrindaban Bliss, and then, ascend to Their Divine abode. There is also a word *'janm'* used for Krishn. *Janm* word means 'to appear' (प्रादुर्भाव). So, you can say that **Krishn appears or descends, and then He disappears** (अन्तर्धान) **or ascends.**

> "कृष्णस्तु भगवान् स्वयम् ।" (भा. 1/3/28)
> "तदात्मानं सृजाम्यहम् ।" (गी. 4/6)
> "जन्मकर्म च मे दिव्यम् ।" (गी. 4/9)
> "सम्भवाम्यात्ममायया ।" (गी. 4/6)
> "जानन्ति पुरुषोत्तमम् ।" (गी. 15/19)
> "पुरुषं शाश्वतं दिव्यमादिदेवमजं विभुम् ।" (गी. 10/12)

**There are hundreds of such quotations and instances of the Gita and the Bhagwatam, etc. that explain that Radha Krishn descend and live on the earth planet in Their original Divine body and in Their full Divine glory** ( यद्यपि साकारोऽयं तथैकदेशी विभाति यदुनाथः। सर्वगतः... शं.). **The third chapter of tenth canto, and sixth and thirty-first chapters of eleventh canto of the Bhagwatam explain, in detail, about the descension (appearance) and ascension of Krishn. God Shiv, creator Brahma, celestial king Indra and a number of other gods and goddesses along with Devki and Vasudev confirmed and witnessed the Divine descension of Krishn in His actual Divine form and paid their homage.**

In spite of all that information in our scriptures, if someone still uses the word 'incarnation', it shows that, either he deliberately does not want to believe in Krishn's Divine descension, or his knowledge about our *Bhartiya* philosophy, religions and scriptures is very little. The Gita says,

> "अवजानन्ति मां मूढा मानुषीं तनुमाश्रितम् ।" (गी. 9/11)
> "मूढोऽयं नाभिजानाति लोको मामजमव्ययम् ।" (गी. 7/25)

"Ignorant people do not understand the secret of My Divine descension, because their minds are clouded with the effects of *maya.*" Our scriptures further say,

" अनेकचित्तविभ्रान्ता मोहजालसमावृताः ।
प्रसक्ताः कामभोगेषु पतन्ति नरकेऽशुचौ ॥ " (गी. 16/16)

" आसुरीं योनिमापन्ना मूढ़ा जन्मनि जन्मनि ।
मामप्राप्यैव कौन्तेय ततो यान्त्यधमां गतिम् ॥ " (गी. 16/20)

" प्रमाणतोऽपि निर्णीतं कृष्णमहात्म्यमद्भुतम् ।
न शक्नुवन्ति ये सोढुं ते मूढ़ाः निरयं गताः ॥ " (मधुसूदन, गी. 15)

In general, it means that those who disregard the Divine supremacy of Krishn's descension enter into darkness and are severely punished for their transgressions. This is the truth of Krishn's *avatar.* **The same Radha Krishn of Divine Vrindaban descend, according to Their scheduled time, on the earth planet in Their original Divine body and in Their total Divine love glory, charm, Grace and beauty.** All the Saints who were in Braj in those days saw Them the same way.

## Devotion.

We teach devotion to Radha Krishn according to the *raganuga* tradition of Vrindaban based on the teachings of Lord Chaitanya Mahaprabhu.

Chaitanya Mahaprabhuji appeared in India 500 years ago. The Divine history tells us that he was the descension of Radha. He himself, along with other Divine associates (Saints) of Divine Vrindaban, came to teach us the path of pure devotion to Radha Krishn. His disciples Jeev Goswami, Roop Goswami, and Sanatan Goswami wrote most of the books on Krishn devotion based on the philosophy of the Bhagwatam, which already includes the philosophy of the Gita, the Upnishads and the Brahm Sutra.

Soul maintains its eternal identity as a fraction of *jeev shakti* ( जीव शक्ति ) of Krishn ( ममैवांशो जीवलोके जीवभूतः सनातनः । ), which means Krishn is the supreme Soul of all the souls of the universe. The Ved says, " तस्येदं शरीरम् ." It means that Krishn is the Soul of your soul, and Radha is the Soul of Krishn (आत्मा तु राधिका तस्य ।).

That's why a Saint loves Radha and Krishn more than his own soul. So They are the soul-loved Divine beloveds of all the Saints of Golok and Divine Vrindaban.

During the descension period of Radha Krishn, all the *Brajwasis* were descended Saints. They naturally loved and adored Radha Krishn as their heart and soul ( तत्सुखे सुखित्वम् ). Their love was called *'rag.'* Thus, following their style of adoration, and loving Radha Krishn more than your own soul, is called *raganuga bhakti*. All the *acharyas* of Vrindaban showed the same path of *raganuga* devotion to Radha Krishn.

Chaitanya Mahaprabhuji said eight verses (Shikchashtak) telling the practical process of devotion to Radha Krishn. He says that every name of Radha is Radha Herself, and every name of Krishn is Krishn Himself, which has already been graciously revealed on this earth planet through the Saints of the *raganuga* tradition. A devotee, not desiring for any kind of material gain from God, should only seek for selfless Divine love, keep the name of Radha Krishn in his heart all the time while doing his normal duties in the world, remember the *leelas* of Radha Krishn, be humble, be respectful to others, develop a deep loving yearning to meet Radha Krishn without being disappointed, have full faith and confidence in Them, and wholeheartedly listen to or sing the Divine name or *leelas* of Radha Krishn (every name of Radha Krishn is *'mantra'*). This is devotion *(bhakti)*.

Mahaprabhuji says that such a devotion purifies the heart, reduces the mental anxieties, agony and attachments, fills the heart with the sweetness of Radha Krishn love, opens up the true insight of the pure intellect ( प्रज्ञा अथवा विज्ञान ), reveals the nectar of ever-exciting love of Radha Krishn, and produces such a *virah* (constant true longing) that unites him with Radha Krishn forever.

After correct understanding, when you really begin to feel the need of God in your life, you will naturally be inclined to do devotion *(bhakti)* to Radha Krishn as explained above. After some time (depending upon your faith and past *karmas*), you may begin to feel a kind of 'affinity' for Radha Krishn and Their names and *leelas*. This affinity is called *'bhao'* or *'divine-love-consciousness'*.

Affinity with material beings is only on the physical and mental level, and it is transitory; but, affinity *(divine-love-consciousness)* to Radha Krishn is on the soul level. It is a divine energy which evokes and evolves the dormant divine love power hidden in the depths of the human heart and brings him close to God.

In the material world, words or names are just sounds that are assumed to refer to an object or a person. They are mere sounds. They have no proprietary virtues of the object. But Divine names of God are eternal and Divine and have full Divine powers. Thus, the names of Radha are synonymous with Radha Herself, and the names of Krishn are synonymous with Krishn Himself.

Radha's name represents the most exciting ultimate form of the absolute nectar of the limitless ocean of Divine love that contains the absolute Divine charm, beauty, love, Grace and kindness ( पूर्णानुराग-रस-सागर-सार-मूर्ति:). In short you can understand that **Radha Krishn are the absolute loving forms of God. They are for every soul of this world and any soul can worship Radha Krishn.**

Remembrance of the name, singing or listening to the names or *leelas* with a desire to gradually increase the affinity and longing for Radha Krishn (without being disappointed) is the only thing one has to do. This should be done regularly, twice a day for at least half an hour.

There are no stepwise rules or techniques to follow in this path (as it is in Yog Darshan). The same name and the same chanting will take you up to God realization. A devotee has to maintain and deepen his consciousness of Divine love of Radha Krishn in his life.

If you remember that the goal of your life is to receive the selfless love of Radha Krishn, you cannot become careless in your life. If you remember that Radha Krishn are always with you, you can never do anything wrong. If you realize that this life of yours is given to you with the Grace of Radha Krishn, you could never be leisurely wasting the time of your life; and if you really understand the eternal reality of your soul-relationship with Radha Krishn, you will be naturally remembering Them all the time.

**This all happens only through the correct understanding of this Divine truth that Radha Krishn are truly the Soul of your soul.** 🙏

# The Divine lineage of *raganuga* devotion.

🙏

The eternal knowledge of this path of devotion as revealed by the Vedic words " कृष्णएवपरो देवो तं भजेत् ॥ रसो वै सः रसँ ह्येवायं लब्ध्वाऽऽनन्दी भवति ॥ " was introduced by the supreme personality of God Krishn Himself to the creator Brahma 155.521793 trillion years ago, even before the creation of our planetary system.

Brahma again introduced it to the Saints of the earth planet 1,972,819,497 years ago. Around 3202 B.C. Krishn Himself descended on the earth planet in His original Divine form. Ved Vyas related the *leelas* of Krishn and re-established the same knowledge of Krishn devotion through the Bhagwatam. *Rasik* Saints and *Jagadgurus* continuously maintained the tradition of Krishn devotion in the world.

Shree Chaitanya Mahaprabhuji further glorified the magnificence of Krishn *bhakti* and called it *raganuga bhakti* which continues until today. We teach the same authentic form of loving devotion to the supreme form of God, Radha Krishn, called *'divine-love-consciousness'* ( रागानुगा भक्ति ).

Barsana Dham represents the abode of Radha Krishn that radiates the Divine love of God which any faithful soul could come with open heart and experience.

🙏

# 6.

## Guidelines and Disciplines for a Devotee of Radha Krishn (as Explained by Shree Swamiji).

1.  Remembering the name in the heart and feeling the presence of Radha Krishn near himself, a devotee should do his devotions regularly, every morning and evening.

2.  He should follow his path wholeheartedly but he should not disrespect other religions or their *acharyas* (Spiritual Masters).

3.  Our path of devotion is authentic, natural and very effective. When a new devotee starts doing regular devotions, sometimes it may happen that the past negativities of his mind may come in his way of devotion in the form of some kind of uncomfortable feeling, during the course of purification of the heart. It is like scrubbing and cleaning a floor which was neglected for years. In such situations, the devotee should still keep on doing his devotions whole-heartedly, without being disturbed. He should know that it takes some time to be fully settled in Krishn devotion.

4.  A devotee should not enter into unnecessary philosophical or devotional arguments with the followers of other paths.

Devotional advice should be given to the one who respects your feelings.

5.   A devotee should not study such philosophical or religious books which are not helpful in increasing love for Radha Krishn. He should learn more about the philosophy of Krishn love, *leelas* of Radha Krishn, life history of *rasik* Saints and their humbleness, dedication and devotion, etc.

6.   Fault finding and criticizing fellow devotees should be completely avoided. One should look into his own faults and try to remove them.

7.   Food affects the mind. A normal, healthy and easily digestible vegetarian meal helps to improve pious qualities of the mind. Non-vegetarian food does the opposite.

8.   A devotee should be away from illicit lust, all kinds of intoxicants, and smoking, as they directly affect your body and mind.

9.   A human mind naturally leans towards more bodily comfort, laziness, gossiping, and prideful talks. A devotee should observe his own weaknesses of this kind and try to overcome them.

10.   *Titikcha* should be maintained. It means a devotee should increase his physical and mental tolerance. He should not be disturbed with undesirable physical situations like weather, etc., and he should not feel hurt if some other devotee says something which he does not like. He should keep his mind calm and devotional. He should know that **every devotional thought has a value**, and every negative thought adversely effects the devotional feelings.

11.   Living moderately, he should improve his faith in God and the Master and humbly do his devotions.

12. Sometimes some devotees receive some extraordinary blissful experience in their devotion due to their dedication and good *sanskars*. Such experiences may or may not stay for very long. It may subside down. Then they wonder what has happened. One should know that devotional experiences are influenced by the devotee's own good and bad *sanskars* of past lives. A Saint, by his own nature, Graces his devotees all the time according to their dedication. When you already have the Gracious hand of the Saint on your head, what else do you want.

13. Sometimes strong bad *sanskars* of past life come in this lifetime and effect the dedication of the mind. Accordingly, unnecessary confusions and questions may enter the mind. His faith in the supremacy of Krishn love and His Grace, etc. may appear to be less than before, and he may feel less affinity in doing devotions. When such things happen he should know that his old *sanskars* are playing with his mind. He must, then, firmly keep doing his devotions and service, and pray Radha Krishn and his Master to overcome this situation and to improve his faith and dedication.

14. 'Inferiority complex' is an enemy of devotion. You should not let it enter your mind anytime, even for a short while.

15. Prejudiced, depressed, or negative thinking of any kind adversely affects your devotions, instantaneously creates negative *sanskars*, hurts the feelings of your Master, and restricts the Grace. It could be really devastating if it persists in your mind for a long time. A wise devotee foresees the consequences and immediately avoids such a hazard by replacing it with loving and positive thinking. You should know that a negative thought could only be cancelled with a positive thought.

16. The most important thing is, that even in adverse situations, a devotee should not feel disheartened. He must have full faith and confidence in the gracious kindness of the Divine Beloved of his soul, Radha Krishn and his Master. He should use all the available time (in 24 hours) in remembrance and try to increase affinity and longing for Radha Krishn.

17. Time is valuable, it should not be wasted. Past is bygone, and future is unsure. Present is in your hands. Use it for the attainment of Radha Krishn love, before it is too late.

**(Devotees who are living in an *ashram*.)**

18. *Ashram* living is different than individual living. In the *ashram* you have to be much more tolerant and more accommodating and cooperative with other devotees. Never pick on the faults of others. Even if some devotee opposes you, you have to be tolerant and forgiving. This habit will improve your devotion and bring you closer to your Master.

19. Cooperation among the devotees is very important. Think of yourself, how much you cooperate with others. **Try to be giving, not demanding**. Everyone does things for himself, but if you help your fellow devotees in some way, it will create more harmony and will improve your devotional humbleness.

20. Never hurt the feelings of other devotees out of your vanity or rudeness. Think, before you open your mouth. Never try to find an excuse for your mistakes, and never try to blame others for your mistakes.

21. Some devotees, while regularly doing their devotions, very happily do a lot of service in the *ashram* or to the Divine mission. Their dedication appears to be great to other devotees but, in some corner of their mind, they hold an important part of their personal attachment which they don't want to release or submit to Krishn. That situation defaults their single-mindedness, and thus, restricts their devotional experience of

**Radha Rani Rath Yatra Celebrations held on the Sharad Poornima of 1997**
(Above: Starting the Rath Yatra. Below: Shree Swamiji doing first *arti*.)

**Radha Rani Rath Yatra Celebrations held on the Sharad Poornima of 1997**
(Above: Rath Yatra near Prem Sarovar and Govardhan Hill.
Below: Close up of Radha Rani on the chariot.)

*bhao.* As time goes by and the devotee comes closer to his old age, this attachment deepens, and it could be observed by other devotees. This all happens because of lack of faith and confidence in Radha and Krishn Who are truly yours and are always willing to embrace you and to Grace you with Their vision any time. Please don't let it happen to you.

22. **When two devotees quarrel or criticize each other, it directly hurts your Master, which you don't want to do.** So, be forgiving and try to recognize the good qualities of that devotee for whom you have some kind of grudge.

23. If you make a mistake, tell it to your Master before it is too late to rectify. Holding it back may be disastrous.

24. Sometimes, attraction to the opposite sex becomes the main cause for a devotee to fall from his devotions. Specially, for a single devotee, it is most important that he must keep himself away from such situations, associations, and attractions. Even a moments mistake may prove disastrous. If he is doing any service in the Temple or *ashram,* he should not share his services with a person of the opposite sex. Men should work with men, and women with women.

25. Some devotees wish to do service but they wish to do it in their own style. You should know that service is not a job to do. Service means leaving your habit of carelessness and improving your humbleness through offering some kind of service. It is also important that a devotee should maintain his health, don't sleep too much or too little (6 to 7 hours sleep in 24 hours is enough), and maintain a discipline in his living pattern. A physically sick person can neither do his devotions properly nor service.

26. Radha Krishn love, *bhao bhakti,* should be carefully protected in the heart. Don't let it decline due to your own uncompromising nature and personality problems.

27. When you hide or withhold something from your Master, with this hesitation or fear that he may not approve it, you are defaulting your faith in him, and that may become the cause of your downfall during bad *sanskars*. You should know that you receive his Grace on the base of the sincerity of your dedication. The Grace of the Master originates from Radha Rani Who knows everything that is in your mind.

28. Devotion also includes discipline, self-restraint and simple living. Live with minimum requirements. Don't unnecessarily waste anything, and don't misuse any available facility. Our *rasik* Saints of Vrindaban have already established the discipline of devotional living. Learn from their life history.

29. A *sanyasi* sets the example of renunciation, devotion, discipline and loving-devotional-humble benevolence for others. He must be aware of that, and maintain it in his behavior.

30. A *sanyasi* preacher must not waste his time idly. He must use his time either in devotion or service. Renounced living, keeping good health (so he can do better service), experiencing the Grace and closeness of the Master, keeping the love of Radha Krishn in his heart, contributing to the mission whatever is needed and being alert in service, are the virtues of a *sanyasi* preacher which he must maintain.

## Barsana Dham Ashram disciplines.

Barsana Dham represents the ancient *ashrams* of India. *Ashram* is a Sanskrit word, which means a place for worship and Divine adoration where a true seeker of God's love feels at home and receives guidance and inspiration to proceed on his Divine path.

We teach devotion to the supreme form of God, Radha Krishn. There are many devotees who live in Barsana Dham. Visitors also come for a short stay. We have *satsang* for the general public at 7:30 p.m. on every Sunday. We also have *satsang* (especially for the Indian community) from 11:00 a.m. to 12:30 p.m on every Sunday.

(a) Anyone can join our *satsang* and experience peace and devotional bliss. When Shree Swamiji is present, he gives a chance to a newcomer to ask any devotional questions he may have.

(b) Apart from *satsang* for the public, we also have *satsang* every day, morning and evening for the devotees of the *ashram.* Our morning *satsang* starts at 7:30 a.m. with prayer and *arti* followed by quiet meditation. Then we have chanting meditation. Evening *satsang* at 7:30 p.m. starts with a prayer and chanting meditation, followed by a speech by Shree Swamiji (video). Again we have chanting meditation, and *arti* and homage. Our chantings are very special. They open your heart to receive God's love. When Shree Swamiji is at Barsana Dham he comes in *satsang* to give his *darshan* and blessings, and we have an opportunity to listen to his teachings. Visitors, who come for a short stay in Barsana Dham, are mostly guests of our life members. They come to enjoy the devotional atmosphere of Barsana Dham. They are supposed to join our regular *satsang*, every morning and evening.

(c) Those who permanently reside in Barsana Dham join our *satsang* every day. They are such devotees who are doing devotion of Radha Krishn for many years under the guidance of Shree Swamiji. There are families who live in their houses and their children go to local schools. There are some single people and there are some married couples who have their own residences. All of them are fully devoted to God. In gist it could be said that **one has to be an evolved devotee of Radha Krishn to live in Barsana Dham.**

There are many spiritual resorts, *ashrams* and communities in the West where people go, relax, socialize, and enjoy physical-mental happiness in their own style. Barsana Dham is totally different from those. **It is like a Divine university where devotees come to experience pure devotion to the personal form of God.** Although everyone is welcome to join our public *satsang*, but those who wish to stay for some time in Barsana Dham as a guest have to have faith in the personal form of God, Radha Krishn.

Devotees living here have already devoted their life for God realization. The Divineness of Barsana Dham corresponds to the *ashrams* of our historical Saints of Vrindaban as they were 500 years ago. To maintain its purity we have made these disciplines according to the Hindu (*Bhartiya*) tradition as explained by our great Masters.

## Do's and Don'ts:

A devotee living in Barsana Dham, (a) should attend our regular morning and evening meetings every day (except when he is given some other service at that time), (b) keep the remembrance of Radha Krishn throughout the day and night (as much as he can), and (c) have full confidence in the Grace of Radha Krishn. The rest of the disciplines, which he has to follow, are already explained earlier in this chapter.

Smoking, intoxicants and non-vegetarian food are prohibited. Other religious groups using our facility should also follow these rules.

# 7.
# Our Contributions to the World.

It is seen that even the most affluent people suffer from mental anguish and anxiety, and they look for the peace of mind which cannot be bought by money. 'Peace' is the effect of spiritual Grace, either you earn it through proper devotion to God, or receive it through the Grace and blessings of a Saint. Shree Swamiji has already Graced us with his teachings and has given us direct blessings in the form of his chantings of Radha name. 'Barsana Dham' itself is the embodied Grace of Shree Swamiji. These Divine contributions, which he has given to the world, are invaluable.

(1) **Speeches and books:** Shree Swamiji's speeches and writings are direct revelations of the Divine philosophy, explaining the secrets of all the scriptures and dispelling the blind faith or intellectual dogmatic fallacies which have prevailed for centuries. Thus, giving us a crystal clear simple path to God, he has brought the material science and the Divine science together by clearly explaining and demarcating their respective fields of action.

(2) **Chantings:** Shree Swamiji's chantings are a free boon to any sincere open-minded person desiring to feel the closeness of God, and so are his speeches. His voice goes deep into the heart of the listener and fills it with the love of God. This is

something very special. In our *satsang,* we play these speeches and chantings.

(3) **The advent of Barsana Dham that reveals the undivided love of God which is the soul of all the religions:** The speeches of Shree Swamiji on the Gita tell us that the philosophy of all the major religions of the world is already in the Gita along with its prime message of *divine-love-consciousness.* The philosophy of the Gita is the origin of all the religions of the world. Today we are facing great diversity in religious faiths. Some people are trying to harmonize it through interfaith movements and conferences, but after so much talk and extensive paperwork, the situation remains the same. It appears that there is something missing.

**Shree Swamiji introduces this missing link and says that the prime aim of all the religions is to experience the blissfulness of God which is Divine and undivided. The religious diversities may automatically disappear if their followers (keeping aside their ritualistic and cultural differences) begin to desire to experience that undivided love of God.**

With the Grace of Shree Radha Rani and the effort of Shree Swamiji, a Divine nucleus has already been formed in the form of Barsana Dham, where a follower of any religion, who is humbly and sincerely looking for Divine love, may find peace, happiness and God's love.

It is the Grace of Shree Swamiji who has imbued Barsana Dham with the Divineness of Radha Krishn love which is vividly felt in its atmospheres and is experienced by God-loving people, even by the visitors who come for a short visit to Barsana Dham.

(4) **Meditation meetings, services and celebrations:** There is no charge for joining our public meetings. It contains Shree Swamiji's video speech and chanting meditation. Anyone can join and experience 'peace of mind' and 'devotional bliss.'

We also celebrate all the major Hindu religious festivals like Holi, Divali, Ram Navmi, Shiv Ratri, Krishn Janmashtmi, Radha Ashtmi, Sharad Poornima, Guru Poornima, etc., where thousands of people enjoy the festivity of our devotional celebrations in the devotional environments of the Temple and the *ashram.*

Barsana Dham is a place in the U.S.A. where Spiritual energy permeates the atmosphere. Thousands of faithful visitors have experienced the presence of this blissful energy. You feel peaceful and relaxed without doing any meditation as you enter Barsana Dham, which is the effect of the gracious presence of His Divinity Swami Prakashanand Saraswati.

**God's love (Divine love) is desired by all the religions of the world, and Barsana Dham is a place where God's love is eminent, that is what the world of today needs.**

*Divine-love-consciousness* will establish social harmony and peace in the world.

# Glossary.

*acharya*. A historical descended Saint in whose name a religion is formed.

*advait vedant*. The philosophy of impersonal aspect of God, also called absolute monism.

*arti*. Waving of light in front of a Deity, altar, or a Divine Personality to offer his hearty salutations.

*ashram*. The residential place of a Saint and the devotees (whose prime aim of life is God realization) and also a place where a seeker of God's love receives devotional guidance.

*bal leela*. The childhood plays of Krishn or Radha.

**Bauddh**. The philosophy or the religion, which is related to Mahatma Buddha, is called Bauddh ( बौद्ध ).

*bhakt*. The devotee of a personal form of God, like Krishn *bhakt*. The plural of *bhakt* is *bhaktas*.

*bhakti, divine-love-consciousness*. Devotion, adoration and loving remembrance of Radha Krishn (or any other form of God) without desiring any worldly thing from Him.

*bhao*. The devotional emotional states of an evolved *bhakt* devotee.

*Bhao*. The Divine ecstatic states of a Saint.

*Bhartiya*. That which relates to Bharat (Bharatvarsh), which is the original name of India, like *Bhartiya* philosophy.

*brahmand.* A planetary system, including the celestial worlds.

*Brajwasis.* The people of Braj (the Mathura district) who lived during the time of Krishn. Wasi means dweller. So *Brajwasi* means the original residents of Braj.

*darshan.* Dedicated vision, or viewing or seeing. It is in relation to a Saint, a Deity of God, or God Himself in His personal form. Like the vision of God, viewing a Deity, or respectfully seeing a Saint.

**Deity.** Statue of God or Goddess specially made and established at an altar for devotion and meditations with Godly feelings ascribed to it.

*divine-love-consciousness.* The consciousness of the closeness of Radha Krishn (or any personal form of God), when a devotee lovingly remembers His name, form, virtues or leelas, is called *divine-love-consciousness.*

*divya prem ras.* Ever-new and ever-increasing bliss of Divine love.

**God.** The supreme, all-powerful Divinity, Who is kind, gracious and omnipresent in His Divine form in His entire creation, and also has an omnipresent impersonal aspect of His Divine being. It is equivalent to the word *bhagwan.*

*Gopis.* The maidens of Braj during the descension period of Radha Krishn.

*gyani, gyan, gyan marg.* The followers of impersonal aspect of God are called *gyani* and their impersonal concept and understanding is called *gyan. Marg* means 'the path'.

*Jagadgurus.* The eternal Saints who specially descended on the earth planet with the will of God, wrote the explanations of the Brahm Sutra, the Gita and the Upnishads, and established their religions.

*jeev shakti.* A formless (*nirakar*) Divine power of God of absolute nature which contains all the unlimited number of souls. It is just a dormant Divine intellect, called '*chit.*'

*karmas.* Actions of a person.

*leela.* The Divine loving plays of Radha Krishn and the *Gopis* or *Brajwasis.*

*leelasthali.* The place where a *leela* has happened.

*maharaas*. Once Radha Krishn fully revealed Their Divine love on a particular Sharad Poornima night (5,000 years ago), and unlimited number of associating *Gopis* experienced the same Divine love while playing, singing and dancing with Radha Krishn. That was *maharaas*.

*mahatma*. A holy person.

*mantra*. A Divine name of God or a Sanskrit phrase with the Divine name of God which a person lovingly remembers or repeats in his mind to purify his heart.

*maya*. The original cosmic (material) power that manifests the whole universe. It is lifeless so it has no mind of its own but it works in a very systematic, computerized manner. It has its own inherent qualities called pious, impious and devilish (*sattva, raj* and *tam*).

*mayavadi*. A materialistic person, sect or ideology.

*mayic*. That which is related to *maya* or which is a product of *maya*.

*nirvikalp samadhi*. The *sattvic* (pious) transcendental state of the mind with no thought or vision of any kind.

*pragya, vigyan*. The conscience of a very pure nature which reveals the closeness of soul or God.

*raas*. *Gopis* singing and dancing with Radha Krishn. It is a kind of short version of *maharaas*.

*raas mandal, maharaas mandal*. The place where *raas* or *maharaas* happens.

*rag*. The natural love of *Brajwasis* for Radha Krishn.

*raganuga bhakti*. Divine-love-devotion to Radha Krishn that follows the pattern of *Brajwasi's* love for Radha Krishn.

*ras*. The Bliss of Divine love is called *ras*.

*rasik*. The Divine personality who has attained the vision and love of Radha Krishn is called a *rasik* Saint.

Saint. The one who has visualized and realized God in any form, and whose teachings are based on the themes and the guidelines of the Gita, Bhagwatam and Upnishads which are our prime scriptures. There are three categories of Saints: *gyani* Saints, *bhakt* Saints, and *rasik* Saints. (1) *Gyani* Saints are those who have attained the impersonal (*nirakar*) form of God. They are of two kinds: *gyani* Saint and *yogi* Saint, (2) *Bhakt* Saints are those who have attained a personal form of God like, Vishnu, Durga, Shiv, Ram, Krishn etc. (3) Those *bhakt* Saints who attain the Divine love form of God like, Ram or Krishn, are called *rasik* Saints (*ras* means the Divine love), but generally speaking the *rasik* word refers to those Saints who have received the vision and Divine love of Radha Krishn.

*samadhi.* The ecstasy. The quality and the depth of a *samadhi* depend upon the *sattvic* purity of a devotee.

*sanyas.* The renounced order of life meant for the service of God and God realization. The one who takes this order is called *sanyasi.*

*satsang.* Devotional speech and chanting programs for the upliftment of *divine-love-consciousness* of a devotee.

**Sharad Poornima.** The day when Radha Krishn revealed the Divine bliss of *maharaas.*

*shastra.* The scriptures relating the general, social or devotional discipline of a spiritual living.

*teerth.* Holy places in India that are related to a descension of God, or a great historical Saint lived there whose Divine presence made it holy.

*titikcha.* To improve physical tolerance from heat and cold and to improve mental tolerance if someone says anything to you which you don't like.

*Vaishnav.* A humble devotee of Krishn, Ram or Vishnu.

*Vaishnav darshans.* The explanations *(bhashyas)* on Brahm Sutra, Gita and Upnishads by *Vaishnav Jagadgurus* and *acharyas.*

*varnashram dharm.* The Vedic ritualistic and devotional discipline for the four castes and the four orders of life.

*virah.* The deep longing for Radha Krishn (or any other form of God) is called *virah.*

# Scriptural References.

| | |
|---|---|
| ऐ. | Aittariyopnishad |
| अपरो. | Aparokchanubhuti |
| भा. | Bhagwatam |
| भ.र.सिं. | Bhakti Rasamrit Sindhu |
| भक्ति सं. | Bhakti Sandarbh |
| ब्र.सं. | Brahm Sanhita |
| ब्र.सू. | Brahm Sutra |
| ब्र.वै.पु. | Brahm Vaivart Puran |
| बृ.भा. | Brihad Bhagwatamrit |
| चै.च. | Chaitanya Charitamrit |
| छां. | Chandogyopnishad |
| दे.भा. | Devi Bhagwatam |
| ग.सं.गो. | Garg Sanhita, Golok khand |
| गौ. महा. | Gaurang Mahaprabhu |
| गी. | Gita |
| गो.पू.ता. | Gopal Poorv Tapniyopnishad |
| गो.उ.ता. | Gopal Uttar Tapniyopnishad |
| ई. | Ishopnishad |
| जा. | Jabaldarshanopnishad |
| कलि. | Kalisantaranopnishad |
| कठ. | Kathopnishad |
| कृष्ण कर्णामृत | Krishn Karnamrit |
| महो. | Mahopnishad |

| मां. | Mandukyopnishad |
| मुं. | Mundkopnishad |
| पद्म. | Padm Puran |
| प्र. सु. | Prabodh Sudhakar |
| प्रश्न. | Prashnopnishad |
| रा. उ. | Radhikopnishad and Radha Tapniyopnishad |
| शं. | Shankaracharya |
| श्वे. | Shvetashvataropnishad |
| त्रि. महा. | Tripadvibhushit Mahanarayanopnishad |
| वि.पु. | Vishnu Puran |
| वृ. म. | Vrindaban Mahimamritam |
| वृ. | Vrihadaranyak Upnishad |
| यो. शि. | Yog Shikhopnishad |

## Other referenced scriptures:

Brahmand Puran
Krishn Sandarbh
Krishnopnishad
Mathamnaya
Muktikopnishad
Narad Paribrajakopnishad
Nyay Darshan
Panchdashi
Parmatm Sandarbh
Purusharth-bodhinyopnishad
Radhopnishad
Ramayanam
Samrahasyopnishad
Sankhya Darshan
Sanyasopnishad
Sarvnirnaya Prakarn (Vallabhacharya)
Shikchashtak
Shukrahasyopnishad
Vivek Chudamani
Vrihannaradiya Puran
Yog Darshan
Yog Vashishth

# Index (English).

**Braj** *leelas*  *See also: leelas*
 definition of  60
*braj ras*
 definition of  308
*Brajwasis*  60, 65, 69, 73, 76, 79, 80, 91, 162, 237, 241, 320, 329, 340
 definition of  37
 during the descension of Radha Krishn they were all descended Saints  361
 their love for Radha Krishn was called *rag*  361
*buddhi*  102

**C**

**celestial abodes**
 also called *sattvic lokas*  213
**celestial gods and goddesses**  104
 are *mayic* powers  131
 serve Krishn during His descension period  119
**Chaitanya Charitamrit**  53, 181, 307
 describes Radha Krishn as supreme *brahm*  124–125
 gives a description of the powers (*shaktis*) of God  86–87
 the absoluteness of all the aspects of *prem ras* is *Mahabhao* who is Radha Herself  308
 the prime disciples of Mahaprabhuji were all descended Saints  53
**Chaitanya Mahaprabhu**  72, 74, 275, 288, 297, 321, 322.  *See also: achintya bhedabhed vad*
 a list of some of the writings by his disciples  181
 accepted the Bhagwatam as the explanation of the Brahm Sutra  53
 advised to stay away from philosophies that don't teach selfless devotion to Radha Krishn  293
 appeared in West Bengal in 1485 and ascended to Golok in 1533  180
 appeared with his associates to teach the path of pure devotion to Radha Krishn  360
 brief biography of  180
 his definition of devotion  361
 did not establish a *math* or religion  173
 freely distributed the Divine love of Radha Krishn through chanting of Divine name  53, 180
 gave the total understanding for a devotee in one verse  81
 in his Shikchashtak explains *bhakti*'s seven stages in one verse  235
 mainly introduced *madhurya bhao* of Krishn along with all the other *bhao*  185
 said every name of Radha Krishn is *mantra*  361
 the *raganuga bhakti* tradition of Vrindaban  360
 told about the supremacy of Shree Raseshwari Radha Rani  54
 told the practical process of devotion to Radha Krishn in his 'Shikchashtak'  53, 180, 181, 235, 361–362
 Ved Vyas mentioned his descension in the Puranas  53
 was the descension of Radha Herself  53, 173, 180, 285, 286, 297, 360
*char*  105
*chetragya shakti*.  *See also: jeev shakti*
 definition of  86
*chid brahm*  168, 296, 311.  *See also: nirakar brahm*
 as omnipresent *chit* power of Krishn  95, 97
 does not even recognize its own identity as *chit*  137
 is affiliated with *jeev shakti*  95, 137
 is dormant like the dormant intelligence of an unconscious mind  138
 is established along with *maya* and *jeev shakti* in *sagun sakar bhagwan*  138
 is the *nirakar* aspect of God established in *swaroop shakti*  86
 *jeev shakti* resides parallel to  138

**D**

*darshan* 326, 330, 334

*darshan shastras*
explain that the soul's pain is the effect of *mayic* involvement 152
explain that there is no everlasting happiness in *maya* 152
five of its six *darshans* relate to renunciation and refer to soul only 150
the goal of Nyay, Vaisheshik and Sankhya is the elimination of pain only 152
the most important philosophies of God, soul and *bhakti* are explained in the Brahm Sutra 153
Yog Darshan teaches renunciation and introversion and is the practical side of Sankhya 153

*dasya bhao*
a brief description of 74

**Deity Establishment Ceremony**
as seen and experienced 329–332

**descension** *See also: avatar*
definition and translation of the word '*avatar*' 347, 357, 358–360
Krishn as *premavatar* 358
of eternal Saints to the earth planet to teach the path to God described 354, 357
three main types of descension: *anshavatar, gunavatar* and *poornavatar* 357–358

**destiny** 151. *See also: karm*
collective and individual 108
of individual souls 41, 109, 110, 313
of lower species 108
of the earth planet 108
of the galaxy 108, 110

**Devki** 79, 359

**devotee**
admonishments according to the Bhagwatam 224
all *bhaktas* of every class and kind are technically related to Krishn 256
an example of a *bhakt* approaching Saints of different forms of God for help 288
can receive the blessings of his Master no matter how far away he is 282
following the advice and instructions of the Master is the best service he could do 281
forms a loving spiritual relationship with the Saint as his Divine father 294
his devotional love is beyond physical boundaries and is related to the soul 234
his faith and love for his Master attracts the Master's blessings 281
his original form of worship is replaced by Krishn devotion in the presence of a *rasik* Saint 278
his present devotion and future rebirth are influenced by God's Grace 300
his style of devotion and selflessness corresponds to differences in Divine attainment 230, 233–234
indications of *bhao bhakti* in his daily life described according to Roop Goswami 239–240
it is up to him how much Grace he receives from the Master 282
lack of longing means lack of understanding 258
must desire Radha's Grace with firm determination and hope 275
must maintain and deepen his consciousness of Divine love of Radha Krishn 362
must maintain humbleness to overcome pridefulness 265
Naradji gave the example of how a Krishn devotee should be 65
of Krishn does not need to study *vedant* and Upnishads 220
of Krishn only has to learn devotional philosophy to maintain his faith and love 221
of Shiv or Vishnu feels devotionally elevated in the presence of a Krishn *bhakt* Saint 277
on his own cannot undo his own misfortune (*durdaio*) 275
prays from his heart 259

**devotion** *(cont.)*
    advice to married and single people regarding sensual attraction 264
    as described by Chaitanya Mahaprabhu in Shikchashtak 54, 361–362
    avoiding the study of such books that don't teach the path of *raganuga bhakti* 268
    avoiding the wrong association of people who create conflict in your path 268
    both the *sakar* and *nirakar* forms of God are attainable through 121
    correct understanding and firm faith are equally important for steady progress in 236
    depression, dejection and prejudice default devotion 267
    in the *raganuga style* is not a disciplinary act of concentration in the brain area 261
    is done with a healthy and sound mind 240
    is prescribed in all the stages of life 228
    is the essence of all spiritual practices 54
    it is for receiving His love and vision and not for family prosperity 248
    its discipline described 262
    its goal and procedure described 54, 182
    meditation and remembrance in described 261, 262, 263, 362
    not just any kind of devotional discipline will give God realization 54
    only if done wholeheartedly to a personal form of God is related to God's Grace 300
    relational feelings described 261
    subtle vanity hampers a devotee's humbleness 264
    the Bhagwatam says other forms of God are naturally rejoiced with devotion to Radha
        Krishn 249
    the five main aspects described 261–263
    the obstacles of the path:
        - bad *sanskars* 263
        - fault finding 264
        - pridefulness, etc. 265–267
        - sensual attraction 264
        - wrong association 268
    the sequence for receiving devotional affinity described by our scriptures 275
    the six main things to remember and observe 283
    there are no stepwise rules or techniques to follow in 362
    to multiple forms of God is classified as a good deed, but is not *bhakti* 288
    understanding, renunciation and longing happen simultaneously through 258
**devotional expressions**
    or *sattvic bhao* of a devotee as described by Roop Goswami 242
*dharm* 70, 118
    is of two kinds, *par* (primary) and *apar* (secondary) 70
    Vallabhacharya said *brahm* is the source of 183
*dharna* 197, 205
**Dhruv** 211, 230
*dhyan*
    along with *dharna* and *samadhi* is for introverting the mind into pious thoughtlessness
        197
    as *sabeej samadhi* 201
    definition of 201
    the process of engrossing the mind is described 202
*dikcha* 288. *See also: initiation*
**dissolution** *See also: maha pralaya*
    celestial gods and goddesses remain in a *nirakar* state 104, 253
    is controlled by the force of *karm* of the souls 107
    *kal, karm, maya* and souls remain in God in a *nirakar* dormant state 103, 131
    the eternal cycle of creation and dissolution 103
**Divine abodes**
    always remain eternally the same and unchanged 253
    and forms of God exist eternally in the Divine dimension 35, 298

**Gita** *(cont.)*
    God's impersonal form is subordinately established within His personal form  296
    ignorant people do not understand the secret of Divine descension  359
    is in simple Sanskrit in 700 verses  42
    is the short and simplified essence of the Upnishads  42, 231, 355
    its main theme relates to selfless devotion to Krishn  231
    its philosophy is the origin of all the religions of the world  374
    *karm yog* defined  225
    the path of devotion to God's personal form is easy and simple  296
    the path of *gyan* or *nirakar brahm* is extremely difficult  296
    the style and practice of the path to God is revealed  354
    was reproduced by Ved Vyas  42
    was said by Krishn Himself when he descended on the earth planet 5,000 years ago  32, 41
    with the Upnishads and Brahm Sutra comprise the *prasthan trayi*  172
**God**  *See also: brahm*
    a diagram depicting His relationship to soul and *maya*  298
    a diagram depicting the qualitative superiority of His Divine abodes  308
    a diagram depicting the simultaneous omnipresence of all His forms  298
    a reconciled definition  122
    *ahladini* is His supreme power whose most intimate state is Radha  52
    all *dharmas* are established in Him  121
    all Divine powers form the supreme absoluteness of one single God  139
    all forms of God are substantially one and absolute  52
    all forms of God worship each other at certain occasions  48
    all of His forms have a particular style of related to a Divine abode  298
    becomes everything in the universe  155, 184
    *chit*-soul and anti-*chit maya* dependently reside in God  99
    created the universe so the souls could come to Him through *bhakti*  121
    definition of  44–45
    descends in His glory and Divine form that only Saints recognize  357
    descends out of kindness in the world in His original Divine form to reveal *bhakti*  123
    engulfs the unlimited expansion of the whole universe  117
    eternal associates of God '*nitya siddha mahapurush*'  128
    exists in His own glory unaffected by the creation and *maya*  120, 134, 181
    facts about Him should be taken with faith  133
    fulfills every desire of His *bhakt* who visualizes Him  211
    has amazing powers that unfold incomprehensible Divine states  122
    has amazing unlimited Divine powers and self-contradictory Divine situations  117
    has both personal and impersonal forms  117, 122, 296
    has many kinds of sweet relationships with His devotee souls  121, 123
    has many omnipresent forms of a mono-dualistic nature  81
    has no material-like senses yet is the enjoyer of all five kinds of Blissfulness  117
    has three categories of Divine blissfulness  34
    has three eternally existing forms as *brahm, paramatma* and *bhagwan*  62, 120
    has three main categories of His Divine attainment  231
    has uncountable Divine virtues  134
    His absolute beauty and Divine love form is Krishn who did *maharaas*  232
    His absolute supreme power is called *para shakti, swaroop shakti, atmmaya, yogmaya,* etc.  138
    His Bliss cannot be experienced through vanity elevating practices  255
    His devotional philosophy is understood by a faithful and devoted mind  45
    His Divine Bliss is not experienced unless He is perceived  134
    His Divine body is beyond the limitations of a material body  117, 133, 358
    His Divine body is omnipresent and eternal  358
    His forms are eternal, unchanging, and exist in their own Divine dimension  104

**Indra** 37, 359
**initiation**
    description of 288–289
**International Society of Divine Love** 343, 352
    a list of its published books 351
    founded in the USA 352
    its four aims described 351
    teaches devotion to Radha Krishn based on the *raganuga* tradition of Vrindaban 360
    teaches the same *bhakti (divine-love-consciousness)* as shown by our ancient masters 287, 356
    welcomes everyone who sincerely loves God and desires to visualize His Divine form 356
*Ishwar*
    as defined in the Vyas Bhashya of the Yog Darshan 207

**J**

*Jagadgurus* 72, 177, 251, 347
    accepted God as the cause and effect of the universe 154
    definition of 172
    descended on the earth planet from the Divine abodes 186
    described the Divine theory according to their Divine status 186
    emphasized the greatness of Radha Krishn 33
    examples of the similarity of their devotional philosophies 286
    Krishn is the supreme *Jagadguru* 276
    names of the five *Jagadgurus* with brief biographies 173–180
    *nirakar brahm* is established in *purushottam brahm* 43
    reconciled philosophies of soul, *maya* and God 185
    Shankaracharya himself worshipped Krishn 33, 66, 161–165, 170, 287
    the common themes accepted by all the four and Jeev Goswami 181–182, 185
    the general theme of their *bhashyas* is *bhakti* 182
    their differences in describing the states of *brahm* and the revelation of Bliss 182–185
    wrote *bhashya* on *prasthan trayi* 172, 347
*janm See also: avatar*
    definition of 358–359
*jap* 269, 314
**Jeev Goswami** 33, 36, 43, 285
    a brief description of soul, *maya* and God of *achintya-bhedabhed vad* 180, 183–184
    defined the functions of *sandhini* and *ahladini shakti* 184
    described relational closeness with Krishn 64
    described the form of souls 95–96
    described the self-submissive unity and qualitative differentiality of Krishn's powers 184
    elaborated the self-submissive Blissful superiority of the personal forms of God 43
    expounded the philosophy of *shakti shaktiman* 184
    expounded the teachings of Chaitanya Mahaprabhu in Shat Sandarbh 53, 173
    improved the theory of soul and *maya* 183
    Krishn is the supreme *brahm* 44, 185
    Parmatm Sandarbh explains the three forms of one supreme *brahm*, Krishn 62
    the description of soul and God is clearer in his writings as compared to others 43
    was the disciple of Chaitanya Mahaprabhu 175
    writings of 33, 36, 43–44, 180–181
*jeev shakti* 129, 130, 137, 139, 183, 304. *See also: tatastha shakti*
    all the souls maintain their individuality even after liberation 96
    and *maya shakti* are the associates of *chid brahm* 137
    as described in Chaitanya Charitamrit 86

**Krishn** *(cont.)*
Shiv, Vishnu and Lakchmi cannot understand His greatness  142
the absolute *nirakar brahm* is established within Him  118
His appearance and length of stay on earth  356
the Blissful lusciousness of the ocean of His love is the glory of Radha's personality  284
the Divine miracle of His absolute greatness as described by Shankaracharya  162–165
the essence of Brahm Sutra and Upnishads is devotion to Krishn  165
the eternal *(apar* and *par) dharm* is established within Him  118
the reason why He is called the main form of *brahm*  144–145
took the permission of Radha Rani before doing *maharaas*  320
Vishnu and Shiv emanate from Him  245
with no personal preference gives you the conception and quality of your devotion  257
**Krishn** *bhakt* **(Saint)**  167, 291–292. *See also: rasik* Saint(s)
**Krishn** *tattva*  286
*kunj*  164, 330

**L**

**Lakchmi**  56. *See also:* Maha Lakchmi
appeared from Radha  147
can enter Vrindaban but cannot taste the Bliss of *maharaas*  50, 78
felt so happy in doing Her service She forgot to sit down and watched *maharaas*  78
Her desire to enter *maharaas* established the absolute supremacy of Divine love  78
in the form of Rukmini  307
is the *sandhini* power of Krishn  143, 144, 307
the distinction between Lakchmi and Maha Lakchmi  77
Who is the supreme Goddess of Vaikunth longs to serve the Queen of Her heart, Radha  78
*leela purushottam (brahm)*  143
definition of  136
is the highest knowledge of the Puranas  145–149
Krishn drowns in the beauty and love of Radha  143
the three forms  136, 141
*leelas*  67, 97, 120, 125, 136, 140, 143, 145, 164, 187, 222, 261, 294, 327, 343, 361
are described in a dry manner in the Puranas with no real feelings of love  67
are eternally happening in uncountable styles in Divine Vrindaban  75
are revealed by Radha Krishn for the souls  75
Bliss of Radha Krishn is of four kinds:
  - *braj ras*  188
  - *nikunj ras* of Golok  144, 188
  - *nikunj ras* of Vrindaban  188
  - *nibhrit nikunj ras* of Vrindaban  188
definition of  33
of Radha Krishn are very easy to remember in Barsana Dham, (USA)  324
*leelas, nikunj See: nikunj leelas*
*leelasthali*  320
*leshavidya*  213
**liberation**  95, 96, 122, 137, 141, 152, 161, 168, 171, 182. *See also: brahm sayujya; gyani*
  Saint(s); *kaivalya mokch; mokch*
as defined by Madhvacharya  177
*brahmatva* of Shankaracharya  168
eliminates forever the possibility of experiencing *prem ras* (Divine love)  211
for a *bhakt* of Radha Krishn  303
for a follower of *nirakar brahm*  304
for *gyanis/yogis* means receiving a Divine similarity with *brahm*  96
in *bhakti marg* means the soul receives a Divine body  94, 122
in *gyan marg* means the soul stays in *nirakar brahm* without a body  94, 122, 129

**Mahabharat war**
    the time of its occurrence 348
*mahan* 151
*mahapurush, nitya siddha* 128, 289
*mahapurush, sadhan siddha* 289
*maharaas* 51, 143, 165, 170, 329, 337, 339
    a brief description of 326
    definition of 321
    it was manifested with Radha's Grace 73
    Krishn asked for Radha's consent 51, 320
*maharaas mandal* 334
*mahat-tattva* 202
*mahayuga* 246
*man* 102, 151
**Man Mandir** 323
*mantra* 270, 286, 288, 289
    every name of Radha Krishn is 361
**Manu Smriti** 194
*manvantar katha*
    the total history of India and the earth planet related in the Bhagwatam 348
*maryada marg*
    its definition according to Vallabhacharya 180
*maryada purushottam*
    definition of 136
*math* 172, 173
*maya* See also: *avidya; bahiranga shakti; maya shakti*
    a constantly changing state of *maya* 45, 104, 295
    a diagram depicting its relationship with God and souls 298
    a summation of the distorted knowledge and understanding of the *mayic* realm 150
    any form of God can give liberation from the bondage of 33
    as defined by Shankaracharya 101
    as described in the Bhagwatam 100
    as described in the Brahm Sutra 100–101
    as described in the Gita 99
    as described in the Upnishads 99
    creates extroverted understanding that takes souls away from God 87, 101, 149
    creates illusive blissfulness of a short-lived nature 86
    defined as *mool prakriti* 102
    definition of 101, 130, 149, 295
    evolved in the form of this world on the base of God 157
    evolves mind, body and its senses 109
    evolves the universe with God's help 100, 181
    exists as an affiliate to the *chid shakti* of God Krishn 101
    forms an unbreakable knot that stays until the soul is liberated 101
    has 3 forms of ego and 5 kinds of perceptions that relate to *mayic* energies 102
    has a totally distorted existence 149
    has four aspects of aging which form the cycle of birth and death 105
    has kept unlimited number of souls under its bondage since eternity 99, 101
    has the power of attraction 102
    is a *nirakar* lifeless power of God that assumes a *sakar* shape of this world 253
    is a power of God and controlled by God 99, 100, 101, 181
    is an abstract existence of *sattva, raj* and *tam* 99, 100, 101, 156–157
    is anti-Divine and anti-*chit* power 129, 130, 138, 149, 154
    is dependently established in *chid brahm* 130, 138
    is eightfold: earth, water, fire, air, space, emotional and intellectual mind and ego 99,
        102, 357

*nirakar, nirakar brahm (cont.)*
    definition of 302–303
    does not even recognize its own absolute identity 62
    followers of *gyan* and *yog* are believers of *nirakar brahm* 204
    has no apparent virtues because these refer to the Divine Personality of God 206
    has some Blissfulness but it is not experienced after liberation 302
    is a state of no-experience 63
    is *chid brahm* 129, 138, 143
    is established in the *sandhini* form of *purushottam brahm* (almighty God) 62
    is live but dormant and is mere Divine intellect 137
    is omnipresent Divine existence with no Divine virtues 302
    is the formless, inactive and virtueless state of God 62
    it is *avyakt shaktik nirgun brahm* 62, 136
    *jeev shakti* as part of 167
    only the personal form of God recognizes its absolute identity within Himself 62
    Shankaracharya describes this path as being very tough 166
    Shankaracharya made the rules for a follower of this path 303
*nirakar brahm tattva* 167
*nirakar samadhi* 303
*niranjan* 123
*nirbeej samadhi* 201. *See also: samadhi*
*nirgun, nirgun nirakar* 123, 162
    definition of 116, 134
*nirgun nirakar brahm*
    is mindless and doesn't recognize its own identity as *chit* 137
    soul in its pure state is an exact replica of in a tiny form 137
    *yogis* and *gyanis* have a neutral relationship with 127
*nirgun nirakar nirvishesh brahm* 136
*nirvikalp samadhi* *See also: samadhi*
    definition of 199
    is the limit of *yog* as a transcendence of the highest kind of *sattvagun* 202
    its stages described 200, 201, 202
    the 5 blockages a *yogi* has to cross 201
    the practice of *samadhi* does not take one to God 203
    the Yog Darshan of Patanjali is the main scripture 198
*nishkriya nirvishesh* 167
**Nityanand Prabhu**
    was the descension of Balram (Krishn's older brother) 223
**Nyay Darshan** 110
**Nyay-Vaisheshik** 42, 150, 158
    describe logical analysis and introversion through *samadhi* 151
    describe two substances: material and Divine 151

**P**

*pad* 73
*panch gyanendriya* 151
*panch karmendriya* 151
*panch kosh* 152
*panch mahabhoot* 151
*panch tanmatra* 151
*pandit maninah* 196
*par dharm* *See also: dharm*
    along with *apar dharm* is established in Krishn 118
    definition of 70, 71, 73, 119

**scriptures** *(cont.)*
  their five main categories described:
    - Darshan Shastras  42
    - Puranas, Uppuranas, Ramayanam, Mahabharat  42
    - the writings of *rasik* Saints  44
    - the writings of the *Jagadgurus*  43
    - Upnishads, Gita, Bhagwatam  41
  to understand their secret a longing for God and a true Saint's guidance are compulsory
    346
**service**  282
  quickly purifies the heart and brings you closer to your Master and Radha Krishn  282
  suggestions for making it more valuable and effective  283
*seva*  292
**Seva Kunj**  339
*shakti, ahladini  See: ahladini shakti*
*shakti, aishwarya  See: aishwarya shakti*
*shakti, anand  See: anand shakti*
*shakti, antaranga  See: antaranga shakti*
*shakti, bahiranga  See: bahiranga shakti*
*shakti, chetragya  See: chetragya shakti*
*shakti, chit  See: chit shakti*
*shakti, gyan  See: gyan shakti*
*shakti, jeev  See: jeev shakti*
*shakti, maya  See: maya shakti*
*shakti, para  See: para shakti*
*shakti, prema  See: prema shakti*
*shakti, samvit  See: samvit shakti*
*shakti, sandhini  See: sandhini shakti*
*shakti, sat  See: sat shakti*
*shakti, swaroop  See: swaroop shakti*
*shakti, tatastha  See: tatastha shakti*
*shakti-shaktiman*  189
  can never be separate  188
  definition by *Jeev* Goswami  184
  in the dimension of Golok and Vrindaban both become one  188
  is beyond comprehension as explained in *achintya bhedabhed vad* by Jeev Goswami  184
  is only up to *prema shakti*  188
  Nimbarkacharya and Vallabhacharya accepted the theory of  184
  Radha has two forms: as Radha and Krishn, both are *shakti* and both are *shaktiman*  188
  the absolute supreme *brahm* Radha is both *shakti* and *shaktiman*  188
**Shankaracharya**  43, 137, 158, 221, 253
  a brief biography of  173
  a brief description of his *advait bhashya* concerning soul and *brahm*  137
  a summation of his *advait bhashya*  160
  accepted the spark-like individuality of the souls  169
  accepted Vedic scriptures as the authentic authority  159
  admonished and cautioned the followers of *advait vad* not to enter into sanctimoniousness
    166
  altered the meanings of scriptural verses to suit his requirements for promoting *advait vad*
    158, 169, 171
  an example of his devotional similarity with other *Jagadgurus*  286
  contradicted Bauddh, Jain and Naiyayiks  159
  contradicted his own *advait* philosophy in Prabodh Sudhakar  169
  defined *maya*  101
  described his love for Krishn  66, 165
  described Krishn's greatness in Prabodh Sudhakar  162–163

**soul** *(cont.)*
    in its pure form is *avyakt shaktik* like *chit* 149
    initially it is a dormant *nirakar chit* (impersonal) 129
    is a fractional part of the *jeev shakti* of God Krishn 90, 92, 95, 360
    is a neutral onlooker of the mind 91
    is an eternal, pure, unadulterated, individual form of Divine intellect 90, 91, 95
    is eternally blemished and influenced by *maya* 92, 95
    is eternally ignorant, indestructible, individual and non-changing 90, 91, 95
    is freed from *mayic* bondage when it receives God's Grace 94
    is infinitesimal *chit* 89–90, 95, 97
    is non-stationary and spot-existent 93, 97
    is not Bliss or part of the *swaroop shakti* of Krishn 92, 95
    is not related to the consequences of the body 90, 91
    is of two kinds: beyond the bondage and under the bondage 181, 354
    is related to God but mind and body are related to *maya* 299
    is searching for absolute Bliss which isn't the character of this world 129
    is separate from Blissful God 92
    is substantially the same and constitutionally a fraction of God 128
    is the form of Divine intellect (Divine *chit*) 89, 91, 93
    is the subtlest and minutest thing in the universe 89, 91
    is unchanged in any situation including liberation 95
    its *chit* aspect is exactly the same as *chid brahm* 128, 181, 185
    its *chit* aspect is negatively distorted by *maya* 149
    its *chit* quality is dormant until it receives a personal identity 128
    its ignorance obscures its Divine relationships with Krishn 91
    maintains its individuality even after liberation 96
    receives a material identity during creation 129
    receives a personal Divine identity with God's Grace 129
    receives a pure *chit* form when *mayic* bondage is broken with God's Grace 95
    receives the Grace of God through selfless devotion 94
    remains the same in all the forms or bodies it takes even during *maha pralaya* 90
    resides in supreme God during creation and dissolution 90
    resides in the heart of a person, not in the brain area 90, 94
    takes uncountable forms of life 90
    the three categories described 149
    travels from one body to another 93
    was never created 90
    who receives liberation (*kaivalya mokch*):
      - enters and remains in the Divine *chit* of God 94
      - loses his personal identity 94
    who worships a form of God:
      - enters the Divine abode of his beloved God 94
**space energy**
    as described in the chronology of creation by the creator Brahma 111
**spiritual transgressions** 264, 270
    associating with a transgressor is also a transgression 223
    block the heart to experience relational closeness with Radha Krishn (*durdaio*) 275
    definition of 222
    disrespecting God, Vedas and *shastras* in any way 159
    disrespecting God's kindness and Grace 223
    of this lifetime can be redeemed to a certain extent by a Saint according to your
      dedication 314
    of those preaching misleading doctrine and having sanctimonious behavior 222, 223,
      224, 292
    their effect upon the mind 224
    to criticize or condemn any form of God 49

**uncertainty principle**
and *karm* described  106
**universe**  120
evolves from, exists in, and dissolves back in God  101, 155
functions through time energy  102
has two stages: evolved and unevolved  100
is the manifestation of *mayic* properties which form the body and mind of souls  155
is virtually God Himself  155
**Upnishads**
almost all of them tell about liberation or becoming like God in His abode  51
among thousands of their verses only a few reveal the truth of Radha Krishn supremacy  51
are all powers of *sandhini shakti*, the *purushottam brahm*  67, 144
constitute only 7% of the Vedas  46
dedication of God Vishnu for Radha Krishn  246–247
describe God's omnipresent Divine form and personality  133–135
describe the almost impossible difficulty of following the path of *gyan marg*  197
describe the characteristics of absolute supreme *brahm*  116–118
describe the characteristics of *maya*  99
describe the characteristics of *mayic* and liberated souls  89–90, 94
describe the characteristics of supreme *brahm*  143–145
explain the process of creation  103, 111
explain the relationship of *maya* (*bhogya*) and soul (*bhokta*)  109
express the existence of *nirakar brahm* in denial form  136
Krishn is described as the supreme Blissful form of God in only one place  51
Maha Vishnu is only a fraction of Krishn's personality  50
mostly use personal pronouns for God  135, 146
Radha is the absolute supreme *brahm*  143, 145, 147
relate an extensive description of Radha Krishn's Vrindaban in the words of Maha Vishnu  118
say that all that exists is *brahm* and there are three eternal things in it  85
supreme *brahm* Krishn has two eternal forms, Radha and Krishn  146
tell the story of the blind leading the blind  293
the Blissfulness of Divine Vrindaban is beyond their reach  148
the Divine love of Krishn is indicated by the very important verse "*raso vai sah*"  72
the glory of the name of Raseshwari Radha Rani and Her supreme absoluteness  31, 148
the most valuable theory of graphically described  305
the style and practice of the path to God is revealed through  354
the supreme Divine truth is attainable through *bhakti*  207
their whole concentration is on renunciation and liberation from *maya*  146
there are about 250 available nowadays  41, 51
were introduced by Brahma in the very beginning of human civilization  32, 41, 355

**V**

*vahyasamudaya*  159
*vaidhi bhakti*  *See also: anushthan*
definition of  262
**Vaikunth**  139, 140, 142, 143, 187, 277, 297, 307. *See also:* almighty forms/abodes of God
Durga's Divine abode is a part of  297
is the abode of all the almighty forms of God  56, 307
is the dimension of *sandhini shakti*, the abode of Divine almightiness  139, 140
is the eternal abode of Maha Vishnu and the personified excellence of Bliss  118
its Divine Bliss is uncountable times greater than the Divine euphoria of *brahmanand*  56
Vishnu's Grace reveals the Bliss of  277

# Index (Sanskrit).

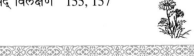

# Illustrations.

# Books and Tapes
## by
## H.D. Swami Prakashanand Saraswati.

### The Shikchashtak
Shree Swamiji reveals to the general public, for the first time, the treasure of devotional secrets imbued in the eight verses of the Shikchashtak (said by Chaitanya Mahaprabhuji). Every description in this book is a direct and precise statement of the truth. It is an indispensable guide to all the souls seeking the path of *divine-love-consciousness*.                    (138 pages)

### The Philosophy of Divine Love
These 15 speeches, given by Shree Swamiji, show the path to God. They reveal the Divine facts that enlighten your consciousness, enabling you to cross the net of spiritual confusion and cynicism of today.        (142 pages)

### Towards the Love Divine
"The riches of the world are pleasing but not satisfying; material attainments increase worries instead of peace, and sensual pleasures multiply ambitions instead of satisfaction." Towards the Love Divine explains how to receive perfect peace and happiness while living in the world.    (132 pgs.)

### Biographies of Rasik Saints
The *rasik* Saints came on the earth planet with the will of Krishn to guide the souls seeking God realization. The descriptions of their love, dedication and renunciation leave an unforgettable impression on the reader's mind.                                                 (170 pages)

### The Sixth Dimension
The connecting energy between physical science, e.s.p. and the Divine, the development of human virtues, the evolution of an individual's potential, and the path to experience ecstatic states of *divine-love-consciousness,* are revealed in this book.                                     (92 pages)

### The Path to God
A simple and exact revelation of the Divine philosophy of God realization in a nutshell. It also tells about our Society (ISDL), Barsana Dham, its devotional places and Shree Raseshwari Radha Rani Temple.    (56 pages)

# VIDEO TAPES

## The Upnishads - Series I
Introduction to the Upnishads.
*36 speeches.*

## The Brahm Sutra - Series I
As said by Ved Vyas 5,000 years ago.
(General theme of the Brahm Sutra.)
*32 speeches.*

## The Brahm Sutra - Series II
The philosophy of *sagun brahm.*
(Explaining the truth of *advait vad.*)
*40 speeches.*

## The Brahm Sutra - Series III
The preface of the Bhagwatam.
(Explaining the 25 most important *sutras.*)
*36 speeches.*

## The Gita.
• Gita Series I, Introduction to the Gita, *24 speeches.*
• Gita Series II, Basic Philosophy of the Gita, *32 speeches.*
• Gita Series III, Secret Devotional Philosophy of the Gita, *36 speeches.*
• Gita Series IV, The Gita and the Religions of the World, *12 speeches.*
• Gita Series V, The Gita is a Complete Darshan Shastra, *12 speeches.*
• Gita Series VI, The *Bhakti tattva* of the Gita, *12 speeches.*

# AUDIO TAPES

(There are more than 200 audio speeches that are available on
the philosophy of Divine love, Krishn *tattva*, devotional humbleness and
the *leelas* of Radha Krishn.  Some important series are mentioned here.)

### Krishn, God the Divine
*10 speeches.*

### *Maya*, Soul, Universe and God
*12 speeches.*

### Gita Series VII, Chapterwise Explanation of the Gita
*18 speeches.*

### Charm of Krishn's Flute
*6 speeches.*

### Radha Krishn Name, Form, Abode
### and Virtues are Absolutely One
*4 speeches.*

### Explanation of *"Rangeeli Radha Rasikan Pran"*
*6 speeches*

### Udhao Meets the *Gopis*
*5 speeches.*

❀

### Devotional Chantings by Meera Devi and Ranjana Devi
• Mere Pranan Pyare aja, Shree Krishn Chaitanya,
Jai Shyama, Bhajo Giridhar Govind Gopala.

• Aja Pyari Bhanudulari, Jai Shree Radhey Jai Nandnandan,
Man nish din gaiyo, Giridhari Nandlal.